The Moral Habitat

In *The Moral Habitat,* Barbara Herman offers a new and systematic interpretation of Kant's moral and political philosophy. The study begins with an investigation of some understudied imperfect duties which, surprisingly, tell us some important but generally unnoticed facts about what it is to be a moral agent. The second part of the book launches a substantial reinterpretation of Kant's ethics as a system of duties, juridical and ethical, perfect and imperfect, that can incorporate what we learn from imperfect duties and do much more. This system of duties provides the structure for what Herman calls a moral habitat: a made environment, created by and for free and equal persons living together. It is a dynamic system, with duties from different spheres shaping and being affected by each other, each level further interpreting its core anti-subordination value. In the final part, Herman takes up some implications and applications of this moral habitat idea, developing the resources of this holistic agent-centered Kantian view of morality by considering what would be involved, morally, in recognizing a human right to housing to meta-ethical issues about objectivity and our responsibility for moral change.

Barbara Herman is the Griffin Professor of Philosophy and Professor of Law at UCLA. She previously held appointments at the University of Southern California and the Massachusetts Institute of Technology. She is the author of *The Practice of Moral Judgment* (Harvard, 1993), *Moral Literacy* (Harvard, 2007), and *Kantian Commitments* (Oxford, 2022), and was the editor of John Rawls's *Lectures on the History of Moral Philosophy* (Harvard, 2000).

The Moral Habitat

BARBARA HERMAN

OXFORD
UNIVERSITY PRESS

Great Clarendon Street, Oxford, OX2 6DP,
United Kingdom

Oxford University Press is a department of the University of Oxford.
It furthers the University's objective of excellence in research, scholarship,
and education by publishing worldwide. Oxford is a registered trade mark of
Oxford University Press in the UK and in certain other countries

© Barbara Herman 2021

The moral rights of the author have been asserted

First published 2021
First published in paperback 2023

All rights reserved. No part of this publication may be reproduced, stored in
a retrieval system, or transmitted, in any form or by any means, without the
prior permission in writing of Oxford University Press, or as expressly permitted
by law, by licence or under terms agreed with the appropriate reprographics
rights organization. Enquiries concerning reproduction outside the scope of the
above should be sent to the Rights Department, Oxford University Press, at the
address above

You must not circulate this work in any other form
and you must impose this same condition on any acquirer

Published in the United States of America by Oxford University Press
198 Madison Avenue, New York, NY 10016, United States of America

British Library Cataloguing in Publication Data
Data available

Library of Congress Cataloging in Publication Data
Data available

ISBN 978–0–19–289635–3 (Hbk.)
ISBN 978–0–19–890622–3 (Pbk.)

DOI: 10.1093/oso/9780192896353.001.0001

Links to third party websites are provided by Oxford in good faith and
for information only. Oxford disclaims any responsibility for the materials
contained in any third party website referenced in this work.

For Theo and Zoe

Contents

Preface ix
Acknowledgments xiii
List of Abbreviations xv

Introduction 1

PART ONE: THREE IMPERFECT DUTIES

1. Framing the Question (What We Can Learn From Imperfect Duties) 9
2. Gratitude: A System of Duties 13
   2.1 The Duty of Gratitude 13
   2.2 Middle Work 1: A System of Duties 24
3. Giving: Impermissibility and Wrongness 29
   3.1 Doing Too Much 29
   3.2 Middle Work 2: Impermissibility and Wrongness 43
4. Due Care: The Importance of Motive 50
   4.1 The Duty of Due Care 50
   4.2 Middle Work 3: Motive 58

PART TWO: KANTIAN RESOURCES

5. Making the Turn to Kant 73
   5.1 A Revisionary Interpretation 73
   5.2 What's It For? 74
6. The Kantian System of Duties 80
   6.1 Ground Clearing 80
   6.2 Setting the Stage: The Priority of *Right* 87
   6.3 From the Juridical to the Ethical 102
   6.4 Provisional Universal Right 112
7. Kantian Imperfect Duties 122
   7.1 Imperfect Duties and Obligatory Ends 122
   7.2 Kantian Beneficence: What's It For? 134
   7.3 Beyond Relational Beneficence 145
   7.4 Imperfect Duties in the System of Duties 153

8. Tracking Value and Extending Duties — 164
   8.1 Casuistry, Due Care, Tracking Value — 164
   8.2 A Note about Juridical Imperfect Duties — 170

PART THREE: LIVING IN THE MORAL HABITAT

9. A Dynamic System — 181

10. A Right to Housing — 189
   10.1 Property, Hybrid Value, and Second Stage Questions — 189
   10.2 A Housing Story — 198
   10.3 Housing Across Borders — 203

11. Incompleteness and Moral Change — 208
   11.1 Moral Change and the Determinacy of Moral Requirement — 208
   11.2 The Duty to Be an Agent of Moral Change — 217

   Conclusion: Method and Limits — 228

Bibliography — 231
Index — 235

Preface

This book covers a great deal of territory. It begins with an investigation of a few understudied imperfect duties, which, somewhat surprisingly, tell us some important but generally unnoticed facts about what it is to be a moral agent. The second part of the book launches a substantial reinterpretation of Kant's ethics as a system of duties, juridical and ethical, perfect and imperfect, that can incorporate what we learn from imperfect duties and do much more. This system of duties provides the structure for what I call a moral habitat: a made environment, created by and for free and equal persons living together. It is a dynamic system, with duties from different spheres shaping and being affected by each other. The last part of the book takes up some implications and applications of this moral habitat idea. From what would be involved, morally, in recognizing a human right to housing to some meta-ethical issues about objectivity and our responsibility for moral change, *The Moral Habitat* explores the resources of this holistic agent-centered Kantian view of morality.

To help traverse this much territory, I've taken some liberties. Although Part One of the book starts out in a familiar way, as the discussion of three imperfect duties proceeds it collects some striking and controversial elements—about system, discretion, wrongness and motive—that do not fit standing assumptions within much contemporary moral theory. Or most readings of Kant, for that matter. They are, I believe, natural ways of looking at important moral phenomena, if we come to them without preconceptions. Much of their defense comes in Part Two where their lessons direct an inquiry about the nature and conditions of lived moral practice that I aim to show Kantian theory can address when interpreted as a habitat system of duties. If we lose some truisms about Kant's ethics we gain a better way of understanding and assembling the normative pieces of Kantian theory, one that puts the deliberating and morally active person at the center of a generative moral enterprise. In order to lay out such a large idea, I've had to forego some of the usual scholarly apparatus of addressing alternative readings and counter-arguments. It is also a holistic theory, whose parts can't properly be assessed independently. There's a cost to asking a reader to suspend judgment while the pieces are put in place, which I accept, and ask for a certain measure of good will and trust as I stage this foray into Kant's work. I think of the book as an essay—in the sense of an *attempt*—to introduce and defend the idea of a Kantian moral habitat. The last part of the book aims to be bold in a different way. If a moral theory is any good, it should help us address real problems that we face. So I put the moral habitat idea to work on a range of front-page examples, about homelessness and housing but also issues concerning refugees, reproductive rights, education—subjects I know something about, but where I would hardly claim expertise. In a way this seems to me a virtue: very few of us are experts, and none of us are expert in all the things we need to think about. If I can show that even so there's productive thought to be had about these issues using the Kantian moral habitat's program, that is strong evidence of its value.

Alongside these two ambitions of the moral habitat project—rehabilitating imperfect duties and reinterpreting and extending Kant's normative thought—is a third, concerning the fit of the ethical and the juridical, or the moral and the political. Historically, there have been a variety of ways in which the pairs have been connected. The (just) polis is sometimes seen as the necessary setting for virtue, sometimes as the very idea of virtue writ large. Law and morality have been taken to have a common root in natural law. In social contract theory, promising (as real or hypothetical consent) legitimates and is a condition of the state's authority. Much less prominent in the Western tradition is the idea that the pairs are related as two parts of a common moral enterprise, together articulating and realizing a division of moral labor. That imbalance in theorizing strikes me as unfortunate, for our theory and our practice. Our moral lives take place in the terms of some political order or other, whose concepts enter into our understanding of what we do, on whatever principle, from whatever motive. And what we as individuals take to be right and wrong isn't just about a private space, constrained by law, from which we emerge from time to time to take a public action. How we care about and care for each other depends on what we value and on the resources we're afforded by public institutions. The moral enterprise can be organized in different ways without either domain owning it. The heart of the moral habitat idea is an account of the moral in which its work is done by two cooperating parts, interconnected yet differently structured. In one we each separately do what we ought; in the other the same we, only now acting together, are tasked to do something that we cannot accomplish acting one by one. It's what Plato thought impossible, Marx thought unnecessary, and, I want to show, Kant thought essential if we are to realize an order of free and equal persons.

Does the moral habitat idea need Kant? Probably not. Or even, hopefully not. The focus on Kant is only partly explained by my own sense of mission to produce a textually accurate and sound version of his ethics. For the other part, the exposition of the moral habitat idea required a theoretical framework, though not just any one would support it. It is a notable result that the revised Kantian theory can succeed at this task, and further, that taking on the moral habitat idea extends the real-world application of its fundamental values and principles.

During the (too) many years I've been working on different parts of this project, I've collected many debts. For helpful discussion at the very beginning of the project I thank Henry Richardson's Moral Innovation Seminar at Georgetown University. For the kind of engaged critical discussion that keeps one going, I'm greatly appreciative of the law and philosophy groups at NYU, UCLA, University of Toronto Law School, Queens University Law School, University of Chicago Law School, and University of Michigan Law School, and equally, for stimulating discussion at Princeton University's Center for Human Values, University of London's Institute of Philosophy, and the philosophy departments at Amsterdam University, University of Antwerp, Columbia University, Cornell University, Stanford University, University of Kansas, University of Vermont, USC, and UCSD.

Much gratitude to Helga Varden and Stephen Darwall who refereed first half and then the whole of the book. Both were generously encouraging and helpful in their comments.

I expect that many readers of this book will be frustrated that there isn't more argument—or sometimes less—with fewer topics, more engagement with critical literature, less self-generated dialectic. This is the curse of its programmatic ambition crossed with my own need to get Kant right. That makes me especially sympathetic to frustration at the lack of sustained encounter with others' arguments that take the Kant material I look at in different directions than I do. I have two lines of defense here. One is that I have read too widely, benefited enormously, built my understanding on the backs of many others' labors, especially about Kant, in ways I cannot now disentangle. I thank most of them, I hope, in the list below; some others are lost to me because I read their work long ago when I didn't appreciate how much it meant to me. And second, I believe that it would have been impossibly awkward to write and unbearable to read the to-and-fro of debate at the very many points I have felt the need to go off on my own. Better, I thought, to try to make a more self-contained argument that would stand or fall on its merits. Sometimes, I am sure, I have just rediscovered what someone else argued first but that I did not in the moment recognize as the very point I wanted to make. It would bother me if the tables were reversed. Still, I feel that what I've written is in extended conversation with a host of people, many of them friends, whose work will continue to speak to me. In that spirit, I want to acknowledge debts to a community of Kant scholars: Lucy Allais, Henry Allison, Karl Ameriks, Marcia Baron, Katerina Delgiorgi, Janelle DeWitt, Kyla Ebels-Duggan, Sonny Elizondo, Stephen Engstrom, Katrin Flikschuh, Paul Guyer, Rafeeq Hasan, Thomas Hill, Louis-Phillipe Hodgson, Pauline Kleingeld, Christine Korsgaard, Rae Langton, Ben Laurence, Onora O'Neil, Japa Pallikkathayil, Andrews Reath, Arthur Ripstein, Tamar Schapiro, Oliver Sensen, David Sussman, Jens Timmerman, Jennifer Uleman, Helga Varden, Kenneth Westphal, Marcus Willaschek, Allen Wood, Ariel Zylbermen.

Closer to home, I owe a great deal to several seminars-worth of graduate students and post-docs who struggled along with me to make sense of Kant texts that resisted our friendly approach, and those who read and discussed the next to penultimate draft of this book. My thanks also to colleagues Herbert

Morris, John Carriero, and Gavin Lawrence who attended some of the seminars, for reasons only they understand, and always improve things when they are there. I have been especially fortunate to have as a friend and colleague Seana Shiffrin, whose support, insight, and critical acumen have made my work better in more ways than I can say.

At home, I am grateful to Mickey Morgan, for allowing many dinners and car trips to be overtaken by my need to describe this or that part or even the whole of the book. It's not something I take for granted that I am with someone who both understands me and the philosophical work I am doing. And thanks to my son, Dan, whose new book is a couple of months ahead of this one, and who has graciously shared and commiserated with me all along the way.

This book is dedicated to Theo and Zoe. They are my grandchildren, and the future; a future so dark just a week ago, showing a little bit of light today (as I write we are one week to the day after Trump's loss in the 2020 presidential election). They make it both possible and necessary to continue writing philosophy in an aspirational mode. I am waiting for the pandemic to ease so that I might hug them again, soon.

10 November 2020

Acknowledgments

Permission from the publishers to reprint all or parts of the following is gratefully acknowledged.

Chapter 2. 'Being Helped and Being Grateful: Imperfect Duties, the Ethics of Possession, and the Unity of Morality,' in *The Journal of Philosophy,* Vol. 109, 5/6, 391–411 (2012).
Chapter 3. 'Doing Too Much,' in *The Journal of Ethics* 22, 147–162 (2018).
Chapter 4. 'Being Prepared: From Duties to Motives,' in Mark Timmons (ed.), *Oxford Studies in Normative Ethics Volume 9,* 9–28 (2019).
Chapter 6. 'Juridical Personality and the Moral Role of Juridical Obligation,' in Tamar Schapiro and Kyla Ebels-Duggan (eds.) *Normativity and Agency: Themes from the Philosophy of Christine Korsgaard,* Oxford: Oxford University Press (2022).
Chapters 7. 'Making Others' Ends Our Own: The Challenges of Kantian Beneficence,' in *Proceedings and Addresses of the American Philosophical Association,* Vol. 93, 191–207 (2019).

List of Abbreviations

Kant references in the text are to page and volume numbers of the *Akademie* edition, *Kants gesammelte Schriften: Herausgageben von der Deutschen Akademie der Wisssenschaften*, 29 Vols. (Berlin and Leipzig: Walter de Gruyter, 1902–). Abbreviations, volume numbers, and English translations used or consulted are noted below.

G 4   *Groundwork of the Metaphysics of Morals* (1785), Mary Gregor and Jens Timmerman (eds.), Cambridge: Cambridge University Press (2012).

KpV 5   *Critique of Practical Reason* (1788), Mary Gregor (ed.), Cambridge: Cambridge University Press (1997).

MM 6   *The Metaphysics of Morals* (1797), Mary Gregor (ed.), Cambridge: Cambridge University Press (1996).

R 6   *Religion Within the Boundaries of Mere Reason* (1793) in Allen W. Wood and George di Giovanni (eds.) *Religion and Rational Theology*, Cambridge: Cambridge University Press (1996).

Introduction

This is a study that took its lead from thinking about imperfect duties. It eventuated in a book that aims to revise our understanding of Kant's ethics and to offer in the course of that a brief for the value of thinking about duties, from the juridical to the ethical, in a systematic way.

The first steps involved a set of small-bore investigations into the puzzling nature of imperfect duties (duties, like beneficence or gratitude, that are incomplete, and so imperfect, in giving us a required end and not a requirement on action). It is not clear what kind of guidance they give or how they interact with each other or with perfect duties; it's just false that they are always the lesser duty; and they can, sometimes, be demanding. It has, as a result, been hard to assess their place or importance in the moral scheme of things. There are also reasons to find imperfect duties interesting. They seem to give moral agents a more active role in determining what to do: unlike the limits and restrictions of perfect duties, imperfect duties involve required ends that offer individuals some say in how they are to be realized. I have come to believe that working through the issues that come with imperfect duties has a transformative effect on the way we should understand moral activity more generally in both public and private fora. That larger trajectory is the target of investigation of this book.

The book has three parts. The first part examines a small collection of imperfect duties with the aim of identifying common features that account for their imperfection. One of the things we find out is that imperfect duties are embedded in a network of other duties, perfect and imperfect, that they complement and complete. Another is that imperfect duties do provide guidance, not by a rule for acting, but in their connection to duty-supporting value. The shift from rule to value has wide-ranging practical ramifications that call for some rethinking of the elements of a moral theory that includes these duties. Issues it puts on the table include the role of motive in moral action, the relation between moral wrongness and impermissibility, and the sources of moral content across the range of interconnected duties.

The second and largest part of the book turns to Kant. Partly this is because Kant's view of imperfect duties is interesting in its own right. But mainly because the study of imperfect duties in Kant opens out into the transformative idea of a broad *system* of duties—a perspective that's been missing from most interpretations of Kant's ethics. As I will argue, the guiding idea for the system of duties is the construction of a *moral habitat*: a made environment in which persons can, individually and together, express their nature as free and equal rational beings.

One of the most interesting features of this revised interpretation is its exploration of the dependence relations between the duties of public morality and those of private or interpersonal morality to which imperfect duties call our attention. A basic structure of right (*recht*) sets the first terms of moral content for a wide array of duties—juridical *and* ethical. A formal idea of innate right sets conditions for realizing the moral status of persons. It shapes a juridical institution like property so that in addition to making possible the usual claims and liberties concerning material stuff, it affects, through its value, not just how we conceptualize justice, but also how we understand such duties as beneficence and gratitude, partly shaping important and even intimate relations between persons (in giving gifts, for example). The resulting system of duties is also dynamic. Because duties located in different regions of the system have shared content, there can be burden shifting—a moral division of labor. Whether a moral task belongs to public morality or is a matter of interpersonal duty is sometimes determined by the nature of the moral work that needs to be done, sometimes by empirical facts about the social world. So if too much moral work in a domain, or work of the wrong kind, is left to private individuals—about welfare or safe working conditions, for example—the fact that we cannot as individuals do what morally needs to be done doesn't diminish the force of moral requirement but can indicate a possible demand at the public level of morality.

As these ideas are worked out, we come to see not only how this familiar moral theory can accommodate the desiderata that come with imperfect duties, we can better appreciate its strengths as a theory. Indeed, while many of the standard criticisms directed at Kant's ethics are apt for the theory as standardly read, they do not have purchase on the revised interpretation.[1] Since making good on this involves a serious adjustment to the way many key texts and arguments are understood, it perforce occupies a large part of this book.

You don't need to be a Kantian to care about these arguments. They take aim at a number of philosophical commonplaces that call for critical attention. Here are three that have played a significant role in moral theorizing. (1) A now entrenched reading of John Rawls' later work has it that the (interpersonal) ethical and the political need to be kept separate; they are different moral spheres requiring different concepts and arguments. There is some truth in this. But it can obscure the plain fact that it is moral agents who make their way through the public landscape. The structures of just institutions don't just constrain, they give form to the moral personality.[2] (2) It is typically thought that a deontological moral theory

---

[1] I am thinking especially of criticisms about the source of the content of duties, skepticism about the nature and role of the moral motive, and the difficult idea of exceptionless rules of duty.

[2] This would be no news to the Rawls of *A Theory of Justice* (1971).

must not look to moral (or other) value in its rules, and relatedly, that a moral theory with rational foundations lacks resources to manage cultural diversity. What is true is that a deontological theory is not a good-promoting theory in a consequentialist sense. For sound deontology, however, the right relation between duty and value is form to content. And if the rational sets the form, the content can manage diversities of many sorts. (3) It is held that the rational, in anything like Kant's sense, stands in an adverse relation to the natural, or that rational principles resist the emotions and passions. This is an ingrained prejudice, not a truth. If it can be shown that none of these views have traction in Kant's moral theory, often regarded as their source, we will gain good reason to suspect their cogency anywhere.

The third part of the book takes up some of the challenges and issues that come with the moral habitat idea: that it is a *system* of duties; that the system is dynamic and hermeneutic; that although the habitat is oriented locally, it is in every iteration an active moral presence in the world. The focus is on what it's like to be a denizen of the habitat: from possible anxieties for agents who are to act for duties under hermeneutical pressure (what are they responsible for?), on out to the preservative and proactive duties members have towards their own duty-generating institutions. An extended example is introduced in section 10.2 as an aid to imagining the system in action. It explores what it would mean for the Kantian system of duties to acknowledge a right, perhaps a *human* right, to housing. For many traditional views a first question is whether their notion of a property right allows for such an extension; on the revised Kantian view, the idea of property is itself responsive to the work such rights are to do in the system of duties. If there is a right to housing, it has a system effect on our interpersonal duties of assistance and hospitality, both towards co-citizens and towards refugees seeking a place that includes a home.

But why a new approach to Kant? There are several reasons. For those who share my sense that the enterprise of extracting a viable moral theory from Kant's writing has stalled out, having a new point of entry should be a welcome development. In general, there has been greater success in work directed at Kant's foundational project than at his accounts of our duties. Too many interpretations of the duties and obligations fiddle with examples and details, cherry-pick arguments, and tend to seek confirmation of independently favored results. Some of this is explained by a tradition of demanding more from the *Groundwork of the Metaphysics of Morals* arguments than is there. If one assumes that the formulas of the categorical imperative are templates for moral judgment, ingenious arguments massaging details to make the formulas yield known duties are to be expected. It has not been a generative enterprise. Success in getting results in one area rarely translates to others, unless the path taken pretty much abandons the detail of Kant's arguments. There is good reason to think this enterprise of deriving duties from the categorical imperative formulas is a mistake, and, as many critics have argued, a fatally flawed project. The first interpretive question should be about whether Kant intended that role for the formulas. I argue he did not (section 6.1).

The addition to the working canon of Kant's *Metaphysics of Morals* and to a lesser extent the *Lectures on Ethics* has greatly expanded the Kantian moral landscape so that it now encompasses duties of right and a rich collection of ethical duties to self and others. However, the picture that has emerged remains unsatisfying. The different pieces don't cohere, and the foundational theory doesn't sufficiently inform the practical part. One wants to know *what* it is about the human as an end-in-itself that gives *this* relation to their body in duties having to do with happiness and *that* relation when it's a matter of right or self-defense. Or, how it is that the rationale for the morality of promise is both about truth in speech, a duty to self, and a performance exchange, sometimes, in contract, a matter of public right? Are there different overlapping duties? Multiple sites for the same duty?

Where a moral theory treats each duty as a separate and complete entity, such questions are hard to answer. However, if moral duties do not stand alone but instead inflect and complete one another in systematic ways, even across the boundaries of duty-types, we gain a line of argument that helps answer such questions. The spheres of ethical and political (or juridical) duty are not fundamentally separate, intersecting only as limits on each other. I can't out of care and concern share with you what isn't mine; I can't be juridically compelled to lie. We get a much more interesting account of morality if we regard the two halves of the *Metaphysics of Morals*, the *Doctrine of Right*, and the *Doctrine of Virtue*, as together providing the first principles of a unified system of duties for beings like us: with our natural and rational capacities, situated in (roughly) our material conditions. One example of interest will be the supposed right of self-defense (section 6.3): figuring out whether as private individuals we have such a right (there is reason to think not), whether there is juridical protection for our bodies from assault (there has to be that), and what determines what counts as our body for the purposes of defense or protection (it is a mix of juridical and ethical functions). By keeping the arguments from the two spheres in conversation with each other, and by recognizing the role of the juridical norms in the derivation of ethical content, we gain a more coherent regime of moral deliberation and judgment.

Missing from most Kantian and deontological accounts of duty is the role of moral or morally salient value in setting a duty's content. As befits the idea of the habitat project, we only understand a duty when we know *what it's for*, or what good moral action under its direction might bring about.[3] This is not a question

---

[3] Here and elsewhere I talk about what is good and what is of value almost interchangeably, and both with an objective inflection. Neither has its seat in what is subjectively valued (which can be no good at all, of no value). We speak of instrumental goods of value as means, and moral goods of value as expressions of free rational agency (or of some other prized moral condition). It may be that what is

about agent reasons—why *I* should keep my promise. The reasons for keeping a promise are not the reasons for promise-keeping being a duty. Up a level we should be asking whether the goal of a system of duties is to protect us from abuses of power, preserve equality, or realize some cooperative potential in persons or for the species. The answer, and the arguments for it, matter to the way we articulate duties (what they require, what exceptions they permit, how the duties coordinate with each other).

On such a view, our duties and obligations are not in the first instance directives for action and end adoption. They are rather nodes in a scheme of moral value, points of attention and concern whose interactions are managed by a more fine-grained practical matrix. A duty introduces a proprietary form or structure of practical reasoning that articulates some moral value in different practical contexts (deliberative if ethical, rights-determined if juridical). What results is a system neither linear nor simple, not about summing or balancing. The different duties and obligations stand in both vertical and horizontal relations to other duties and obligations: one duty can stand at the head of a chain of subordinate duties (so that a duty is only fully understood by looking up and down); a duty can engage or trigger other duties, incidentally, as conditions are altered by actions taken for its sake (in saving myself I put you at risk), or systematically, as a result of common content (what truthfulness and fidelity share). As a result, a duty's deliberative or directive import is not free standing, even if in typical cases it can seem to be so. Having promised, I ought, if I can, do what I promised, and most often that's the end of it. That this is not the last word is acknowledged, if not always thought through, in *ceteris paribus* reminders. Suppose keeping a promise makes things worse for all concerned. That's not enough to make the promise go away, but deliberatively, things may go forward differently for those in the duty's orbit. Perhaps I should sound a warning. Here a perfect duty might need to be managed by an imperfect one. As we'll see, such added complexity can be liberating.

Was anything like this Kant's view? At least in the abstract, I think it was. That is of course a contestable claim.[4] Nevertheless, I think, and aim to show, that it is the view that best fits and makes sense of his moral theory as a whole.

---

good ought to be valued (or is suitable to being valued); it is not the case that what is valued is good, or of value, just insofar as it is valued. Some goods, like happiness, are to-be-promoted; others have their value realized only in a way of acting (e.g., respect).

[4] Among the many reasons Kant is difficult to interpret is that he tends to ignore collateral issues if they are not obstructing the road to where he is going. He will for dialectical purposes work with a view (e.g., about pleasure) that he does not hold because leaving it in place will strengthen his arguments. And he simply does not think about a range of questions that are obvious to us. Nonetheless, his attraction to the architectonic, his view of reason as a unifying principle, and suggestions throughout the critical works that the domain of the moral law is an order that reason would bring forth in the world, these all suggest that the system view of the moral fits his larger purposes.

PART ONE
THREE IMPERFECT DUTIES

1
Framing the Question (What We Can Learn From Imperfect Duties)

Imperfect duties have had an intermittent but continuing presence in the history of moral thought, showing up most commonly in nonconsequentialist accounts of morality that want to include in addition to duties of right or justice, duties that take the good as their object. They also offer a site of resolution for substantive problems in the accounts of some positive duties, e.g., how to manage the scope of beneficence or allow the personal inflection of some otherwise impartial duties in light of our attachments (to persons and projects). If, as it is thought, imperfect duties allow for individual choice in their execution, there is room to argue that we may justifiably turn away from others' need if we choose to (so long as we don't altogether neglect them) and may also select those to whom we direct attention and resources according to considerations that track our relationships. This position has always seemed to me both right-headed and unhelpful. The right-headedness comes with the recognition that many good-promoting obligations are, by the nature of their requirement, so entangled with our private activities that unless some priority is afforded to the interests of the agent of obligation, she is in danger of becoming a creature of morality rather than a person living a life, even a moral life. The problem is that the template of the solution is in essence a reciprocal projection of the problem: imperfect duties are duties that both obligate and leave room for whatever living a life amounts to. It's more the form than the substance of a solution, leaving unanswered on what terms we may carve out room for our lives and attachments. One might well think that if this is all imperfect duties add, we don't really need them.

And indeed, many would proceed without them. The idea is that one can, on the basis of intuition and overall plausibility, simply include relational duties in the census of our obligations, and argue that these introduce limits to the demandingness of impartial good-promoting requirements (by their nature? by their weight?). Sometimes one kind of duty, sometimes another dominates. To the extent that one also holds that duties either directly reflect a balance of reasons, or are inputs in an all-things-considered calculation, it may seem that we can manage deliberative tasks: aid for tsunami survivors outweighs some number of nice family dinners; either surplus funds are better spent on researchers tracking the effects of global warming than on famine relief—or not (and "surplus" here means...?); and those piano lessons for one's child?... Well, given the importance of music in cognitive and affective development, and given the importance of responsible parenting, the balance tilts. Except, of course, for the existence of some child who could be saved from...(name a life-threatening condition).

Further moral resources can be wheeled out. There are substantive questions about who is responsible for what, and about justice and the distribution of wealth. Answers to these questions will manage some of the issues, often by burden-shifting from the obligations of separate individuals to those of social and political institutions. I think this can advance the debate only if the explanation of the relation between individual and institutional obligation blocks the devolution of unmet institutional obligation back onto the individual (or, in different terms, only so long as there is a good argument about why the relation between individual and collective obligation is not essentially instrumental). We will return to these questions later.

Given all of this, why focus on imperfect duties? I think they offer a missing middle term in a complete account of moral obligation that knits disparate elements together into a usable moral garment. I don't mean to say that they do it all on their own. They are, methodologically, gateway duties. When embedded in a system or ordered structure of duties, public and private, imperfect duties open up a principled solution to many familiar, often intractable difficulties. The key to understanding them is the nature of the license imperfect duties provide. As we shall see, the discretion they offer is not a benefit for the agent of the duty but something necessary for realizing the duty's point or object.

There are two routes that lead to imperfect duties that I do not take. One of them reads imperfect duties through a contrast with the supposedly clearer idea of a perfect duty. Perfect duties, it is said, impose requirements on actions; imperfect duties on ends. Perfect duties are strict about what they require; imperfect duties sanction a latitude of choice. But the moral reality is not so tidy. Sometimes a failure to perform an action is a failure of an imperfect duty; the strictness of perfect duties does not bar exceptions; and the latitude of choice, such as it is, is hard to limn—"I don't want to," the plainest expression of choice, is rarely a sufficient reason not to act as an imperfect duty directs. There are still more ways of making the distinction, none satisfactory. Perfect duties are in the realm of right; imperfect direct us toward the good. Perfect duties are negative; imperfect duties positive. Performance of perfect duties can be claimed; imperfect duties are not owed to persons. But when we look at cases, from harmings to promises to gratitude, they don't sort easily with any of these ways of classifying things.

The second route not taken is one that allows the account of imperfect duties to be hijacked from the outset by beneficence. Although it is the poster child imperfect duty, our understanding of the duty and what it requires is under pressure from consequentialist responses to the moral arithmetic of need. It is hard to resist the idea that, prima facie, meeting more need is better than meeting less, and that this sums across persons. This makes the primary questions about the duty turn on its scope, its demandingness, and making room for the partiality of our private concerns. I think the assumptions that drive these questions can and should be contested. But even if they turned out to be right about beneficence, they are not a natural fit with a wide range of imperfect duties.[1]

For these reasons, I think we do better to start our account with other, less central imperfect duties, ones that don't carry so much deliberative weight or so many preconceptions. If one aim is to understand the choice or discretion that imperfect duties allow, seeing where it shows up in the casuistry of these other duties should be instructive. Like people we think we know well, we often understand them better when we meet their relatives. The three duties I will present in some detail are (1) the duty of gratitude, (2) the duties that come with gifts and some other free transfers of goods (i.e., without expectation of return); and (3) the duty of due care (or non-negligence). Each is tremendously interesting on its own; all are understudied. Though not about matters of life and death or the grand questions of justice, these duties are representative of concerns that make up a moral life, the weave, as it were, that can give ordinary life a moral texture. I take the metaphor seriously. In working out their less familiar puzzles we come to see the advantages to be had in viewing duties in general, and imperfect duties especially, as set in a fabric or tapestry of reciprocal moral elements. It moves us past the obfuscating atomism in much modern moral analysis and relies much less on hyper-refined intuitions about matters of life and death which have by now lost touch with the rest of ethical theory. To appreciate this will require that we spend more time with these "lesser" duties than would be necessary if our aim were simply to elicit the elements that suggest they are imperfect.

The plan of Part One is to lay out the contours of each of the three duties along with some of the puzzles they generate. Canvassing provisional solutions will sometimes be enough to enhance our idea of what an imperfect duty is like. Given the larger project, I will be attending to Kantian contributions where I can find them. Sometimes an account of a duty will require that we go beyond it, calling for pieces of background theory that will require their own investigation. In between the accounts of the three duties there are shorter sections I refer to as "Middle Work." They develop and defend some of the more controversial elements for moral theory that the discussions of the duties bring forward. What should become evident by the end of Part One is that to finish the investigation, to draw out the consequences and make things more precise, turns out to require the resources of a larger moral framework into which the duties can be set. That's because, as we will see in the details of the accounts of them, imperfect duties often

---

[1] There will be a sustained discussion of beneficence in Chapter 7.

complete the work of other duties, and so depend for content and structure on surrounding moral elements. While other kinds of duty will move to center stage as we move on, it will be a continuing theme to look out for the place of imperfect duties in the different strata and divisions of the system of duties that shape the moral habitat. They tend to show up, or are needed, where the business of morality is in the hands and judgment of its agents, not merely in conformity to its rules.

2
Gratitude
A System of Duties

2.1 The Duty of Gratitude

In the central, ordinary case of gratitude, you do something for me—provide a benefit—and in response I owe you gratitude (leave to the side for the moment just what I owe you in owing it). For all the apparent simplicity, it is really rather puzzling. Suppose the benefit is something you have given freely ("Happy to help!" you say as you lend a hand pushing my car out of the snow or carry in my groceries or give me a ride to the airport or feed me when I'm hungry). You provided the benefit because you wanted to; you did not act in expectation of anything in return. And yet, were I to accept the benefit and just go on with my business, were I not to do or say something in response (something in the register of gratitude), you would have cause to find fault with me, and you might even feel hurt or insulted or aggrieved by my omission.[1] So what started as a free act on your end winds up producing an encumbrance, reflected in talk of *debts* of gratitude, on mine. And curious debts they are, since they are owed to benefactors, but cannot be claimed or waived by them. It is an odd mix of features of both perfect and imperfect duties. (I am for now leaving it open whether the providing of benefits itself is a duty. But suppose you provided a benefit out of duty. You helped me because you thought you ought—stopped when you saw the accident, called 911, and waited with me until help came. Gratitude seems in place. But why would *I* incur a debt because *you* did what you ought to have done?)

There is much more to find curious. One extreme of the gratitude spectrum is managed by politeness and etiquette (thank-you notes and return dinner engagements); nothing is demanded of us beyond the performance of an Emily-Post-appropriate gesture. At the other extreme there is *ingratitude*, a vice that is not just a failure to make the right gestures, but an attitude of hostility or indifference to a benefactor long thought to be among the gravest of moral offenses (philosophers and moralists used to get quite purple about this). The extremes can seem too wide

---

[1] There are cases where we benefit another and manifest gratitude is not appropriate or not possible: where benefits belong to the texture of relationship, announcing a debt of gratitude can be a sign of estrangement; because of depression or disability, there may be no fault to find. The central, ordinary case provides terms for identifying the limits of the gratitude relation.

to encompass a single moral idea. Some debts of gratitude are thought to have the further oddness of not being dischargeable. While a note or a return invitation closes the books in some cases, in others providing a benefit appears to create an open-ended channel of reciprocation. Suppose you helped me out of a financial crisis, or worked on my behalf to resolve a costly bureaucratic error (that was neither your doing nor your responsibility). I have expressed my gratitude (effusive thanks; flowers; whatever seemed called for in the situation). At a later date, the tables turn: you have a comparable need that I could meet. It would be odd to say: well, you helped because you wanted to, and I was duly grateful for that and showed my appreciation, but I don't want to offer help to you now, and I don't see why your having freely helped me in the past in just such circumstances should, by way of past gratitude, make a difference to what I do now. In the classical literature on the subject, at least from Seneca to Kant, it is worse than odd: not only do I owe you help in return (regardless of earlier acts and expressions of gratitude), but I should regard myself as permanently in your debt, and be prepared to step up more than once, if that is needed. (There are limits—but they are not at the point of equal benefiting.) If the classical view is at all right, it is not obvious why it is (it is sometimes said to be about being the *first* benefactor in a chain; but that is no explanation; and should we then hasten to provide benefits to get to the head of many chains of benefaction?).

Not everything one person might do on another's behalf is something that *should* have gratitude as a response.[2] Some goods are unwanted (you and I differ about whether something is a benefit;[3] or I want to get out of the fix I am in by myself and regard your benefit as ruinous meddling); some goods are burdensome (trying to shed possessions, I am not wanting to receive your aunt's collection of small porcelains, however valuable they may be, and however much I coveted them years ago); some goods involve costs that I may not want to bear (you send

---

[2] If you return what you had no right to borrow, gratitude is the wrong response (except, perhaps, ironically). If you return what someone else had no right to borrow, it could well be in order. If you remove your private barrier to a public right of way "just for me," my gratitude would treat a right as a service and is therefore inappropriate (though wanting the continued benefit without hassle one may find pragmatic reason to treat a right as a "free" benefit). There is no space for gratitude in normal debt repayment or other contracted acts; if we informally coordinate, but without agreement or acknowledgment, then I might be pleased that you plowed as usual left to right, but there is nothing in your so doing that calls for a response from me (though were you to know that I rely and act because you know it, things change; I think this is true even if there is no special cost to you: it is the *place* of my informal coordination expectation in your reasons that makes the change). There is nothing to be grateful for in the course of breathing the clean air in your living room; though we might suppose in some smogged-over dystopia it would be a real benefit. In a world where we took turns—this year, the car or the field is mine, next year it's yours—we would not have occasion for gratitude for a timely transition, though we would for an improvement left in place for our sake (though not for one that you made for your sake but now was a permanent part—indeed, if it were truly a turn-taking form of ownership, my permission might have been needed for any change). And so on.

[3] And what if the benefit is imposed (you leave a turkey on my porch every Thanksgiving); should one be grateful for something one would have, if one could have, refused? Even when the benefit meets a need?

me tickets to a recital by a favorite pianist, but it will be expensive for me to get to the venue; I might be grateful for the thought, but hardly owe you gratitude for what you did).[4] This much tells us that there is a complex ethics of benefiting and receiving that needs to be sorted out. But we are still far from understanding the core case, where the benefit in question is timely, useful, and not unwelcome. And freely given. Why is *anything* owed in return?

Putting the question that way—why owe anything in *return*—might suggest that the benefit is the first move in a reciprocal relation, or that it is a kind of action that is only completed when it receives the appropriate (re)action. When we are engaged in cooperative activity and I do not do my part, you have grounds to feel put off and I owe something (my share; an apology). But it changes the nature of benefaction to regard oneself as engaged in a cooperative venture—the standard view has us encountering need, not being enmeshed in an ongoing project within which needs arise (intimate relations are different).[5]

Perhaps reciprocity enters with the *receipt* of the benefit. My papers fall from my hand and start to scatter in the wind; you, with hardly a thought, retrieve some of them and give them to me. Looking at such cases, some have suggested that the absence of gratitude is hurtful since it chills generosity, the will to give freely, either in general, or just in the present benefactor; or that, correlatively, gratitude greases the wheels of free helping, a great good to us all. But the first suggestion already assumes that the absence of the grateful response is a disturbing deficit, and the second that gratitude's role is to secure something like a practice. Not all free giving requires a climate of grateful receiving. We give anonymously and arrange for giving posthumously. I leave my keys in the seminar room and someone puts them in my mailbox. (Do I owe gratitude to "someone"? I am certainly grateful.) And, however important the reinforcement of the good, it comes too late in the sequence to ground or make sense of the duty.

Gratitude plainly involves some kind of acknowledgment. Since it can be impaired when the benefit had to be wrung from someone or is offered grudgingly or comes with condescension or contempt, that suggests it is the will in the giving that gratitude aims to acknowledge.[6] Face to face, I can tell you with my "Thanks!"

---

[4] Owing gratitude and feeling or being grateful are quite different, though sometimes coinciding, responses. We speak of being grateful that something happened—the rain stopped on the day of the picnic—or that we live in interesting times or among kind people. Perhaps it's a metaphoric response, or an atavistic display of animism. The duty of gratitude, as the tradition considers it, is a required moral response to intentionally helpful acts of others. Ordinary usage may not be precise here, but the distinction is clear enough.

[5] Some of course have viewed beneficence as a common project, that persons are united in one dwelling place so that they can help one another. Such a view does not make the duty of gratitude more intelligible.

[6] Though Aquinas seems to have thought otherwise: there may be an issue here about motive and what I call "free giving" which is compatible with some grudgingness, and even some contempt, e.g., helping an alcoholic who repeatedly relapses, avoids therapy, etc. Gratitude to someone simply for "staying the course" makes sense.

that I know I had no claim on your action and that I am appreciative of your attention to my good. We say "thank you" often and easily, sincerely and also cravenly (sincerely to the postman who is careful not to leave packages in the rain; cravenly to the voice we finally reach in the call center who might help rebook our flight). Just about anyone can offer thanks (we teach it to and demand it of children very early). But just because it comes easy and often, it is not always in order: it is *not* in order to thank the thief who takes someone else's wallet instead of yours, and it is not appropriate, though hard not to say, when one is given as a favor what all should have by right (a symptom of our awkward liking for special treatment as such).

Thanking is or is close to being performative: just saying the words provides routine acknowledgment of the good will of another in benefiting the speaker or those the speaker speaks for. As in other social forms of gratitude, a convention allows the beneficiary to act as required without having to negotiate the things that can make expressing gratitude difficult or its receipt fraught.[7] I would rather you hadn't invited me to dinner; I am embarrassed to have been helped by you; we all do better to act as if we believed what occurred was the result of good will which we will acknowledge. While this allows easy movement through a variety of circumstances without much thought, it can also make the expression of gratitude difficult where sincerity matters and there is reason to doubt its presence.

But why is saying "thank you" often not enough? It is natural to suppose that the expression of gratitude is sufficient in cases where the benefiting was easy, involving little effort or cost. The further burdens of gratitude—the debt—would then be incurred when the benefiting act was in one way or another more demanding (though it's not clear from whose perspective the demandingness is judged). The verbal expression of gratitude would be too slight—but too slight for what? It cannot merely be about acknowledgment. So it is still not clear why from the fact that I had a need and accepted a benefit from you, I am now obligated to benefit you in turn, if needed and if I can.[8] (While we demand the verbal expression from children, we don't expect them to assume the further burdens of gratitude [at least not while they are children]. It is not clear whether it is because they in general lack material resources—though sometimes they have them—or because what is involved in "returning a benefit" demands resources of moral agency that are not yet developed.)

Perhaps gratitude is a justice-like requirement to restore a balance of goods. You gave me goods or services that I had no claim on, but that I lacked and

---

[7] In general, and especially where securing hierarchy or equality matters, rules of speech and action can minimize awkwardness and clarify appropriate behavior. There are times when "Thank you" said in the right way, is the only possible response to an unexpected or large benefit.

[8] Gifts and presents can also generate a mandate to respond with more than thanks; however, these are duties of reciprocity, not gratitude. But see Emerson's "Gifts" to glimpse the moral difficulties surrounding giving. And also Chapter 3 here.

accepted for the sake of some need. The result is something like a conditional debit.[9] You were willing to provide for me, diminishing your resources, without requiring return—that's the goodness of the act the verbal expression of gratitude acknowledges—but if it turns out that I can do for you what you did for me, then I should, to bring you back to the condition *ex ante*. Subject to my ability to provide the benefit, you would then have gained something like a rainy day fund in me (an advantage that morality creates but that one would be wrong to aim to have).

Were that the nature of the duty, it would explain why there is no failure of gratitude if the opportunity to reciprocate does not arise. And it would explain why the debt can't be claimed. But it would not easily account for the fact that a debt of gratitude can be fulfilled with a benefit different in value and kind (a service in return for a material benefit; I take you to a fancy dinner after you have expended time and effort working on my manuscript; and what do I owe if you fire me, intending and succeeding in giving me a much-needed kick in the pants?); nor can the justice-like account tell us why, although someone else can restore the goods you used to help me, that does not reduce my debt, even if the goods are restored in my name and for that reason. It makes more puzzling the idea that some debts of gratitude endure beyond what looks like full reciprocation, and stranger still that on a justice-like account, you cannot waive or forgive my debt of gratitude.[10] (Perhaps it is just the logic of the imperfect duty at work here: what you cannot claim by right you cannot cancel or nullify; nor can you assign or sell the benefit to others; I owe the debt of gratitude to *you*. But reasoning this way begs the question about gratitude as an imperfect duty.) And there is also no place in the justice-like account for a familiar element of the phenomenology of gratitude: the feeling or belief that where I cannot pay *you* back, I should provide something like the benefit you gave me to others, even strangers.

I have been focusing on the gratitude side of things, but there are interestingly related issues that arise prior to it. There are people from whom we do not want to receive benefits. We have a need; they could and would provide the benefit; we say no. In some cases we refuse a benefit because its being given would harm the giver. A beneficiary has responsibilities on the receiving end: e.g., not to accept benefits that are the fruit of wrongful actions; not to allow generosity to cause disproportionate harm. It may be that I do not want to receive a benefit from a particular person: we have a complicated personal history and being in your debt is where

---

[9] Though not one that has the form of returning something, as if borrowed: there need be nothing conditional in the giving of the benefit.

[10] You can say: "Think nothing of it!" or "You don't owe me anything." You can say it strategically or sincerely. But to my ear, at least, you don't thereby cancel the debt so much as express your attitude towards the benefiting. So saying can sometimes make a mere "thanks" enough; but it can also make the right response in gratitude that much more difficult to fashion. Receipt of gratitude can be embarrassing. Yet another topic.

I should not be.[11] Some benefits come with strings (something adolescents obsess about). But even a free benefit from someone who is an enemy or a rival may occasion resistance or resentment. We do not want to be in *that* relation to *them*. But what relation is that?

(i) Let's back up and reposition. If B had a need that A met with a benefit (and B accepts it), and A's act was unforced—that is, from A's point of view, B's need gave her sufficient reason to act and she acted for that reason—why is there anything left dangling on A's side? That suggests that the problem gratitude resolves might lie with B. Here is one way that might be. Because of the benefiting, A and B are no longer equals: there is an alteration of status. Before, although A and B were differently positioned (A possessed something; B had a need), they weren't unequal because of that difference.[12] The inequality inheres in the giving and receiving: with respect to some end or goal that B has, A has become a surrogate for B's agency, providing what B was not in a position to provide for herself. B has become dependent (albeit in a limited way). And that might call for remedy. The question about gratitude would then be whether its work is to re-establish equality and to ensure that in being benefited (or in accepting a benefit), there is no compromise to B's independent and authoritative agency. The paradoxical effect of an act of free giving would be the introduction, alongside the benefit, of something like a threat—something that gratitude can neutralize.[13]

How plausible is this? Surrogate agency has a necessary place in the development of children. But the arc of development is to displace surrogate agency with the growing child's own. As we come nearer to adulthood, free benefits (especially from parents) are a temptation and a threat to independence. There are adults who turn away benefits even when they need them. If the only way for me to get around for the next month is to accept freely offered rides from my friends, then I might try to stay home more. It is clearly not just the burden (I don't think my friends are lying when they say they are happy to help). If the condition of my realizing significant ends of mine is that you make them yours, then I am so far dependent on you—and I do not want to be that person or in that position. So I cannot regard the valuable free benefit as an unqualified good.

---

[11] Cases where the asymmetry is extreme, where the benefit is large and nothing I as beneficiary could do would benefit you in return, pose real problems. My gratitude has a helpless quality. We may not be able to have the same relationship afterwards that we had before—the free benefit becomes an obstacle where reciprocity is inconceivable. The point of anonymous giving need not be humility (it is often a form of self-protection).

[12] All things considered A might be much poorer than B, but not poorer with respect to B's specific need. (That the possibility of being in this condition is inescapable for humans is the backbone of the argument against a maxim of nonbeneficence in Kant's *Groundwork*.)

[13] This might explain why small children are not piling up debts of gratitude towards their parents—their dependence comes with the territory. But even as children, they begin having these debts to their peers.

I think these must be the issues that lie behind Kant's curious instructions about the special care we must take when the need that calls for a benefit is not a result of illness or misfortune, but likely the effect of some injustice.[14] Then we should not represent our act as a free benefit, but rather act as if we were providing something that is owed (not necessarily owed from us, *as if* we had done some wrong, but owed nonetheless). Anonymous helping in such circumstances is even better, he says. The instruction would make no sense unless status inequality threatened (or appeared to) when one adult has to depend on another to take care of her needs. It becomes a moral challenge to prevent the benefactor from appearing to be superior. The problem dissipates if the beneficiary can regard herself as being treated as she deserves to be, or as somehow having been dealt a good hand.

This view of the problem also fits the general cautions about the giving of benefits: they should not be intrusive, usurpatory, or pre-emptive. It explains why it is that an excess of generosity can verge on stalking rather than showing an abundance of good will.[15]

Now if the moral issue in benefiting results from surrogate agency, how would gratitude manage the recipient's side of things? It would if, in acknowledging a duty of gratitude I am to be taken as saying: "Although I can't act for myself now, my agency is unimpaired and I have not by accepting your benefit become your dependent, in proof of which I can and do accept a burden of response to your need into the indefinite future."[16] Only an independent agent can assume such a debt. The duty of gratitude would then allow one to assert and maintain status, securing a relationship of equality with a benefactor that they are not free to refuse.

Here's a different way of looking at the situation. Rather than accepting a benefit and then being grateful, I do just one thing: *in accepting your benefit I assume a debt gratitude*. By moving the duty of gratitude into the acceptance of the benefit, I make it the case that we are doing something together, as moral equals, no matter the indeterminate time and kind of reciprocation. In the way I receive the benefit I make it now true of me that I am prepared to meet some need of yours, as I can, and regard your future need as obligating me in a way that is different and more demanding than the comparable needs of others. The *expression* of gratitude acknowledges your good will; the *duty* of gratitude involves an alteration of my ends. I thereby assert that I am not your dependent, that your agency does not stand in for mine, but that as equal persons who may at times have needs we cannot meet, we stand together. If this is right, the barrier to

---

[14] Immanuel Kant, *Metaphysics of Morals* (hereafter *MM*) 6:453. I say more about the helping duties in circumstances of injustice in section 7.3.

[15] If you know my ends and get to them before I do, I may have good reason to object: I am working on my house; you judge (correctly) that you can finish the stairs better than I can and do so while I'm at the market. "It's *my* project," I complain.

[16] Assuming a debt of gratitude is then, like promising, a performance, where, in asserting my ability and will to play a role I make it true that I am obligated.

releasing someone from the debt of gratitude would not follow from the logic of imperfect duties, but is there because the aim of release would amount to a rejection by the benefactor of the equality of agency that comes with taking the duty of gratitude seriously. This is one of the reasons why the free benefiting is not so free. Not only does the beneficiary incur a debt, the benefactor has obligations to recognize and manage the change in relationship brought about by her giving.[17] If benefit and responsive gratitude create a new relationship, failure to act out of gratitude when appropriate makes the beneficiary's default, and so the relationship, like a lie; and that is something it makes sense to resent.

We can also now make sense of the desire to "pass on" or pass forward the good done to us when we cannot act out of gratitude to our benefactor. In directing our frustrated gratitude to others, we both affirm our status as independent agents and make it true that being a beneficiary of help was an amplification not a diminution of our agency. (We do not have the same response to goods that come to us as manna from heaven.)

And what of *ingratitude*? Were gratitude a matter of righting a balance, ingratitude would be or be like an offense against justice. But it seems more intimate than that, more important than a failure to take one's turn in righting an imbalance. Ingratitude is a refusal to admit the new relationship, denying that the benefactor is worthy of one's attention. It is as if the benefactor is not regarded as a person, just a happenstance source of a good, or a sucker. There is in ingratitude an active insult to the benefactor. I rather like Kant's explanation of the cause of ingratitude as in a mistake about a duty to self (*MM* 6:459). We have both a duty and a drive not to be dependent on others. The ingrate thinks that to admit owing gratitude is to accept an inferior position; so he refuses to acknowledge the changed relation in order to "hide the inequality." The moral cost is not just the mistake and the self-deception, but that he comes to hate the cause—the benefactor—turning love of humanity on its head. This ingratitude is not merely an attitude of indifference to a debt, but a refusal to recognize the co-dependence of human agents.

(ii) Some of the detail I have pointed to in the central cases fits the quasi-justice model of benefit and gratitude, some fits better with the relational status account.

---

[17] It would also seem that having benefited someone we would be under some obligation to let them return the favor. Perhaps allow them, rather than someone else, to benefit us. Does the return benefit generate a duty in gratitude as well? Since the reason *I* act for your need is not merely for the sake of your need but in completion of my accepting the prior benefit, it would seem not. The mutual recognition in gratitude would be lost if the chain just continued. This kind of account also gives a hint of an explanation of the odd (to my ear) claim that in the land of benefits and gratitude, it is better to be the first benefiter. If we imagine two persons starting as equals, and one accepts a benefit from the other, although they can return to a position of equality, the work of securing that equality belongs to the first beneficiary—she has a kind of permanent encumbrance to make her claim of equality (non-dependence) true. This makes some sense if gratitude is a mark in the register of dignity and not material economy.

While I think the second model goes deeper and explains more, I do not think that is enough to decide the issue. There are other cases, competing intuitions, different explanatory conjectures. I see this as a natural and not unhappy outcome of the discussion so far. The point of the extended interrogation of the central cases was to indicate how much work an explanation has to do, so it is not surprising that at this stage there are remainders and recalcitrant bits whichever way you go. One way to go forward might be to generate more carefully contrived cases, to test competing hypotheses by shifting variables. The problem with relying on more casuistry at this point is that in constructing the cases we would need a better idea of what the stakes are than we have. A different and I think preferable strategy takes off from something we do know: that while the different ways material goods move between persons—free benefiting, exchange, borrowing—call for different kinds of moral response, the set of responses must make sense together. And that suggests we might do well to change tack and begin examining the place of gratitude within a larger set of duties and requirements. My conjecture is that much of both benefiting and gratitude do work negotiating issues specific to a moral regime of possession. If I am right, we shouldn't be able to resolve the puzzles about gratitude by considering it on its own, or as an independent element of private morality.[18]

Gratitude arises as a moral phenomenon because persons have needs that may be met through other persons providing benefits, principally material goods and services. These are our "possessions": property in the usual sense, but also the skills and abilities we have and can use for various purposes, ours and others'. We only get to gratitude because there are differences in possession (or entitlement to possession) that are independent of need. I am grateful to you for lending a hand because you made available to me what is yours, whether it was literally your hand or material goods that you own and that I needed. So then the new question: Shouldn't the moral significance of our making available what we possess to others when they have needs—and so the thing to which gratitude is a response—reflect something about the moral nature of what is provided? A "yes" puts the ethics of possession prior to the ethics of gratitude.

Suppose we had the Lockean thought that the moral point of possession was to create private holdings so that each of us might securely use bits of the material of the world to pursue our own purposes. The system of property exists to manage acquisition and holdings. Through industry and good fortune, some of us have more than others. Given the contingencies of human life, some of us sometimes land in trouble that we cannot manage ourselves. This is the *locus classicus* for free

---

[18] Part of this conjecture is that material benefiting is the core case and the ethics attendant to personal services (e.g., retrieving someone's spilled papers) derivative, at least with respect to the debt of gratitude. Even if the conjecture turns out to be wrong, fitting the various types of case together makes it imperative to resolve the strict bookkeeping impulse that seems to prompt gratitude in kind in the cases of material benefiting.

benefit or beneficence. So, yet again, I am one of the needy. You step forward and provide me with what I need from what is yours.[19] I gain; you are less well off than you were before. True, it was your choice to act, and you did so without expectation of return. But we do not think that in acting to benefit me you were simply pursuing another one of your private projects (as you might be when helping a friend). So the benefit to me counts as a loss to you. And since that loss is something I am responsible for (absent my need, you would have kept what you had), I should make it up to you, if and when I can. Thus, the debt of gratitude. But here is the thing to note: the idea that I should make it up to you depends on the prior thought that the moral point of possession is to enable each to pursue her own purposes.

Now change assumptions. Suppose an efficiency argument for private possession that comes from communitarian values of equality and general welfare. Private benefit is then a back-up transfer mechanism of surplus possession to someone with a deficit: it has the role of cleaning up inefficiencies of the system. Where would gratitude fit? Consider a similarly structured smaller group, such as an orchestra. Although participation by others is needed by each for a performance, the violins do not incur debts of gratitude when the woodwinds play the score. The activities belong to a shared or common end. Suppose each of the oboists starts the year with an equal and ample supply of reeds, but one player runs out or his reeds happen to be defective and another player makes a transfer so the playing can go on. Is there a place for gratitude here? We share a common end; your action allows me to sustain my role in promoting it; I am grateful to you for that. But it does not look as though I owe you anything more than I already am committed to in virtue of our common end. If in providing me with a reed you put your own future performance at risk—because no new reeds will be delivered this month—would I have a special responsibility in gratitude to help you? It is not clear why I would. Each member has the same interest in the performance of all and the same reason to respond to faultless need with available surplus. So where benefit is transfer of possession within the framework of a common or cooperative project, gratitude as acknowledgment of a benefit has a place, but debts of gratitude might not.[20]

We get a very different picture of possession and its duties in Kantian theory. Previewing the account to be given at length in Part Two, gratitude will reside, for Kant, within a set of ethical duties that are to shape the actions and relations of

---

[19] And if what you give me is "your hand" to extricate me from some trouble, your hand and labor are yours, and their use in providing a benefit is an opportunity cost for you.

[20] But suppose someone stayed up all night to repair my damaged reed. It is true that the benefit is larger (it cost more); but I think *I* have no special debt as a result. Perhaps *we* do? If, again faultlessly, our supererogatory benefactor and another oboist both lose reeds tomorrow, should we act for the supererogatory benefactor first? I cannot see why we should. There is some analogy here with Rawls' lottery of natural talents, which, on some accounts of it, include the will and ability to do more.

persons *already* acting under the governance of duties of right (that is, of *recht*: the moral institutions of a legitimate state).[21] The positive work of rights of property and possession, about owning and transferring material things and about the integrity of our person (body and mind), is directed neither at material equality nor at welfare. Their purpose is to empower and extend the agency of persons—that is, to enable our forming and adopting practicable ends (unlike the Lockean view in which purposes are prior to right). Although rights introduce limits on what other persons (as individuals or in private groups) may do, they are not sources of absolute entitlement: both the state and morality itself can make claims on persons—on their services and material goods—that neither violate nor constrain their rights. The state can tax for its legitimate purposes (roads and bridges; welfare; education), and it likely can make direct claims on persons for public service (of both military and non-military sorts). Such state powers are part of the conditions of right. The powers and liberties of right together make up a large part of public morality.

The ethical duty of beneficence introduces a moral claim on action and possession on behalf of individuals in need. In circumstances where one's property or a service can relieve another's urgent need, one may not refuse to help *on the grounds that* what is to be done involves what is, by right, one's own to use as one pleases (consistent with the rights of others). In blocking this response, beneficence does not violate or override rights. Rights tell individuals where they may not go, what they may not use, without the consent of the right-holder. They are not, however, the last word about the moral relations between persons with respect to possessions. The claims of right are rather first members of a system of moral principles and duties to which beneficence also belongs, all of which share the aim of securing the conditions for effective agency (and are compatible with various schemes of distribution). There is order in the system: e.g., we cannot articulate beneficence until we understand property (to tell us which benefits are ours to give); we cannot know what is ours without the background of public law. But while the order is necessary to articulate our duties, it is not an order of normative importance, as if the priority of property rights in the system made any property claim superior to any claim of need. Indeed, the set of rights has to be formed with an eye to what might come downstream. A property regime that made duties of beneficence too cumbersome (because, say, of elaborate co-ownership conditions), would on those grounds be defective.

The overall aim of this portion of public morality is to create a social space of laws and rules that make living a life of one among many, equals among equals, possible: the system of property and taxation can manage the moral effects of material inequality; the state provides public services and protections. In such a

---

[21] So, no duty of gratitude in the state of nature? Since, for Kant, the state of nature is not a morally possible place, the question is unintelligible, like asking about weight where there is no gravity. See section 6.2 for a discussion of the difficulty of conceiving of moral relations in a state of nature.

moral environment, most adults most of the time should be able to take care of themselves independent of the largesse of the powerful, who control resources, or anyone's lenient favor, just to get on with things.[22]

But of course human life cannot be made entirely safe, nor fully adequate to persons' purposes as they develop and pursue their various projects. Fortuitously, we live among persons who are able to help us and who in turn may need our support. Morality requires that the needs of others not be indifferent to us: they are to enter our deliberations about what to do alongside our entitlements, private preferences, projects and commitments. So we help and are helped.

Now again we ask, in this moral social world, where does gratitude fit? The idea that any provision of a benefit counts as a loss of protected possession doesn't seem to have a place—here the helping *is* among an agent's ends—her moral ends. We do not typically incur debts when someone does what morality directs her to do. It is true that you might have done everything you ought to have done and not helped *me* if someone else had been equally needy. Surely it would be perverse to think that I owed you gratitude not for your help but for choosing me instead of him. But if, as in the Kantian view, the moral point of possession concerns self-governance, and being benefited raised an alarm about that, then the duty *would* make sense if its purpose was to resolve issues about status and independence: the assumption of the debt of gratitude making it true that the beneficiary is able to stand for herself despite the alteration of their relationship that benefiting implies. And that would also explain the importance of *expressing* gratitude: why the saying matters apart from any other response that may be owed. As with apologies, something has transpired between agents that calls for speech: some outward and formal recognition that their relationship has changed.[23]

2.2 Middle Work 1: A System of Duties

For a full account of gratitude, there is obviously more that could be said, more cases to canvass, other issues that intersect with its peculiar requirement. I have offered no argument that gratitude must be understood as belonging to the moral nexus of status and possession;[24] what I have argued is that so regarding it makes

---

[22] A duty of self-management is not here an invitation to stoic virtue.

[23] For the classical view of gratitude I have drawn on common elements in the works of a variety of authors, chiefly Cicero, Seneca, Aquinas, Adam Smith, Hume, and Kant. In the contemporary literature I have benefited from Claudia Card, "Gratitude and Obligation" (1988), Terrance McConnell, *Gratitude* (1993), Houston Smit and Mark Timmons, "The Moral Significance of Gratitude in Kant's Ethics" (2011), A. D. M. Walker, "Political Obligation and the Argument from Gratitude" (1988).

[24] There will be cases where issues of possession and dependence seem out of place in explaining an episode of gratitude (we could construct one). Such cases are not counter-examples to the thesis; the question is whether they make sense within an evolving moral practice which will inevitably include side-tracks and deviant cases.

good sense of the core cases, and allows us to see its puzzles not as residue of stale practice or procrustean anthropology, but as a site where interesting moral work is being done.[25] In the larger scheme, we have seen how gratitude functions as a telltale, pointing towards the place of imperfect duties in a more holistic account of public and private elements of morality. The next two examples of imperfect duties will further fill out this picture, as well as clarifying just what it is about a duty that makes it imperfect. But before moving on, we should pause and collect the features of gratitude as we now understand it that seem to make it an imperfect duty and also begin a roster of questions whose answers will shape the emerging account of imperfect duties.

In the best-known accounts of imperfect duties, the marks of imperfection are choice (about when and how to act) and noncoercibility (action on an imperfect duty cannot be claimed by right or externally compelled). Neither mark figured centrally in our preferred account of gratitude. What we saw instead was that gratitude is expressive and importantly personal (though the person on either end need not be an individual human person). It is due (due to?) one's benefactor (though not owed), but its moral work is to make the grateful *subject* whole by way of benefiting the recipient of the act of gratitude. The act of gratitude is responsive to another's need, though not just any need. The need acted for is to be in *some* way analogous to the need met by the original benefaction, though maybe not a need one would have responded to for just anyone (even though that might be true of the initial benefaction). To realize gratitude's moral point, one might have to do more (and one might be fine doing less). It's also not necessary that the person materially benefited by the act of gratitude be the person who provided the original benefaction. Cases can readily be imagined in which it would be inappropriate or impossible to direct an act of gratitude to the original benefactor (perhaps she has turned corrupt or is unavailable or has died; honor and gratitude can get tangled in Dickensian complexities). In such cases, the duty can (sometimes) be redirected towards someone else.[26] Although "paying it forward" or to

---

[25] When I began reading about gratitude, I was a bit startled by the first sentence of Seneca's treatise *On Benefits*. He says: "Among the numerous faults of those who pass their lives recklessly and without due reflection...I should say that there is hardly any one so hurtful to society as this, that we neither know how to bestow or how to receive a benefit." That now seems to me exactly the right way to begin, whether we are, as Seneca was, thinking primarily of the favors public officials give and receive, or wondering how we might ever repay our parents, or how we should negotiate helping and being helped by friends and neighbors, or how we are to design social institutions consistent with the equality and dignity of persons.

[26] This is yet another piece of evidence that the moral point of gratitude is not the benefiting of the benefactor, though it is a responsive benefaction. When the original benefactor is out of the picture, it's an open and interesting question whether the other options (benefiting someone related, paying it forward) are genuine acts of gratitude or measures that indirectly resolve the status question. It fits with this account that feelings and expressions of gratitude cannot be redirected, though they also don't require a living or perhaps even a virtuous target. In an extended sense one can be grateful for the opportunity to pay forward, although another's misfortune is not to be wished for regardless of the moral opportunities it affords.

someone else is sometimes a possibility for the original beneficiary, the original benefactor cannot redirect the act of gratitude (that's part of having no right to it), and the beneficiary cannot simply choose to help someone else *out of gratitude*. The "gratitude relation" has practical primacy. This remains a feature even of the paying forward cases since the cause of action has to be connected by respect or honor to the original benefactor.[27]

As we've also seen, gratitude is not a free-standing duty. Other duties figure in the conditions that specify what the obligation amounts to—principally duties having to do with independence and with the moral significance of property and possession (including the use of one's body and abilities as means). We could also say that gratitude lies at the confluence of two streams of value. One stream has to do with the point and purpose of possession: that persons have the wherewithal to pursue ends; the other has to do with the maintenance of our moral independence: that we neither become nor appear to become subject to another's will as a result of their acting for our ends. It is the articulation of the two values in the context of response to benefaction that determines the content of the duty of gratitude, both what it requires of us directly, as well as how the duty is inflected where other duties share moral space.

For example: Even if the debt of gratitude gives one's benefactor a place in one's articulated sphere of beneficence, the benefactor's subsequent needs do not trump everyone else's. Suppose at the time my benefactor has financial need that I could meet, I have a child with urgent and expensive medical needs. We should expect the child's needs to come first (an order that might reverse if those needs were discretionary). The casuistry here will be guided by the surrounding structure of value and obligation. While the expression of gratitude is a signal to the benefactor that our relationship changed when I accepted benefits, it is part of the effective assertion of equality that gratitude involves that I not relinquish other duties and responsibilities because I have a debt to a benefactor. Otherwise gratitude might move us into the normative world of the Sopranos, where accepting a benefit from Tony gave him the authority to dictate when and in what terms the debt should be paid. I am not arguing that gratitude's recipients have no say about what counts as a suitable response. In some contexts a conversation ensues in which the beneficiary asks what she can do in return. In other contexts the benefactor might resist

---

[27] Obligation-survival has different trajectories depending on the obligation. If I promise A to take care of B, and A dies before the caretaking is called for, I am obligated *by the promise to A* to take care of B. If the promise was to A to drive him to the airport, the obligation evaporates. However, if I promised A to pick up his mail, his untimely death leaves me with some responsibility for the mail—maybe to at least make sure it's taken care of. There's an ought implies can issue, but also the fact that the promises to A made B's care and A's mail my responsibility separate from any further involvement of A. Now if out of gratitude I was going to shovel the snow in front of C's house, I needn't shovel after C's demise. However, if C's family lives in the house, I might take myself to be obligated *by my gratitude to C* to shovel the snow—conferring the benefit that my shoveling for him would have provided them. More of the casuistry of obligation-survival will come up later (cf. Chapter 7).

the attempt to repay, perhaps out of generosity or embarrassment; out of respect one might feel bound to honor that. If the resistance reflects a desire to retain superiority, one might ignore it. What the benefactor does not have is final authority over what is done. That follows from a value scheme that makes independence the central issue for acting out of gratitude.

The tradition makes much of the obvious fact that gratitude is a response, not an initiating act. It is therefore not possible for gratitude to match the original benefaction. Even if later on the grateful person comes to have an abundance of resources and can do a great deal out of gratitude, she cannot match the authorial initiative of the original benefactor. Their relationship is asymmetrical; the initial intervention plays a special role in the life-narrative of the beneficiary. (Think of the difference in stories of the moment when "you were there for me" and when "I had a chance to do something in return for you.") The asymmetry is no threat to the independence restored in the act of gratitude. Gratitude asserts a competence where there is no exact measure of amount or kind. It may be the thought that counts; it may be that the beneficiary has to do more than she would have had to had she been the first to act. Hers is not an act of pure benefaction: neither in its target nor the need to be met. What's required is that she be ready to act within her means, as and if the occasion arises. As an act of respect, the potential recipient may need to make herself available for the act of gratitude to be completed. Because help and gratitude are often in play within a relationship that is changed by the initial benefaction and needs to be reset, we may have to do moral work to sort through benefaction and its seemingly indeterminate narrative arc. This is not a burden on but a part of being in an ongoing relationship.

We do not hesitate to have friends knowing that once we are friends our friendship may tax us (though knowing this, we may hesitate before becoming involved with someone we know is needy). Each kind of relationship—parent, friend, colleague, benefactor—has its own norms of connection and its own levels of demandingness. The help that one gives to a child or parent is given with love and is relatively open-ended; the help provided to a benefactor is more discrete, given with and out of gratitude. Appropriate gratitude is a function of the nature of the relationship one is in even as it changes that relationship. In a common project, we may owe no more than is already involved in doing our share. Gratitude at stranger benefaction may express an altered relation to persons in general—a recognition of our shared need. In friendship, alongside the risk of inequality is the opportunity for deepened trust. At the limit is the giving and receiving of benefits between intimates, where love and trust can do a great deal to sustain equality in the face of dependence, making gratitude more a part of the weave of the relationship than discrete episodes of indebtedness. Though even here it can be hard to get giving and benefiting right, and sustained asymmetry of need with illness or aging may introduce new threats to dignity that leave little room for either intimacy or gratitude to work repair.

It is obvious from even these slight sketches that there is to be no full account of the duty of gratitude that is independent of the array of moral relationships in which benefiting and its return take place. These are what I think of as the horizontal extensions of a duty. However, the moral complexity we have been looking at goes deeper—it has a vertical dimension as well. I have tied gratitude to something like an ethics of possession, connected in ways to be determined to the system of property in a political order. This suggests more value interdependence than we normally entertain between the public and private sides of morality. Beyond the expected idea that public morality provides permissibility conditions for private morality, here the elements of public morality enter into and shape the deliberative potentials of private morality. We've already seen how our understanding of gratitude is partly a function of prevailing ideas of property and public standing. We'll need to see how far this vertical structuring goes, and what to make of movement in the opposite direction: is there something about gratitude, its importance in its own right, that puts pressure on the principles of public morality? If private beneficence engenders debts of gratitude, what of public acts of welfare? Are there equality-related reasons to limit gratitude, or limit it to expressions on grounds that status-equality should not be at stake between persons because secured by just institutions? This is the kind of question that we should expect if public and private morality shape and complete each other.

Running alongside property rights, there is a complex lattice of moral considerations that attend the different ways possessions are held by and move between people. Formal economic exchange will make up only a portion of the ethics of possession. What we do with what we possess is central to what we are like as friends and neighbors, co-workers, partners, and citizens. All sorts of duties, perfect and imperfect, will have to reflect that. In the next chapter, I look at some ethical issues surrounding gifts and returning what's owed that exhibit more of this moral structure.

3
Giving
Impermissibility and Wrongness

3.1 Doing Too Much

The topic here is the ethics of gifts (and to a lesser extent, repayment). I came to it by an odd route: thinking about whether the defining feature of actions governed by Aristotelian virtue—that they abide in regions of activity where persons tend to go wrong by both mores and lesses—still plays a role in the way we look at norms of wrongful action. It's easy to think of cases where we go wrong doing less—less than what we promised or what we owe. But what of the other side? Do things go wrong in the same sort of way when we would do more? I'm not asking about the supererogatory, of doing more than we have to, or worrying about achieving the right balance between competing goods. Rather, it is a straight-up question about the morality of *doing too much*.

In what follows, I develop the question through two deceptively simple cases. Some will find the cases too slight, not raising any pressing moral issues. They are not cases where anyone is betrayed or killed or caused to bleed. They may seem to be cases of agent-failure, where someone acts less well than he should, or from a non-ideal motive, but does no wrong. I will agree that the actions I am interested in are not impermissible doings, but I will argue that they are wrong nonetheless. So I will need to be arguing against the common view that an action that is not impermissible cannot be wrong (this is the topic of section 3.2). I believe it's a position that the cases make credible. So I ask you to suspend disbelief and bear with me as I worry my way through the details. However we come out on the issue of moral wrongness in acting, I think you will find that there is something morally surprising here. Spending some time in the less strenuous parts of morality can be pretty interesting.

(i) Here is the first of the two cases. Suppose I owe you $10 (I borrowed the money to pay a cab one day when I was short of cash). The next day I thank you again for the loan and hand you $12. What I did was not impermissible; it was not a burdensome cost to me; and it is surely of value to you. Still, something in the doing is wrong. I did something I should not have done: I gave back to you *too much*.

The second case is this. You and I have been academic colleagues and friends for a while. We occasionally go to the movies together or out for a meal. It is your birthday; last year I gave you a card; this year I give you a new car. I can afford it; you can make use of it (you've been talking about getting a new car for months). Nonetheless, once again, something in the doing seems wrong; I should not have done what I did.[1]

I don't claim that what is wrong is the same in both cases. But what is true about both cases is that I did too much. Too much of a good thing, one might say. How could that be wrong? It's not "wrong because rights or perfect duties are violated," or "wrong because some cost is not balanced by a greater good." So the first task is to get the cases to raise the right questions.

(ii) Staying with the first case, let's continue by asking: What might I have been thinking when I gave you $12 as repayment of your $10? What might you understand me to be doing? That I felt an additional debt of gratitude I valued at $2? Or thought $2 a fair price for the burden of your being without the $10 I borrowed? These thoughts lie somewhere between odd and offensive, or disrespectful. The placing of a dollar value on gratitude; the precision; the implicit comparative judgment. Then there's the implied sense of wanting to be even. Just this much extra and I owe you no more; we're quits. As if in addition to borrowing money from you, I took a measure of good will that needs to be returned as well. Or was the $2 a tip—a gratuity for a service? Then I treat you not as a friend who helped me out but like a service employee. The tip alters our relationship, transforming a voluntary loan into a compensated service. So the two dollars buys a moral mess.

But maybe I am making too much of this. Why wasn't the $2 just a bit of generosity? An exuberance? So pleased was I by your loaning me the money that I felt a need to express my pleasure, and did so by giving you more in return. How could that be wrong?

Suppose you come over to my house to help me plant my garden (it would be hard to get it done on my own). I offer heartfelt thanks at the time, and then later in the spring, when you begin work on your garden, I come over and help you, out of gratitude. Say I work for two hours more than you worked on my garden. Nothing here seems off. It was good of you to help me and vice versa. We got the gardening jobs done. The extra two hours doesn't cause the puzzle of the extra two dollars. So why is that? (We are not doubting that the extra $2 is a benefit.)

---

[1] If the car case doesn't do it for you, up the ante until you feel the constraint; the conjecture is that at some point, the gift is not just excessive or in bad taste, but, for reasons we will explore, it is wrong to have given it. This is a good point to note that the norms of *too much* that I am assuming may well be parochial. I am trading on shared intuitions. I hazard, though can't prove, that the phenomenon I'm interested in will show up wherever there are norms about appropriate exchange.

The natural thing to say is that the gardening case is about beneficence and reciprocity; the troubling $2 case is not. $10 owed for $10 loaned leans on the form of contract, not beneficence; there are moral rules to follow. But why would they block the extra $2? Why not a rule telling us not to return *less* than we borrow; why interfere with my handing over more? The rule preserves the nature of the original interaction—borrowing to be followed by repayment, *simpliciter*. In borrowing, a moral narrative is initiated; one assumes a role. While the role allows for personal expression—flourish, annoyance, amusement, matter-of-factness— the rule requires that performance not subvert the role or be an act in a competing narrative. A subversive performance would be repayment with a sack of 1000 pennies, or a penny a day for 1000 days (to be sure, we can always imagine cases where these things make sense; in any normal case, they are a little or a lot transgressive—a sharp "What are you doing?" would be a reasonable response). I think that the extra $2 is also subversive, though in a different way. It is one thing to come to recognize that what looked to be a simple transaction has unexpectedly involved us in complex and unexpected costs and to want to do something to sort that out (your having loaned me the $10 on Monday made you incur an unexpected extra expense). But in the $10 case, everything is as we thought it would be, and that makes changing the terms an imposition on the person who loaned the money.[2]

The initial terms—$N borrowed, $N to be returned—mark out a relationship characterized by trust, equality, and the mutual recognition that the duty to repay is the coin that keeps everyone whole. That is what makes the debt not, in a moral sense, a deficit—no one is *morally* worse off or better off at any time in this relationship—so there is no call for any sort of compensation or repair (were it a debt with interest charged, the moral equivalence would simply be a different number).[3] The $2 then has to be about something else. If it is an expression of gratitude for money loaned, then it mistakes the nature of a loan. As a response to the good will of the lender in making the loan, it's inappropriate: the wrong sort of response, putting money where it doesn't belong. The loan was not $N plus an amount of good will worth $2. (There is room for gratitude for the willingness to make the loan, but the appropriate response to that, beyond thanks for doing it, is a reciprocal willingness to benefit the lender in similar circumstances.) I think that, if there is insistence that it is just a part of the repayment of the debt, the $2 mistreats the lender. In doing too much, in returning too much, the borrower subverts the moral relationship between equals that repayment was to preserve.[4]

---

[2] There are curious cases in the vicinity. We are out for dinner and I've forgotten to bring my wallet. I ask to borrow $10, but instead of loaning me the money you say, "Let me pay for this." I later send you $2 "for your trouble" (the $2 that I would have added to my repayment had you lent me the money). This is surely weird; maybe a bit nasty. It's certainly not generous or gracious or grateful.
[3] It would be a different relationship if usurious, in the sense of money for hire.
[4] One might want to say that one simply cannot repay too much—$10 did all the repaying there was to do since that was all the debt there was. I agree. The example of "repaying" too much is meant to explore the moral effects of that limit.

Is this unduly rigid or moralistic? Could returning more than one borrowed be regarded as an improvement, making the relationship a better one? Perhaps allowing for greater spontaneity and expression, turning debt into an occasion for generosity? Or making good on the injunction "Neither a borrower nor a lender be"? Granted, if you are a borrower you need to make a lender whole, but why not also do more, especially if the debt is between friends?[5] While we might expect greater ease about when a debt is repaid or even forgiven when it's between friends, the "what to do" here belongs to a social practice whose form or terms are out of reach of the individuals involved. The argument is familiar. There's need for a practice that manages both possession and use by others, and the moral rules are its social possibility conditions. The heart of the argument is about security: it is only rational to make loans if we can count on a return of what we lend out; the practice ensures that use doesn't trump possession. The feature the "too much" case points to is also about security, but of a different sort—security of equal status, not of performance. And indeed, one might argue that it is only security of status that the practice itself can establish: compliance will follow, or not, as a result of voluntary adherence or effective sanctions. In making possessions available through the practice of lending, we have a form of transaction that avoids the risk that one's possessions or one's person, through one's possessions, will become an extension of the other party's will.[6] By including the $2 as part of his repayment the borrower counter-asserts authority over what is owed. The fact that no material loss is involved masks the moral loss; formally, it is in the same register as theft.

If this seems a bizarrely strong claim, it is consonant with relevantly similar cases. Were the borrower to repay with *less* than what was owed, claiming it as full repayment, no one would hesitate to reject the claim and its basis in the will of the borrower. It does not seem off to regard repaying *less* as a kind of theft. I am not claiming the $2 case *is* theft, but rather that the borrower assumes the same authority over the debt in both cases—she would have it be up to her what counts as repayment. If I include extra money with my car payment, the bank will either return it to me or credit it to a future bill. My will is blocked, not by the bank but by my contract: I am not able to repay too much. In the informal case there is no mechanism for rejecting the usurpatory will, but the form of borrow-and-repay is the same: in borrowing, as in promising, you accept constraint on how you will act on this matter in the future.

Now mostly we don't have an overtly usurpatory will. But the emphasis should be on "overtly." Suppose one is moved to repay too much by the exuberance in

---

[5] There are cases on the other side as well. I ask to borrow $10, you give me $12. Was your thought that I didn't know what I needed? Eccentric generosity? A lesser wrong than our $2 case, but absent more to the story, still something you shouldn't do.

[6] Debt default is a material not a status loss.

feeling flush after the troubles leading to the borrowing. "Not only do I now not need your money, I will repay more than I borrowed (to prove it!)." What could be the fault here? Consider where it leaves the lender. If he takes the money, he has accepted as repayment more than he's owed. Win-win? Doubtful. Since there has been no change in terms or shared understanding, it's more like taking advantage of weakness or confusion. If he says no, rejecting or returning the extra money, he thereby challenges or (implicitly) criticizes his debtor, taking on interpersonal burdens he was entitled not to have. The only paths available to him are unwelcome and the result of the debtor imposing his will (whether or not things turn out as he wills).

Cases that have to do with mistakes and confusions about gratitude—monetizing the value of the good will or regarding the loan as a service calling for a gratuity—are different. Although there is no presumption of authority over the practice, they also involve insult and disrespect. So again one is put at a disadvantage. Even if correction would cause discomfort or embarrassment, it is no kindness to preserve the insult, and worse to benefit from it.[7]

That these are small or trivial actions can make a difference. While an action that does not have seriously bad consequences is not less wrongful for that, it may be easier to overlook or forgive. It's not something that must be prevented because of harms, or that is in your face every day like a neighbor's planting his tomatoes in the corner of your garden. The ease of passing over small things is an undeniably important psychological fact about us that lets us live with each other despite missteps. We can have good reason not to want to make a big deal out of something. The fact that mostly you and I get on fine may encourage you to take this instance of mistreatment to be an idiosyncrasy, more about me than about my relation to you.[8] But even if you come to think it best to take the view that I just didn't act well in this case, or didn't act well towards you, it remains true that what I did was not just inapt or inept; my doing was in some way wrong. As I would put it in a more Kantian vein: there is no route of valid reasoning from available moral premises to my way of repaying you. And if the possibility of co-reasoning is the condition of morally correct action, the source of the impossibility here is in my way of acting, which is, for that reason, wrong.

One might have thought that the rules of a practice functioned as a limiting condition on action, locating fault on one side of a barrier, leaving it open how to proceed in the space of nonviolation. The "too much" case suggests that rather

---

[7] This is one reason why any acts of gratitude in such cases are typically separate in kind and time from the repayment of the debt. I repay the money and later invite you out for a drink. The repayment manages the debt; the drink acknowledges your good will. Separate goods and separate responses. (Suppose I didn't have time to go out with you and instead gave you money for the drink when I repaid the debt; this verges towards a tip.)

[8] These are moments when we may be inclined to psychologize: were there problems in the family about debt, or legacies of religious scruples?

than merely regulating *action* by a barrier, the function of the rules of the practice is to close off certain patterns of reasoning: we go wrong if we regard doing either more or less as options available for our purposes. Focus on and tighter regulations of the *doing less* side of things is natural in the practice of borrow and repay, given the practical consequences of default. But it can be a mistake to go directly from practical concerns to the nature of the wrong involved.

(iii) Let's go back now to the second example, an act of giving too much. This is the case where I give you, my casual friend and colleague, a new car. Even if we are not worried about ulterior motives, absent a special story, the car-giving is "over the top" and somehow for that reason morally inappropriate. Again, not just inapt or inept, but wrong: I shouldn't give it; most likely you shouldn't accept it. The mere fact that you'd like to have a car doesn't make it all right for me to give you one (or for you to accept it).[9] And why not? After all, your need for food is reason to feed you; your need to catch a plane is reason to drive you to the airport. You want to know the time and I tell you. That there is a reason in the need does not, to be sure, make it all right to provide the thing needed; there are all sorts of further conditions that have to be met (the food is mine to give; I haven't promised to drive someone else to the airport; and so on). But that's not the issue here. If there is a problem in the gift of the car, it is either about its size, or about the difference between wanting and needing, or about something else in the moral logic of giving.

In meeting need, the benefit provided is shaped for the most part by the need; some needs require large benefits. Gifts, by contrast, are to a much greater extent shaped by the interests of the giver, often initiated by the giver's desire to please or do something good for the recipient (which may then involve attention to the recipient's needs). If I provide what you need in the form of a gift, that it's a gift changes the nature of the benefiting. In an act of beneficence, that it's me who does the benefiting can be an incidental feature of the benefit (it could equally have been someone else who was on the scene; I simply did what needed to be done). If the helping is in the form of a gift (not just willingly given), it is part of the benefit (the benefiting) that it is from me. (Parallel things can be said about the identity of the beneficiary—how much it matters to what is done that it is *you*.) While there may be no bright line distinction between wants and needs, we recognize that some needs call for providing their object (chronic hunger; remediable illnesses);

---

[9] It may take some doing to get on board with this. It certainly goes against the grain of television fantasy where extravagant giving is the essence of the drama (*The Millionaire*, if you are my age; extreme makeover shows in recent times). But it is a telling feature of the genre that the giving is anonymous, as if manna from heaven, with or without an exhortation to use the gift wisely, or from some entity with whom the recipient had no connection and will have no future contact. It's important to the case being discussed that the giving is not of this sort.

mere wants, however much space they take up in the desiderative life of their subject, lack that urgency; however, they are often the target of gifts, though only as satisfying some person's want is an interest of the gift-giver.

Gifts or gift-giving, for the most part, belong to relationships (ones that already exist or ones that the gift is to help establish, typically, though not necessarily, between persons).[10] Parents and children, relatives, friends, co-workers, all give gifts to each other in the course of things. Gifts can be perfunctory, creative, abstemious, generous. They are expressive even when conventionally set and expected (think of the holiday "gift" to the person who delivers the morning newspaper), exhibiting appreciation or affection or regard. The success conditions for gifts are complex. Expecting a small token of affection, you are surprised by the bottle of wine—something you *must* taste, I say. Gratification on both sides. There's lots of calibration that goes into the gift to make it work. It can be off if I know that you don't like wine or the kind of wine I would give; it can fail if it carries an implicit criticism of your taste. A gift can be straightforwardly inappropriate (wine to a recovering alcoholic; lingerie to a subordinate employee). The attraction of the simple gift, such as flowers, is that it avoids many of these perils— flowers are beautiful, hard not to like—though even the giving of flowers can succumb to extravagance and commerce.[11]

The complexity of even ordinary gift-giving comes from the mediation of expressive intent by the nature of the gift and the reception of the giving. We want, in giving, to please or delight or impress, meet expectations or surprise, and we want those wants to be read through the gift. Suppose I gave my son a car on his sixteenth birthday. The gift expressed trust and supported his desire for greater freedom. But it was a lot to give (our history of gifts didn't lead up to it—Legos, transformers, a new baseball glove, a phone). Once I mention that we live in Los Angeles, it makes sense. It will still make sense (though maybe with a little more strain) if I give my son a car on his fortieth birthday (though you might want more of a story, both about me and my son). And I might, without raising an eyebrow, give my old car to a neighbor's child or to one of our students when I'm about to buy a new one for myself. But when it's a new car for *you*, my casual friend and colleague, it really doesn't make sense: it's too much. Too much for what or whom? It's too much for what we are. Relationships are weight-bearing, and possessions are among the things whose transit they support. Too great a load causes damage.[12]

---

[10] I will stay with gifts between persons, but there is much to be said about gifts to animals, possibly gifts between animals, and gifts to gods. Charitable giving to persons or institutions is a different kind of thing.

[11] Seventeenth-century Dutch fascination with exotic flowers and fruits in both gifts and paintings signaled wealth and imperial reach. Cf. Norman Bryson, *Looking at the Overlooked* (1990).

[12] In the O. Henry short story, "The Gift of the Magi" (1906), the material cost of giving (his watch for hair combs for her, her hair for a watch fob for him) would produce tragic failure were it not for the simultaneous nonmaterial gift of sacrifice that, in the same acts, confirm and celebrate the relationship. Nothing here is simple.

But why should this be? Why the difficulty in moving things about freely—that is, so long as no one's rights are threatened and there's no significant distributive impact? We might appeal to what's not good for us: one kind of "too much" is pure excess, like the calories in junk food. Too much can bloat and disable. But that's not the kind of too much at issue.

Treatises on "the gift" in economics or anthropology start with the proposition that a gift is a transfer of possession without expectation of return.[13] That proposition is sometimes taken to mean that gifts are given without expectation of anything, which engenders puzzlement about the complex social conditions of giving that so often are about cementing relationships, seeking favorable treatment, displaying power, and so on.[14] There should be no puzzlement. What the proposition asserts is that a gift is a one-way transfer; unlike a sale or exchange which is done with expectation of return, in the case of a gift, there is no equivalent that must be offered to complete the transfer.[15] But not expecting payment in exchange doesn't mean that there aren't other expectations and obligations that attend the receipt of gifts.

It is no news that gifts are communicative, and also that we cannot, humpty-dumpty-like, fix their meaning at will. We are hostage to conventions about giving, not just about scale, but when and to whom we may give different kinds of things. State gifts, wedding gifts, retirement gifts, all labor under clear standards of appropriateness.[16] In the case of gifts to public officials and employees, though we may feel and want to express gratitude, or want to use a gift to facilitate needed services, we may not do much.[17] The gift can suborn the rules that constitute public relationships. A gift isn't a bribe because of its size, but because of the role it plays in securing good will. The virtue of the parties is irrelevant. It's not just that appearance is the reality that counts; public roles block the parties from entering a wide range of privately obligating exchanges that would compete with the relations their roles dictate.

The moral impact of the gift is also serious in private relations. Even just the proffer can transform the connection between persons. It forces the recipient to assent to or to reject the gift *and* the giving, a situation she might not want to be in.[18]

---

[13] The theme is first sounded in Marcel Mauss, "Essai sur le don: forme et raison de l'échange dans les sociétés archaïques" (1925).

[14] The extreme is Jacques Derrida's idea of the gift as "the impossible" discussed in his "On the Gift" (1999).

[15] As we'll see in a moment, making the transfer complete and making the gift complete are not the same thing.

[16] Some will recall the wince factor when the Obamas gave England's Queen Elizabeth an iPod loaded with American music (and not, e.g., a museum quality piece of early American silver). It was also sort of thrilling.

[17] The US Postal Service permits mail delivery employees to accept baked goods, but not money or purchased gifts.

[18] In many kinds of relationship, small gifts are part normal life: I might routinely give a friend a DVD or a book I think he would like. Consent is an issue where a gift appears to challenge authority, where it might signal a change in relationship, or is a burden to the recipient.

We are prepared to worry about the coercive effect of offers that cannot be refused, but any offer introduces options that may be unwelcome. The proffer of a gift is already presumptive. And further, in accepting a gift, and especially a large gift, you cannot at the same time reject the new line of connection with the giver: the gift object is not all that comes with accepting the gift. Although Lockean labor-mixing may not generate first possession, actual possession carries something of the possessor: in taking my large gift, you to some extent take me as well.[19] We are familiar with talk of, or worry about, strings attached to gifts; sometimes we are surely right to worry that in giving the giver's aims go through and beyond the gift. But it would be a mistake to think that there is something special, or particularly untoward, about a gift carrying a sphere of influence.

Especially in private cases, we might well ask, when there are or might be strings attached to a gift, where would they come from? What attaches them? If there is anything beyond those conventions that underlie giving, it is the parties" mutual awareness of the stakes and conditions of the gift and the relationship within which the giving occurs.[20] If you give your child your father's watch, he knows how much it means to you, both for what it is and for your being able to give it. The watch will be a stage on which your relationship is enacted. If your child doesn't know what it means, or couldn't care, then you probably shouldn't give it if you will care what happens. But if you give me your extra copy of a book by a novelist we both like, we both understand what the gift is, and I am free to do with it what I will (though, to the point, you're not wrong to expect I will tell you, if I've read it, what I thought of the book).

It is often part of a giving to take an interest in the fate of the gift given and enjoy some entitlement to seek information about it that would otherwise invade privacy.[21] In accepting the gift *and* the giving the recipient assents to an alteration in the relationship to the giver that opens this door (recognizing this sometimes gives a reason not to accept a gift). It need not be a determinate alteration of the relationship; it can be something worked out in the accepting ("I can accept this only if..."). Absent such an agreement, the giver's enquiry into the fate of the gifted object may still be rebuffed, but there now is a risk of rudeness and ingratitude that there would not have been had you kept the giver at a distance,

---

[19] There's an additional conveyance in small gifts too, but it's often realized as affection or good will. I don't mean to say that one can't make a psychological separation between gift and giver—as in refusing to acknowledge from whom a gift comes. But the refusal is just another way of dealing with the connection. Lest one think this is all too much to be credible, recall the comparable moral minefield in helping and its response in gratitude.

[20] Competitive gift-giving, like the potlatch, is an interesting case: its role can be redistributive; but it can also establish relative rank by displaying a willingness to disperse wealth. To work, all parties must know the script.

[21] I give you a film subscription and want to know how you like it; you may have many reasons not to respond, but I think your desire for privacy has less claim once you accept the gift. Gifts are (usually welcome) intrusions.

saying no to the gift, or better, having the opportunity to say no to the giving, or put conditions on the acceptance (not always an available neutral option).[22]

(iv) Because gift-giving (the gifts and the giving) imposes on recipients in these and related ways, it falls within morality's purview. That's why consent can make a difference. Of course if it is up-front impermissible to offer or to accept something as a gift, consent is impotent. We may not give or receive stolen goods, or protected plants and animals. In such cases the wrong is about the object's status as "givable" (morally speaking, the giving can't be completed because it can't be rightfully started). Whatever the wrong in the giving-too-much case might be, the transmittal is not impermissible—that is, the giver gives what they are free to give and the receiver is not prohibited from accepting it. If there is wrongdoing, it is something further about the *giving* of the thing, about the way the gift exchange affects the relations between persons. It is a wrong that can be difficult to make out because it would seem to be of an action-kind that is permissible (part of our license to give to others what we rightfully possess, other things being equal).

Suppose I raise rare orchids and occasionally drop them off as presents to friends. Some of my friends love them; some regift them; the orchids make one friend acutely sick. So my giving is sometimes successful, sometimes inept, and sometimes something I ought not do, at least once I know the effect on the friend who gets sick. It is wrong to continue with that giving, a violation of an "other things equal" condition that belongs to the action-kind: that is, knowingly causing harm violates a restriction on the permission that belongs to gift-giving. That's the point of the "other things equal" clause.

By contrast, if a parent consistently gives extravagantly to the one of her four children she likes best, she does something she is entitled to do, and yet there can be good reason to judge that what she does is wrong.[23] It is the same when a pattern of giving plainly encourages the dependence of the recipient. The problem is that these actions violate no "other things equal" clause: each is a free use of what the giver has and it is not a moral condition on giving that gifts be fair or even overall beneficial. Yet the giving action is wrong. We make no mistake in saying, "You shouldn't do that." What I suggest is that in these cases the wrong comes from something in the family of an abuse of authority.

Here is how that might be. In certain regions of activity, across a wide range of possible choices, we have the freedom to act as we judge best. Having that

---

[22] Though of course the sound of this is instructive: Yes, thank you for giving me X, but I accept it only on condition that you not ask about whether I enjoy having it.
[23] Think of Lear's fateful division of his kingdom. It was not just an expression of weakness of character or an old man's desire to control the sexuality of his daughter, or... That is, it was all of those things, but as a doing, though done by kingly right, it was wrong: wrong to do. (That there may be reason to think the kingly right itself is impugned by the case would be a welcome step.)

freedom, that authority, allows us to realize an important value. Property and parental rights are obvious examples. The cases I am highlighting are ones where an exercise of discretion draws on the rationale for having it—so not about the enjoyment of an absence of rules or of free play, but acting in a practical space where it matters to what we are doing that our action reflect our judgment about what to do.[24] The space of discretion is also a space of risk. Specifically, when an exercise of discretion is inconsistent with its justifying rationale, then the action that follows can be wrong. Self-defeating in a moral sense. Not strictly impermissible, not a violation of a constraint, but still wrong: it should not be done. (Let me be clear: this is *not* to say "permissible and wrong"; rather the action is "*not impermissible* and wrong."[25])

Using the contrast with a conditional wrong, which violates an *external* limit of the sphere of authority, in the problematic or self-defeating cases, the wrong comes from a violation of something *internal* to it: that is, the wrong is *embedded* in the sphere of authority. It is because the risk of wrongdoing is integral to what's valuable about the action-kind, *and* because the moral boundary cannot be independently identified by a rule, that it makes sense to regard the wrong done as a misuse of authority and not just a bad choice. Why this should be true about giving too much will take some explaining.

(v) The back story for giving too much might go like this. The moral value of possession or property is not undermined if we cannot use what is ours to violate the rights of others. It is also secure if there are limits to the terms of permissible contract. However, it would be undermined if we could not exercise extremely wide discretion in the one-way transfers that mark gifts. We might support this by following anthropologists who regard the gift as central to the way individuals and groups create and sustain various kinds of sociality (both private and more broadly social relationships). The discretion available in the gift exchange is essential to this work. If we are to bind ourselves to one another through meaningful gift exchange, we need the freedom to choose that allows us to express ourselves in and through the gift while tailoring the gift both to the recipient and the social purpose the gift is to serve. Getting things right is thus often dependent on the individual's powers of discernment and vulnerable to practical facility. We will just about inevitably get things wrong. This is one reason why such a region of interaction is a magnet for convention: most of us much of the time want not to

---

[24] This can include deferral to someone else's expertise, as when, on the occasion of my burgundy-loving friend's birthday, I consult with her favorite wine store about her preferences.

[25] The conjunction of "wrong" and "permissible" offends moral logic. What I am claiming here, and argue for in the next section (3.2), is that there is space for "wrong" and "not *im*permissible" if "permissible" and "impermissible" are contrary terms not contradictories. T. M. Scanlon acknowledges this region of cases in *Moral Dimensions* (2008). But because he holds that an action that is not impermissible cannot be wrong, he has to develop a separate domain of moral assessment for them that he calls an action's "meaning."

depend on our own resources of discernment (and we express *that* as well when we give a socially sanctioned gift). One way we go wrong here is in making gifts that affect relations between persons in ways not consonant with the moral point of having discretion about giving.[26] The parent who consistently favors one child over another or whose giving reinforces another's dependence on her undermines the conditions for persons' regarding themselves as they are, as equals.

In general, relationship-affecting actions can be morally wrong if they cause or threaten to bring about or maintain status inequality between persons. There can be a dominant party in a relationship, but not domination. One person may serve another, but may not be her slave. Advice-giving should not morph into oppressive rule. This is familiar moral terrain. Now, in making gifts we standardly express or enhance connections we have or build connections we would like to have. On the dark side of gift-giving are gifts that aim to humiliate or mock or to reinforce subordination in a relationship. Vicious gifts. I want to leave these aside, since the case that is puzzling is well-intentioned and, at least on the surface, friendly to the recipient.

Across the range of well-intentioned gift-giving, some giving calls for a reciprocal gift, some not. In most cases, the recipient of a gift should respond in some way, conveying recognition of the good will or thoughtfulness or appropriateness of the giving. The actions in the exchange form a set, one completing the other. A gift object that lands still-born in the hands of a recipient is some kind of failure.[27] In a successful giving, we recognize one another in the gift and the giving, taking something of the other into our lives through the gift, however modest or grand the exchange may be. In giving too much we disrupt this mutual recognition: to use the language of another time, we put the recipient at a disadvantage. Of course such a position is uncomfortable, but it's the further claim that it affects the equality of persons in the relationship that matters morally.

Consider for a moment and by contrast sacrificial or supererogatory actions, where more is done than could be expected or required.[28] So, in the usual kind of case, some person, A, faced with a choice between losing his leg or B's losing his

---

[26] Where the wrong is embedded in this way, an action that might in other locales be fine is here wrong. Paradoxically, it is the sphere of permission that creates the space for the wrongful action. Other cases share this form: to value autonomy is to give agents discretion over decisions they may make poorly; to value speech involves accepting and protecting foolish or hurtful speech. The justification for protection does not inoculate the actions protected from being wrong to do. Such a distinction is often made between law and morality (one may do a moral wrong acting on a legal right); the distinction here is inside morality.

[27] This resists the idea that a gift is complete in the giving. It's like the throw in playing catch. Anonymous gifts are a special case: someone has reasons to block the normal narrative arc of giving and receiving.

[28] It is action over which the agent has discretion, though I am less confident than most that one is always free not to make the sacrifice.

life, sacrifices his leg. A does something extraordinary; supererogatory. But now let's go on with the story. B is of course incredibly grateful, but at a loss about how to make an appropriate response; nothing she can do or say is adequate to what A did. A's action is for B the first movement in a set she cannot complete. To this extent, the sacrificial action also disrupts the relation between persons. In friendship we can stretch the boundaries of what we can accept from one another, as a matter of course and in special circumstances. But there are limits. If A and B are friends it is possible that their relationship cannot survive the supererogatory sacrifice. That's regrettable, but surely a bearable cost, given the greater good of the life saved.[29] It is no paradox of friendship that the relationship might be the source of reasons to act in a way that makes the friendship no longer possible. It's a movie script; maybe a tragedy; not a paradox.

In the case of "giving too much," the problem is not that the good given is too large absolutely, but that the burden created by the gift is too great: out of proportion... to something. In a supererogatory action, it is the burden of providing the benefit that makes the action discretionary, but it is the benefit that makes sense of the action. With the gift, the burden of giving it isn't an issue, nor is the benefit one that would otherwise obligate. But like the supererogatory action, this action, the giving too much, introduces a burden. Unlike the supererogatory action, imposing that burden is wrongful. At least that's the claim.

Now, it is true that even if gifts create burdens, the burdens are often welcome: they give us opportunities for further communication, make it easier to share things, transmit values, build social connections. These are opportunities which if not given by giving can be harder for us to find. Which brings us back to the discretion we have in making (and receiving) gifts and the task we have of managing the burdens that come with them. We won't always do it well.

Suppose I give something significant to you; you start expressing your gratitude; I firmly waive it away; there is nothing to thank me for, I say. Why would I do that? The most natural read is that I don't want you to feel that my gift or my giving burdens you. I wanted you to know: "It's a gift! There's nothing you owe me." I don't have the power to waive away your feeling, but I can clarify the meaning my giving was to convey. You may or may not wish to hear this. Suppose I take it a step further. Having waived away your gratitude, I also refuse to accept a return gift from you. I didn't want, and didn't want you to think I was aiming at, a return gift—I really just wanted you to have something. And I'm hurt that you don't see this. That's why, faced with the material shape of your thanks, I rebuff you. Now you are hurt. So it turns out that both parties, wanting to act well, have moved into the space of mutual insult by mismanaging the moral burdens that come with giving and receiving. There were things to say, things that could have

---

[29] Here the note of proportionality sounds clearly.

been made explicit, that would have avoided the unhappy outcome. There's no easy explanation for why things go wrong. Once we find ourselves on this sort of terrain, a lot of different things can be going on.

What makes giving too much wrong, when it is, is that it disables the recipient as a full and equal participant in the exchange: it overwhelms resources of response. The recipient becomes, as it were, morally speechless, unable to perform the acknowledgment that would complete and secure the gift as a transaction between equals. There is nothing the recipient can do or say that is sufficient, but he must respond. Refusal of the gift is possible—a kind of exit that keeps the problem from compounding. But it can't resolve the difficulty the gift introduced, and in its counter-assertion, it overtly contests not only the giver's will but her generosity.[30] If the gift is not refused, and the recipient, unable to fill the role of a full participant in the exchange, cannot complete the giving act, he becomes, in a sense, subject to it (it imposes on him). Of course sometimes that is the intention of the giver—to overwhelm, to show power, to shape the life of the recipient through the gift. The giver's aim is to put the recipient in a position of deference, to establish or exhibit their inequality.[31] But the effect can also occur without the aim. Giving too much, even if motivated by an impulse of generosity, can alter the relation to a recipient in a status-demeaning way.[32] Good intentions are compatible with mismanaging a region of interpersonal connection that morality calls on us to get right: that in our interactions and transactions, we maintain our and others' status as equals. When we fail, it's not that we will suddenly begin violating each other's rights, but rather that we may no longer be able to reliably act from a fair evaluation of one another's interests as equals. A sense of disadvantage may be manifested on the one side, of resentment on the other, that clouds or impedes judgment.[33]

Now what counts as giving too much in one situation or relationship might not in another. Since we are not in a region governed by rules of action, it is to be expected that some of us will be able to act or react safely in circumstances where others cannot: sensitivity and self-knowledge, a grace in giving or receiving, can

---

[30] One can imagine friends of unequal wealth whose gifts to each other are never comparable. They know and accept this. Part of the work in maintaining such a friendship is to ensure that economic inequality doesn't distort the relationship. Giving unequally is not as such a problem. But giving too much might be.

[31] Anthropological accounts of elaborate ceremonies of competitive giving have rich detail about this sort of thing.

[32] This connects giving too much with other areas where doing too much turns a good thing into something we ought not do. Help is a good thing; too much help undermines initiative. Praise and criticism are good; too much of either creates damaging confusion about merit. And so on about food or exercise, though not about health or wisdom, as Aristotle reminds us.

[33] I should emphasize that I don't mean to be making claims about how people must feel in these circumstances. If you turn out to be someone who is untroubled by the receipt of exaggerated benefits out of sense of entitlement or obliviousness, the status problem is already present.

extend the limits of what may be done.[34] Conventions of appropriateness exist on both sides of the gift exchange to protect the cautious, the young, and the insensitive, among others who find themselves for some reason unable to negotiate the region's issues on their own. The closer we are to one another, the easier it can be to move things without a moral fuss ("what's mine is yours"). Of course there are also special problems about gifts between intimates—more is communicated, there are opportunities for collapsing difficulties elsewhere in the relationship into the gift exchange (though, as we also know, gifts done well can be healing). Given the nature of the gift exchange, and the way it interacts with other activities and relationships, this degree of variability and compounding was to be expected.

(vi) This discussion has done little more than peel back the cover on the topic of gifts. Just below the surface there are fascinating issues about anonymous gifts, charitable giving, bequests, public and state giving. There are gifts that deplete the giver, and those that don't (artistic production is sometimes regarded this way). Outside the narrow confines of analytic philosophy, the gift and the gift-exchange are of enormous concern, in anthropology, economics, feminist thought, and continental philosophy (mainly French). I have no definite idea why this isn't a larger topic in our tradition. Perhaps the reason for philosophical neglect has been the tight focus on distributive questions, and in giving, on philanthropy. The relational issues that arise in directly benefiting another may seem secondary, and gifts a private, not a moral matter. It should be clear that neither view can be right.

3.2 Middle Work 2: Impermissibility and Wrongness

The obvious question going forward is about the controversial meta-normative claim about the relationship between the impermissible and the morally wrong (more precisely: the possible consistency of *not impermissible* and morally wrong). Before answering it, one might want to be sure we have to go there—whether all that is necessary in the moral data might be captured in a less worrisome way. We often say than an action was permissible but bad of one to do (we sometimes talk this way about cold assertions of rights); or permissible but inconsistent with a commitment to virtue (or inconsistent with attitudes necessary for virtue); or permissible but in tension with two people having a minimally decent relationship ("I get it that you didn't *have* to help, but how can you call yourself my friend if you wouldn't do this?"). I could have said things in this vein about the embedded wrong cases that raised this issue and said something morally informative. I didn't

---

[34] Great gifts from strangers are confounding, sometimes inspiring. Like sacrificial gifts, they are extreme cases whose rationale and moral status depend on and can't explain the ordinary moral norms of giving.

because none of them capture the sense in those cases where *what* the agent did was wrong, not just that in her acting she was less good as a person than she might have been, or that she could have done something better. That's not the correct metric of moral assessment in the cases that raise the meta-normative question.

Although the cases that got us to this point may not seem of maximal moral importance, it would be a mistake to think fundamental moral distinctions show their face only in matters of life and death. Hard cases are often encumbered with procrustean presuppositions (often used as data points for any theorizing, thereby tightening their hold); working away from their gravitational field can provide liberating perspective on basic moral notions. With that in mind, I will offer two approaches in support of the meta-normative space I want to claim. The first develops the conjecture introduced in section 3.1 that the pair impermissible–permissible is not exhaustive with respect to moral wrongness (that something can be "not impermissible" and yet wrong).[35] The second (taken up in Chapter 4) considers the way the imperfect duty of due care (or non-negligence) introduces an additional circumstantial element in the moral assessment of action that puts similar negative pressure on the idea of impermissibility as the sole mark of moral wrongness in action, this time through bringing motive into the account. In enough ways to be significant, the two approaches inform each other and should provide sufficient reason to reorient several key moral assumptions.

We typically do not mean the same thing when we call an action impermissible as when we say it's wrong. In saying that an action is impermissible we often imply that it is all things considered ruled out, not available to the balance of reasons. It's a verdict forbidding a kind of doing: killing the innocent, even to produce a large benefit, is a paradigm example of the impermissible. That's not what we must be saying when we judge an action wrong to do. A possible action strongly opposed by the balance of reasons might be wrong to do (if the reasons tipping the balance are moral ones), without yielding a final verdict of impermissibility if more of some kind of consideration that entered the balancing could reverse the judgment.[36] Further, impermissibility is not a verdict about an action *simpliciter*. An action is said to be impermissible when it's an instance of a forbidden or impermissible *act-type*: e.g., killing the innocent, torture. But then to say of an action or related act-type that it is *not impermissible* is *not* to say *ex ante* that a performance of the type is morally neutral—to be performed or not as the agent chooses. Rather, it is just to say that it is not *ex ante* or all things considered already ruled out. It is open for further consideration. In some circumstances, an action that is not *im*permissible—not an instance of a forbidden type—can

---

[35] See page 39 (and footnote 25).
[36] In this spirit we might say that the balance of reasons speaks against breaking a promise for a small benefit, but if the benefit is large or significant enough, the balance of reasons is recalculated and the promise-breaking may not be wrong. Of course we do not need balance of reasons talk to reach this conclusion.

nonetheless be wrong to do.[37] Judgments of moral wrongness are context sensitive in a way that impermissibility is not.

If we follow this line of thought, we get a tripartite distinction: impermissible, not impermissible, and permissible (I leave it open whether the third might be an empty class). Despite their surface form, I am suggesting that we regard impermissible and permissible as *contraries*, not contradictories. We could then say an action is morally wrong *either* if it is of an act-type that is impermissible, *or*, if not of an impermissible act-type, ruled out in particular circumstances or conditions.[38]

I am not supposing that pointing out a possible resorting of categories makes the case for accepting it. My point is that the familiar pairing of permissible–impermissible as exhaustive terms of evaluation for the moral status of actions is not *necessarily* true, not true as a matter of concept or meaning. Since there is reason in the moral data to reject it, we might want to consider where the commitment to the exhaustive pairing comes from.[39]

A natural thought is that the pairing mirrors the exhaustive distinction in positive law. But part of the point of the exhaustive legal pairing is to eliminate middle ground: what is not forbidden by law is permitted by law. In principle, "not legal" designates a zone of enforceable prohibition. But there is no comparable idea or regime of moral policing. We have at most imperfect duties to prevent others' wrongdoing and are not typically in a moral position to impose penalties for wrongs done. One might offer other moral or practical reasons for the exhaustive pairing on the moral side—e.g., that morality must be narrow in its requirement, leaving the agent free to act however she wants to so long as she doesn't violate a directive moral rule. But that would involve a substantive normative argument about the nature of moral requirement, not just an excavation of the logic of the terms.[40]

A similar issue obtains between moral and legal uses of "right": that is, I think we should resist the idea that it is a matter of logic that if one has a right (not) to do X it cannot be wrong (not) to do X (on the grounds that having a *right to* implies it is *permissible to* . . .). If "having a right to" is an independent moral and not a quasi-legal notion, we might understand its point in a different way. For example, we might instead say that to have a right in this sense is to have a sphere of

---

[37] An action can be morally okay if done to a stranger but not to a friend. We will say it's wrong to treat a friend that way, but not that the action is impermissible.

[38] This also gives a natural way of treating exceptions—as belonging to a class of actions that are typically but not necessarily wrong.

[39] It may be that introducing a gap between the "not impermissible" and the "permissible" won't fit well with traditional deontic logics. If so, that's a consideration not an objection if the moral data call for having it.

[40] "Blame" is a more complicated marker. There's pressure to say that however unsavory an action is, if it is within an agent's rights to act in that way—so not impermissible—she cannot be blamed. And if no blame can be launched, her action is not wrong. No blame and no interference playing the same role. But the aspect of blame that goes in this direction is responsibility for consequences, not the blame of "how could you!"

discretion, or a sphere of authority, something that is one's own to use (versus another), which is not the same as having conditional license to act as one wills. Indeed, as we have just seen in the "too much" cases, the grounds for there being a sphere of discretion or authority are often part of the explanation of how actions may go wrong in its exercise.

The general thought is that within a sphere of authority, the moral status of an action can be connected to an agent's judgment and choice. If one has the relevant authority, taking Saturdays off or assigning a plum job to employee George rather than employee Martha seems to make it the case that one does no wrong in not coming to work on Saturday and in not giving the job to Martha. Abuse or misuse of authority can change an action's moral status. Some abusive actions live in the shadow of authority and go straight to impermissibility: making it a condition of giving Martha the job that she provide a sexual favor, for example. Morally, no one has the authority to do that. In other cases, the fault is about misuse rather than abuse. Always assigning Saturday off to oneself, or to one's pal George, when others have equal interest or need is an exercise of authority carried out in a way that undermines the authority's rationale (viz., using one's discretion as a supervisor to make work schedules efficient). That makes the action *in this context* wrong, perhaps not the first Saturday one takes off, but as the sequence of self-dealing goes on.[41]

There are all sorts of good reasons to grant or cede authority to someone in some sphere of activity, sometimes even to give them free rein. We might give Arthur authority to manage our investments and Mary authority to determine the first cut in some competition. Absent the authority granted, Arthur and Mary would be acting impermissibly if Arthur sold my stock or Mary put candidate *a* in the reject pile. But if they do have the authority, they may make these choices as they see fit. We balk, to take an extreme case, if Arthur and Mary exercise their respective authority using a method of random selection (or by consulting a spiritual medium). Arthur then sells my stock and Mary puts candidate *a* in the reject pile. If being given discretion were the end of the story in the grant of authority, then while we might be disappointed in the outcome and learn a cautionary lesson, we could not complain: no wrong was done. But in real life, if what was intended was that they use their expertise, then even if there was no contractual or fiduciary expectation, if Arthur and Mary acted within their remit without due care, what they did was wrong. A secondary and imperfect duty was violated whose purpose is to keep the exercise of discretion in line with the value that supports granting or having it.[42]

The moral puzzles in the giving-too-much cases arise because part of the value of ownership is having authority over both free and contractual conveyance. Such

---

[41] It will be debated whether the first Saturday, if taken as the *first* Saturday (as in an intended sequence), is wrong, regardless of what is done on subsequent Saturdays. I would argue that it is.
[42] This is the duty of care, discussed in Chapter 4. Cases of this sort can be difficult because terms of exercise of authority aren't spelled out, and because of the point in reliance on authority, can't be.

authority respects, indeed expresses, the equality of persons. It's not surprising that if, over time, permissible exercises of the authority over possession introduces substantial inequalities, it may be morally necessary to employ the correcting machinery of distributive justice to prevent the authority (based in the equality of persons) from undermining its own legitimacy. While gifts (especially untaxed inheritance) can disturb the social distribution of wealth, it is their disruptive force in interpersonal relations that we have been examining: when a gift imposes on someone, or puts another at a disadvantage, or creates unwanted intimacy. If the giving action is wrong in such cases, it is not because we are not free to give what we have, but because we will have failed to attend to the effects of the giving on our relations or on our status as equals, something we have a duty to do that belongs to our having the discretion to make gifts.

Bringing together the elements of the discussion here and in the previous section, we should say this. In the case of repaying too much, we start with the fact that repaying less than you owe is, other things equal, impermissible. It violates the rule that defines the relation of debt-exchange for whoever is in that relation. The importance of the rule is that it sustains the equality of the parties across the time of the debt: the lender needn't act independently to secure his loaned goods because the borrower is in his person security for the loan. Repaying too much doesn't seem to violate this rule—not literally, anyway. However, the over-repayer mistakenly assumes that there is discretion about the way the rule is to be adhered to, in that it allows him to bring other considerations to bear on what counts, for him, as repayment. One might argue that in usurping the final authority of the rule, the agent acts impermissibly. Suppose you thought that goes too far. Even if we accept that the action cannot be impermissible because the debt is repaid, we should still find it wrong—it is an exercise of discretion that the rule doesn't allow, and it is the rule, not the agent, that is the authority here.[43] Unlike the case of gifts, where discretion is of the essence of the activity—and we are to secure equal relations through successful exercises of discretion in giving and receiving gifts—equality of status in the debt-relation depends on the rule. In the gift case, the wrong involves a misuse of discretion; in the repayment case, the wrong is in assuming discretion where there is none.

Where to go from here? We've looked at some complicated cases that introduce questions about the moral guidance that flows from duties, perfect and imperfect. I have offered some explanation of why the questions arise and a conjectural outline of a moral-theoretic response to them. To get beyond conjecture will require several interlocking pieces of argument. The first involves taking a close look at the duty of due care, a secondary duty that begins to fill out the moral component of agent discretion by making a motive-involved connection to the

---

[43] It is here that we find a rationale for the separate duty of gratitude. The debt and repayment are in one moral register.

values that underlie primary duties, especially but not exclusively imperfect duties. This will in turn require a rethinking of the role of motive, indeed, of what a motive is, in an adequate account of moral and practical rationality. The second piece extrapolates from due care to primary duties more generally, focusing on their mode of regulation, and especially on the way the values that undergird different kinds of duty affect deliberation in complex or challenging circumstances of action. The third and most ambitious piece is to provide a framework in which the relationship between primary and secondary duties, and between perfect and imperfect duties, makes sense and can be laid out.

As the project proceeds, I will take increasing advantage of the resources Kant's moral theory has to offer in securing the systematic connections among types of duty. We should not be surprised that it's a natural fit. Kantian morality articulates norms of respect for persons as reasoning agents. The norms of correct reasoning are common to us; no one's reasoning is privileged. In satisfying co-reasoning norms in acting, we respect each other as equals. If we act well, we reason in a way all others can recognize as valid (validity implies universality). You can wish I would act differently while acknowledging that there is nothing morally flawed in my doings. There are, however, some kinds of action to which there is no valid route of reasoning. Engaging with another on those terms is to impose one's willing on them. The impersonality of this co-reasoning failure is the mark of impermissibility. It sets the *first* question about the wrongness of actions, but it is not the only one. If an action-type is not impermissible in this sense, the region of choice left open may yet contain positions that should not be occupied, typically, though not necessarily, because of the effect on actual relations people are in, or because of specific moral harms so acting would bring about (some of these are what I earlier called embedded wrongs). Open-ended permissibility is not impermissibility's complement. Rather than a morally vacated or empty notion, we now have reason to consider whether permissibility might mark a kind of substantive permission that follows from a rationale for discretion. Even modest personal choices—whether to exercise in the morning or the evening, alone or with friends—are ours to make not merely because they don't violate a principle of impermissibility, but because having discretion with respect to that sort of choice matters—personally and morally. That is, it matters not just because I want to run my own life, which to some extent I do, but because it is integral to the development of rational agency in individuals and to the sustaining of agency-supporting relations between persons.[44] It is that piece that is well accounted for by Kantian

---

[44] We register these differences in the ways we criticize wrongful actions. "It wasn't yours to give" looks at the action-kind and judges the action impermissible; "he already depends too much on you to ease his way" looks to the relational effect. In the first case the wrong is independent of the particulars about the parties; not so in the second. More is expected of an agent in judgment and action when she would enter one of the risky places in a sphere of permission. The same geometry creates opportunity for virtuosity and improvisation.

moral theory, which posits rational agency values as a necessary premise in (all) practical deliberation. From that perspective, actions may be stupid or futile or inefficient, but not for such reasons morally wrong (just as there need be no failure of reasoning if there's a mistake of fact). But an action will be wrong if *in the conditions of my exercise of discretion* it has the effect of subverting your (or my) status as a reasoning agent, even if only in a situationally confined way.[45]

---

[45] Practices, like institutions, give persons additional powers, and with them come opportunities to do more things well or badly. Once it is clear that there is a well-defined syndrome, we are like doctors. The task is to find the mark or defining symptom of things going wrong. In the case of gifts I have focused on the interpersonal effects on equality of status. It is possible I am wrong about the mark. Not wrong that there is one, but about the particular moral stakes involved. Even if so, it is unlikely that the general shape of the argument would be different.

4

Due Care

The Importance of Motive

4.1 The Duty of Due Care[1]

Among the things we found in examining the use and misuse of discretion in the giving cases, as well as the perturbations around beneficence and gratitude, were regions of morally significant activity in which a person either takes on or finds themselves in a position where they may without malign intent go wrong in acting, and yet what should be done or avoided is underdetermined by the applicable moral rules or duties. There are sometimes local solutions to generic cases. Pieces are carved off into etiquette and thank-you notes, conventional gifts, precalibrated scenarios of reciprocal giving and receiving. Outside the carved-off region, the issues that arise may be or seem to be novel or personal or tangled with other matters. We may have to proceed on our own, knowing that we are responsible for getting things right. And even where the rules and duties are clear, there may be different ways of doing what we must (how we tell a truth or keep a promise) and the context into which we are to act is freighted: perhaps a situation is evolving such that doing the right thing one way may turn out to be the wrong thing to have done when the dust settles. Among the moral resources available to the deliberating agent is a secondary imperfect duty that can help identify a course of action that will fit the moral circumstances when the primary duties are insufficiently directive. This is the duty of due care, sometimes called a duty of non-negligence. As a secondary duty, it extends an agent's deliberative reach by tasking them to integrate the value that underlies a salient primary duty with the values that belong to other duties with which their acting will interact. How this works will take some explaining.

But before describing the duty, I want to flag in advance two noteworthy features of due care that challenge assumptions often made about the nature of moral requirement. One is that the duty can require our being motivated in certain ways. This poses an obvious challenge to a rarely questioned moral-theoretic dictum—that because motives are not in our control, we cannot have a duty, a moral requirement, that depends on motive. If, as I think, the moral

---

[1] I first explored this fruitful subject in a seminar co-taught with Seana Shiffrin on moral negligence. For some of her views on the topic see "The Moral Neglect of Negligence" (2017).

phenomena we are about to examine are compelling, they will lead us to some hard and revealing questions about the account of motive on which the dictum relies. The second noteworthy feature is that what due care requires of an agent can depend on who the agent is, or what she brings to the occasion of action. This introduces some novel connections between responsibility, contingency, and moral inventiveness, requiring as a matter of duty that we figure out for ourselves how to respond to nonstandard or specific-to-the-agent circumstances. Due care may start out in the microspace of applications, but it ends up reshaping some of the structure of moral theory.

(i) Let's begin with a brief survey of the work of the duty of due care. The agential tasks of attending, remembering, preparing, taking care, and the like, are often also moral tasks, at least in the sense that failure at them can be moral failure. Something I failed to do yesterday makes me unable to do what I ought today. Aiming to take care of business I act in haste and don't get things quite right. I don't think about the fact that the gift I am giving will cause embarrassment. My expressions of gratitude are too public. All of these are instances of moral negligence, showing a deficiency of due care.

That there is a moral duty of non-negligence or due care is obvious once you think about it. But if you try to find a literature on the subject, there's hardly anything there. Negligence as a wrong *and* as a subject-matter is pretty much owned by the Law and run by the department of Torts. It's not hard to guess how that came about. The law has the huge task of managing the large class of actions that harm persons and property: it needs to say in what conditions the relevant harms occur; who owns them; what remedies are appropriate; who pays. However, if we think about negligence away from rights and remedies and instead in the more ordinary space of things we do, it's clear that it isn't always about harm, though it is about acting responsibly.

When you and I interact, on the street or in my front room or even over the Internet, lots of things can happen. We pass and make room for one another, we exchange ideas or gifts, we make plans to meet—and we intend things to go a certain way. But we also bump into one another, fail to notice a salient change, make an offending remark, miss a meeting—without intending these outcomes. Suppose we could have done better. We were negligent. Of course, even if we take the care we could and should take, failure happens. There are hazards that we can't anticipate; others' actions may alter the circumstances in ways that defeat our cautions. So it matters how things come about. Failure isn't proof of negligence; success is consistent with it (ordinary morality doesn't require harm to find negligence).

Suppose one makes a promise to A to do X, where X is complicated enough to require some planning and care to execute. I promise to bring bread; I forget the bakery closes at 6 and arrive at 6:30; it turns out the bakery is, for today only, open until 7. I bring the bread, as promised. I also acted negligently. Have I succeeded in one thing and failed in another? One can't succeed negligently, only despite one's negligence. Had I forgotten the promise and brought the bread for some other reason, we would not say I kept my promise. The same is true when the happy result is owed to luck.

Knowing that negligence lies in failure to direct the right kind of critical attention to our acting doesn't tell us what we are required to do. Even so, it's not hard to identify carelessness: the right turn made without looking; loudly voicing a criticism without attending to who can hear it; closing a valve or a latch, but not all the way; relying on memory rather than writing down a complex schedule. If these acts all seem to involve taking for granted something that shouldn't be, we don't, in acting with due care, need to pay attention to everything, just to those areas where absence or misdirection of attention is a fault (one could be attending very carefully to the identity of the birds in the branches while making the right turn). When we say, "Pay attention!" we assume that it's obvious where attention isn't being directed—that the target already knows where the spot is in what she is doing that might warrant the warning. It's as if we are primed for failure to take due care.[2]

It's important to be clear that the duty of due care is not a special case of the requirement to take necessary means, though it often does its work in tandem with the instrumental requirement. Having a duty to repay, I must gather and then convey funds in a timely manner. But servicing the duty instrumentally is not all that is required.[3] I should not, for the pleasure of it, act in ways that lead you to doubt that I will repay. That's a kind of negligence. Likewise, if I have a duty to be truthful about something, I should try to make the truth accessible (not deliver medical advice in an overly technical manner). I put out the fire but in a way that needlessly damages your property. Failures of this sort are not instrumental failures; they rather undermine the value of the dutiful performance.

So why not a duty to help *and* a duty not to cause damage; a duty to speak truthfully and a duty not to obfuscate; a duty to pay debts and a duty to appear to

---

[2] Getting it right is not quite a matter of more or less caution. Or of moral luck (as if at any moment we might find ourselves stumbling into a Chuck Jones constructed universe). It is true that the world of our acting causally outstrips our ordinary vision of it. Knowing that, we learn caution. But not too much caution, else we become paralyzed. As with many regions of activity where the "right amount" is for good reason under-specified, a responsible agent acquires the habits of caution suited to the range of activities she engages in, alone and with others. How we hand one another tools or put out a grease fire or maintain the brakes on our car. We monitor what we say to whom, try not to drive when we are sleepy. We also knowingly play games where someone is likely to get hurt and engage in productive activities whose footprint will not be light. And sometimes we throw caution to the wind. Much more than a grasp of efficient causality is needed to judge that what we are doing is good and sufficient to the occasion.

[3] Instrumental failures are typically regarded as a species of irrationality, not negligence. In some cases, failure to take the *best* or *better* available means is negligent: e.g., a doctor who maintains an entrenched regimen when newer medications have fewer side effects.

intend to pay one's debts. There are of course circumstances in which one has and must act on multiple independent duties.[4] But in the cases at issue, the supposed second duty somehow belongs to the first. We do not have straight-up duties to be transparent or not to obfuscate or to act without incurring costs. We also have no standing duty to remember. We have a duty to remember (or to take steps so that we remember) when forgetting is a foreseeable impediment to fulfilling another duty. We have a duty not to obfuscate when lack of clarity undermines the point of the truthful communication. And so on. When our not taking steps to remember, or not making the effort to speak clearly, incapacitates us with respect to the primary duties we have, it makes sense to describe these situations as failures to take due care.

Suppose that you do not fail in doing what your duty to repay requires, but the manner of conveyance introduces other kinds of difficulty. You repay the debt with a check, but after the banks have closed, and I needed use of the funds today. We know each other well enough so that you knew that. If it was easy, or easy enough, for you to have avoided the difficulty, then you should have. While I have no claim on you to do that based in the duty to repay, there surely seems to be a failure of due care here. But if so, with respect to what? Plausibly, the standing duty you have to be mindful of a friend's welfare. So not a *conflict* of duties; it was possible to attend to both duties with the same action. And although there is only one claim on you—were you able to attend only to the debt you would violate no duty—there is some kind of requirement that in the servicing of the debt you not do less than you easily could to avoid serious inconvenience to your friend. If you do less than you could, it would seem to be a failure of due care *in the exercise of one duty with respect to another duty.*

I think the data from the cases tells us that as a moral requirement the duty of due care has no content of its own, but is a secondary duty whose application and content depend on independent or primary duties. There's a nice term for it that Kant uses (though doesn't invent): an *accessoric* duty—a duty that comes into play when another duty is to be acted on.[5] The duty of due care implies a standard for action but does not provide one. Failure in its sphere means that *something* that required attention on the occasion of acting for a primary duty was not managed effectively. This is what divides negligence from pure accident.

---

[4] The literature tends to focus on cases where duties conflict, but, as we'll see in a moment, there is interesting work to be done on the effects duties have on each other when they can be co-instanced.

[5] See his *Metaphysics of Morals* 6:448. There's a question whether due care is a separate secondary duty or a secondary part of what is required of us by a duty (any duty). One of the things we see in the examples is that in acting in the space of even a quite narrow duty like debt-paying we may touch various things. There are lingering effects of the way we chose to act, effects that may interact with other duties—things that the narrow description of what we have a duty to do won't capture. That the moral fault in negligence is distinctive across cases suggests a category of duty. The lack of any content of its own suggests due care might be a formal or structural element of what a duty is. We will be in a better position to think more about this later.

Due care demands that we attend to and avert the effects of a wide range of foreseeable sources of failure (both generic and personal) that impinge on dutiful action, and that we manage the intersections of action on a primary duty with other duties (possibly but not necessarily conflicting duties). The duty calls for no specific action or action-kind; it is not owed as a matter of right. Indeed, due care can sometimes be satisfied without our doing anything, though not in the manner of negative perfect duties, e.g., not to murder, which we can satisfy simply by not considering it; due care requires our judging correctly that what needs to be done is being done. There is no single standard of due care; not everyone faces the same demands of due care in similar circumstances. It often calls on us to manage our own agency.

The duty of due care's indeterminateness and dependence on contextual judgment align it with imperfect duties in the standard sense. Other features suggest it is a poor fit. It doesn't seem to be directed at an end, or not an independent end. It may not leave the agent with any choice about whether to exercise it. (If it is ever a reason not to help someone that you helped someone else yesterday, it is inconceivable to think that exhibiting care in acting yesterday has any bearing on whether you should be careful today.[6]) Taking due care is often demanding and its importance in the moral scheme of things can be greater than many perfect duties. Further, its sphere of application ranges across all duties, from the most public duties of state institutions to the intimacy of personal relations. The negligent agent can be the private individual, someone acting in a defined public role, but also a court or a corporation or a battalion. The directing of non-negligent attention can be a matter of individual judgment or of institutional design. Due care can prompt creativity or dependence on checklists. I don't see any of this making due care a problem child as an imperfect duty. To the contrary, it alerts us to how much we may need to revise our idea of what an imperfect duty can involve.

(ii) Now here is the controversial claim. In the way that due care is something like a managerial requirement, it concerns not just our actions but also our motives. Think of it this way. There's a volunteer weekend, and some dozen of us want to spend it refurbishing an inner city playground. A site has to be identified, materials purchased and transported, assignments made, and so on. One of us agrees to act as the group's manager. She knows what the group is aiming at, as well as the values and resources of the members. She knows that it matters to the group that the task be finished in the one weekend. Several people really care about repurposing old materials. There is a budget; they all want the playground to be attractive and safe; it would help get the work done if there were decent food

---

[6] Except in the limited sense that being worn out by care yesterday, I choose projects for today that require little care from me in execution.

nearby. The manager has a list of things to do. She also has a different kind of list—of things to attend to, to balance, to anticipate. Quirks and rules and relationships, missing tools and disagreements. She will need to be flexible and creative, focused on and able to focus others on what matters to the project and to the group. She must, in effect, organize her agency around their shared values.

If we suspend for a moment the dictum about duty and motive—that because we can't choose our motives we cannot have a duty that depends on them—and just look at the case, I think the natural thing to say about the second list, the one that organizes her agency, is that the manager must take on a motivational burden in accepting her role.[7] If her decisions are made and expressed in ways that ignore the group's values, she will be negligent *because* she failed to be motivated as she should have been. Of course the manager is a volunteer, so we could say that the negligent manager's failure was in assessing her motives when taking on the job. Perhaps she should have declined it. That would resolve the issue about duty and motive. The problem is that this response is not available for the moral agent's obligation of due care: she is not a volunteer. We can't decline the job of effectively managing ourselves as we act for the duties and obligations we have.

How, then, should we proceed in the face of the conflict between data and dictum that comes with due care? We first need to get clearer about just what the connection between motive and duty is supposed to be. The managerial idea helps, but it's an abstraction that locates rather than explains the connection. We'll do better if we return to the related problem about the range of concerns the agent responding to a duty might have to have in order not to be morally negligent. We've seen that the duty of due care itself offers the agent no rule of action. Primary duties are in play—a duty about harm or a debt to repay or a requirement of fair treatment—but circumstances are such that how to act is not fully fixed by straight-up appeal to the rule or directive of the primary duty. If the success of the

---

[7] Since I know this claim will provoke resistance, I want to go "offline" for a moment to anticipate a bit. One source of resistance might be the idea that "being careful" isn't something that takes a special motive any more than directing one's attention or listening does. It's part of doing what the situation calls for. Or if a new motive is needed, it could just as easily be a crass one: say, being motivated to be careful in just these ways by the prospect of a reward. But consider two scenarios. (1) I'm attaching the battery cable and you say "Be careful!" and I say "Yes" and take a breath as I go on doing what I was doing only now more slowly and deliberately. And yet for all that I may be acting negligently. (2) On the 1980s TV police show *Hill Street Blues*, the shift sergeant would close every morning briefing with "Let's be careful out there!" He could have meant to include not slipping on a banana peel, avoiding junk food, or keeping grease stains off pants, but he didn't. He was alerting his officers to the special care they needed to use in doing their duty: managing the risks to themselves while protecting others. That they exercise good judgment *as the values they served* warranted in whatever crazy situations the city served up. Not that they do *more* of something, or do it more slowly, but that they approach things in a value-guided way. That seems to me to call on a motive. Might a resister contend that what's in play here is a *competence*? I wouldn't disagree. What I'm claiming is that the competence involves a motive whose task is to track and respond to multiple instantiated values. My conjecture is that resistance comes from thinking of motive as some kind of activating force with an object (desire-satisfaction, or even rule-following), so it couldn't play the role I want to assign it. But as I argue in the next section (4.2), the reasons for insisting on such a view of motive are not compelling, and certainly not necessary.

non-negligent agent is not a result of better instrumental reasoning, what guides her? It has to be *something* related to a primary duty that gives the agent direction.

The first thing to note is that there is more to a duty than a rule of action. Duties provide guidance in virtue of both their *content* and their *value*. Sometimes all that is required of us is that we avoid doing what a duty forbids (by its rule or content)—not to take more than our share or violate a right or fail to show up as promised. At other times we need to look to what makes the requirement of a duty matter: its *value*. It's the duty's value that sets the agenda for due care and that can make a demand on motive.[8]

Consider the promissory duty. It contains sub-duties about promise-making, promise-keeping, and promise-breaking. They are the content conditions (or rules) of promising. There is also what promising is *for*—its object or value. Our grasp of *that* is what orients due care. If we take the point of promising to be about securing cooperation without depending on altruism, that puts the focus of due care on avoiding promise-breaking since defection defeats promising's point. But if we thought the point of promising is to enable us to give another limited authority over what we do, our attention would be on trust as well as security of performance: that both parties act in good faith; that defection plus compensation is not an equivalent; that the promisee will not take inappropriate advantage. If it's the first, the focus of due care is on preparation and performance, and perhaps in anticipation, on possible repair. If it's the second, the concern is about maintaining the relationship that the promise brings about, or its fit with other relationships the parties may have.[9]

Or take the right to privacy and different accounts of what it, or the correlative duty, protects. There need be no disagreement about the kinds of actions that invade privacy, but different accounts of what the right of privacy is for (its value) can yield different contents for a related duty of due care. If the right protects a valued interest, compensation for violation (for the sake of other interests) is within the horizon of the right, and that would affect how careful one needs to be. But if privacy matters as an integrity value—because it partly constitutes the social boundary of who we are, of our identity—then due care will call for a high threshold of alertness so that privacy concerns are kept separate from other interests. As with promising, without an account of the value of the right or the duty, we do not fully grasp the terms of compliance.

---

[8] This is why moral negligence can't be regulated by an analogue of strict liability. The rationale is not about risk responsibility—who should bear it—but about norms of correct action.

[9] This contrast in interpretation exhibits an important difference in what it means to point to a duty's value. On the first, or securing cooperation account, the value is independently specified, with promising its instrument. On the morally safe transfer of authority from one person to another account, what that value amounts to is partly constituted by the content of the duty of promising. Not just any transfer of authority, e.g., at gunpoint; it has to be a respect or autonomy preserving transfer, and promise, so interpreted, can secure that.

If, as the examples indicate, the requirements of due care are that we be *responsive* to the interpreted value of a duty, they make a demand on the agent's ability to draw the value of the duty into her practical deliberation and proactive attitudes. And if this is, as it seems to me to be, a practical ability that is rooted in motive, we see the work motive is to do, and the location of the problem posed by due care.[10]

A friend of the dictum might respond: Must we read the requirements in this way? Why motive? Couldn't someone be schooled to act as a duty's value directed? Well, how? The point is that there is no finite list of actions to be taught, no lessons to practice: due care can call for an indeterminable variety of duty-relative responses that outstrip any fixed curriculum. Since this is a significant point of resistance, let's walk through one more extended example.

George knows that one should be on time to meetings. He tends to rush in at the last minute, which counts as being on time but is also disruptive. If he made a little extra effort with bus schedules, he could arrive a few minutes early and the meeting would start smoothly. We tell him that. We haven't told him he had a second duty he was unaware of—that there's a duty of being on time and one of being considerate. What we've alerted him to is that the point of being on time is being considerate. But it isn't *always* inconsiderate to arrive in the nick of time. One could imagine a group indifferent to hurried arrivals so long as everyone is seated when the gavel is struck or the movie starts. But if the point and value of being on time in this meeting context is to facilitate a multi-person activity, it's a disrespectful lack of due care not to make the extra effort. That's what the just-on-time negligent George fails to see.

I want to say that George does make a mistake about what the being-on-time duty calls for. He misses something. But since the duty is not a set of performance requirements with George missing one of them (it's not like missing a step or an ingredient in a recipe), the failure is not in the province of belief. If George had a grasp of the value of the duty he would be alert to how he should adjust his actions to meet the contingent needs of different settings. Correction does not add due care to the being-on-time duty as an extra rule of orientation; what is wanted is George, *as an agent of the primary duty*, motivated to exercise due care in realizing the value of the duty in his acting.

In light of this, it might be tempting to take a page from negligence as the law manages it and assess George using a reasonable person standard. After all, the point of such a standard is, in a way, to evade the problem at issue: how to hold someone responsible for something he doesn't see or recognize. But the reasonable

---

[10] This would seem to conflict with the ordinary sense of what we are asking about when asking for a person's motive. Aren't we asking about the psychological back story—what her motive was in taking the job—not about the organization of her agency? But we *are* asking about the back story when we ask this more complicated question about motive. The ordinary question (with its presumption that there's something hidden that needs to be revealed) masks the work motive does as a cause of action.

person standard is part of a theory of juridical accountability for harms, and the rationale for that doesn't fit George's very ordinary case. I think we make better sense of George's having done something wrong if we can allow that his failure involves a motive he needed to have had for him to track the moral values in play.

To make this a real possibility, we will need to take a step to the side and open a line of inquiry into the very idea of a motive and its role in practical agency. It's not a simple notion, not just a "that which moves us to action." It couldn't be that if it has to play the value-tracking role in moral action *and* support a view of wrongdoing that remains sensitive to the dictum's challenge to any connection in moral requirement between motive and will.

4.2 Middle Work 3: Motive

Here's a way of resetting the question about motive. We need a way to hold two apparently conflicting positions. On the one hand, there is the widely accepted view that we can't love or feel pity or be outraged by injustice at will. Knowing we should be otherwise, we can take steps to change, but we can't get there by bare choice. So no duty directly to have a feeling or an attitude *or* a motive that we might lack. On the other hand, I believe, and have been arguing, that *as* moral agents, *as* bearers of duties and obligations, we have a duty of due care even though satisfying due care can require our having some motive. I take the first position to be undeniable. I find the second supported by the moral data. So what to do?

In the back of my mind is this thought. If we are not troubled by Strawsonian reactive attitudes as a necessary element of our moral agency (attitudes that are beholden to norms of appropriateness), why be troubled by a connection between moral agency and motives (think *proactive* attitudes) that organize the agent, connecting her actions and attitudes to what matters in having a duty?

This suggests a strategy and a crucial distinction. Strawson's point is that as moral subjects we have reactive attitudes: those we regard as moral agents we judge according to attitudes we impute to them about how they regard us (and, reasonably, themselves). We don't demand of human beings that they have attitudes they may lack; however, in taking another to be a normal moral person "we demand some degree of good will or regard." Analogously, we might say, due care doesn't require of someone that she have a motive she lacks; nonetheless, a motive can be a condition of our doing what due care requires.[11] We might think

---

[11] If there could be a kind of agent that negotiates the terrain of due care by means of higher order of cognitive processing (a moral variant of Deep Blue), I doubt its primary duties would have the same content as ours.

of it this way. You couldn't have a duty to have hands or sight, although having them, you can have duties that depend on their use, even duties that require you to *right now* do more with them than you have done before.[12] Now, you can't have *any* duties unless you have certain practical capacities. If having the right kind of motive is among them, the argument is on its way.

Now, not just anything we might call "motive" will do. Whatever its neurophysical or rational nature, whether it involves a responsiveness to reasons or is something independent, *motive*, as I want to use the term, designates an action-oriented organization of the whole agent.[13] Instinct, not desire, is the better model. When we think of a desire, we tend to think of an affective state with an object (or object-type) that moves the agent to activity when an object-related instance is encountered or recognized. When we think about instinct, we think of a *system state* involving arousal, heightened attention, quickened activity, focused on an object *as* fits the instinct, moving the subject towards its object in a characteristic way. It's the global aspect of the instinct model that I would have "motive" inherit. It puts the emphasis on activity, on the causality of agency, and on value.[14]

Because motive in the system or agency sense is about how things go from the point of view of the responsive and active agent, it's a model that suits the complexity of moral action. In the face of a duty, say repaying a debt, a suitably motivated moral agent is active, focused on a task that means something, aware of how she should act and ready to do so. The debt is on my mind; I'm already on my way to taking care of it even if it's not due until next week; I am, if the debt is personal, grateful; and if I know you are uncomfortable about such things, also already seeking a way to show my gratitude without embarrassing you. If on the day I come to pay my debt you turn out to be out of town and I have to leave what I owe in your mailbox, with no way to express my gratitude, it's not merely one among the many things I planned for that I now cannot do, my debt-paying activity is now incomplete (leaving a sense of loss and regret). Of course if the debt is to my bank, my attention is fixed on making the payment on time, period. The different responses don't imply a different duty or a different motive.

---

[12] That I've never used my hands to perform a water rescue or to staunch a flow of blood is no reason to think I can't be called on to use them for that purpose if the need presents. I may be surprised by what I can do.

[13] I hear in "motive" something from the French *motif*: the subject of a painting or a melodic phrase which provides structure to a musical work and acts as a unifying element.

[14] I speak of models here because "motive" and "desire" certainly and "instinct" to some extent are terms of art. We say that Hume has a desire theory (the complexity of which is often not reflected in modern desire theories), and Kant has a motive theory, though when he speaks of motives, especially the moral motive, it tends to be mistakenly read as, functionally, an odd sort of desire. Neither Hume nor Kant needs to be read as hostile to motive in the system sense. Treating motive as a kind of disposition is a more plausible move from the Humean side. It's not a counter-direction for this discussion because what counts as a disposition can range from primitive and isolated response features of the organism to tendencies to recite romantic poetry.

It's awkward to capture this with a desire model.[15] Since the role of desire is to orient the agent to bringing about its object, the work of a desire-modeled moral motive is to identify and secure the performance of a required action (paying the debt), as if an object of desire; there is no natural connection with the value content of the duty.[16]

I find it helpful in thinking about this system idea of motive to look at *the person* from the perspective of the active human body. Consider the difference between thinking of hunger as a motive (or as motive-like) and hunger as a desire. I think of the desire as an activity-inducing physical module that turns on and off in response to calorically significant bodily changes. The prompted activity that began as an infant's rooting develops soon enough into seeking breakfast and then even interesting or desirable breakfast. The structure remains the same: in a healthy person, some physical change or state triggers some kind of food-seeking activity.

That's not wrong, but there's something odd about the modular picture. We do have responsive modules that relate to hunger and its satisfaction. The pancreas is one. Its function is to help with the digestion of food and to regulate blood-sugar levels (that in turn affect feelings of hunger). The gastro-intestinal tract is another: it secretes ghrelin that arouses appetite and affects when a person reaches satiety. But hunger is neither just a response to the presence of ghrelin nor just a response to the presence (or absence) of food. Hunger involves multiple systems and organs, triggers, arousal, attentional focus, perception and seeking, engagement with memory, and a characteristic (though not necessarily reliable) feeling. In priming the agent for an object, it may depend on past experience (infants suckle at all sorts of knob-like objects until they are organized enough to put smell and feel and familiarity together to actively seek the breast). Given its complexity, hunger may also be interfered with at different points in its emergence and by the demands of other systems. Associations are formed that cancel attraction to earlier desired objects; development and learning change and enlarge the available array of responses, leading in the higher mammals to the possible exercise of active choice. Hunger, so described, involves the organization of an active being's agency. That's hunger as a motive.[17]

When we tell this kind of story about motive we are at once naturalist and psychologist. Suppose we were interested in competitiveness as a motive: it affects perception, judgment, and physiology in certain settings. Not a desire for winning

---

[15] Awkward, not impossible. Ptolemaic effort can align the results of very different models. One may, however, wind up with something like Hume's double relation of impressions and ideas.

[16] It's not just a problem about desire. Dispositions set to track the balance of reasons are usually expected to latch onto the action or effect the balance favors, not the value.

[17] And what of desire? It will still make sense to talk about desires in the way we talk about urges—that middle-of-the-night desire for chocolate. And we might want to see desire as a kind of resultant—an action-prompting state caused by the motive system honing in on an object. What is abandoned is the belief-desire model of explaining the generation of action.

or a desire for self-advancement. It involves a complex social relation to an opponent that one seeks, though need not expect, to beat. Competitiveness doesn't make sense in all creatures. Some are natural cooperators; some go it alone; some will struggle with others if a resource is scarce but don't seek or need the struggle. An agent moved by competitiveness looks at the struggle in a positive way. We should say that something in the creature's nature, its make-up, tends this way or can be shaped that way. A naturalist will tell a story about how the tendency serves the species. A psychologist will locate the drive in the economy of the individual, marking the difference in the competitiveness that belongs to mate-seeking and that of playing chess. It's of interest where the sources of pleasure are, where danger is sought or tolerated. Both instincts and motives have vicissitudes. In humans, the work of mechanisms like repression and sublimation can mask the deep structure of a motive: we trace out how mating drives lead to shoe fetishes, or competition to a monastic life.

This seems to me a natural way to talk about motives. We say that self-interest leads Mary to focus on a goal, ignore a loved-one, lose sleep. Patriotism makes George susceptible to fear-mongering by politicians and to suspicion of his neighbor, to wear funny clothes, even to give up his life. In each case motive does not point to an object, even a vague one, that instrumentally shapes subsequent response and activity, but describes a potentiality of the agential system as it responds to some value.

If we add "rational" or "moral" to the naturalist's account, we are not merely adding something to a response set or object-palette. (As if to be rational is to be an animal +.) Both norms introduce distinctive cognitive and affective organization of agency, involving their own triggers and forms of arousal, attentional focus and a suite of responses. Rational concepts and forms of reasoning have a role in the organization of agency: in coming to judgment, in the way we act, and in the mix of appropriate responses to all stages and perturbations of the practical situation. To be in the grip of a rational motive is not just to be under pressure to do something or realize some outcome or even to instantiate the directive of some principle. It involves an organized response of the person to a principle-involving value.[18] So, likewise, when we compare the agent moved by sympathy with another moved by the moral motive it's not just that the former motive attaches to pain and distress and the latter to the principle of beneficence, the two agents read and respond to need differently, each of their motives carrying a different organizing value. A *moral* response to the pain of a person calls on us to give her some say about how and even if her need is to be met. "How can I help you?" is not just a *façon de parler*.

---

[18] I see shortness of breath, the EMT sees the early stages of a heart attack. I am moved to calm the agent; the EMT acts aggressively to initiate preventive measures.

This gives us an idea of why in terms of content and structure, the candidate moral motive as a system responsiveness to moral value better fits the data than something modular that provides directed energy for moral action. That still leaves a possibility question: is our nature such that it supports a distinctive kind of agential responsiveness to a principle-informed judgment that articulates a rational or moral value? There's some mystery about how even to approach such a question. I take it to be about the existence conditions for a kind of being. Here's what I mean.

For a living being there must be a significant match between its needs, its capacities, and its environment so that, actively or passively, it is able to sustain itself through generation and change. If it's an animal, it has basic systems that manage pain, hunger, and thirst, as well as response to danger, each able to trigger life-supporting activity. They are, in the language I am using here, system motives (or their precursors). Some animals have strong social motives that lead them to patterns of feeling and behavior that are not always optimal for the individual's material well-being. They will engage in dangerous mating practices, forego eating for the sake of their young. If, as with African elephants, herd attachments leave them mourning their dead, the fact that mourning depresses life does not show that there are conflicting systems of desire, one for intimacy, one for life, that vie for dominance. It makes good or better sense to posit a complex principle of affective organization or a system of motivation that we would expect to manifest in a variety of context-appropriate ways across individual and social behaviors.[19]

I think it is not implausible to regard the moral motive as in this sense an element of the existence conditions of a kind of rational being (as reflected in its perceptual, cognitive, and affective systems, as well as in its habitat). So if the existence conditions for *us* as a rational life form involved morality, understood as respectful relations that involve recognition of the value of persons as such, then

---

[19] An implication of the system view of motive that I'll note and then set aside for future discussion is that you don't have to be a natural agent to have motives—i.e., you don't have to have a psychology. What matters is whether an entity's causality is organized by principles that express and are responsive to value. So a basic structure that adheres to Rawls's two principles in lexical order has a motive in that its activity is oriented by and responsive to values of equality and fairness. Strict scrutiny in law is a structural expression of a motive that tracks the value of some due process protections. Not surprisingly, moral negligence arises with respect to institutional motives and values. Consider, for example, the circumstances around *Brown v. Board of Education of Topeka*. The research findings of psychologists Kenneth B. Clark and Mamie Phipps Clark about social disadvantage and segregation challenged the idea that the formal equality of separate but equal met constitutional standards for equal protection. Though not discussed in these terms, the argument addressed to the Court was about due care: *if* the Court accepted the Clarks' empirical findings *and* was motivated, as it institutionally had to be, by the value of equal protection, it had to take steps that would alter existing educational arrangement in the direction of the value. The assignment of motivation to the Court as such seems to me uncontroversial. Had the Court refused to consider the Clarks' findings, it would arguably have been negligent (or worse) because badly motivated. The evidence for this would have been the Court's arguments, not the motives of its justices. (Note that an institution needn't be in its defining purpose a moral institution for it to be or have the responsibilities of a moral agent. In a just state, one of the effects of legal incorporation is to introduce the moral motive into an institution's organizational structure.)

human beings would have to have, at least in potential, a distinctive agential organization unlike other natural agents, one that can be responsive to the normative demands of duties and the values that support them.[20] Although I think we have evidence that supports this (despite the painful present), I regard the argument as transcendental, not empirical.

If you thought we were nothing so fancy, just smart animals with complex welfare-functions, that might speak against our having a moral motive of this kind, though not against the idea of system motive as such. I believe the moral data points to a richer conception of our nature.

It is no counter-argument that it can take experience, relatively benign circumstances, and a morality-supportive social environment to get the motivational system of the moral agent working right. After all, we don't think that health is self-generating either, though we assume a desire for it. Perturbations and distortions are normal; a motivational system is typically robust enough to allow for self-correction, though not always or easily or in all circumstances. We expect mature persons to take a fair amount of responsibility for their cognitive and their motivational system's functioning well. If I'm prone to anger, or overuse insult as a form of humor, I should and can make adjustments (perhaps with others' help). We are expected to self-regulate as we entertain risky behaviors (not to drive after drinking).

Suppose we find that racialized anxiety affects someone's practical judgment and action. We don't infer an absence of a moral capacity; we instead recognize the role of this kind of fear in distorting a person's practical organization. Even when the region of failure is not first-person accessible or even first-person correctible, we are not excused. Think of the discussion around implicit bias—the idea that persons can sincerely avow a standard of impartiality that they not only fail to meet, they also cannot identify the source of failure in themselves. Correction may have to be drawn from a non-agential source: we can use procedural devices to approximate a morally defensible outcome, or seek a change in contributing social conditions.

It matters to response and correction what the nature of the defect is. It could be that an agent's motivational system is deformed or corrupted. This might show in a sense of satisfaction at the confirmation of a bias-determined outcome (consistent with an official rueful attitude). It's also possible that a person can be moved but not motivated by her bias, so a more directly causal rather than an agential

---

[20] This is in fact Kant's view. The moral motive is a system motive, an organizing principle of the human will as the capacity for good willing (Kant speaks of "determining ground"). It is a source of our pleasure in respectful relations and our sense of offense at intentional cruelty. It is constituted by, not attached to, moral principle. This sort of view is, happily, confirmed in integrative behavioral and neuroscientific studies that track the emergence of moral behaviors in system-developing stages. See, for example, Katherine McAuliffe et al. "The Developmental Foundations of Human Fairness" (2017).

explanation is warranted (as is the case with our tendency to vote for the taller candidate, or buy the item to the right in our visual field). Noticing this can cause surprise and distress, though also greater openness to change—we have less at stake in some of the things that merely move us.

We cannot always tell whether we are moved or motivated. We sometimes discover after the fact that what moved us was other than a motive: we unwittingly got caught in a cultural stereotype or were swept away by social pressure. It is on us to be alert to these effects, and where tools of resistance or correction are available, to make use of them.[21] Sometimes what merely moves us is something of value. Someone finds he has a fascination with form and color that intrudes on his career as an X. The fascination can develop into a principle of his activity, a motive, if he becomes a Y. Managing the tension between being motivated and being moved is an ongoing project of acceptance and sublimation. It helps us make sense of our vulnerability to akrasia and phenomena like adverse preference formation. This sort of complexity is not an unwelcome cost of adopting the system view.

To get us back on track, recall that the problem that set us on the path of a system motive was the awkward finding that the duty of due care had regions of requirement where the duty's satisfaction depended on a motive—viz., to self-organize in order to manage an open-ended, value-directed, moral task. The thought was that a different understanding of the sort of thing a motive could be might eliminate the reason for the blanket prohibition on motive-dependent duties. The target for the inquiry was then a motive that does not need to be summoned at will, tracks relevant value, and is both sufficient and appropriate for its object, dutiful action, and in particular, the duty of due care.

If the moral motive is a system motive, it is also a species of rational motive and thereby inherits much of its structure, though not its content or its connection with moral necessity. Normal human agents have a capacity to carry intentional action into circumstances they neither control nor fully grasp (circumstances that include opaque features of their own agency), while adjusting their actions to both the goal and the point of their acting. This calls for more than instrumental resiliency. Persons also need the ability to remain alert and responsive to the values that make their ends and actions worthy of choice. Both abilities direct an agent's causality to an intended effect; both are embedded in practical skills that involve attention to working around unanticipated obstacles; but it is the value sensitivity that keeps the agent's activity anchored in her rationale for setting her end in the first place.[22]

---

[21] We can ask a parallel question about the surrounding society that encodes bias in its institutions and culture—how much is passive legacy, how much living value.

[22] As I was writing this, there were fires burning in the Los Angeles hills a few miles northwest of my office. It was the end of term; I had scheduled office hours for nervous students with a paper due. The

Responsiveness to value in acting is not something extra, not something about our character or the meaning of our actions in some larger sense; it's about getting things right. I may play tennis because it matters to my health or I just enjoy it or it's a venue for maintaining a friendship. Whichever is the case affects how (and sometimes whether) I proceed. If it's health, I might do something else equivalent—or, if I have a tendency to flake, take extra vigilance; if it's enjoyment, I might decide "not today"; the connection with friendship introduces a host of things I need to be attentive to, including, though now for a different reason, being on time. Negligence, carelessness, and the like, are threats to end-pursuit generally. Part of our maturation as a rational agent is to develop both instrumental discipline and non-instrumental managerial skills to stay connected to what matters. It is one's motives, be they a concern for health or pleasure or friendship (singly or nested), that provide the connection—a normative connection—between end, value and action. Of course I have significant latitude in the face of the value of my discretionary ends. There may be cases where the costs of staying with what's of value makes a project or pursuit not worth maintaining. We lack this freedom with ends or actions that fall under moral duty.

The point is that when we turn to the moral case, the foundation of due care is already part of the fabric of rational action. That there is a *duty* of due care of the kind I have described reflects the nature of the values that give rise to the different duties and the kinds of practical problems they pose for us. We can have such a motive-dependent duty because we already have in place the capacity to be responsive to value in a motive-involving way. The agent who fails at the duty of due care does not err because she lacks a motive; she had the motive as a part of her capacity for moral agency, a potential that she failed to deploy.

In focusing an agent's attention on a primary duty's value, the duty of due care sets terms for reasonable response to the situational complexity that comes with our acting as duty requires. We may need to see, feel, anticipate, plan, leave ourselves vulnerable, take our time, engage others even when, if we were just

---

campus was open and safe. I'd checked my traffic app and saw that I could get to my office without too much delay. My instrumental reasoning was done. But I had other concerns, of a different sort. Some were about contributing to the traffic nightmare unfolding; quite a lot about what my students needed and how my decisions would affect them, about the contours of my responsibility and what else I might do that could make a difference. Coughing, I was reminded that there were health issues for me (I was just getting over the flu). I want to say that what set this mix of concerns in motion was a motivational engagement I have with my work as a teacher. It both prompted my projected end—getting to my office by 1:30—and injected it into my deliberation a lattice of values that not only affected my decision about what to do in these circumstances, but also about what to tell my students, what new options I needed to make available if the emergency continued (did I really need them to bring in hard copies of their final paper?), and so on. It was an extreme situation, but formally entirely ordinary. What it shows is that failure to give adequate attention to the array of values in play (I think of them as saturating deliberation), not only risks our reaching the wrong conclusion about what to do, we may then mismanage, because we fail to notice, options and collateral needs.

thinking instrumentally, we could realize the bare object of a duty directly and by ourselves. A morally competent agent comes prepared.

To be sure, not every moral agent is motivationally alive to the array of values that belong to her duties, and even if she is, she may not pick up on all that matters in her situation. We have structural limits and we are not always in peak form. The question is whether, given the presence of a capacity sufficient to engage with the relevant elements, failure that has its source in motive is any more problematic than failure of cognitive capacities that lead to moral mistakes. If we can be responsible for failing to put two and two together, we can be responsible for inattention to privacy concerns as our beneficent actions blunder into information that should not be shared.

None of this is to deny that there is a third- or second-personal evaluative perspective from which we may be indifferent to motive. An insensitive, under-prepared, or hasty agent may tell the truth, return what's owed, violate no rights, indeed meet all the demands of the moral situation. We might think of this as a view of moral requirement from the perspective of acceptable complaint. The point is that things look different from the perspective of the duty-responding agent. She borrows a book; intends to and does return it. The episode of borrow-and-return has a middle period—an arena of agent responsibility. It doesn't govern the order of chapters read, or who you talk to about what you read, but it does have something to say about wear and tear and about at whose convenience the return is made. A specific duty gives us a target *and* a forward-looking sphere of responsibility much of which is managed by the duty of due care. It's the task of the moral motive to prime the agent to meet these demands.

In fact, much more than due care is involved in a motive-involved moral competence Think about what happens when we acquire a region of duty. The concept that something belongs to someone else is not, when we grasp it, just another bit of sortal moral information. Understanding that some thing could be "not mine" and instead "yours" changes a person's orientation towards the physical world of things she encounters. Some things can be used but must be returned (it's Mary's truck); other things can be used but then must be left in place when you're done (those trucks stay in the playground for whoever wants to play with them); still others can come to be yours (through gifts or purchases or chance finding). The objects may all be the same, but their place in the scheme of moral relations is quite different. For the person acquiring the moral concept, it's not just about whether something can be kept or has to be returned. There are matters of delight, the enjoyment of possession and the different possibilities of sharing. The issues around using public common objects together are not the same as when we share privately owned objects (e.g., playing under the implicit threat of Jane taking her ball home). The spaces owned objects occupy look and feel different to us; we move among them in distinctive ways; love and aggression are directed at persons via their owned objects. We act to preserve what a loved one values; we give gifts. We need to manage envy.

Since we are talking about a system motive whose elements need to be actualized, we should expect the same motive to manifest somewhat differently in different agents. Moved to help, how readily one responds to some need can depend on past experiences. One person has vivid memories of earlier successes at rescue; another carries the painful imprint of a complex failure. The one reinforces practical confidence; the other creates space for hesitation. These are not additional motives but factors, like one's degree of physical strength or dexterity, that the motivated agent works with. She may seek a tool or support from someone else to take up the slack; knowing her own anxieties, just like knowing her physical limitations, may give her reason to decide *not* to be the one who acts. One can manage one's limits with respect to motive well or badly. Barring something unusual, difficulty in keeping track of one's money is not an excuse for failure to pay debts. Morality has its own reasonable person standard. Where one is unable to meet the standard, there may be spheres of activity that are off limits.

When we correct a child who does the right thing to get a reward or to avoid the disapproval of their parents, we are in effect telling them that what they've done is not enough: they have gotten only part of the way there. When someone acts as they should "by accident" (say, solely from convenience), it rings false to say that they were lucky (no moral police will catch them?). We are accustomed to saying of the morally motivated person that they perform the right action *plus* they had a good motive. I think we should instead regard the "from convenience" actor as doing the right act *minus* something. Their act is a kind of simulation of the real thing. We may have good reason not to regulate or interfere with the simulated right action, but it doesn't follow that anything that was done is correct, except in the sense that we grade as correct some answers on a multiple-choice test where every answer offered is "b."

If one thought the moral motive was just one among many possible causes of right action, tying action assessment to motive would not make sense. We should draw a different conclusion if the moral motive is a system motive responsive to moral value. Such a motive can be essential for securing the correct arc of dutiful action. It will follow that in some cases, motive can affect the moral valence of an action. This will be the case if a wrongful performance can be the result of a failure in value-tracking.

Consider two contested cases. The first case is of a landlord who uses his discretion in selecting tenants to avoid renting to someone because of their ethnicity or race.[23] Even if he is acting "within his rights" the action is clearly wrong. I think what makes the action wrong is a motive that draws an "externally rightful" exercise of discretion into a deliberative schema that tracks contrary-to-duty value. It subverts discretion, turning it into discrimination. In the second case motive makes an action wrong because the controlling value it introduces in the

---

[23] The example is drawn from T. M. Scanlon, *Moral Dimensions* (2008), 71–73.

acting puts someone at unjustified risk. Derek Parfit describes a gangster entering a coffee shop poised indifferently to pay for his coffee or shoot the barista as fits his mood and the moment. As it happens, he pays. Parfit concluded: bad attitude (bad motive), but nothing wrong done.[24] I think it's more like driving without using brakes: wrong to do even if no one is injured. So not a case of "no harm no foul." Acting on the bad motive violates the secondary duty of due care.

Typical instances of motive-involved wrongdoing occur when an action of a type not in itself *im*permissible has its source in a motive that causes a mismatch between the value of a governing moral requirement and the value the agent's motive in fact tracks. Think, for example, about keeping a promise to create a false sense of trust (like a long con), or acts of competitive gratitude. By subverting the action's apparent value, the motive can in effect make the action a lie. What looks all right isn't what it seems to be; as what it really is, it is wrong to do. Motive in such cases is essential to action description. We are to keep in mind that although a duty's rule, its content, orients our deliberation, it is the value the duty directs us to realize in our acting that is morality's point. Ignoring motive can make us miss that.

In the lead up to the duty of due care I indicated that I would be turning to Kantian moral theory to identify resources for managing a variety of questions that arose in the survey investigation of some imperfect duties. What to make of the fact that these duties are not free-standing? That they make best sense as parts of a system of duties? Whether this system feature is true only of imperfect duties? How important is it to have discovered that some violations of duty can be wrong, involve wrongdoing, and yet not be impermissible? Because imperfect duties are frequently encountered in contexts that contain multiple moral elements that are in no fixed order, what guides appropriate response to each and all of them? In some cases, due care orients the deliberating agents. But due care has its own issues. Because it seconds primary duties (both perfect and imperfect), it can inherit a determination problem if more than one duty is present in a context of action. And further, for due care to guide at all, it must access a primary duty's value, not just its rule. So we need an account of the connection between duties and their values that can guide action *and* make sense of duties as a system. In the Middle Work chapters of Part One, I have offered some answers to some of these questions that I believe are consistent with core Kantian claims (in some cases I did no more than open up space for an answer). But I did not use the Kantian apparatus to explicate or defend them. In Part Two I propose to begin doing that. It may seem an eccentric ambition since the Kantian theory most of us know, and even find compelling, has not been especially resourceful when taxed for answers

---

[24] Derek Parfit, *On What Matters Volume I* (2011), 216.

to questions it doesn't entertain. My thinking now is that this failing may be more a function of interpretive rather than theoretical limitations.

A theme that will emerge going forward is that we do well to regard both our moral rule-following and our more situational moral responses, like those called for by due care, as part of an ongoing project of inquiry. As moral agents, we are charged to affirm and extend moral knowledge through our duty-guided deliberation and actions. If we are engaged in inquiry, whether in morality or science, we have very good reason to hold that accidental results lack value, even if they get it right about what counts as "correct." Moral actions that are not guided as they should be lack authority to express the truth in moral action that our inquiry and practice depend on. This makes the structure and perspective of human moral agency central to an account of the system of duties.

Before initiating the full-on discussion of Kantian moral theory, I should say a word about the upshot of the way of talking about motive that I recommend for the famous *Groundwork I* account of moral worth (4:397–401). It will give a sense of things to come.

A first thing to note about the *Groundwork* text is that moral worth is a matter of "acting from duty" (versus acting from inclination), not quite the same thing as acting from *the motive of duty*, as we tend to think of it. There is a form and content issue here. On most accounts of moral worth, the "motive of duty" is taken to be a modular constant, attached to duty as a volitional or action incentive (of a special rational kind), whatever a duty's content. So promise-keeping, gratitude, truthtelling—all the same from the point of view of motive: doing the right thing because it's the right thing to do. But, as we've seen, if what a duty requires of us is deliberative, attention-directing, and being responsive to intersecting saliences, the modular motive seems a poor candidate. In acting *from duty* we appreciate and reason to the performance keeping an eye on the relevant aspect or aspects of moral value that are present in our circumstances of action. We might see a reason relevant to realizing the point of the duty to hurry or delay, or to act with an explanation why we are doing *this* thing and not *that*, or be prepared to manage fallout. If that's what acting *from duty* involves, then Kant requires a kind of motive that tracks the value in the content of a duty, not just the bare fact that there is a duty in play. When later on Kant talks of "moral personality," he moves us into this space of motive as the organizing principle of an agent's practical system.[25] I think it is latent in the *Groundwork* account; as is often the case in Kant's work, he elaborates no more than he needs to move an argument forward.[26]

---

[25] Cf. *Religion* 6:26–28 Concerning the Original Predisposition to Good in Human Nature.
[26] There is confirming material in Kant's *Lectures on Metaphysics* (28:247–259; 29:896–903). For rich accounts of the Kantian faculty of desire, which is, as it has to be in us, partly a cognitive and value-tracking faculty, see Stephen Engstrom, *The Form of Practical Knowledge* (2009) chapter 3; Janelle DeWitt, "Feeling and Inclination" (2018).

Whether the human being can ever fully realize this norm of good willing in their dutiful actions is an open question. But what they are aiming for is not a kind of purity of will; what they are to do is engage with all the morally relevant determinants that objectively bear on their choice of action. Persons who merely act according to duty fail at this task: their maxims lack moral content (a representation of the value of a duty) and so their actions do not have moral worth. Agents who act *from duty*, however, could swim in a soup of desire and inclination so long as they are able to keep their eye on what matters. It might be easier for them if the soup were less rich, but not better from the point of view of good willing.

PART TWO
KANTIAN RESOURCES

5
Making the Turn to Kant

5.1 A Revisionary Interpretation

The plan for Part Two is to introduce and argue for a revisionary interpretation of Kant's ethics (broadly understood). I am guided in this by two lodestars: that the resulting reading be convincingly *Kant*'s ethics, in both letter and spirit, and that the revision justify itself by giving us a better theory, in its own terms and in ours. The interpretation will be taxed to get us past some of the standard objections, to make the account of duties usable, and to show how the revised theory can incorporate desiderata that arose in the discussion of imperfect duties. The revision will be deep and sometimes surprising. It will present a unified and dynamic account of juridical and ethical duties; add a juridical dimension to the idea of moral agency or moral personality; allow for the content of duties to be partly shaped by circumstance, open to change, and yet be objective; explain how the object of a duty can pass from one duty-type to another, even sometimes be in the province of both, as in a division of moral labor; and, overall, present the practical part of morality—the system of duties—as an ongoing common human project, something we are to do together even as each does what they ought. Not exactly the Kant we thought we knew.

Some *ex ante* resistance to be overcome lives in assumptions shared by both friendly and hostile interpretations of Kant. One that is especially tough to root out is a rigidity in the account of moral duties that, among other things, rules out exceptions, resists the role of value in the articulation of a duty's content, and as a consequence, both disallows adjustment in the face of social and historical contingencies and is insensitive in the setting of duties to the strains or costs, as well as the creative opportunities, in realizing a moral condition. When it comes to the account of our duties, what they are and how they guide action, there remains an ill-fated emphasis on generating duties and obligations by way of the *Groundwork*'s "categorical imperative procedure." I believe and will argue that there is no such procedure. For the derivation of duties, we have to look elsewhere. When we do, we find an account of duties that presents their function not so much as rules for action or volition, but as nodes or transit points on a deliberative map to a coordinated system of ends and actions and institutions whose shared aim is our realizing the value of free and equal persons in a morally supportive social world.

A word about my method going forward. It is standard and sound practice in revising a reading of well-known texts to engage with competing accounts, debating comparative strengths and limits. The problem I face in Part Two is that many of the revisions I propose depend less on a new reading of some sentence or paragraph (though sometimes they do) as on an argument about fit with *other* proposed readings of texts not often taken to bear directly on the immediate interpretive question. Where that's so, I've felt that extended engagement with the immense scholarly Kant literature could obscure or swamp the arc and larger implications of the moral habitat project. So except in a few cases, where the line of interpretation I favor goes against an established and author-identified position, or when a line of argument I join is clearly indebted to someone else, I don't pause to argue with competing views. It has allowed me to tell a complicated theory-story that a reader should be able follow and be in a position to assess on its merits. That doesn't mean I think accepting the whole is a condition of finding parts valuable. Or that I think my way of sorting Kant's categories of duty is the only credible way. I regard the arguments and interpretations of Part Two as, in architectural terms, the schematic design phase for the Kantian moral habitat idea. More work will be needed to test the functional capacity of the proposed design elements, to assess moral costs and feasibility. Going to critical deconstruction too early risks losing sight of the point of the endeavor, and possibly missing the support that a strut or truss to be introduced later on provides.

Because I begin by casting some doubt on the way Kantian morality is generally understood, I assume the reader has some familiarity with the *Groundwork of the Metaphysics of Morals* and perhaps with parts of the *Metaphysics of Morals*. As the positive argument develops, engaging Kant's theory of 'action under law', his view of moral assessment and imputation, and, centrally, the role of innate right as a source of moral powers, I will change tack and show in some detail how the interpretations I favor emerge from the text.

5.2 What's It For?

Rather than tiptoeing around the issue, the best place to begin is with a first question about value.[1] It will help orient expectations.

It should be obvious, though I know it's not, that any account of our duties has to answer a "What's it for?" question. If we are to be bound by duty, there has to be

---

[1] As I noted at the outset (cf. Chapter 1, note 3), I am comfortable talking about "good" and "value" together so long as we keep the following clear: what's good is of value, but it can be open whether it ought to be valued; what's valued may or may not be good. The value of persons, we might say, is their dignity. Is that a form of goodness? You might think "no" if you think it's to be respected, not promoted. But that's a view of goodness we can reject.

something we are aiming to do in acting morally, something we would now or later, alone or with others, bring about or realize. In acting we aim to and do change the world. We accept that our individual actions may not always be successful; it would be intolerable if the conjoint effect of all of us acting well was in no way beneficial. Taking the question seriously does not mean, *pace* Prichard, that we are looking *beyond* morality for an answer—that we regard the "What's it for?" in terms of our interests. What we have reason to want is a characterization of our duties that shows the actions they require to be intelligible and good, a potential source of reasoned conviction that can engage attention and commitment—that they be able to organize and direct real persons, both individually and collectively.

The "What's it for?" question seems easy for the consequentialisms—they are designed to answer it. But their kind of answer, where duties are about outcomes and nudges are as good as motives, makes it hard to capture many of the features of moral action we've canvassed. The focus on a palette of current options threatens the ongoing connectedness of action and attitude that some duties call for: we sometimes have to carry the legacy of past actions into current choices in a non-outcome-centered way (the demands of gratitude are not outcome optimal). So there's a cost that comes with the ease of answer. Of course, consequentialist theories find ways to include some of these odd features of ordinary morality, often by going up a level where it can be argued that their inclusion is itself optimal.

A certain amount of theory construction is inevitably *ptolemaic*. Most any plausible theory will, by way of epicycles, accommodate itself to objections from common sense and to the compelling bits of competitor theories. In the hands of those who set them out, moral theories learn from each other. Can most consequentialist theories make room for duties of gratitude or due care? In a sense, of course they can. If having dispositions to take greater care, or care of a certain sort, would be overall beneficial, then on consequentialist grounds, persons ought to have those dispositions. If returning a benefit with gratitude in action or expression promotes the good, then we should do that. And also not, if not. And that's the start of a problem.

Ptolemaic solutions tend to be unstable because they are reactive, not generative. We see this in the history of rule utilitarianism as a response to common-sense moral objections and to the exclusion of independent first-order moral considerations such as fidelity and the value of truthfulness. Rule utilitarianism *is* a better moral theory. It is, however, under destabilizing pressure because it has no good story to tell about when to make the move to a rule, or what should limit a rule's content (if it ever absorbs exceptions, why not always?). There are workarounds. The worry is that if the move to a rule blocks reapplication of the underlying "What's it for?" value, then the ability of the rule-level theory to respond is compromised. More rules can of course be introduced to manage the difficulty, even meta-rules to regulate the adoption of new rules. In the end, epicycle fatigue spawns a tendency to bite the bullet and embrace counter-intuitive results, perhaps sweetened by an error theory.

The ptolemaic problem is hardly confined to the consequentialisms. It is more conspicuous for them because they are good-promoting theories with a moving target. One might think Kantian theory is immune precisely because it is not a good-promoting theory. But recall how the so-called deontological paradox creeps in: if we should not lie, then it must be better if we can minimize lying, for which telling a lie might be a means. There are other ptolemaic pressures. Kantian theory needs to find principles of duty that can speak to the cumulative effects of large numbers of agents acting, where each action in isolation is permissible, but taken together they seem terribly wrong. It needs a way of including nonhuman animals in its account of the subject of moral concern. Kantians may then feel compelled to expand the theory's terms of assessment, and compromise with the foundational claim that the source of moral wrongness lies in the quality of agential willing. That's a very high cost.

I do think that Kantian theory has to say something about the way we regard and treat animals and something about managing the effects of large numbers of agents acting. And I believe it can, once the system of duties is up and running. Moral theories are like scientific theories in that their principles and laws are used to generate an explanatorily sound account of their respective fields of data. Since their premises partly pick out the data to be explained—as what they can explain—there is tension between the impulse to treat the system as closed and the pressure that comes from phenomena that seem to challenge the straight-on application of the theory's principles. Together they generate the ptolemaic tendency. And where there are different theoretical approaches to a region of inquiry that make salient different aspects of moral concern, the challenge for any one theory is often how to take up and absorb salient elements that are not, in a manner of speaking, native to it.

If a first tendency in response to such challenges is ptolemaic, it should rarely be the final posture. A theory is resilient when its acknowledgement of a challenge deepens and extends its basic principles, making it a better and more complete theory in its own terms. The interplay between new data and first principles can prompt a revision that creatively changes how one takes the point of the data and interprets the principles. It's a hermeneutical, not a ptolemaic, view of theory development.

As a practical and a moral matter, the normative arm of a moral theory cannot be a closed system. A moral theory includes an account of the possibility conditions of a kind of practice (as far as we know, a human practice), and an account of the values that call for and make sense of the practice, articulated in principles (of duty or best reasons) that apply to particulars. Because the descent from principles inevitably involves the incorporation of local and social facts, there is permanent pressure on a moral theory to be able to reflect and take account of them. We come to know more; the problems we are compelled to address change as knowledge or available means develop.

One effect of hermeneutical adjustment can make it seem, after the fact, that anything new already belonged (perhaps only implicitly) to the theory as it was pre-adjustment, so not new after all. But that's misleading, and ignores the further fact that the accommodation of the seemingly new will often change the way we understand the theory as it was, as well as make us question the innocence of what was taken as a given. Adjustments are often not just about correction. As it emerged that the very terms used to express respect for persons were coded for class, gender, and race, more than the language of respect had to be rethought. The very idea of what it is to be a person is contested as there are changes in how gender identity is understood and named.[2] Some will argue, not implausibly, that this teaches us that the notion of "person" was always fluid, reflecting what emerges historically and socially as of fundamental importance: so, property-owner, worker, citizen, human... If there's a Copernican takeaway, it's that there is a standing recursive obligation on those who are moral agents not just to maintain but also to renew basic terms of the moral enterprise.

Such an idea of moral theorizing may seem to take us far away from the core Kantian enterprise of setting out rules of duty as standards of good willing. I see it as a welcome part of the transformative effect of taking the "What's it for?" question seriously. It adds to the core enterprise inquiry about why a duty has the object and content it does, not in the sense of immediate effects, but in what it brings to human living. Suppose being treated as an equal made no difference in the way human beings went about their business, or worse, provoked depression and distaste for the company of others. Or if, when we imagined the world that "reason would bring forth," we found it cold and hateful, a source of despair, not hope, or bad for the children. It's not just that it would be difficult to discipline oneself to acting morally in the face of this—people have done worse for themselves. Kantian morality, as a practical regime, would be incoherent: in following the principles said to be constitutive of their active power, persons would undermine the value of their active lives. Which is not to say that morality exists to promote our interests or that in acting morally we should expect to benefit. Rather, it's that it makes sense to ask of the promising or the truth-telling or any duty what value or values our acting for it will realize. Which *is* to say that arguments *to* duties should have such value claims as premises. And if such

---

[2] In the face of this, *who* it is that is doing the theorizing loses its appearance of neutrality. Whose voices are being heard? How much of moral theory is captive to ideology? One of the strengths of the moral habitat idea lies in the way it makes these dynamics of moral practice central to the philosophical project.

premises are about forms of human living, they will have to be able to reflect changes in our understanding of what human beings and their relations are like.

Kant himself sees the "What's it for?" question as appropriate and inevitable.[3] There is ample evidence of an answer in the Kantian corpus that the point of our duties and permissions is to create a habitat for free, equal, and self-directing human persons to develop and express their rational natures. As a habitat, it is an environment suited to such persons, together, over time. As a created habitat, it has laws, but they are moral laws, not laws of nature. It is, in the Rousseauian sense, a second nature. Its fate is to a large extent in the hands and wills of those who inhabit it. The duties associated with positive law along with the duties governing interpersonal relations and duties to the self are the vehicles for habitat construction.

A Kantian idea of making something together supports an agency-centered account of morality, with duties that are deliberative and orienting in their requirement, not just productive of beneficial effects. Moral action is a mode of address as well as an efficient cause; duties elaborate terms of standing between persons. It can therefore matter in moral action how the agent reasons to it—whether and how her acting is anchored in the duty's value, reflected in her motives—perhaps not for all dutiful performance, but for more than one might think.[4]

As befits the ecological metaphor of a habitat, duties are interdependent and morality is holistic: it has to be a *system* of duties. Even if action taken for one duty can interfere with action called for by another, the overall point of two duties—their value—cannot be incompatible (so we should not expect that we can be required to be helpful to one another and yet allowed to be indifferent to the collateral effects on well-being of what we do for other duties). A duty approached in isolation from other duties is often deliberatively incomplete. It is not just that one may not be finished once one has dutifully performed because success with one duty threatens another. What we are to do in the first place can depend on our foreseeing that a duty might come to intersect with other duties. If what I would say to you is, though true, gratuitous and hurtful, a duty of truthfulness does not

---

[3] See, for example, Kant's *Religion*, 6:5. After reminding us that right conduct requires no separate end to motivate it, he says: "Yet an end proceeds from morality just the same; for it cannot possibly be a matter of indifference to reason how to answer the question: *what is then the result of this right conduct of ours?* nor to what we are to direct our doings or nondoings, even granted this is not fully in our control, at least as something with which they are to harmonize." This is "the idea of the highest good in the world." I am not here concerned with the conditions of the highest good, but of the necessity of the idea as a part of the rational structure of morality.

[4] This characterization applies even to duties associated with positive law. Not every moral agent is a natural person; some are institutions. And as I argued earlier (Chapter 4, n19), not every motive is an element of natural psychology; some motives are encoded in constitutions and other authorizing documents. Juridical obligation is a species of moral obligation. Though realized through political and legal institutions, it enables a wide range of activity that would otherwise be morally impossible for individuals. For an account of this see sections 6.3 and 6.4.

give me reason to speak, leaving me with a need to repair; in its system-based interpretation, that very duty gives me reason to stay silent. If we have agreed to meet and it's known between us that the arrangement is not consequential, I don't violate the promissory injunction not to defect if I signal the meeting is off because compliance would be very costly to someone else.

When looking at the ethics of gratitude and gift-giving, we saw how duties that follow from or are connected to property rights are internally attentive to other moral considerations in the way they direct action and attitude. The value of personal control over material resources (what property is about) stretches well beyond self-interest to matters of independence and self-shaping, and on to beneficence, and the material wherewithal to express and develop relationships. If property is also (in part) an instrument of dispersal for justice and some welfare concerns, this affects how we think about beneficence, or even taxation: not calling for a sacrifice or a legal taking, but different kinds of contribution to the common work of what a system of property holdings is for.

The alternative is to take the import of other duties and moral considerations to come from outside the deliberative catchment of the duty whose authority one is acting on—say, a promissory or property-respecting obligation. It is then hard to avoid weighing and balancing. One asks: Over against the pain that will be caused if I keep my promise, how much weight does a promise have? It's hard to imagine a metric for managing this sort of thing that isn't ad hoc. How would we assign different promises or kinds of promise different weights? On a more holistic view, by contrast, practical concerns coming from other duties and moral concerns are already in the catchment area of the promissory duty; the promise isn't weighed against them. Neither the specific directives of the duty nor its practical valence (its importance or stringency) is set for all circumstances.[5] A default deliberative structure is put in play by the duty, marking that we are in the orbit of a specific region of moral value. It is the geography of the region that tells us what the moral ecology will permit.

But this is all highly metaphorical and abstract. To bring it down to earth, we need to dig into the details of what I'm calling the Kantian habitat project.

---

[5] This is not any move to particularism. Context sensitivity isn't paired with anything like atomic reasons. There are still duties; duties provide deliberative schema; the schema are not blind to the co-existence of other moral features (you would never know a priori that people who ski can do ballroom dancing; we absolutely do know that people who claim property can make promises).

6
The Kantian System of Duties

6.1 Ground Clearing

My aim in the four sections of this chapter is to lay out the elements of the Kantian system of duties in a way that resists the recurrent worry that Kant has a "derivation of duties problem." Through no lack of interpretive effort, it remains unclear how to use Kant's arguments to explain our having the duties we do (or any duties). Commentators switch back and forth between the *Groundwork* and the *Metaphysics of Morals*, especially its second part, the *Doctrine of Virtue*, in search of arguments that can explain or generate duties, but the efforts have not, to my mind at least, yielded up an account that is not ad hoc, riddled with cherry-picking strategies, ultimately relying on the results one wants the arguments to provide. There is an adjacent question that also needs an answer: why we have *duties* at all—as opposed to reasons or values with respect to which "duty" might represent a summary directive report. I will be arguing that duties are a moral kind whose members together form a system of rational practical requirements, perfect and imperfect; they provide deliberative schema for negotiating regions of fundamental concern for securing the equality and independence of human beings (understood as rational, finite, embodied agents). Since this argument makes use of assumptions that are both broad and atypical, it will be helpful to see why the interpretive tradition's more narrowly framed arguments fail, and have led to there being a derivation of duties problem for Kant.

Although the *Groundwork* speaks of "deriving" duties from the categorical imperative "as their principle" (*G* 4:421 ... *abgeleitet werden können*), commentators have failed to find a reliable method for following the maxim testing recipe that Kant's subsequent examples suggest (the so-called CI procedure associated with the formula of universal law or law of nature). The procedure is unreliable (generating both false positives and false negatives), and dependent on moral premises that it assumes and cannot derive. Added to that is the multi-faceted action-description problem for specifying maxims: the procedure's input. Faced with all this difficulty, many *Groundwork* interpreters have turned to the other formulas of the categorical imperative—humanity, autonomy, the kingdom of ends—which avoid the maxim-specification problem, and, in introducing more content (e.g., the idea of treating persons as ends-in-themselves), look to be able to avoid the difficulties associated with the formula of universal law. I have come to think not only do none of these strategies work, none of them *should* work since they depend on a mistaken reading of the *Groundwork*'s argument and apparatus.

Most efforts that turn to the *Metaphysics of Morals* to account for our duties focus on the *Doctrine of Virtue*. Although Kant lays out an array of duties to self and others, from truthtelling to beneficence to friendship (with even richer portraits of the related vices), left out are many duties that belong to morality as we usually understand it: duties about assaults on life and body, promises, possession, even familial duties. Left out or relegated to the *Doctrine of Right* whose juridical duties apply to these regions through positive law enforced by coercive state authority. But even if we would or could have no promissory duties without contract, surely the ethical duties of promisor and promisee are not just analogues of the regime of juridically enforceable contract. And although most intentional injury is antithetical to beneficence, the wrong in it doesn't seem well explained as a failure to promote another's happiness. Worse, when the *Doctrine of Virtue* points to a source of duties, it's the idea of humanity as an end in itself that does the work, but with humanity spelled out in richly empirical anthropological and social terms which would seem to violate the "no empirical grounds" strictures the *Groundwork* makes central to the Kantian idea of duty. And of course any problems with the *Groundwork* account of the formula of humanity as a source of duties will reappear here. So the *Doctrine of Virtue* arguments founder, and the *Doctrine of Right* is not a source of truly *moral* duties at all.

Some who see these problems regard the conjoined parts of the *Metaphysics of Morals* as either a philosophical mule, or, more kindly, as an artifact of late-in-life ill-advised publication decisions. To the contrary, I see in its twofoldness an argument that the complete moral project of duties and obligations is not to be had in the application of a *Groundwork*-driven theory of good willing. Well-founded institutions of public law provide necessary background conditions in the explication of the connection between good willing and moral or dutiful action. Such an argument would make the *Metaphysics of Morals* as a whole a good fit for the habitat project: it calls on us to do something together that is a necessary condition for us each to act well. The theory of the habitat project engages with how things go from the point of view of a well-formed person *in the setting of a larger collective moral project*. It makes possible coherent deliberation across the various domains of obligation. Assumptions at work in the background that make moral judgment possible—about the status of persons and institutions, specifically—aren't normally elements of deliberation, yet they have to be deliberatively accessible to and coherent with the active elements of moral judgment. This turns into a *moral* requirement on institutional design.

This means we need a new reading of the argument structure of the *Metaphysics of Morals*. But before offering that, it will be useful to walk through the broad claims I've made about the limits of the *Groundwork*'s moral formulas and theoretical strictures. Limiting the scope of what the *Groundwork*'s central arguments can do is not a negative or deflationary project so much as a clearing away of misdirected interpretation that occludes its real contributions to the system of duties.

It's not hard to see the cogency of the criticism that comes with taking the *Groundwork* to be engaged in deriving duties. In order to elicit the rational fault in actions contrary to duty—making a lying promise, betraying a trust left in one's hands, taking others' property—Kant famously argues in the *Groundwork* (and again in the *Critique of Practical Reason*) that the subjective principles (maxims) of so acting would be, if universal laws, internally contradictory. Critics then point out that Kant uses the logic of the moral concepts the wrongdoer employs in their maxim to reveal the form of wrongdoing: making another's possessions your own assumes a system of property; the lying promise assumes a convention about reliance; and so on. The criticism is that even if Kant's arguments can show inconsistencies in universalized willing, the arguments assume and don't derive the duties.

The critics are right—*if* Kant was, by those arguments, aiming to derive duties. As I see it, the critics, and not only the critics, read the *Groundwork* in a way that conflates two very different philosophical tasks that Kant kept separate: one is a radical approach to a metaphysical question (what would it take for a principle of morality to be possible for rational beings?); the other is a generative normative project (given what *we* are like—a specific kind of rational being capable of moral agency—what are our duties?).[1] The *Groundwork* has powerful things to say about the former, and despite appearances, almost nothing about the latter.

Kant is in fact quite clear that the *Groundwork* is not a text in normative ethics. Its announced purpose is to search for and establish the supreme principle of morality; its method of argument, Kant insists, will forego the advantages of application. Of course, the *Groundwork* uses examples, and Kant allows that the formula of universal law can be used in moral appraisal.[2] But we make a mistake if we then conclude that the examples are models of duty-derivation. Their role in the text is clarificatory: to confirm at each stage of a very abstract argument about an a priori rational principle that it really is tracking morality by showing that familiar contrary-to-duty maxims are not consistent with the form of universal law. Finding out that a maxim fails does not tell us what the content of the relevant duty is, or even, as legions of counterexamplers have shown, that it is a violation of a duty that is picked out—e.g., when we would be "first through the door." Typical

---

[1] That is: the possibility of morality depends on there being a source of action other than self-interest (a principle other than happiness), one connected essentially to our freedom or autonomy as rational beings. But the matter or content of morality, of our duties and obligations, is about us as human beings. If human rational nature can't explain our duties, nothing can.

[2] The idea of appraisal assumes some value as a measure, as when a diamond is appraised for purity, or an art work for authenticity. Moral appraisal involves the evaluation of the reasoning in a maxim that contains moral concepts, like promise and honesty: it asks whether a maxim's reasoning is consistent with its moral content.

moral failure, Kant notes, involves our exaggerating the urgency of our interests or assuming that making an exception to a known moral duty is, in the instance, trivial (G 4:424). With all such maneuvers, reasoning from self-interest leads to contradictions under universalization: the so-called "categorical imperative procedure" functioning as a kind of moral validity test for maxims, but not as an argument deriving duties. It's a proof of concept for the idea of universal lawgiving as the form of good willing.

We should also note Kant's care in presenting the examples. Each argument is triggered, *not* by a question about the permissibility of some random maxim, but by an agent fully aware that their proposed action might be contrary to duty and inquiring whether it actually is. It is no accident that only maxims overtly about something already taken to be morally significant are in play (promising, helping, self-neglect).

There are other warning signs. Suppose duties were generated from a procedure that assesses agents' maxims. We might then wonder why it isn't the case that each person's duties can be generated through the exercise of each person's judgment and will. That might well yield great diversity in outcome, which could be a threat to morality, or an opportunity for free expression of sound values in action. On the threat side, we should worry because moral action, claims, and complaints need to make common sense for all who affect one another. Some will argue we can get to a common ethics—they might call it a kingdom of ends—because each of us as a free rational being is under the common rule of reason and that implies common laws. But Kant's idea of a kingdom of ends abstracts from the matter of ends (and so maxims) under common law, and so gives us a compossibility condition and not a common set of duties. While the shared rule of reason could show that for any two agents with the same maxim it must be evaluated the same way, nothing in the *Groundwork* shows that each of us must approach our promises or the material goods of others or their needs with the same maxims, or the same understandings of what we are doing. Others might argue in semi-Rawlsian terms that we can get to a common ethics by each of us reasoning from the point of view of a representative person, or behind a veil of ignorance.[3] But there is nothing in the *Groundwork* argument to support such a Rawlsian move. On the other hand, if, as seems reasonable, there is no uniquely correct principle of property, or marriage, or promise—that is, common reason is not sufficient to get us a common set of duties—perhaps that's a good and creative thing. Common reason can rule out some principles, but any rationale for convergence must come from elsewhere. So, quite apart from the many familiar mechanical problems encountered in getting the formulas of the categorical imperative to work without

---

[3] Rawls himself modifies Kant's ethics in this way. See his *Lectures on the History of Moral Philosophy* (2000), 175–176. His immediate worry is to block maxims targeting populations to which the maxim-holder does not belong.

begging hard questions, it is not clear how a *Groundwork*-type argument could get us to the basic duties of ordinary morality.

We do get some general moral guidance from the patterns of wrongful reasoning revealed in the first run through of the *Groundwork* examples. In one class of cases, violations of a perfect duty for the sake of self-interest, we learn that such failures result from an over-estimation of the justificatory reach of the maxim's premise: e.g., there is no valid course of reasoning (i.e., consistent with universal law) from self-interested need as a premise to deceit as a permitted means (G 4:424). The failure is formal, a fault in a sequence of steps presumed to be valid, though what is reasoned about is a bit of material human activity that includes the conditions for reasonable trust. In another class of cases we learn that although we have discretion about the content of the necessary end of happiness—of what counts for us as our life going well or badly—we are not free *on grounds of our own happiness* to ignore the needs of others or the development of our own general abilities to pursue ends. Happiness may be a necessary end for us, but neither in idea nor content is it rationally authoritative. Saying what's involved in the non-neglect of others' happiness—what the relevant duties are—is not part of the argument's brief.[4]

If this view of the formula of universal law examples is right, it is not surprising that Kant was never bothered by the possibilities of maxim tailoring or eccentric maxims. You would only fend off challenges of that sort if you were trying to build a duty-generator or elaborate a sure-fire test procedure for any maxim whatsoever. A better assumption is that Kant was not doing either thing with the *Groundwork*'s first formulation of the categorical imperative.

Efforts to generate duties using the idea and formula of rational nature as an end in itself fare no better.[5] We do get a more resonant self-conception in the idea (and so a formula closer to intuition, Kant says [G 4:436]), as well as a vital piece of argument showing how an unconditioned principle can have a non-analytic yet necessary connection to a rational will. But the standard of evaluation in the formula of humanity is and must be that of the formula of universal law. The idea of humanity as an end in itself tells us that we must regard each person as an in principle authoritative reasoner: no one's reasoning is superior to anyone else's in virtue of being theirs. And that means that we may not act on a principle that *could not* be reasoned to correctly by the person affected (self or other). But that "could not" can only point to reasoning that encounters a contradiction, and the formula of universal law has already exhaustively set out that part of moral logic.

---

[4] The examples fit the idea of using universalization as a moral compass (G 4:404). However, as any scout will tell you, a compass without a map, or some other means of orientation, is of limited use. It can tell you "that way" is *not* north, but not how to get where you want to go. What's missing from these arguments is the account of *what* promise involves, or *why* the needs of others should be ends for us.

[5] The points I make here are developed more fully in my "The Difference that Ends Make" (2011).

What we get is an interpretation: If I act from an idea of promise or property that includes you as someone acted on or with but excludes you as an independent reasoner, I fail to regard your humanity (your rational nature) as an end in itself. There is nothing here that could be generative of moral content: e.g., nothing that can tell us whether a social practice involves a moral concept or is merely a piece of a social convention that ignores or has room for false speaking.

There's no help to be had from the other formulas. The formula of autonomy explicitly depends on the argument of the formula of universal law; the kingdom of ends re-presents this same argument in the idea that the aggregate of agents' good willing is formally compossible. Why? Because the form of good willing—its law—makes formal compossibility necessary. So again, we don't get past the formula of universal law's argument structure.

If we do set aside the *Groundwork*'s arguments as a generative source of duties, that doesn't mean the *Groundwork* makes no contribution to our understanding of them. We learn, at the least, that the content of some duties will have a connection to common reasoning and the nature of willed action. It may tell us that the form of moral reasoning will be different when it is about kinds of action whose existence is dependent on a moral regime of some sort (promising, property) than when it is about kinds of action that involve giving shape and direction to activities that we are anyway or naturally engaged in (beneficence, self-perfection).

By contrast and design, the two parts of the *Metaphysics of Morals* together give us the wherewithal to derive duties consistent with the *Groundwork*'s account of the authority conditions of moral requirement.[6] As we will see, its arguments are generative, supplying something like the categories or first principles for duties and exhibiting some stretch of what they look like *in concreto*, as Kant likes to say. Just as the categories of understanding supply a priori concepts that make our ordered experience of nature possible, so also do the moral categories introduce order, this time the order of a rational, law-governed system for how human persons ought to live consistent with their rational nature (their rational *human* nature). It does not tell us about the life form of rational natures as such. Its arguments to duties reflect the nature of human persons as they are known to be, and are about situations they have to negotiate given the human life form. Some things, our mortality and dependency, our communicative abilities, our need to use the material world to live, the drive for happiness, can be assumed for the kind. Other assumptions will have to be made but are permanently contestable, e.g., the social and technological contingency of what counts as able-bodied.

Now, in performing the task of deriving duties the *Metaphysics of Morals* uses two distinct principles—one about free action, one about necessary ends—that

---

[6] That the principle of a duty not support an invalid form of willing; that what is required of agents be something they can do; and that duties reflect and express the autonomous and free will of persons.

establish what appear to be two independent spheres of duty: of RIGHT and of ETHICS.[7] This would be a problem. If the two principles establish independent moral spheres, they would need a principle of communication and ordering to balance their interests. We find nothing like that in Kant's discussion—not even an argument for the priority of duties of RIGHT when duties conflict.[8] Some argue in what they take to be a Rawlsian spirit that Kant's sphere of RIGHT is something other than moral, in the narrow sense: that because it is concerned with juridical institutions and not the will of the individual, it frames the moral but is not part of it.[9] Such a view might claim support in the fact that the *Doctrine of Virtue* makes appeal to the principle of "humanity in a person as an end in itself" while the *Doctrine of Right* relies on the *sui generis* Universal Principle of Right, which isn't any sort of categorical imperative.

Kant doesn't speak directly to this question, but what he does say strongly supports the view that both principles are instances of the moral law, though only one is (or could be) a categorical imperative for willing.

We should then ask: what relation do the principles and their duties have to each other? The view I will advance here is that the two principles *together* generate a system of duties. Not just two kinds of duty—juridical and ethical—that complement each other, but duties whose content is determined across the boundaries of the kinds. We should think of them as principles of a unified and dynamic system of duties anchored in something like a *moral basic structure*.[10] The elements of the moral basic structure set categories for duties of RIGHT that then extend into the self- and other-regarding morality of individuals. ETHICAL duties, derived from obligatory ends, introduce their own requirements, but also often complete the duties of RIGHT and further articulate their regions of concern as the effects of juridical institutions are manifested in our relations to self and others. And because the content of RIGHT has to adjust to make ETHICAL life possible, it is a truly a system of duties.

The next section will look in some detail at Kant's approach to the duties of RIGHT. It is one thing to endorse the idea that political and juridical structures are

---

[7] To help with tracking terms, I will from here on use RIGHT for Kant's *recht* when it describes the system duty (also RIGHTFUL for *rechtliche* and in describing the class of duties of RIGHT), but the ordinary "right" for e.g., the right to property. I'll also use ETHICS for *tugend*; the usual translation of *tugend* as "virtue" takes the contemporary ear in an overly Aristotelian direction. The font shifts aren't pretty, but they hopefully make things clearer.

[8] RIGHT relates to ETHICS as form to matter (*MM* 6:380), but not as the form of a duty to its matter. RIGHT is about "the formal condition of outer freedom" whereas ETHICS is about the matter in the sense of objects of choice.

[9] Read through the lens of liberal and libertarian thought, the *Doctrine of Right* is often taken to provide Kant's answer to the justificatory question about the coercive state. The duties of RIGHT are duties of coercible obedience to positive law. It is a Rousseauian story. The coercive state is a necessary condition for rights (their existence, not just their security). Human freedom requires rights, especially property rights, and so freedom requires coercion. No nonjuridical moral action is required; no content of ethical duties is affected. I think that is not Kant's view.

[10] Both parts are "metaphysical first principles" *of morals* (*MM* 6:205).

part of the conceptual background of moral duties generally, and quite another to take seriously the project of a unified system of duties. How Kant carries the second project out is both novel and instructive. It changes the way we regard the moral agent, adding an element to what counts as "moral personality," and, as a result, introduces new questions about how responsibility for fulfilling duties is assigned (not just as a reflection of agents' maxims). Whether or not all the detail of Kant's argument survives critical examination, the way the project is cast is of sufficient interest and usefulness to make it worth seeing why it has the moving parts Kant assigns to it.

As we proceed, it will be important to keep track of the moments of argument versus the moments of application. The *idea* of RIGHT is not the idea of positive law—of juridical institutions (given shape by positive law)—although juridical institutions are a solution to demands of RIGHT. Solutions for *us*. General features of what we are like, the condition of our existence as rational beings, introduce threats to our independence and equality that we cannot resolve just by each of us willing well. Once we understand the problem and the idea of the solution, the project of generating duties can commence. Moving too quickly from the one to the other, from the demand to the solution, we can miss the point where moral value figures in the genesis of duties of RIGHT.

6.2 Setting the Stage: The Priority of *Right*

The most salient fact about the *Doctrine of Right*'s arguments is also thought to be the greatest obstacle to bringing it into the general project of the derivation of duties: the objects of duties of RIGHT are principles of external action, not maxims, the subjective principles of willing.[11] Deliberative or volitional content in the full moral sense is not a necessary element of juridical judgment or decision about what may be done. While true, there are good reasons to think just this feature of RIGHT makes it the appropriate place to start the derivation of duties and so to anchor the habitat project. Because Kant's treatment of RIGHT isn't obvious, it will be helpful both now and in the evolving discussion to devote some time to setting the stage for it.

A first reason to want RIGHT at the start of the moral system of duties is about the order of moral assessment: accurate moral deliberation depends on prior knowledge of what we are free to do: which efficient means are available for our purposes. Why should it be that if the nearest path to my health is through using

---

[11] Care needs to be taken that this not be regarded as a shift in Kant's moral metaphysics or as an invitation to strict liability. The entity assessed is as it always is: willed action. The aspect of willed action that is the concern of RIGHT is its effect: willed action as a cause, authored in choice, as consistent with a principle of freedom. *Duties* of right, or juridical laws, may have narrower concern still, depending on their purpose.

your prescription meds, I can't break into your house and take them, but if the nearest path to safety in a forest fire is across your land, I may trespass. Since the reasoning looks to be the same, there's a question about the different conclusions that can't be answered from the perspective of rational volition alone. Or suppose we would assess an action that promotes my ends and sets yours back, though that effect on you is no part of my intention or maxim. As we've seen, the *Groundwork* formulas can tell us that *if* rights are involved, then a maxim that includes a rights-dependent concept can be evaluated by the possible universal law standard. But they can't on their own distinguish wrongful from as-it-happens effects of action. Surely this is too fundamental a feature of our interactions with each other not to be at the forefront of the terms of moral assessment. Not every wrong action is wrong because of the way it is willed.

A second reason emerged in the discussion of imperfect duties: many of what we regard as our ordinary ethical duties depend for their deliberative import on the interpreted content of positive law. What is ours to hold or give; who or what has a claim on what is ours; what counts as having made a binding agreement. The laws that make property possible by way of rules of possession, loss, transfer, taxation, and so on, implicitly give an account of what the institution of property and possession is for and in so doing situate us in a materially articulated world.[12] As we've seen, it matters to our understanding of what we may do and what we may have to do whether we see our position as part of a cooperative human endeavor or a merely coordinated one. It may not be easy to read purpose from law, and what it is can be widely contested, but that doesn't defeat so much as reinforce the importance of the connection.

A third reason concerns the role of RIGHT in giving an account of the moral status of persons: not whether they have it, but what kind of standing having it secures. One might think that moral status in the Kantian system is determined by the general marker "rational being." Formally, that's correct. However, while the moral law is universal, duties are not. They can be species-specific and they are sometimes local. And since duties fill out status, there has to be more than the general marker (we already know that "rational being" is not itself a generator of duties). We need to know what about us as human beings enters the space of moral concern. Surely *something* about our bodies, *something* about the kinds of relationships we have (family, friend), *something* about the nature of our projects, private and collective, *something* about the fact that we live in structured social groups. But then we are faced with two obvious questions. What is on the list? Does it include our wishes, our happiness, our spiritual lives? And second, what is the moral significance of items on the list? Do they enter deliberations with some pre-assigned weight? Whenever affecting them affects a person's choices?

---

[12] A version of this sort of argument is found in Liam Murphy and Thomas Nagel, *The Myth of Ownership* (2002).

Answers to these questions require a moral account of permissions and powers—their content, scope, and limits. It is within and in terms of such a framework—a framework of duties—that human persons have effective moral status or standing.

We should think of the *Doctrine of Right* as providing a moral response to the most basic moral fact about human persons in the world: they will do things for production and reproduction that, considered as natural actions (using land, having intimate relations), leave them morally vulnerable (e.g., the way land use by some excludes others; how domestic life creates relations of dependence and subordination). That doesn't mean that without RIGHT things would necessarily go badly for anyone or everyone. It would depend on how people treat each other and they might treat each other well. However attractive that picture is, it wouldn't solve the problem. Dependence on the contingent kind treatment of others is a condition that cannot realize our equal status as persons—how we *should* be treated. I might be willing to share; but may I *on my own authority* include some and exclude others from using what I have or constrain their freedom of movement? Goodness isn't a source of interpersonal authority. So if it is not reasonable to avoid affecting one another in the above ways (and how could it be?), and we have no natural standard for how things ought to go, then there is a moral threat, a kind of moral impossibility, in the bare facts of human existence. Kant's argument is that given how humans live in the world with each other, this threat can only be resolved through the institutions and claims of RIGHT through which persons gain morally supported forms of authority that make equal moral status real.[13]

If one is thinking in terms of a moral habitat for human beings, this makes sense. We first need principles or duties that secure public recognition of what we are—principles of standing—and principles about how we, together, are to use the material elements of the world on which the moral habitat depends. Until we know who we are and what we have moral power to do, what kind of real freedom we have, we are in no position to seek the principles for the actions that express our more particular nature—things from giving gifts to doing favors to making art and raising children. While it is familiar to regard duties of RIGHT as providing a scaffold for the permissions and values on which ETHICAL duties to self and others depend, their connection to the ETHICAL runs deeper and in both directions. This sort of system-effect was at the heart of the discussions in Chapters 2 and 3 where we saw that, independent of questions about fair distribution, the free and unfettered exchange that a system of property makes possible is not enough to sustain the equality of persons. Because we remain vulnerable to the relational

---

[13] In his "Nature and Value of Rights" (1970), Joel Feinberg uses a similar strategy of argument to identify where the need for rights lies, though his conclusion is that with goodness and duties but no rights we have no way to make a "claim" and (explicitly) not that there is a moral need that requires an intermediary institution.

effects of forms of exchange, ETHICAL duties take on the task of making such transfers morally safe. So while standing is first set in the terms of public morality, what it amounts to in the relations between persons is not clear until the full system of duties, public and private, is laid out. In the larger picture, it is only within a well-formed political space that the demands of individual morality show their full value in a human life.[14] Kant is hardly the only philosopher to have thought this.

While these are compelling reasons to endorse the priority of RIGHT in a Kantian system of duties, because RIGHT regulates external action, there will remain a question about the idea of action under obligation that has to be addressed. Here again there is a tendency to over-read the *Groundwork* argument. It can look as though the only way action can encounter duties and obligations is through an agent's maxim—the action as it is willed. But the reason for the *Groundwork*'s focus on maxims is not that they are the sole object of moral regulation or assessment, but to show that the supreme principle of individual morality, authoritative for all rational beings, is a principle of pure practical reason. It *will* follow that maxims whose principle couldn't instance the moral law are not maxims of good willing, and that good willing is not a constraint on but an expression of a free will, but it does *not* follow that all moral laws, or laws of obligation, are directed at *how* an action is willed. So if it turns out that for us there are, because, morally, there have to be, duties of RIGHT, then actions that violate RIGHT do fail laws of obligation, and RIGHT conforming actions don't depend on good willing.

It's then not surprising that one of the tasks assigned to the Introduction of the *Metaphysics of Morals* (in sections III and IV) is to give a formal and general account of action under obligation, leaving it to the substantive discussions of the first principles of our duties to say when and why it matters what an agent's maxim or incentive is. Since this material is less often discussed, and is of considerable importance, I want to use the remainder of this section to set out the philosophical gist of Kant's account of action and obligation.

One possible way a general account of action under obligation might go would be to find principles of alignment between our producing effects in the natural world and moral categories of right and wrong. So if an action A has effects Y and Z, we'd want to know whether one or the other of those effects has moral significance and how, if it all, they combine (Y might be a harm and Z a benefit). A moral sifting of actions regarded as natural events. Kant doesn't take this path. He argues that an action under obligation is a *moral event* in its own kind of causal

---

[14] While injunctions against greed and jealousy, for example, point to a need for self-work, these tendencies of persons also indicate a role for institutions to mitigate inequalities so that persons may more readily manage their possessions (broadly understood) in morally healthy ways. Cf. *Religion* 6:95ff.

order. Just as the connections between natural events are explained by natural laws in terms of which we understand both normal and deviant effects (which events are effects that "belong to" which causes), so in the moral case there is moral causality with its own law (represented in the duties) that offers its own explanatory framework. This follows from the metaphysical foundations of morality. It also reflects a solution to an otherwise intractable problem.

Suppose, concerned with questions of responsibility, we need to know where an action ends. In natural terms, I think there is no clear answer. Is it when an action's causal influence peters out? And does it ever? Is it when it no longer plays a leading role in explaining how things go on? Or perhaps when the counterfactuals play out both ways? But why take any such model of explanation to be what matters morally? After all, even if event E would have happened had I not A'd, that I did A could still matter morally in the history of E. Treating obligation as an overlay on natural causality is a source of paradox and puzzle.[15]

Kant argues instead that principles of moral causality (of duty and obligation) *impute* effects to choice and give completion conditions for action under obligation. An action under obligation is called a *deed*: it is a doing issuing from free choice, typed by a law of obligation. That is, a law of obligation determines what the deed is—e.g., a promise-breaking, an assault—and which of its effects (both natural and moral) can be imputed to the agent as their author and responsible cause. Being open to imputation is what distinguishes a "person" from a "thing."[16]

Imputation does not depend on the intention of the agent acting (a maxim of generosity can yield action that violates RIGHT). If an action, issuing from choice, is typed by a law of obligation, certain things follow, morally, about the action and its effects. *Conformity* of action to obligatory law is a kind of safe harbor. You are where you are (morally) supposed to be, so the *moral* causality of your action is finished, regardless of further *natural* effects, good or bad. One might say that it's the duty, not you, that owns the effects. (It is not a success condition of one's promise-keeping that its effect be beneficial.) If, however, you *exceed* the requirements of obligation and do "more in the way of duty," it is *your doing* that takes the duty's concern (its value) further than was required, and the good effects are then imputed to the deed and to you as its author. Actions that are contrary to duty are still deeds (an obligatory law applies). If they bring about a good effect, it is, morally speaking, an accident (there is no principle of moral causality that connects the deed with it). So no wrongful action can be rescued by an intended or

---

[15] Was the effect intended or foreseen (or what ought to have been foreseen)? Was the effect direct or indirect, the result of an intersecting cause (which could have anticipated? and should it have been?), and so on.

[16] For those agitated by the formula of humanity remark about treating animals as things, this definition matters. The remark is not a claim that there is no morally significant difference between animals and rocks, it is that the actions of animals are not under obligatory law and so not (morally) imputable to them. If imputation is the anchor of Kant's idea of moral responsibility, this is not a controversial claim about animals.

realized good effect, no matter the magnitude. Where wrongful action produces bad effects, because the deed is a transgression there is no safe harbor: having acted on your own authority, you own the bad effects.[17]

Suppose the context is one in which there is the potential for harmful interaction (an overheated argument, say); the subject's moral activity—her *deed*—is to be described according to the relevant duty (respectful exchange) whether or not her choice of words is taken with an eye towards or an awareness of the obligation that applies. The moral perspective of the deed is in that sense third personal: the assessment does not refer back to the subject's maxim. So if, suddenly thinking about something else, the duty-oblivious arguer leaves the scene without saying anything, whatever her state of will, there is no imputable failure.[18]

As a theory of free action, morality looks at what we do in its own terms, including a proprietary order of causes and effects. Keeping a promise, an act of gratitude or one of self-defense, are first-order descriptions of deeds. They are not reducible to natural descriptions; they do not strictly supervene. The obligations that apply make it that some effects of deeds are imputable to agents, some not, depending on the structure of the law of obligation. If I keep a promise or repay a debt and as an eventual consequence the recipient acts badly, that does not count as an imputable moral effect of my action, even if it's true that had I not acted it wouldn't have happened.[19]

One doesn't have to agree with all of the sub-conclusions in the doctrine of imputation to see the deeper point it is making. Morality is a system of laws; the laws are principles of duty and obligation that not only issue permissions and requirements, they shape an autonomous causal field that assigns effects to deeds. Failing to recognize a law that applies does not excuse (though in some circumstances it may mitigate culpability); we cannot self-assign the moral description of our action *or* which effects we will take responsibility for. That leaves the question of incentive: whether the content of *some* laws of obligation require a recognition of their requirement (as part of their value) in moral action. That's an intra-moral question.

---

[17] Even if the transgression is unintentional (the subject fails to see that a known duty applies or makes a mistake about the grounds of obligation), not being where she ought to be, she lacks the protection of the duty; objectively, she is in unprotected waters. How things are *subjectively* can still make a difference. There can be a question about the *degree* of imputation: the extent of authorship of the deed and its effects may be treated differently depending on how easy it was for the subject to have avoided the error (*MM* 6:228). Failure to overcome a natural obstacle—hesitating at a sacrifice—is very different from coolly and knowingly acting contrary to what is required: the latter makes a transgression all the more one's own.

[18] This is not to suggest that RIGHT requires juridical prohibition of disrespectful speech. It is about the point of view of the *deed*—that there can be moral misuse of speech absent a maxim of disrespect, or, it's interesting to note, absent any maxim that would fail the universal law test. Of course it would be better to have a maxim rejecting abusive speech than one that leaves the possibility open.

[19] The "eventual" qualification is in recognition of the intersection of a possible requirement of non-negligence.

We can state this result in more familiar Kantian terms. We are free in one dimension insofar as we are not determined in our willing by natural causes, but we are not free from the constraints of moral causality—a burden in one sense, a source of new powers in another. The rationality that marks us as moral agents is a species capacity: we are in our essence free and equal. Realizing our freedom and equality in our lives as embodied, finite, social, and world-dependent reasoning beings is, by contrast, a shared moral project. Part of the argument of the *Doctrine of Right* is that the problems which initiate the project are knowable a priori and that the form of their resolution, if not the detail, is morally inescapable for all of us. The *Doctrine of Virtue*, by contrast, gives us a common moral project in the form of obligatory ends: a common project but not a shared solution. This distinction will prove important in the derivation of duties.

Again, we begin from the plain fact that human life and action involve doing things that limit the available actions and choices of others. Because I am walking here you need to walk there. Perhaps I even walk here with the aim of getting you to walk there. But things are very different if I pursue my aim of having you walk there by force or threat. In doing that, one person asserts herself against the equality and independence of another, setting terms, by their willing, for how things are to go for both of them, subordinating the other's choice to their own. Subordinated persons may not be unfree in an absolute sense, but they are not equally free in their choices. While use of force or threat is typically at odds with the freedom of persons, not all uses of force or threat subordinate (self-defense is a standard example), and not all subordination comes about by force (think of the conventional structure of family life). Moral distinctions are needed here. But also—if it is ever okay that one of us thrives while a neighbor doesn't, it seems to matter whether it comes about by our hand or by the invisible hand. The relevant difference is not between doing and allowing. For Kant, that difference could not be fundamental; if it can parse moral events, it will be as a consequence of the way laws of obligation type deeds according to kinds of effect on freedom of choice.[20] What's basic is the idea for thinking there has to be a moral domain—of RIGHT— whose purpose is to make reciprocal and equal freedom of choice possible.

Articulated RIGHT marks an order of permission and exclusion. Duties of RIGHT define spaces of morally possible action by flagging whole categories of means (e.g., using what's yours, forcing another to act for one's ends) as inconsistent with the equal freedom and independence of persons. This is the familiar idea of RIGHT as a limiting condition. The underlying structural idea is about protecting something of value—freedom of choice—represented as the formal

---

[20] To prefigure a bit. Exploiting the plight of victims of a natural disaster for profit (making the necessities of life inaccessible) violates the idea of RIGHT. Whether or not actual law holds price-gouging businesses responsible for the resulting harms, the harms are imputable. That is, if it is, because the practice is contrary to a law of obligation that settles matters of RIGHT.

object of what Kant calls *innate right*. The *contents* of the reciprocal duties of RIGHT are drawn from the necessities of human living reshaped to comport with the innate right of persons—embodied, finite, social, world-dependent—to be independent, free, and equal. The less familiar part of Kant's idea of articulated RIGHT, the part that goes beyond the setting and enforcing of limits on action, is the creation of *positive juridical powers* that enable rationally necessary but freedom-restricting forms of human activity in a way that is consistent with the freedom and independence of all human persons.[21] To see how this goes and what it adds to the moral story of RIGHT, we need to follow out Kant's argument.

At the opening of the *Doctrine of Right* Kant defines the idea of RIGHT as "the sum of the conditions under which the choice of one can be united with the choice of another in accordance with a universal law of freedom" (*MM* 6:230). An action is then right if it can coexist with everyone's freedom of choice in accordance with universal law, wrong if it cannot. Kant calls this the Universal Principle of Right. What the coexistence condition amounts to will depend on the nature of the laws of freedom that apply (e.g., about property or family or contract). Unlike the freedom of the will which is about its rational rather than sensible determinability, a kind of freedom whose law is a standard for individual good willing, the standard for RIGHTFUL choice is about how things should go for a community of interacting persons. It is for this reason a law of external obligation, a law that obligates each person, configuring her deeds, without a demand that she should make the law her maxim. This is not because the individual will is bad or weak, but because the conditions of RIGHTFUL action are reciprocal—ways we stand towards each other—not something anyone can unilaterally will.

This fits Kant's starting point: that the so-called state of nature is not a morally neutral place. The "natural" condition of human life is incompatible with the innate equal moral status of persons; we will do things that nominally interfere with the freedom of others. Each enclosed field, each built house, statue, or family, enhances the freedom of some and limits the freedom of others. No one has standing "by nature" to authorize any of that. Yet there are no reasonable grounds to think these forms of freedom-impinging action could all be impermissible.

The point of RIGHT, whatever its details, is to resolve this kind of problem. For external freedom (freedom of choice) to be morally possible for human beings, preventing interference with some exercises of choice—about production and reproduction, centrally—must not violate anyone's equal entitlement to act (their freedom of choice). *If*, for the vexed regions of choice, there were morally sourced laws for free action (laws of RIGHT), there would be entitlement to act even if so acting limited another's choice. Then, interference with lawful exercise in RIGHT would be a choice opposing freedom, would lack the law's protection,

---

[21] So if there were a race of rational beings whose existence conditions involved no such necessities, there would be no need for duties of RIGHT, though the idea of RIGHT would still apply.

and could be opposed or impeded.[22] This is Kant's "hindering of a hindrance of freedom" (*MM* 6:231). Actions violating RIGHT are still under a law of obligation and imputable (being under law is not itself a choice), and if imputable *and* a violation, not entitled to completion as their rightful effect. That's why their impedance is permissible: it is consistent with a law of (external) freedom. That such impeding is not contrary to freedom of choice tells us nothing about *who* can do the impeding. Though we know one thing about who it can't be: it can't be any one of us using personal force to compel obedience to our choices.

Since the reason we can't compel obedience through individual or voluntary joint action is that it would subordinate the willing of some to the willing of others, we are to straightaway see that the solution to the problem of external freedom has to be via a kind of agency whose principle is universal, not freedom diminishing, and yet supportive of interference with wrongful action.[23]

Kant's answer to this challenge is to locate RIGHTFUL interference in the coercive powers of the morally founded state. It is a created or made order of juridical powers (rights and duties) that apply to all in its domain. The *moral* possibility of a state with coercive authority depends on positing the obligatory state-creating action by what Kant calls an "omnilateral will": a bit of transcendental grounding that takes the rational impossibility of the alternative—private force—to justify the conditions, whatever they turn out to be, of freedom preserving rightful coercion.[24] That is, the shared morally vulnerable condition of all who live together requires a shared solution (something they *cannot not will* for the sake of their freedom).

It then follows as a condition of free external action that each person has a moral duty to be a part of, and to be supportive of, the created collective authority. Because no choice outside such an order is free (in the sense that interference with it would be wrongful), being constrained to conform to duties of RIGHT involves no loss of freedom.[25] To the contrary, each person gains the power to compel

---

[22] Like the rules of a game that make certain moves unavailable (the rook cannot move on the diagonal), they also create an arena for choice: we can now play chess. In this rule-governed space, if a player moves the rook on the diagonal, because it is not a move in chess it has to be taken back (i.e., impeded).

[23] There is some delicacy for Kant with concepts around volition that I am heeding and should explicitly flag. What I'm calling a *willing* is typically an exercise of the human faculty of desire (called *Willkür*), determined by a principle, issuing in the choice to do something for some end. In us, the faculty includes a capacity for rational action, and has its own principle for determining choice—the moral law—which functions through an agent's representation of it as a principle determining choice (the faculty of desire so determinable is called *Wille*). An agent who judges their own interests to be a *first* principle of willing acts on a *mis*representation of that law. They can in fact subordinate the choices of another to their interests, but not according to a universally valid principle of willing. (The text for this is *MM* 6:211–214, 226.)

[24] It is obviously resonant with though not the same as Rousseau's general will. Kant reserves the notion of a general will as a moral standard for acts of governing institutions. The general will is in an extended sense the will of the people committed to RIGHTFUL order across generations.

[25] In some domains, like property, Kant does speak of "provisional right" antecedent to any actual rule of law. This is not an independent proto-right. If the coercive state could not be justified, there

others by way of the authority of all, without infringing their freedom of choice. They act in ways sanctioned by a state, or other concatenation of juridical power, whose coercive authority is beholden to a moral purpose.

It is not a task for the Universal Principle of Right on its own to say what the content of RIGHT is. That would be to replicate the derivation of duties problem. The departure point for the duties of RIGHT is a first principle that specifies the idea or value of humanity in terms that reflect the challenge to realizing the idea of free action under universal law. This is where innate right enters. Its function is to identify primary loci of threats to equal status for persons that come with systems of juridical rights and duties whose moral point is, only somewhat paradoxically, to protect it.

In Kant's work, "humanity" names the practical capacity of an embodied being with a rational will to make reasoned choices. The moral law is the law of this capacity. We are familiar with the idea of humanity as a marker of equal respect: no one should (is entitled to) treat the willing of another as subordinate to their own: that is, treat it in their maxims merely as a means. What's at issue for RIGHT is that we also affect one another externally in ways that impact equal status—we may harm others in order to realize our purposes; we form relationships that threaten others' separateness and independence; we effect the exclusion of some from common resources. Innate right marks out humanity's external side, filling out a unified moral conception of the person in a world of persons able to affect one another's choices, actions, and standing.

It follows that innate right is prior to and independent of any juridical order; it belongs to all persons in virtue of their humanity; it sets conditions for any system of laws that takes its authority from the idea of freedom expressed in the Universal Principle of Right.

In spelling out what innate right involves, rather than an analysis of the concept Kant offers what he describes as four "authorizations" (*Befugnisse*) that belong to innate right.[26] They indicate necessary conditions for securing the equality and freedom of persons in a regime of RIGHT: if not met, juridical constraint of choice lacks authorization (i.e., moral authority).[27] (*MM* 6:237–238) As I interpret them they assert: (1) that all forms of freedom-constraining action must be reciprocal (no one can obligate another who could not be obligated in return); (2) that persons are equal in status (there can be no differential status by birth or affiliation affording special privileges and powers over others); (3) that one's *ex ante* status as

---

would be no provisional right. Understanding "provisional" as a stage in a possible moral progression towards a RIGHTFUL condition is the central idea in Martin Stone and Rafeeq Hasan, "What is Provisional Right?" (2022).

[26] Note: they belong to, but are not derived from, innate right. Kant says, instructively, that "they are not really distinct from it (as if they were members of the division of some higher concept of right)" (*MM* 6:237). Not distinct, but not analytic elements of the concept, either.

[27] For an extended discussion of this way of thinking about innate right, see Katrin Flikschuh "Innate Right in Kant" (unpublished).

a person is as innocent (there can be no inherited moral taint; nothing is imputed independent of what one has done or authorized); (4) that there can be no constraint on expressing one's mind (save for speech that infringes rights).[28] Together they specify the basic terms of what it is for persons to have public standing as independent, free, and equal.[29]

One might also regard the four authorizations of innate right as membership conditions of the rule of law. (1) One could not be a proper subject of public law if one were already subject to the rule of a private person. (2) All who are subject to public law are subject to it equally (there can be no legal castes). (3) No one under the law is judged guilty of anything apart from his or her own deeds. And last, (4) no one's standing to speak in public can depend on the content of their speech conforming to any orthodoxy.

The four authorizations are not legal entitlements; they articulate moral conditions of public law's legitimacy. They are also not moral entitlements in the sense of one's being able to make an enforceable claim against another independent of public law (though they do provide grounds for disputing obligations imposed by the law). They are, one might say, constitutive terms of the law-citizens relationship that make public morality a real possibility. They are also the first step in the generation of juridical rights and duties.

A system of juridical rights (and correlative duties) descends from the elements of innate right, ensuring that the activities of free and equal persons going about their lives are morally possible (consistent with their humanity). So, obviously and directly as a first step, no RIGHTFUL arrangement can tolerate slavery or any form of indentured servitude. Some regime of free speech is required. There must be juridical recognition for the human body. Additional protections are to manage the moral perils of the human condition, consistent with innate right. Persons must gain the moral powers to possess and use the material world, make binding agreements with each other, and enter enduring domestic relations, without wrongfully interfering with others' independence and free action. This is the business of "acquired right." It is the second step in the generation of duties, extending the domain of externally free action.

At every step—from setting the domain of RIGHT in an omnilaterally willed civil condition, to the later structures of governing and law-making—the

---

[28] Interpersonal speech is treated separately as a doing that leaves others free to accept what is said or not. (Compare trespass or taking: one is free not to complain, but violation of right is in the act, whereas, according to Kant, since it's up to me whether I believe another's promise or communication, their speaking falsely as such violates no claim of RIGHT. False speaking can infringe another right, as in a false representation that affects the value of my property.) The *ethics* of false or untruthful speech is another matter.

[29] The first and second authorizations capture the human being's moral title of being their own master (*sui juris*). This is the central concept in Arthur Ripstein's original and important reading of the *Doctrine of Right* in his *Force and Freedom* (2009). Its tight focus on how the idea of being one's own master is expressed in private and public RIGHT tends to occlude the view of the broader system connections with ETHICAL duties.

authorizations of innate right stand as possibility conditions for descendent rights, because they include, as part of the idea of rights, a system of public enforcement. Some further detail should help make sense of this.

So first, about the body. If persons are to be subject to RIGHT, their bodies and the use of their bodies must be their own—that is, free from the control or domination of others. As a condition of realizing the value of innate right, my right with respect to my body must be "something internally mine." That is, it is not an acquired right, but a right that "belongs to everyone by nature" (*MM* 6:237), and that informs other rights. Why? There would be no free action, nothing that could count as a deed, unless the person was an independent physical agent of a doing (or one whose physical acting wasn't dependent on another's permission).[30] This is so even if bodily rights ultimately require public specification, and the terms of rightful resistance need to be set by public law (viz., who can do what to protect the body). It is not a matter of natural fact or direct moral judgment what assault or battery is, when harmful contact is incidental or accidental, or when brandishing a knife is assault. Once it is determined in law what assault and battery are and what is incidental contact, we come to have juridically defined bodies, from what counts as parts of our body (natural and prosthetic) to the boundaries of availability and use. We gain a juridical analogue to proprioception: title to claim directly that some kinds of physical encroachment are an offense.[31]

By contrast, rights to extended possession of material things external to our bodies do not arrive directly. While free action is unintelligible without RIGHTFUL control of one's own body, it is imaginable that persons might be, out of respect for free action, blocked from having extended exclusive control over material objects. Kant thinks that would, if conceivable, be a kind of paradox: "[That] freedom would be depriving itself of the use of its choice...by putting usable objects beyond any possibility of being used..." (*MM* 6:246). So an antinomy that practical reason insists must be resolved (*MM* 6:250). To be entitled to remove material from the commons, to exclude others from use, requires an alteration of the reciprocal relations between persons that they cannot make on their own authority.[32] Constraint without subordination is possible only in the juridical

---

[30] Would that mean infants, who cannot perform deeds, have no bodily rights? I see two possible arguments here. One, that infants *do* have bodily rights because Kant's arguments address "the person" generically, regardless of age or occurrent ability. So: infants' bodily integrity is necessary for them to act freely whenever it is that the person they already are is able to act. Or that the bodily rights of small children are *indirect*, flowing from the protective authority of caretakers, which authority they have *on condition that* they protect and direct the abilities, physical and psychological, necessary for eventual adult status. I think the first argument is a better fit with Kant's overall pattern of argument (and provides content for family obligations to dependents). I discuss some other advantages of this argument in section 6.3.

[31] Not something each declares as they will; more like the boundaries of territorial waters.

[32] Acquired right can regulate possession without the actual use of coercive force, but not without the entitlement to coerce.

condition. No private claim to exclude has standing. In Kant's way of speaking: we gain a power to obligate each other with respect to possession of material things without violating innate right.[33]

About contract, the idea is that to be able to form and execute performance agreements, also something we need to be able to do to take advantage of common human powers—enabling the division of labor, for example—it has to be possible for us to obligate others into the future. But to constrain a future performance in a way consistent with another's freedom is not a power we have by nature or by innate right. The juridical regime of *contract* gives us that power, and so allows us to meet this need consistent with our standing as equals (which is then also a moral test for any particular regime of contract). It makes it the case that my agreement to perform doesn't make me your servant, and yet it is not empty or dependent on my continuing interest in the enterprise.

The central issue raised by domestic unions concerns the mingling of what is ours with what is someone else's: e.g., sharing space and wealth, authority, and, to some extent, voice (who speaks for "us" when our interests are indivisible).[34] The conventional members of a domestic union are adult partners and children, but also, as Kant saw it, domestic servants (live-in nannies, in-residence caregivers and housekeepers still fit much of the function if no longer the label). Because of the intermingling of lives, if not bodies, there is, for Kant, something not manageable through contract (which is for delimited goods and services), and so a distinct question about securing the equal status of all members while in the union (which includes determining what counts as dissolving the union, in contrast to fleeing or abandoning it). It is not that one can't find moral terms to describe various kinds of domestic abuse without appeal to juridical status. The juridical is about creating terms of standing—of role, responsibility, complaint, and redress—and that requires juridically defined and protected roles that give individuals determinate rights and powers in a region of human living that in its natural forms threatens innate right. Though Kant was surely too focused on matters of paternal authority and obedience, it is not implausible to see in the juridical boundaries of (relatively) enduring domestic relations a means of sustaining a safe space for persons of varying natural powers and shifting roles to be and be seen as equals. Or not, if the

---

[33] It is noteworthy that this is *not* an argument for private property. It is antecedent to and a possibility condition of any specific organization of possession, including what kinds of thing can be owned—e.g., the means of production. Whether a regime of private and temporally unlimited possession satisfies the moral purpose of the juridically defined institutions is, at this stage, an open question. The apparent embrace of elements of the German property regime is not a defense, but as in other work, a proof of concept. Given what acquired right with respect to property would have to do, "these and those" elements of German law fill the bill.

[34] Intense focus on Kant's views about sex and marriage have tended to obscure the more general moral issue he sees raised by the formation of households and families.

facts betray their rationale.[35] It is of more than passing interest that Kant did not view the family as a purely private entity.

We are now in a position to draw some general conclusions from Kant's idea that the moral point and justification of the state is to create morally secure powers that enable living a human life consistent with the freedom of others. The point is not to secure natural rights or to make us safe from human predation (though it should do that). The acquisition of the juridical powers adds a dimension to "moral personality" *even though* the laws that specify the powers are human made and even though the duties that come with it do not obligate directly but constrain by way of coercive institutions. They are rational powers that enable new kinds of obligation-generating relationships. Unlike the primary moral powers which we have as individuals essentially (as a kind of rational endowment), these are powers that we gain only on the condition that others with whom we must interact do so as well. As an amplification of our rationally determined powers, they alter what it means to be a person under obligatory law.

It becomes a moral duty of each, and of all together, to make it so that all who are in practical relations with one another in a place are under enforceable reciprocal obligation with respect to relations it would be contrary to reason to avoid and which, without our together being in juridical relations, would be inconsistent with innate right. In effect, the moral existence conditions for human persons in a finite material world is that they together make themselves into citizens. When this happens, we become juridical persons with reciprocal rights and powers that permit our acting towards each other—for our own or others' purposes—secure that in so acting we are respecting one another's standing as free and equal.

Although it is tempting to continue exploring Kant's intriguing and provocative arguments for the moral necessity of the state and its spheres of juridically defined powers, I've taken us just this far down the Kantian road for a different purpose. The importance for the habitat project of what we have so far is to give us enough of Kant's idea and ambition to make credible the idea of public juridical right as a moral environment that secures status and sustains innate right amongst persons as they act on the world and affect one another. I will be arguing that it is a fruitful idea, of a created moral space, at once lawful and potentially tolerant of both local and historical variation, so long as its defining purposes as an institution securing freedom in a wide sense are realized. Critical to the project is seeing the footing of the juridical as involving the same value that supports moral duties generally, so that it is possible for dutiful action in one sphere to be morally continuous with action in the other. The task as we go forward is to show how within something

---

[35] Friedrich Engels' work on the centrality of the family in the history of oppression is an historical-materialist descendent of this argument.

very much like Kant's framework of RIGHT, the rest of the system of moral duties can be laid out.

But before moving on to do this, there are a few pieces of Kant business that I need to briefly note, discuss, and then dismiss. They have been taken to block the idea that juridical duties could be integral parts of a *moral* system at all.[36]

There are three related claims to unravel. (1) The Universal Principle of Right is not a categorical imperative or a formula of a categorical imperative, and so not a possible principle of duty for a moral system. (2) Because it is not part of the idea of juridical duties and obligations that one conform to them "from duty," and conformity is appropriately a product of coercion, juridical action is no expression of rational or moral autonomy. (3) The mark of a genuine moral duty or obligation is the potential for deliberative engagement with its source value; juridical obligation, by contrast, is exhausted in obedience to the law. The antecedent characterizations in the three claims are not mistaken. The error is in thinking about what follows as inconsistent with the conditions for juridical duties being moral requirements.

As we have seen, since the idea of a law of obligation is not restricted in its address to the argument form of maxims, there could be laws of obligation for external action (whether there are any for us is a different matter[37]). If there are such laws of obligation, they *could not be* categorical imperatives in the *Groundwork* sense (because not addressed to the principle in willing an action, but to the action willed—i.e., as chosen), and if they *could not* be categorical imperatives for willing, conformity *cannot* be "from duty."[38] They would be categorical imperatives for action that type them as *deeds*. Juridically conforming actions are about freedom of choice, so not, by design, expressions of autonomous willing.[39] The authority of a particular juridical law is that it is institutionally and procedurally made in the right way, about conduct in a region of action necessary for human life but not morally possible through individuals' self-legislation. The value of a juridical duty is conditional on the fact that it can be enforced.[40]

In the case of ethical obligation, one can only stand towards the duty in the correct way if one's principle of choice (maxim) integrates the deliberatively salient value of the duty in question. In a hard case there can be a demand on

---

[36] A more complete discussion of the different parts of this question can be forum in my "Juridical Personality and the Moral Role of Juridical Obligation" (2022b).

[37] For Kant, leaving the human being aside, the answer seems to be yes for a race of devils, yes even for an embodied holy will, and no for God (or any other perfect, self-sufficient being).

[38] Sometimes Kant explicitly refers to duties of RIGHT as categorical imperatives. They are certainly not hypothetical imperatives (because, even if, at the level of individual choice, the incentive is not moral, the condition of application is independent of the agent's valuing of some end).

[39] Though RIGHT is the condition for autonomous willing under the auspices of obligatory ends—the part of ethics concerned with the pursuit of happiness (see section 7.1).

[40] So not like herd immunity, where nonconformers can just enjoy the benefit of others' conformity. If any member of the community is outside the law, the law is not valid.

individual judgment to determine whether the value encoded in, say, the default duty of truthtelling, can be realized in their circumstances of communication or has been hijacked by someone's wrongfully intended speech. If the latter, then there may be a deliberative route to false speaking. In the juridical case, I may not act on my own authority with respect to a juridical duty, even if, in the instance, its value is manipulated for private purposes, and I know it. Catastrophe cases aside, if positive law fails to enable free action for all, deliberative recourse is available institutionally, via legislative reform on out to constitutional amendment. Although we should not take the law into our own hands, we may not be indifferent to legal arrangements that by design or effect produce serious inequality or injustice. Juridical personality gives us specific obligations as citizens to secure and sustain the rule of law.

The juridical order is neither a natural nor an intuitive order. It is a kind of moral order—an order of obligation for choice and action—that does not look to good willing, but instead depends on the coercive (both preventive and remedial) institutions of the state. Like the ethical duties, the target of juridical duties is human freedom. Unlike the ethical duties where the target is the freedom (of will) of individuals, external freedom is only possible in union with others under public law that secures this freedom for all. The conditions of free action are reciprocal.[41]

Is the Universal Principle of Right an instance of the moral law? As the source of laws of freedom in the duties of RIGHT, we should say yes.[42]

The rest of the argument for the inclusion and place of RIGHT in the system of moral duties is best made through setting out key elements of the system and seeing how they work together. We turn to that next.

6.3 From the Juridical to the Ethical

Moving forward, I will assume the general structure of the *Doctrine of Right* argument as set out in section 6.2 and consider what the upshot of the first duties of RIGHT could be for other elements of the system of duties. I am interested in this more as a vertical rather than a horizontal inquiry, less about the details and conditions of RIGHT and the fit of its various parts with each other, more about the

---

[41] The claim is not that there is *some* system of law in which my acting the way I do would be consistent with others acting freely, but that it is consistent under the law that is the case.

[42] Forceful examples of arguments to a different conclusion can be found in Paul Guyer "Kant's Deductions of the Principles of Right" (2002) and Marcus Willaschek "Which Imperatives for Right? On the Non-Prescriptive Character of Juridical Laws in Kant's *Metaphysics of Morals*" (2002). Ben Laurence offers an important argument for there being a role for the moral incentive in RIGHTFUL action in his "Juridical Laws as Moral Laws in Kant's *The Doctrine of Right*" (2015).

way the duties of RIGHT shape and are shaped by the principles of interpersonal and directed-to-self morality.[43]

Here's an example of what I have in mind. Ideally, once there is a regime of RIGHT, once the value of the integrity and independence of the person is articulated in public law, some of the questions about the duties and entitlements of individuals can be answered. In some cases, there is continuity from what the state has authority to do to the reasons individuals have for acting, though not always in the form we expect. Consider in this light the morality of self-defense—taking coercive or violent action to prevent and protect oneself from assault. It is clear that the assault is contrary to RIGHT and so is an action that may be hindered. What is not clear is *who* may do the hindering. As the host of law, the state has the function of enforcement. When the state uses its coercive apparatus to prevent assault, its action, though perhaps violent, does not count as assault because it is not a violation of RIGHT, not a wrongful interference with the freedom of the aggressing person. The state's entitlement and obligation to protect determines the moral status of its actions. It is not interfering with a freedom anyone has title to exercise. This tells us important things about individuals acting privately in self-defense.

The defender of self-defense (or a right of self-defense) might argue that if the wrongfulness of physical assault is about culpable disregard for the independence of the victim's agency, the victim's self-defensive action is, like the state's protective coercion, not itself assault, not an interference with rightful freedom. As a resistance to assault, it is justified. This is not what Kant's view of RIGHT implies. If the action taken in self-defense is in the ordinary sense to protect life or limb, it is a means to furthering a private purpose. A very important purpose, but its importance is *to* the victim, the self-defender. As a private person, they are not entitled to use violence in this way, that is, not entitled to use violence against another for a private end. Justified defense aims to restore the moral condition of RIGHTFUL independence that is the point of public RIGHT. One can hear this in the 'You have no right!' directed at the aggressor (compare: 'Don't hurt me!'). The problem is that the private self-defender can't act to preserve or protect their own or anyone's threatened public status as a not-to-be-wrongfully-interfered-with citizen-person.

Private self-defense in the face of aggression has the same fault as private revenge as a form of punishment for criminal wrongdoing. Just as only the state can legitimately punish violations of the law, only the state can act in a way that preserves a person's public status (which, in the instance, requires forcibly resisting an aggressor). In Kant's formal language, not every impeding of an aggression

---

[43] There is good methodological reason not to embark on the horizontal inquiry. I want to read the *Doctrine of Right* in the same spirit as I recommended for the *Groundwork*—separating the strands of the argument for the elements and limits of RIGHT from the elaborations of duties which, in the juridical case, are clearly dependent on contemporary German law. We should regard the appeal to specific rights or duties not as argument for a particular regime of property or contract but as showing that constituents of an actual legal system can be understood as if an application of the theory of RIGHT.

counts as a hindering of a hindrance in the relevant sense. The problem is that there are *two* injuries, one material (the threat to life and limb), one juridical (an action contrary to RIGHT). All the formal "hindering of a hindrance" argument does is signal the absence of a barrier *in* RIGHT to impeding the exercise of wrongful choice. Who can, with RIGHTFUL authority, interfere remains a question: there is no state of nature entitlement to self-defense. A threatened material loss does not give one title in RIGHT to act.

Would this mean the threatened individual can do nothing RIGHTFUL in the face of a threat to life? It would mean that for the private or "natural" person, there is no *right* of self-defense, and no enforceable entitlement to take whatever measures are necessary to repel a perceived threat. That leaves room to argue that if the arm of the state is not nearby, the self-defender could act as the state's ad hoc deputy. Acting as a state deputy, a person's coercive defensive actions can be about status, not just life-saving. But we should note that this justification applies equally to the defense of *others*. *Self*-defense is not privileged.[44]

It would then seem to matter how the self-defender is motivated, or how she regards herself in her acting. I think that's right. It's not about her having a specific psychological state vis-à-vis the action, or that she would have acted even if the defensive action didn't also serve a private purpose (either protecting herself or, in other-defense, say, eliminating a rival). In taking on the role, it is motive in the regulative and system sense that is engaged.[45] To be an ad hoc deputy is to have taken on certain deliberative constraints: e.g., giving fair warning, if possible; being prepared to defer to the police were they to arrive on the scene; aiming to minimize one's use of force; accepting responsibility for harm to innocents. There are different responsibilities and liabilities than there would be were there a private right of self-defense.

Continuing down the vertical axis, the next level down from duties of RIGHT are what Kant calls, using a traditional term, nonjuridical *perfect duties*. These perfect duties are distinguished from duties of RIGHT as duties conformity to which cannot be compelled. Some want to call duties perfect that require a discrete performance or omission. I don't see Kant dividing things that way.[46] Perfect

---

[44] We can regard this justification of self-defense as an element of public reason. The terms of public reason delimit what one is entitled to make public complaint about, what demands one can make, how one can describe an event (in terms of public reason, in this sense, it's not wrong to call it rape if the woman says no, even if, in the event, interpersonal things between the parties were murky). Public reason determines standing, who has responsibility, etc.

[45] The so-called right of necessity defense might block the state's prosecution of suspected private actor self-defenders (because to no possible effect), but that does not eliminate the moral distinction. For a fascinating account of the issues that arise in this kind of case, see Arthur Ripstein's "In Extremis" (2005).

[46] Note at G 4:421 when Kant introduces the distinction, what makes a duty perfect is that "it admits of no exception in favor of inclination." He says: "It must be noted here that I reserve the division of duties entirely for a future *Metaphysics of Morals,* so that the division here stands only as one adopted at my discretion (for the sake of arranging my examples). For the rest, I understand here by a perfect duty

duties are duties of persons (natural or artificial) that constrain reasoning to action in a specific way. I am in particular interested in the class of perfect duties whose content descends from duties of RIGHT. They are nonjuridical duties of individuals in the sense that what is required does not (even in principle) depend on securing general conformity, either by unanimity of will or by external constraint. They descend from duties of RIGHT in the sense that their content continues the work of RIGHT, protecting a fundamental value by limiting what we may do for the sake of our private purposes (in a sense, this is just the idea of deontology).[47] Some perfect duties flow directly from duties of RIGHT; they are a kind of shadow juridical duty. There will be perfect duties not to take a life and not to steal running alongside and informed by corresponding juridical duties. The difference between them is not just that a juridical duty constrains action directly and externally (this kind of doing in these circumstances will not be allowed: it has no juridical existence), while the perfect duty is only a deliberative constraint (reasoning from considerations of self-interest to this kind of action-type is not valid: its principle is not a possible law of rational willing). In taking the content of RIGHT into the arena of nonjuridical moral duties, the perfect duty inherits and translates the value protected in a juridical duty's articulation of innate right. It will be useful to have an example of what this looks like.

The law that reflects the value of innate right makes the human body off-limits as property: it is part of what a person is, and so not among material things available for acquisition and use (in the juridical sense). In *nonjuridical* morality, to regard the body as not a mere thing or means is to look at its needs and vulnerabilities as a human being's needs and vulnerabilities, to regard it as a source of positive claims for respect (we regard the body in whatever its form or function as the locus of the person). It therefore enters deliberation as more than that aspect of a person that cannot be used or engaged with without her consent. It is the agent's vehicle of action and expression and identity—a condition not just of free choice but of free willing. This is why the related perfect duties extend more broadly than duties of RIGHT. Body-shaming is a violation of a perfect duty that has this origin. There are also perfect ethical duties to self against actions that negatively affect the agent's practical powers (e.g., self-maiming). This brings us to the border of imperfect duties: how one lives, uses, and develops one's body as the body of a rational and moral agent. We have discretion; we may not be negligent.[48]

---

one that admits no exception in favor of inclination, and then I have not merely external but also internal *perfect duties;* although this is contrary to the use of the work adopted in the schools, I do not intend to justify it here, since for my purpose it makes no difference whether or not it is granted me."

[47] Note how on this account the law-like nature of these perfect duties is not a reflection of their location in the CI procedure but instead follows from their being the individual's portion of support for the value of humanity in public RIGHT—a matter of content and purpose, not mere form. The argument structure of the formula of universal law is sensitive to that: that is, were one to use the test, such as it is, it will work with this moral content.

[48] There is a more general account of imperfect duties to the self in Chapter 7 (section 7.1).

All of this opens a question about the provenance of the moral concept of the body. On the juridical side, the primary focus is on the material thing that a person is, that aspect of the person that can be engaged in and engaged with in external action. But is the "material thing" protected in RIGHT only the biological body? Both restraining my hand and taking my glasses impair my external agency. Surely my glasses are, whereas my hand is not, my property; yet functionally, in terms of the value of innate right, they seem on a par. The questions get harder around implants and prostheses, even if, as with a possible implant, its function depends on a proprietary smartphone app. The point to take from the spiral of questions is a reinforcement of the idea that the specification of innate right will be an ongoing and contested task for positive law. It is certainly not about nature or limited to the subjectivity of being embodied. It's a third-personal account of the body. Like other external objects, it can be both divisible and one. Prostheses wear out and need replacement; they can get lost or stolen, purchased, improved on; one can have different kinds of prosthetic limbs for different purposes. Are they, juridically, *my body* only when in use? The documents will have been signed by my hand yesterday and again today, even if I've swapped devices, though not if the device is used by someone else.

From the ethical point of view, things will look different. My body is the material vehicle of my will, my mode of access to the world, that through which I first learn to make my desires and interests real. It is integral to what it is to be an agent of duties and obligations. It is that through which I most often exhibit respect and show care. The commodification of the body is inconsistent with the ethical idea of embodied agency. It would be to regard the body merely as an instrument for use, of value as it fits one's purposes. Thus the difference from the ethical point of view of amputating a limb to preserve oneself as an agent and selling a body part for profit: a difference in deliberative role, not functional outcome.[49]

The juridical body looks like an assemblage of means; the ethical body is a source of ends. That can make it seem that the decline in usefulness of a body-part is like the breakdown of one's car—an unwelcome loss of means—and not a juridical concern (unless there was a taking or a wrongful injury). But if the condition of free action is a body (natural or prosthetic), then there is pressure on the juridical side to ensure the path to purposive activity is open in order to secure independence, even if it is by means of amplifying a bodily constrained power of choice through services and devices.[50] The ethical body requires still more—from us, and from the social world. It needs more in the way of protection

---

[49] So it's not just the ethical wrong that speaks against a market in body parts; the atmosphere of commodification is toxic for human moral agents.

[50] It is important in this regard to flag the absence of *work* as a distinct category in RIGHT. Kant regards having a trade to matter as a condition of positive citizenship, in contrast to day-laborers whose

(e.g., from nonvoluntary social forms that wear it out), and more in the way of expressive power and control.[51]

Some of the contestation around the gendered body can be understood as an attempt to negotiate these two moral spaces: the body as expression of agency and identity and the body as our third-personal presence in public space. They are separate and yet not separable. The ethical need to determine one's own ends puts pressure on the juridical terms of equality—of how one is present to others in public space. Typing the public body by categories of race or class or gender can risk turning juridical protections into sources of oppression. Given that how a person inhabits their body—what kind of agency they can see for themselves—is not all of their own making, it makes sense that the body, in both of its moral dimensions, will be contested.

The priority of juridical RIGHT in the descent of duties does not insulate it from extra-juridical moral need. This is in general true, even for the a priori elements of innate right. Understanding what it is to be a person susceptible to imputation or someone who expresses thought in speech has to be worked out and adapted to the contingencies of the social world in which moral action (both juridical and ethical) takes place.

The content shift from juridical to descendant perfect duties is reflected in their practical logic as well. Unlike duties of RIGHT, where a violation of a proscribed act-type may be justified by appeal to its effects (breaking into someone's home during a fire to rescue a trapped child) or excused if not entirely voluntary, nonjuridical perfect duties do not generate prohibitions on act-types. There is a perfect duty not to deceive, yet in some circumstances the duty itself permits false speaking; there is a perfect duty regarding promise-breaking, but there are circumstances in which the promise does not obligate. None of this is as paradoxical as it might seem. What *is* exceptionlessly prohibited by perfect duties are deliberative schema (certain maxims or patterns of reasoning): certain act-types are not available as means to a private end. This sets a default requirement which can look from the outside like a juridical duty, forbidding an action-type. However, where adhering to the default requirement of an ethical duty would undermine its own supporting value, there can be reason *based in that value* not to act on the default rule.

---

bare labor made them an instrument of others' wills. He seems not to have had a sense of the value of work in a human life (supporting something like a right *to* work). Also missing is awareness that issues of discrimination and subordination could arise in the workplace, or that the conditions of external freedom—living wages, health-care, freedom of speech—could depend on the will of profit-driven owners or international corporations. However, even if Kant was in no position to recognize the moral issues around work, the terms for amending the account of RIGHT are already set. Is work a sphere of moral vulnerability that cannot be resolved by good willing (or decency, as we might say), but requires a regime of freedom-infringing constraint? Labor laws, unions, OSHA, and other safety regulations belong to a positive answer to that question.

[51] Just as autonomous vehicles may make driving available to a wider range of persons, so might descendants of virtual technologies create new avenues for expressive powers.

Kant illustrates the difference in his examination of the perfect duty to self not to identify living with life's pleasures and pains in such a way that when the balance goes harshly negative, one regards oneself as having good reason to end one's life (*MM* 6:423 and also *G* 4:422). This is the form of the default rule against suicide. As the casuistry shows, this is not an absolute prohibition: *some* other reasons can rebut the default, as when, for example, one's continued life is an unavoidable threat to others (rabies is Kant's example [*MM* 6:424]). The satisfactions (or lack of them) of continued life are not at stake.[52]

A very different kind of case involves the duties of a public person. Kant offers the case of a great king who, to avoid capture in battle and being forced to make terms of peace harmful to the state, would voluntarily end his life (*MM* 6:423). Kant suggests that such a self-killing would not be an exception to the default rule against suicide because it would be supported by a different order of reasons—reasons of state—and thus engage a different ground of obligation. A king whose ongoing life would destroy his state would violate the conditions of RIGHT. And if the only escape from this crisis of state was through self-killing (biting a poison pill), then the public role could call for the sacrifice of the person who is the king, and that person might permissibly take the fateful step. Because a different order of value and obligation apply, this is neither a violation of nor an exception to the default ethical rule against suicide.

There is a parallel structure of descent from juridical duties to the perfect duties concerned with lying, deception, and truthfulness. Anchoring these duties is the innate right to speak one's mind. Its first role in public right is that we be free to speak truth to power (saying what we see).[53] If we could only say what someone else thinks or permits us to say, or if all effects of speech were juridically imputed to the speaker (with liability), then we could not freely represent our ideas to others, and our speech would carry no authority. In the public sphere, freedom of speech is a necessity. Beyond securing the conditions of public reason, this aspect of RIGHT also lies in the background of how we regard giving one's word in contract (that it could be authoritatively self-binding), of why consent can make a moral difference, and it is a starting place for intellectual property (it is because we can be original authors that there is something to protect). Ethics, or interpersonal morality, takes up the rationale for the innate right in a general presumption of truthfulness in speech (only if I speak my mind can we reason together) and perfect ethical duties of communicative integrity (that I not regard myself or cause

---

[52] The idea that perfect duties provide default directives and not exceptionless requirements is consistent with the claim that moral requirements necessitate. It marks the difference between "one must always speak truthfully" or "never lie" and "the principle of lying from self-interest is morally invalid."

[53] Kant argues in "What is Enlightenment?" (8:37) that although one may because of a social role not be free *in that role* to dispute and disobey authority, because one is also potentially a scholar (the citizen about taxes; the soldier about the military, etc.), one must in *that* role be free to speak one's mind.

myself to be regarded as a mere speaking machine, uttering words that look like communicative speech, but are sent out simply for their effect). Down further is an imperfect duty about what and how much to say when "more truths" obfuscate or defeat communicative purpose. Some of the Platonic railing against rhetoric has purchase here.

To say that primary duties of communication are perfect is, first, to say that truthfulness trumps private interest: false communication betrays the common rational endeavor.[54] However, if by eliciting your honest speech I would co-opt you in wrongdoing—think of the murderer at the door—you may speak falsely to me. Here the speech context lies outside the orbit of the default rule of the duty, and truthful speech won't serve the duty's value. The point and purpose of truthfulness is to make common reasoning possible, something no longer available once the murderer sets things in motion.[55] The inquiring speech of the murderer at the door is not an invitation to common reasoning but a device to subvert it. That makes resisting the subversion with untruthful counter-speech a defense of the moral value of truthful speech. That is, the *same* ground of obligation supports apparently opposed kinds of action.[56] False speaking to the murderer is not a lie, not wrong, not an instance of instrumentally justified wrongdoing. And also not justified if done for an altruistic purpose.

Imperfect duties of speech and communication continue the trajectory of support for common reasoning. Think of when it matters how we tell stories; the perils of groundless criticism; what counts as fair humor; the sensitivities at issue in communicative micro-aggressions.

We find the same vertical structure in Kant's central argument for property rights. Recall that the argument to property rights arises in the intersection of the practical necessity of our using the stuff of the world and innate right's demand that any exclusion of others from use be consistent with equal freedom of all. The solution is to tie the very idea of property to the enforcement condition of innate right—the juridical state. Thus, descending, the argument for property can support the state's power to tax to provide social moral necessities like roads, clean water, healthcare, and education (but *not* as welfare goods). A regime of RIGHT may restrain or tax gift-giving or other free transfers consistent with its values (e.g., to avoid creating the kind of inequality that undermines the state's claim to express the will of a community of equals). Juridical duties about contract and perfect duties about promising follow.[57] The values of the property system drawn

---

[54] If one's partner in a scientific inquiry brings false data to the project, even if the effect is neutral (in the end, it does not in fact skew results), the project is now a failure.

[55] For fuller discussion of this kind of argument, see Seana Valentine Shiffrin, *Speech Matters* (2014), chapter 1.

[56] By contrast, the RIGHTFUL resisting of a violation of RIGHT is not a counter-action in the same register of obligation but a juridical rejection of the completion of the RIGHT-violating action.

[57] The connection between contract and promise is not self-evident—whether promise involves a transfer of an entitlement or some other shift in authority. Whatever the origins stories, they will come to share moral space.

from innate right continue, shaping the imperfect ETHICAL duties with respect to free giving and gratitude, as we've seen, the duties of assistance or beneficence, as we should expect, but also influence such things as the material structure of the family.

Although it won't be clear what is required and what is protected until the full system of duties that express the values of innate right is laid out, the initial stages are especially important for their terms of inclusiveness. The requirements to treat persons as separate and independent, as having bodies that require protection but also space for movement and expression, as innocent, and as free to make their minds public—these hold of all persons, regardless of condition. Innate right is not a temporalized right that first applies at the age of reason, or a conditional right that depends on achieving any degree of accomplishment. Innate right applies to the person as such, awake or asleep, acting and thinking well, or not, neurologically or developmentally typical, and not. It is a kind of presumption. It will not follow that every element of the descendent rights and duties applies in the same way to everyone in every life station or situation; it *does* follow that every person has an equal claim to be counted in the generation of descendent rights, and any limits in the extension of rights must rebut the presumption of equality in its own terms.[58]

Starting from innate right therefore secures a first line of response to the chronic complaint, efficiently expressed by Bernard Williams, that "Kantian theory makes the beneficiaries of morality co-extensive with its agents," when not all of those who should be the object of our duties are moral agents in the full sense.[59] The human being in all its variety and condition is, in Williams' terms, the beneficiary of morality, or in mine, a denizen of the habitat. The source of the worry about Kantian theory is the interpretive muddle that comes from ignoring the fact that the *Groundwork*'s arguments address the possibility conditions of moral *agency*—for rational beings as such *and so* for human beings—*not* the scope of moral duties or concern.[60] If none of us are moral agents, there are no duties. If some of us are, some things follow about how moral agents must treat each other, but it doesn't at all follow from the conditions of moral agency who "the beneficiaries" of morality are.

When, in the *Metaphysics of Morals*, Kant takes on the project of duties for human beings, the first order of business is securing the external conditions for the free action of a community of interacting human persons. Second is determining

---

[58] Persons have cultures and history that are important to who they are, but may not mark anyone's moral status as other than equal. That a culture or group may in its own way create a dependent class or caste would not defeat the presumption: there is no independence from the basic terms and authority of the juridical condition as such. It follows, juridically, for all groups, that practicable terms of exit must be available and not defeated by past expressions of consent.

[59] Bernard Williams, *In the Beginning was the Deed* (2005), 20.

[60] In fact, the *Groundwork* argument runs in the other direction. It supposes that there are some obvious duties and asks what we, as moral agents, have to be like for them to have practical authority for us.

the moral impact on deliberation of our recognition that we are embodied and sensitive rational persons: what principles or premises these facts introduce in duties to ourselves and others. Whoever turns out to be in the class of moral subjects—those persons or entities that moral agents are accountable for—the conditions necessary for effective moral agency are of paramount importance in the articulation of the system of duties.[61] The duties of RIGHT and of ETHICS reflect categories of impedance to that end as they show in the vulnerabilities of individual human persons as well as the form of their collective life.

Questions about impedance and vulnerability are questions about powers. In this case, moral powers. Thus the "authorizations" that belong to innate right are directed to the conditions that can prevent a human being from acting as their own person: their body could be in another's service, they have a mind whose expression can be controlled and constrained, they can be treated as guilty by association or birth or nature. The argument that I've ascribed to Kant is that unless these impedances are in principle and in fact recognized (as a threat) and removed (as a matter of RIGHT), common and cooperative moral life isn't possible. The protections cannot be private or contingent on good willing; they must be general, public, and enforceable.

Now, from the perspective of innate right there is no specific set of abilities that warrants this protection. If members of a moral community must be free to present what's on their own mind, it is morally arbitrary by what means they are able to do that. The absence of common language is a technical not a moral obstacle. So long as there is something that could be or could come to be their own voice, that could count as or come to count as their being independent of others' power, the protections of innate right make sense for them. We all depend on resources and special opportunities to realize our potential. In none of the stages of life are we invulnerable, not as infants but also not as mature adults. Remediable dependency is the human condition, not a mark against anyone's moral status.[62]

The advantage of a point of view that is neutral about specific abilities is that one needn't tag the absence of one or another ability as something that sets people outside the orbit of moral regard. Within a range, these are, like the effects of age or accident on agency, contingent matters, amenable in principle to amendment or accommodation.[63] From the point of view of innate right we should speak generically: "the human" has a claim for access to the conditions necessary for

---

[61] That the conditions for effective human moral agency might impose costs on nonrational agents is not just a speculative possibility. The point here is that this is a problem integral to and not a defeat of the idea of the habitat project. The human life form has a heavy footprint on any account.

[62] Where Kant saw a problem was with "illegitimate" children—they look like foreigners, at best, having failed to enter the polity through the right kind of family portal, and so lack status. There is a kernel of insight in his eighteenth-century prejudice: children require a social-institutional location that serves their moral interests. But there was no reason, especially given the strictures of innate right, for Kant to think the irregularity of parentage was inherited as a status defect.

[63] Perhaps there are limits that aren't matters of available technology. It might be one thing to have one person be able to give voice to another's thoughts, quite another to impute thoughts the way we

them to exercise external freedom and moral agency. To be under laws of obligation doesn't require a specific set of developed abilities. Because both constraint and protection are external, their form can be adjusted. One wouldn't hold a child accountable in the way one does a fully-formed adult, but we also don't treat their actions with impunity even before they are fully formed. One of the salutary results of anchoring the moral system in RIGHT is the identification of the moral subject with the domain of choice.[64]

If innate right marks the formal conditions of free action for human persons, duties, both juridical and ethical, give free action social and material shape. The elements of innate right make morally justified public institutions necessary. They require constitutional provisions and protections whose procedures embody rule of law values. They set an agenda for the creation of specific public rights and duties (about ownership, public goods, contract, freedom of speech, etc., but also about institutional roles for adjudicating, enforcing, and making law). They also call for a criminal law, with its array of public sanctions, to make it generally the case that protection of RIGHT does not depend on wealth or power or status. And they task the legal system to ensure that exchange and commitment do not threaten RIGHTFUL independence.[65] In extending the work of duties of RIGHT, ETHICAL duties impose additional limits on the authority of preference (or self-interest) in justifying action. We have to respect the integrity of each person in regions of action outside the reach of public right. It is wrong to coerce or deceive for our private purposes; in a promise we stand guarantee for our word. In action and interaction we are to acknowledge self and other as separate and independent, innocent and equal, as persons beholden to moral reasons for what they do and entitled to moral reasons for the ways they are treated. In this way, moral agents, created in and by the conditions of RIGHT, complete the work that RIGHT begins.

6.4 Provisional Universal Right

An important structural issue surfaces here. If a large stretch of ethical duty descends from and completes juridical duty, would there be none of these duties where there is a failed or corrupt state? A corrupt ethics? No ethics in a state of nature? That would be a worrisome conclusion. It's not a question about the possibility of antecedent moral duties. There are duties that are not juridically dependent. Some duties of respect, some duties to self, and, of course, the duty to

---

sometimes impute interests to trees, or landscapes, or works of art. This is in any case a different issue than the intellectual powers and the having of a moral personality in the practical sense that would seem to be a necessary condition for moral agency.

[64] If moral obligation is extended to nonhuman beings, it will not be in terms of RIGHT.
[65] Juridical duties don't exhaust the work of public institutions. They have the further moral role of creating and supporting a variety of public spaces and interactions that allow individuals to be and to see themselves actively participating in a cooperative moral endeavor. These will be some of the institutional *imperfect* duties.

create the juridical condition in which innate right is recognized and respected. The question is about descendent ethical duties such as those surrounding the transfer and use of goods, or that are about the body, where their content draws on juridical rights and duties.

The place to start is with the recognition that the content of articulated juridical duty will inevitably (and appropriately) differ from one public order to another. However, the range of legitimate possibilities is limited by the core values of innate right. So, for example, there are no morally or juridically fixed rules for abandoned property (when it counts as abandoned, when mislaid), but every system of property has to have such rules, and those rules have to comport with the value encoded in the property system (whether, e.g., to increase private means or to support individual agency or for the sake of cooperative life), which in turn has to be a possible expression of the independence demand of innate right. Then, even if, absent an appropriate set of laws, there is no fact of the matter, one can assert a priori that some practices or rules could not be consistent with any legitimate system of property—e.g., that anything out of one's hand or protection will count as abandoned. That would subvert the moral point of a property system to secure possession at a distance, putting users at the mercy of potential property predators. Wherever one is, there is reason to presume that what is fairly regarded as an ownable thing that is not in the manifest possession of anyone is not for that fact either unowned or abandoned. It's not just an arbitrary local convention that we treat found wallets as lost and to-be-returned.

It will follow from the connection of the idea of property with innate right—the "what it's for"—that there is no free pass to plunder in a failed or unjust state, but it won't follow that one must respect all property claims or other "legal" arrangements in such a condition. Things do not become unowned, in the sense of available to whomever, though we might, in Kant's terms, regard their status as reverting to a provisional claim. However, just as it's not wrong to seek shelter in a vacant house in a weather emergency, homeless victims of severe injustice may have warrant to inhabit unused living space. But if squatting is not impermissible, it does not give rise to a property right, even where relevant property claims are the creatures of an unjust system. The necessary (though possibly limited) temporal stability of possession suggests that if persons find themselves compelled to use what is not their own, they cannot use it wantonly: they have a duty to take care of what is being used, treating it as if it were on loan and needing to be returned in good order. It is an imperfect ethical duty attached both to the moral idea of stable possession (not to render the usable unusable), and to the presumptive value of what is used for the (provisional) owner (so different standards for an apartment and a hammer).[66]

---

[66] The provisional owner in a generic sense, not some particular Donald Trump.

Other descendent duties follow. What one may justifiably use in an emergency one may provide for others, though not as a free gift (or as an object for sale), and with continuing responsibility for what is being used. The limits to beneficence in such circumstances will in turn limit and reorient gratitude, the guiding value in the provision being closer to sharing what one has rather than supporting another's ends.[67] There will have to be a casuistry of consumption, about whether recompense should be made where to use is to use up. Even without a juridical prohibition, there are ethical barriers to hoarding. And so on.

It is not hard to see how analogous arguments might secure limited descendent ethical duties with respect to the body, promise, speech, and intimate relations. If there are some types of action in a domain that would not be morally possible in any practice regulated by RIGHT, that is sufficient to support truncated ethical duties. It is a kind of limited negative contractualism for failed juridical conditions.[68]

Where what's at issue is violations of innate right, whether encoded in bad law, or where persons are outside the law,[69] we can speculatively take the above line of argument further. Each and every person has an entitlement based in innate right to being treated according to the core values that frame juridical duties by those with whom they interact, directly or indirectly. For Kant, that introduces a moral duty on people interacting in a place to create the conditions of RIGHT.[70] Our world is interconnected to a degree beyond his imagining. If connection and interaction are the moral measure triggering the duty, we should conclude that failure to establish the conditions of RIGHT anywhere is a failure imputable to all of us.[71] And if all of us have a duty to realize RIGHT in circumstances where we cannot live without interacting with others, we couldn't both share responsibility for that failure to protect *and* take ourselves to be free in the meantime to act as if the moral claim for protection of innate right had no force.

With this, the Kantian account inches towards something that looks like universal human rights. We might, in a Kantian spirit, call them "provisional universal rights."[72] They are not state-of-nature rights, conceptually independent

---

[67] See Chapter 7 (section 7.2) for the account of beneficence that lies behind this distinction.

[68] Kant uses an argument that has this form at *MM* 6:329 as a test for law that violates its own condition.

[69] There are (too) many examples—slavery, forced statelessness, internment, caste—to just start a list.

[70] The "duty to create" marks an analytical, not a temporal, priority.

[71] It's an extension of the thought that were a group to decide to form a state that includes people on the left bank of the river but not their regular trading and marriage partners on the right bank, they would not thereby be released from the obligation to act with the others to secure the general condition of RIGHT for both. This also suggests an opening for an argument against any simple model of the unitary state in circumstances where the interactions of persons across borders is sustained, not episodic (Kant's ships passing on the high seas).

[72] This is not a direction in which Kant took his account. But then, Kant's world didn't (yet) look like ours. Talking of "provisional universal rights" rather than human rights is more than nominal: it's meant to mark both that the rights in question are not fully formed antecedent to realizing the juridical condition, in a place, or perhaps generally in an interconnected world, and also that existing regimes of

of the idea of a juridical right. And they are not juridical rights. It is the invariant core of innate right that gives them (formal) content: consistent with the idea of RIGHT, no one may be treated as less than an equal person, subordinated to others' private interest, found guilty independent of her deeds, be denied a voice.

One might worry that in the absence of a real juridical context it is unclear what is owed, who has duties that correlate with provisional universal rights, and whether anyone has title to enforce them. It might seem we are stranded between registering the wrong and having no justified action available. But why think this? We (all) have the moral duty to realize the value of innate right in juridical duties (along with their existence condition, a rightful state). Right now, we have the ability to protect persons who are vulnerable to moral injury because of the absence of articulated juridical right that applies to them (if they are stateless, or in a failed state). While we might not be able to provide juridical protection (imagine failed courts and corrupt police), we *can* often indirectly support persons' entitlement as possessors of innate right to reside in a juridical condition, and we have in the meantime a duty to mitigate the effects of activities of private actors or any unjust polity that violate the claims of innate right.[73]

Here's an example. It is thought to be obvious that child marriage is inconsistent with innate right. It puts girls, especially, at high risk of violence, exploitation, and abuse.[74] It is part of a cluster of social norms and attitudes that reflect and reinforce the low value accorded to girls. What is missing is the relevant structure of realized RIGHT—of legislation, adjudication, and enforcement—as it applies to marriage. Given the claims of girls based in innate right, there is both a general duty to promote the juridical condition (which would exclude child marriage), and a descendent ethical duty to protect young girls from this sort of harm. Those who are citizens have standing and a duty to change marital laws to accord with innate right, and in the meantime, a duty to protect the vulnerable as they can. For those who are not citizens, the same duties apply, although they support different actions.

The ethical duty to protect children from harm is universal, though truncated. That is, we might not be able to say that every social practice that tolerates any harm to children is contrary to RIGHT. There might be reasonable cultural variance about the value of taking risks, some judging it necessary for developing

---

right may not be, as they regard themselves, free standing. In the latter case, even without the idea of a world state, the notion of citizenship and its attendant duties would likely be very different. For a related view, see Katrin Flikschuh "Human Rights in Kantian Mode: A Sketch" (2015).

[73] This seems to me an instance of a more general form of moral argument. If the success of the steps we are each obligated to take to provide protection to persons from a kind of harm depend on the (empirically) contingent cooperation of all (we need to build a fence), I cannot, while waiting for the rest to act with me, regard myself as free to ignore specific threats of that very kind of harm that I could on my own avert.

[74] UNICEF figures have 14 million marriages a year of girls under eighteen, 5 million of whom are under fifteen.

adult coping skills, others seeing the costs in harms to some not justified by the benefits. But child marriage doesn't fall within reasonable cultural variance. Since the duty applies, what may we noncitizens do? The duty is imperfect, realizable in a variety of ways. Many UNICEF projects that target child marriage seem well-designed to fit this duty, tracking the value under threat through interventions that cross no juridical boundaries. Their programs aim to, among other things, provide educational resources (effecting an increase in the value status of girls, for themselves and socially), promote economic development (poverty is a driver of the practice of child marriage), create international campaigns of information and informal pressure (drawing the targeted community into a wider ethical conversation). Aiming more directly at juridical change are programs that support grassroots organizations and that make some forms of non-urgent aid contingent on changes to marital law. There are many levers of action noncitizens can pull.

Most of our nonjuridical duties descendent from innate right are owed by us individually to persons who are co-citizens. If there are provisional universal rights, there is another set of duties that look outward from the same value, now directed to all persons in support of their access to the juridical condition. It is true that much of the work done for the duty is by polities and groups that act on our behalf: they can, variously, take in migrants and refugees, provide resources for permanent settlement, coordinate with other political groups across borders, and provide support for emergent or threatened local institutions that aim to satisfy juridical norms. Nevertheless, the duty belongs to the collective of persons, each and all together. The closing of borders is done by *our* agents, the refusal of resources by *our* government. It is imputed to us. Failure to do what we can to secure the juridical independence of others is wrong, even if we cannot on our own do all that is needed to make things right.

Provisional universal rights are not a shadow list of generally accepted human rights, as if juridical status was just one of many human entitlements. Their role is to signal a systematic deficit of juridical right. We don't need a story about provisional universal rights to identify duties to provide food to people who are starving or education to children. Provisional universal rights make a practical difference when unmet need is integral to system failure: a moral deficit that must be recognized alongside the material need. Caloric provision or Peace Corps classes is then not enough. The way food is provided, the way work and educational opportunities are presented, should promote the transition from provisional to real juridical independence of beneficiaries.

Provisional universal rights are also not a Kantian precursor of cosmopolitan human rights. Their realization condition is in a system of interacting rights and duties that articulate innate right in a place. We might think of this as a moral habitat constraint. Local facts about property, inequality, education, citizenship, all interact, as do the duties and rights that configure a moral social place. This has implications even at the social margins. How, for example, are the provisional human rights of a nomadic people living in the margins of an urbanizing and industrial society to be recognized? It can't be done without reference to the institutions of a state or polity that is to recognize them. Suppose that the realization conditions of rights to education, work, freedom of women from sexual violence, all involve entry into a civil society, a condition that is not preservative of all values that support a nomadic way of life. Education, as we often think of it in a rights-related sense, involves access to sustained training that requires being in one place for extended time. And with that comes the introduction of life forms that disrupt nomadic values. In Tanzania, this has meant Maasai children (mostly the girls) living with one parent or elder in a village while the father and the sons follow traditional herding practices. Family compliance may not be enough. Since the integrity of the group whose life form has been disturbed is at issue, social costs will be incurred that call for modes of education to be imagined that will make taking next steps to integrate into civil society culturally sustainable.[75] There is parallel responsibility for the viability of the community into which the transition is to take place. The responsibility is not to compensate for costs as losses but to ensure that the implementation conditions for effective agency and status show respect for the groups involved. If this means that decision-making should be local, the duty to secure schooling for all Maasai children is not. We are all bearers of a primary duty here: even where what is to be done should be realized through local institutions, they may not exist without the help of others.

In many settings of urgent need that raise human-rights-type questions—resettling refugees, meeting food needs during severe droughts or famines—a balance may need to be struck between acting directly and acting in a manner that, even if it is less immediately effective, will make it possible for those who receive aid to enter or create political communities. What moves refugees may be the ravages of war, ethnic cleansing, or threat of starvation. What they are entitled to is freedom from all that *as part of* movement towards civil life: being in a place where they can work, be respected, have a political voice, raise their children, and so on. These facts about what people are owed have a profound effect on how we understand the duties of aid. Tracking the intersection of material and moral need is required of all responsible actors; it may not always make solutions to either sort of need easier.

A few points of clarification. First, I have been talking about states, occasionally about polities, and loosely about civic and juridical structures. None of this provides a brief for what has been called the Westphalian nation state. Quite the contrary. If anything, the arguments I have sketched suggest that states likely do not have complete sovereignty over their territory or domestic affairs. Nor must there be states in the capital S sense wherever there are peoples or nations or

---

[75] In sharp contrast to traditional missionary schools or Indian Residential Schools whose mission was to "civilize" and integrate by destroying indigenous culture.

geographic boundaries. What the habitat project requires is that there be substantially self-governing and (at least potentially) multi-generational juridical communities. Historically those have tended towards a certain form. At this stage of the discussion, we don't need to know whether there is a single best form of social/political arrangement, or, at the other end, whether the idea of interlocking sovereignties is possible. The point of the habitat project idea is to set standards that can be responsive and directive with respect to both social and technological change in whatever the social juridical form. It might, for example, predict that the juridical form (or parts of it) cannot be realized if the population is too large or too varied. If too large, what citizens can effectively do by way of participation is limited and formal; if too varied, common terms for managing difference call for institutions that reflect no one's local values.[76]

I will be returning to these issues later in discussions of a right to housing (section 10.2) and the moral status of refugees and migrating people (section 10.3). For now, the point to emphasize in the account of the moral habitat is the role of innate right and the system model of duties in setting out substantial moral claims. In the habitat account there are neither natural duties nor natural rights, though there are natural moral problems that require a non-natural solution. As we have seen, that doesn't mean the account then veers across the conceptual street to merely conventional duties and rights, or duties that have no meaning apart from the social condition in which they arise *by contrast with* duties that have natural meaning (what makes a bad father, e.g., for Hume). The system of duties is articulated *in a place* with respect to the conditions for realizing moral duties generally—that is, within a moral habitat, the juridical space that is innate right's essential demand. The idea of provisional universal right introduced in this section is only intelligible on a sight line to the habitat setting.

Second, there is a question, mostly an inside-Kant question, about the status of the obligation to enter the civil condition and the title to compel others' entry. It is a central claim, whose obscurity can mask an important aspect of the universality of the Kantian idea of RIGHT.

The obligation to accept the authority of the juridical state cannot itself be a juridical duty. And it doesn't seem to possibly be an imperfect duty, certainly not an ethical imperfect duty, since one can be compelled to enter (and satisfy the duty merely by so doing). It is also something done only once. At least ideally. Though in a sense it is also constantly reaffirmed. But what does this mean?

The duty to enter the civil condition is a demand of innate right, given the material world as it is, human persons needing to use it as they do, interacting as

---

[76] Technology is confounding. We need to co-deliberate. Do we need to talk? We've discovered that email, texting, and social media posting provide some substitute. But there is something elemental about physically, not virtually, being in the same room talking with others. We need to better understand the importance of our practices of embodied speech.

they inevitably are. It follows from a postulate of practical reason that the conditions of possession, obligating others, be made real, which makes the move to the juridical condition necessary and the positing of an omnilateral willing to make it so. Subjectively, any person may or may not consent to the law. Objectively, they must. If they will to make a claim to exclude anyone from what they design to use tomorrow (as it were), they must also will the conditions necessary for the exclusion to obligate others. And that implies a rational commitment to the juridical condition. That is why resistance to the idea of juridical authority is, as Kant resonantly puts it, wrong in the highest degree: an assertion of the authority of a single will over others. Such resistance is not a moral possibility.

The idea that the duty includes the entitlement to compel people to accept the civil condition does not mean that we are entitled to move anyone into the civil condition with a gun to their heads. "We" have no such authority. I think it does mean that in a region of interacting persons, those who have entered a civil condition do not act wrongfully in refusing to recognize privately asserted claims of possession made by recalcitrant or resistant individuals who assert them. Because the civil condition is, *objectively*, one the recalcitrant already will in making any claim against others, treating them as inside the juridical condition—and in that sense compelling them—is not a forced imposition of the arbitrary will of a collective.[77]

By contrast, the duty to support or reform the civil condition where one is a citizen has to be imperfect. Its goal is maintaining the conditions of reciprocal free action; its source value the conditions of innate right. One acts for the duty in proposing legislation, seeking reforms, and at the limit, in acts of civil disobedience (a meta-juridical act that can only be what it is if its object is securing the value of a RIGHTFUL order).

If there is a general duty to promote the civil condition *tout court*—i.e., not just at home—it too would be imperfect, secured by the same source value. Economic and cultural relations create opportunities to affect the course of civic development elsewhere, modulo substantial due care concerns. Negatively, economic activity that reinforces class or caste or other modalities of inequality is to be avoided. Positively, one might insist on fair working conditions in the venues of economic cooperation, support for educational opportunities for women, and so on. Because the duty is imperfect, there can be variation about *who* is to act.[78] Not all are equally well situated to promote the civil condition everywhere they might

---

[77] So we get an atemporal argument that no one has grounds to complain that the place they reside or were born into has juridical authority over them if it satisfies the moral norms of the civil condition. No appeal to tacit consent is necessary.

[78] This doesn't speak against the right girls have to an education and the not-imperfect duty their own state has to provide it. But where the state fails, and the actors promoting education are from the outside, *their* duty is imperfect. As may be the duties of parents in comparable circumstances. When the Taliban controlled Afghanistan, they banned the education of girls and women. Some families took great risks, putting their girls' lives in danger, to send them to secret schools. The risk-taking parents

have an effect. Given different histories, not every intervener is equally credible. And since not every beneficial intervention is coherent with a culture's trajectory, there is a defeasible anti-hegemonic principle of deference in decision-making and social interventions.

Acts that would assault or undermine the actual juridical condition anywhere violate innate right and have no standing. They can be resisted, though not just any physical intervention counts as hindering the wrongful act so as to assert or reassert the authority of the juridical condition. Since the failure of the juridical condition is a burden on all, international insistence on and supervision of remedial repair should not count as a violation of juridical independence.

Nothing in this sketch speaks to the balancing of domestic and global duties. Its purpose was just to take the first steps in extending duties that have their home in the moral habitat beyond its borders.

*

Having noted that, at the limit, a provisional human right functions like a negative contractualist principle, condemning a way of acting (e.g., denying women an education) on grounds that it would not be morally possible in any practice regulated by RIGHT, it is natural to ask whether the moral habitat project is itself in essence a contractualist scheme.[79] There are deep similarities: a formal modeling of moral reasoning; a value commitment to equality and dignity; a resistance to aggregation. However, the differences are both deep and instructive. If a region of value is brought to the contractualist test—about friendship or family or property or the fair balance of benefits and burdens of a social scheme—the principle can apply and explain considered moral judgments, even separating out some attractive principles (that aggregate or create wrong-reason inequalities) as inconsistent with the assumed dignity and separateness of persons. What contractualism lacks is an *internal* account of the values it manages. Some will view this as a strength. It in any case contrasts with the Kantian moral habitat project which, beginning in innate right's recognition of embodied (human) rational agents' claim to freedom of choice, tells a story of value and vulnerability for the sake of which duties, both juridical and ethical, give principled protection. And they do this not with principles no one could reasonably reject, nor principles everyone could agree on, but with duties that require actual persons to, together, articulate the terms of moral requirement *within a framework of objective value*. Some will see this as a weakness. I have tried to lay out what seem to me compelling strengths of the habitat view: that the internal reliance on moral values

---

acted on an imperfect duty. They did not and could not fulfill their girls' right to education. A family who judged the secret schools too risky violated no right, and in using their discretion, failed no imperfect duty.

[79] I am taking T. M. Scanlon's exposition of contractualism in *What We Owe to Each Other* (1998) as the paradigm.

leads to system connections among duties and types of duty; that there is then the possibility of a principled division of moral labor between public and interpersonal duties; that taking common moral reasoning beyond wrongness as impermissibility offers richer, context-responsive deliberative resources; and, as we'll see, that the room it gives for positive, imperfect duties gives persons a commission to construct a moral habitat in which free and equal persons, individually and collectively, can express the creative potential of their rational nature.

Are these ideas ruled out for contractualist theory? In a ptolemaic sense, no. The point is that even if contractualism can absorb the moral habitat idea, it cannot generate it.

7
Kantian Imperfect Duties

7.1 Imperfect Duties and Obligatory Ends

It is time to reintroduce imperfect duties. So far we have come at imperfect duties in two ways. Part One of the book examined a small set of imperfect duties with the aim of understanding what their imperfection was about, and in light of that, what their inclusion in the lexicon of duties required of a moral theory. Several features came to the fore: the role of moral value in the deliberative discretion afforded by an imperfect duty; the way background moral and juridical concepts could shape an imperfect duty's content; and then the role motive might need to play in providing the structural connection between value and action that supported agent discretion in acting for this class of duties. A task of Part Two has been to present an outline of a Kantian system of duties in which imperfect duties can make moral sense, where they play a central role, sometimes necessary to complete the work of other duties. What we have not yet explored is their origin or foundation.

The focus of this chapter and the next are the familiar imperfect duties to self and others found in the *Doctrine of Virtue*. Of first importance will be getting an account of the idea and role of obligatory ends—ends we have a duty to have— from which the ethical imperfect duties descend. Obligatory ends are not merely a generative source, like a rocket stage, that falls away once the duties are set; they provide the connective tissue, the moral value, that makes discretion the defining mark of these duties.

Once we have in hand a working model of obligatory ends and their relation to imperfect duties, we will be in position (in section 7.2) to look in a fresh way at the duty of beneficence, now as an instance of, not the paradigm for, what an imperfect duty is like. Among other things, we will see that while not indifferent to issues of demandingness, the point of the discretion the duty allows is not about limiting the amount of what beneficence asks of us. Further, as we work through cases it will become clear that not all duties of aid are duties of beneficence, or, if we are fussy about nomenclature, not all duties of aid are duties of the same type. Failure to recognize this may explain much confusion about what morality requires of us when the needs of others are large.

At different moments I have suggested that there is a place for imperfect duties that have a juridical origin, some, a juridical object. They are not found as core juridical duties—determining whether we have a right to some object or authority over our children—but rather set terms for what we do with what we rightfully have or shape how we go about our children's instruction. In the larger sphere of RIGHT they provide terms for the moral duties of citizenship, and perhaps, more broadly still, our duties with respect to the idea of RIGHT across all persons. It is also reasonable to think that there are institutional imperfect duties: that some of the responsibilities that come with the juridical order require the kinds of exercise of discretion that mark these duties. The duty to address institutional injustice may be one of them. Despite their importance, it makes sense to delay discussion of the juridical imperfect duties since they depend on the understanding of discretion that emerges in the detail of the ethical ones.[1]

Stepping back, we might frame the role of imperfect duties this way. If the point of morality were primarily for protection and coordination, most of its work could be done by carefully crafted public right and perfect duties. But if we are talking about a moral habitat for rational persons, something we make together, there will be complex choices we need to make and ends we need to have and share. It's not just that the habitat is a made social place and not a natural object; its origin and maintenance call for our having more than enforceable principled relations and resources for managing wrongful action. Its object—what it's for—calls for principles by which we give our habitat, and our lives, a moral shape.

Consider the familiar list of imperfect duties: taking steps to prevent violations of other duties and to minimize harm generally, benefiting others, self-perfection, due care. Each serves a goal well-suited to the moral habitat project: we add material and psychological resources to make the habitat safe and accessible; we provide one another support and cooperation; we take ourselves on as a moral project; we bring attention to moral value even in our externally lawful actions. Framing the work of imperfect duties this way can give common ground to the interpretive project without assuming that the duties all do one thing.

As we encounter them in the *Doctrine of Virtue*, imperfect duties are deliberative duties, drawn or derived from obligatory ends. There are two pieces: end and duty are not to be conflated. A single obligatory end gives rise to a number of duties. The end of promoting the happiness of others, for example, generates duties of beneficence, but also duties of gratitude, duties to avoid envy and a false sense of virtue, and, indirectly, duties to make ourselves more sensitive to the ways human lives can go well or badly. While the obligatory end serves as a first premise in reasoning to the content of an imperfect duty, the duties we wind up with also

---

[1] The investigation of the idea and the possible source of juridical imperfect duties is taken up in Chapter 8 (section 8.2). Since they are duties that cannot be derived from Kant's familiar account of obligatory ends, we need to know what could anchor them and deliver content, and how they are, if they are, related to ethical imperfect duties. Although in Kant's work we find a "derivation" of imperfect duties only in the *Doctrine of Virtue* (parts of which are foreshadowed in the *Groundwork* examples), there is no argument there or elsewhere that restricts their occurrence to the ethical duties of virtue.

reflect and draw on facts about our personal and social circumstances. We should then not expect fixed action directives. Unlike duties to pay our debts or keep our promises, a duty to develop our abilities may direct each of us differently, and will adjust to our place, condition, and life stage. This class of duties requires that we read our circumstances in light of the value each duty brings to bear on our choices. How we are to manage ourselves and others can depend on accidents as well as past decisions whose effects we could not (or just did not) predict. Even so, imperfect duties are objective in their requirement. I find it a helpful metaphor to think of an obligatory end as introducing a complex, site specific, moral engineering project.

About obligatory ends, we will want to know both what they are and why we have them. Kant argues that for the human being (that is, generically), there can be just two obligatory ends: the end of self-perfection and the end of the happiness of others. Together they amplify the practical specification of how to regard the human being—self and other—as an end in itself.[2] They are general or global ends, capable of setting a variety of tasks. Structurally, they are like many other general ends. If you would sustain an intimate relationship there are demands on attention and concern and action; some are ongoing, some vary as circumstances change. If you would train your dog to be easy around children you must alter a range of its behaviors and responses; what you need to do will depend on the dog's temperament and the socialization of the children encountered. To become proficient in public presentation...; to overcome fear of...; and so on. General ends of this sort identify a target as valuable and to be pursued (though not everything that is valuable as a general end for someone is an end for everyone). They guide the selection and organization of subordinate ends (and related means), providing a forward-looking narrative goal that primes planning.

An *obligatory* end is not only a general or global end, it is both universal *and* an end that cannot be abandoned or even temporarily set to the side when doing so would free us to act for some other end that is important to us. It is an end we are obligated to have and respect in all our acting. This is not the absurd requirement that we never act in a way that has negative consequences for our own perfection or the happiness of others, but the idea that such facts and their moral value have to be given full measure when considering countervailing choices. It is sometimes to be promoted; it is always in play as a deliberative condition or constraint. By acting under the direction of obligatory ends our lives take on a morally inflected shape.

Seeing the kind of thing obligatory ends are, we should ask: Why must we have them? Why does Kantian moral theory need them? The argument Kant offers in the Introduction of the *Doctrine of Virtue* is both straightforward and surprising.

---

[2] This is parallel to the specification that RIGHT provides of what it is to be externally free. It also takes us beyond the idea of the end-in-itself as a limiting condition.

It is, he claims, a necessary condition of freely willed action, and so of any categorical imperative for willing, that there be obligatory ends: ends whose source-value is in reason, not inclination.[3] I take the argument to be this. Suppose there were no obligatory ends. Then all volition and action would bottom out as empirically determined: that is, in the broadest sense, in the service of our needs and desires. If all action were empirically determined, the only practical principle that could apply to our volition would be the hypothetical imperative: its relation to the content of a maxim is instrumental, its directive contingent on the end someone happens to have. So in short: no end(s) from reason, no categorical constraint on willing.[4]

The argument embedded in the *Groundwork*'s formula of humanity makes a parallel claim. We are told that the possibility condition of a categorical imperative for the will of a finite rational being is an end of absolute value, an end in itself, a final end of some sort, connected as a matter of necessity to our willing, but not contained in the concept of the rational will as such. Our humanity, our rational nature regarded as an end in itself, fulfils this role. Represented as a principle for acting, it supports, first, an anti-subordination rule: that we take the standards of good reasoning to have final authority in the pursuit of subjective ends (that we not treat rational nature in ourselves or others as a mere means). And second, that our volitions must "harmonize" with the idea of humanity, requiring positive attention in our actions to self-perfection and the happiness of others. So, while refraining from treating humanity as a mere means is a necessary condition for treating humanity as an end in itself, it is not sufficient: there are ends that serve human rational nature that we must adopt (G 4:430).[5] These two ends are just the

---

[3] "For since there are free actions there must also be ends to which, as their objects, these actions are directed. But among these ends there must be some that are also (i.e., by their concept) duties. —For were there no such ends, then all ends would hold for practical reason only as a means to other ends..." (*MM* 6:385).

[4] Obligatory ends thus introduce the second stage of a single argument whose first stage is the principle of RIGHT. First, compossibility of choice; second obligatory ends. Without a standard for free action and juridically limned moral powers, we would have no specific moral location in the space of positive duties. An instructive comparison is Mill's *On Liberty*: a regime of regulation that does not permit harm to others and otherwise offers wide license for choice. This can look quite a lot like a free-standing *Doctrine of Right*. But the questions and values are different. The Millian question is about how to live if we care about human happiness; the answer is to allow for experiments in living consistent with not harming. There's an implicit trust in human nature to eventually make wise choices, *so long as* there is a socially progressive economic and cultural environment. Kant's question is not about happiness but about the life-form of free rational agency. That's why morality has to constrain choice beyond RIGHT. It's a curious side note that the same progressive environment that Mill's argument requires as a setting that makes his liberty prescription rational for happiness emerges integrally in the Kantian program of support for human rational agency (what I've been calling the habitat idea).

[5] A more direct way to see what's at stake here is through the idea of the categorical imperative as a principle of morally sound or good (practical) reasoning. Maxims of action that lack the imperative's universal form are not valid: they cannot be willed a universal law without contradiction. A principle of validity catches reasoning errors coming from premises, either in their interpretation or in what's taken

obligatory ends of the *Doctrine of Virtue*. They are situated in both arguments as marking conditions of free rational agency in us as finite rational beings.

The *Groundwork* suggests and the *Doctrine of Virtue* argues by elimination that there are only these two obligatory ends. Under happiness Kant includes the ends and interests the satisfaction of which we expect will make our life go well and which we choose for that reason (there need be nothing narrowly self-interested in this). Under perfection he counts both sustaining and improving our capacities, natural and rational, so that we stay or become effective agents generally and morally, without regard to any specific moral or practical tasks. If the happiness of others and our own perfection are obligatory ends, it is obvious why they can be final and general ends. Since practically anything we are considering to do or avoid will affect either self-perfection or others' happiness, or both, the obligatory ends orient us as we factor these effects into our choices.

That leaves us three questions. In order of difficulty: Why is it *others'* happiness and only our *own* perfection that matter? Why are happiness and perfection the content of obligatory ends (and especially, why happiness)? And third, why are there imperfect duties in addition to the obligatory ends?

In answer to the first question: it can't be my own happiness or others' perfection. The one because we already and necessarily have happiness as a natural end—a duty doesn't double-down on a necessity; the other because perfection entails the adoption of ends, and one person can't do that for someone else.[6] Why either remaining candidate is an obligatory end still needs to be shown.

Kant takes this to be a question about the interest reason (that is, Reason) has in the human person's ends.[7] It is an awkward way to speak, but we can sensibly say that a practical capacity is like a natural capacity in the sense of having a virtual interest in working well. So just as we might say the heart (or the circulatory system) has an interest in the health of its valves and its arteries not being clogged, reason insofar as it's a human practical capacity has an interest in its working well

---

to follow from them. Typically, the errors are about what we take to follow from our self-interest. But a validity standard does not tell us what premises to have. So although good willing depends on valid reasoning, it is not unconditionally good if there are no ends good in themselves to serve as premises.

[6] There's thought to be room for doubt about this because, e.g., I can certainly help someone else develop their talents—counsel them, give lessons, sensitivity training. But what I can't do is make them do these things for the right reason—get them to engage deliberatively as they ought—with the relevant value. It will also be argued that many people are unable to pursue happiness due to failures in their circumstances or psychology. Many others undermine their desired happiness through various kinds of self-defeating decisions. Kant's point is technical. "Happiness" names whatever we pursue under the Idea of living a life that we believe will satisfy us. That untoward circumstances or our own bad choices lead to failure does not invalidate the idea of the Idea.

[7] In the deduction of the principle of virtue as a categorical imperative (of ends) Kant offers: "Pure practical reason is the capacity for ends generally, and for it to be indifferent to ends, that is, to take no interest in them, would therefore be a contradiction, since then it would not determine maxims for action either (because every maxim contains an end) and so would not be practical reason" (*MM* 6:395). The two obligatory ends fill out reason's mission.

in us. And since that's about the fitness of our agential abilities, qua rational being we have the end of self-perfection. It is less clear how happiness gets into the story.

You might expect that about happiness, what we have is a duty to pursue it in the right way: go for good ends, not bad ones. We could have such a duty if there were a story about the correct personal ends a person should have, but Kant doesn't seem to think there is one. And that means that when he casts the happiness of others as an obligatory end, it is not in order to bring them to have correct ends either. Kant is clear that it is *their* idea of their own happiness we are to engage, not our conception of what would make them happy, or good. Although it is hard to imagine a moral theory that does not require that we attend to others' happiness in some way, why *Kantian* moral theory should do so, is not so easy to say. Even when we appreciate the necessary deference of the pursuit of happiness to juridical and other moral requirements, what's left is a subjective, highly personal end: what we each separately consider to be a satisfying life for ourselves. How could I, starting from an interest of reason, get to have a duty of any kind to support *your* passion for coastal sailing? It is a question we obviously need to answer, and unfortunately, the answer is far from obvious. We won't be in a position to secure it until we understand how and why obligatory ends give rise to duties. And that will take some work.

We can take a first step towards that goal by looking at the way common or shared ends affect choices. Suppose we are to be working together on some project over an extended period of time; neither of us can accomplish our goal without the other. If you are working too hard, that can be a concern for me; if you are preoccupied by troubles in a relationship or another project, I might need to help out—to ease your mind or to release some time. A failure to attend to the well-being of a work partner can be a failure to do what must be done for the common goal. Likewise with how I regard myself. I have to keep myself alert and engaged, rested, learning new skills as the project calls for them, attentive to my tendencies to procrastinate and undermine my own work. I may need and need to accept support from a co-worker. Although they will see their support as both for me and integral to our work together, they will tend not to succeed if they merely act instrumentally, helping me only as much as is immediately needed for the presenting task of the common goal. In limiting their support of competence in that way, they fail in due care: competence needs to overshoot. (If we are to be hammering, you should teach me both how to drive a nail and how to remove the bent ones.) The takeaway from the ordinary case is that the guidance we get from having common or shared ends is no simple instrumental directive. We should expect something similarly complex in the relation between obligatory ends and imperfect duties.

Recall that in the descent from innate right to the ethical duties against lying and suicide, something of value is first given the protection of RIGHT—the power of speech or communication, having an independent life—juridical rights and duties then articulate the protection, and the rest is left in the hands of individuals to manage. But not left to them in a libertarian sense, as an entitlement to do with whatever they want (modulo the rights of others). Rather, what the regime of RIGHT does is take a natural thing and turn it into a moral power. Animal movement becomes an exercise of free action; talk becomes discursive speech; material holdings become property. The power in each case is to obligate others: not to interfere; to follow certain rules; to cede certain decisions to public authority. But the value that supports the existence of the power continues to have a say about how it should be used. That is: the collective may be obligated to protect the security of the person's body and speech, but it is often up to us individually to sustain the protected value as we go about our business. That's where the ethical duties attached to the obligatory ends are active.

But why do we need a special class of duties for this? That is, if an obligatory end represents a moral value that then serves as a premise for reasoning to free action, why do we *in addition* need distinct duties flowing from the obligatory end? Why wouldn't it be enough to deliberate directly from obligatory ends to action? What do *duties*, mostly *imperfect duties*, add? There are familiar answers. Like rules of thumb, they could be epistemically and practically valuable, pre-sorting morally salient phenomena and pre-selecting appropriate means. Or they might take on the role of secondary rules of conduct: rules such that in following them we better instantiate the value of the obligatory end than we would with no rule, or a different rule. Neither answer yields a duty in the Kantian sense. Although the relation between obligatory ends and imperfect duties is deliberatively directive, not merely limiting, it is not instrumental. We are not to bring about more self-perfection or more happiness *simpliciter*. While it can be useful to have rules of thumb and secondary rules to promote uniformity or negotiate complexity in promoting an end, it is the idea of "promoting" that misses the relation between obligatory end and ethical duty. Ethical duties introduce a moral and not merely an efficient connection between action and end. They guide the use of our moral powers so that we make ourselves and others more effective stewards of human life and habitat.

The point of any duties in the Kantian system is to provide principles of organization in a morally freighted region of practical activity. The regions, and the kind of duty that fits them, are typed by the ways rational agency in persons requires support for its purposes. In the case of both of the obligatory ends, the duties are about the maintenance and development of rational (practical and moral) abilities: the duties manage vulnerabilities that come with or from our pursuit of discretionary ends. They reflect an interest of reason in us as rational persons.

Consider imperfect duties to self. Suppose it is a common feature of human beings as rational creatures with natural appetites that they are susceptible to appetitive deformations of the will such as gluttony and greed. The deformations are two-sided. Qua appetite, they vastly exceed the appetite's natural role in prompting the individual to consume and preserve what's needed for ongoing animal life. In the life of the rational agent, the presence of deformed appetite can heighten certain ideas and senses of necessity that lead the individual to faulty deliberation about what they should do. However, the ways we avoid or counteract tendencies to excess in appetitive pleasure or stockpiling means (often but not necessarily money) are not the same. We need to be sensitive to causes. Is it the appetite itself that is disordered or is it the social milieu that's responsible for the excess? A duty here directs us to attend to a problem area and take steps in light of causes to take preventive measures or make reparative adjustments. How we do this requires more than attention to the governing obligatory end. Inducing anhedonia could fix one aspect of appetitive deformation, just not in a way that recognizes the essential role of appetite in living a valued and productive human life.[8]

So one set of duties enters where we are drawn to principles of appetitive self-abandonment; putting oneself under the rule of another, or an addiction; the threat of depressive self-destruction in suicide. There will be other duties where there is danger of moral corruption: about lying and deception, as well as the cultivation of false conscience. The target of these duties is the known temptation to invert the order of value, the subordination of the rational and moral powers to something else persons are vulnerable to finding compelling. The duties meet a threat to what Kant describes as the "prerogative of a moral being": to act on principle rather than being the plaything of other forces: a thing and not a person (*MM* 6:420).

What the duty provides, what would not be provided, say, by encouraging us to be more attentive to the balance of reasons in our appetitive lives, is a regime of discipline for a region of choice where persons are known to have tendencies to go wrong even when trying to get things right. Some of the duties that follow from obligatory ends look like perfect duties.[9] The structure of such duties is to incorporate the tendency to error by excluding the distorting class of reasons from the balance of considerations, and requiring as a condition of their re-entry that they connect with the value that sets the duty's content. So if a duty manages indulgence, it blocks the pleonexic "desire for more" as a balancing reason, though its restriction is defeasible if presented with some caloric or social urgency. So rather than a duty that calls on us simply to minimize exposure, the duty demands that we come to terms with the appetites as they bear on our capacity for rational agency (temperance not continence). An imperfect duty in this space will remind

---

[8] Just as a headache cure that puts one to sleep fails to register what the cure is typically for—i.e., more than just pain relief.

[9] Disciplinary red flag rules of this form: Don't shop for food in the late afternoon when you are hungry if you want to avoid buying junk food. You are fighting marketers who know that facing a prominently positioned treat, a hungry shopper rehearses the reasons against and buys it anyway.

us of the importance of enjoyment to sustain a will to life. The counter-appetitive ascetic impulses we have also fail to serve the moral project. How we sort this out is to a large extent up to us; we rely on a mix of understanding human nature and updating self-knowledge about how things are playing out in our own case.

The imperfect duties that belong to the end of self-perfection are about the development and care of our practical and moral abilities. They don't dictate the activities we should engage in, no chess over checkers, but instead introduce a deliberative demand that in our choosing of activities we attend to positive and negative agency effects both for the sake of our moral competence *and* for our role in the common project. As happiness-seeking creatures, we will order our lives in ways that we believe will yield satisfaction. Whichever kind of life we seek, we also and always have a duty to avoid self-harm (physical, psychological, moral) and to find ways to maintain and develop practical abilities and skills that serve our own and our moral purposes.[10] In effect, the duty requires that we track two sets of values, shaping the one while remaining attentive to the issues of the other. Such a demand is vivid as we manage our wish to avoid painful self-criticism, our tendencies to obliviousness, to self-serving action interpretation, to blaming others as a mode of self-defense. We are right to seek positive self-regard; we are tasked with a requirement of honesty in self-reflection.

In short: we have ethical imperfect duties because an obligatory end makes salient regions of moral vulnerability in human life. The duties serve as deliberative nodes for managing these regions of vulnerability in light of the value introduced by the obligatory end. There are different duties because the regions of vulnerability have different structures, fault lines and background conditions that we need to attend to if we are to function well. It's both an individual and a system concern. We might think by analogy of the practical attention we give to the vulnerabilities of the body: pulmonary or cardiac problems are distinct foci that involve multiple organs, different modes of diagnosis and repair, as well as complex interconnections, systemic and idiosyncratic. So even though there may be a final end of good health or of the well-functioning body that introduces an encompassing value, the path to it is in terms that fit the functioning of the parts in light of the whole, adjusted, when that is possible, to the particulars of an individual life.

We saw the same pattern of organization in duties of RIGHT. Given the different ways human beings interact, it isn't possible to have single "maximize external freedom" principle. There are different domains with different structures, faults, moral vulnerabilities. There is no single instrument that that resolves the problems

---

[10] This is a clear case where an ethical duty has upstream implications for public institutions. There will be ascendent civic duties about work—that it not be unnecessarily onerous in any of these dimensions, and where it is burdensome, that the burden be mitigated by access to time and resources to engage in more agency sustaining activities.

of possession, exchange, and interpersonal authority, yet the different instruments need to work together, as a system.

If we think of the imperfect duties as providing engineering principles for the projects initiated by obligatory ends, we should also expect them to guide adjustment and repair. If helping someone leads to their having feelings of inferiority, or is experienced as a status insult, it may not be the fault of the help given, but nonetheless adds to the responsibilities of the helper. Leaving the problem with the person in need would just exacerbate their burden. The benefactor then has a duty of due care to seek a way around the negative effect, consistent with the primary duty's guiding value (anonymous giving can sometimes make receiving easier, as can the use of a neutral agency), and to find ways, if needed, to repair relationships (perhaps to be graceful in the face of the complex dance of gratitude). We needn't think of each of these moves as belonging to discrete duties involving separate moral decisions.[11] The structure of governance of an imperfect duty by its obligatory end can make its success condition open-ended. This is part of what makes an imperfect duty imperfect. But the *structure* comes with its being a duty.

It is also obvious, once you think about it, that being directed to engage with self and other in the terms of an obligatory end is rarely a "one-off" event. The nature of the deficits I might aim to remedy through duties of self-improvement often call for an extended project or plan, one that can require flexibility as I or my circumstances change. Likewise with others, as what we are to do enters into and affects an ongoing relationship, whether friend, neighbor, even enemy. The obligatory end marks out regions that matter, that are of moral value. The duty sets terms of engaged attention that carry the value into the circumstances of action.

The practical organization that comes from obligatory ends and imperfect duties does not merely apply to already formed regions of human activity, it partly makes a region of activity what it is. Take something as basic as pain, a condition not welcomed for itself by any healthy sensate being and a source of compassionate distress in others. But there are lots of things we don't welcome. Pain matters morally, on a Kantian account, because it is a mark of impedance with rational and autonomous functioning. We also know that pain can be integral to valuable activities, from gaining a physical aptitude to mourning the loss of a loved one. There can be something very wrong with medicating against grief. Because of its importance, both as warning and as a sign of health, we are obligated to attend to pain, to account for it in deliberation, but should respond to it as its significance is interpreted by the values in play in the context of its

---

[11] As it might be with perfect duties. As we return a book to the library, we don't leave something dangling if we don't want to chat about its lead character. Though out of kindness or generosity or in support of a casual but real relationship, we might.

appearance.[12] Friendship, we say, is not just mutual feelings of attachment or attraction, but attachment that has a reciprocal practical dimension that builds out how friends should attend to and act with and for each other. One doesn't have to have or raise children. But once you start down that path, your choice set and so the shape of your life changes in somewhat unpredictable though also unsurprising ways under the aegis of imperfect caretaking duties.

In these ways imperfect duties offer a kind of inter-temporal and inter-personal regimen that secures and sustains the moral value of a wide array of significant human activities. Through having duties that carry out the work of obligatory ends, this part of morality both tracks and transforms basic features of our physical, psychological, and social lives. It is not a product of morality or of rational nature as such but one of the given facts of human life that persons will form social bonds and want to attend to the needs of those they love when they can. We just do have appetites and various abilities and a reactive emotional repertoire. Imperfect duties introduce standards that are to guide our actions and manage our responses, directing the self-shaping of our given individual natures into a moral form.

This is enough to see why the familiar account of the discretion imperfect duties allow could not be right: that it is a permission to limit the demands morality makes on us. It is true that we do not have to act to promote the end an imperfect duty serves in every situation we could. We have some say beyond selection of means about how and when we fulfill the duty. But the point of the discretion is not about being free to resist the demands of morality. It is about our having an authorial role in giving our lives a specific moral shape and direction. The demandingness objection assumes the duties it would limit would otherwise be unfettered—that they come with an endless list of things we should do. But from what we've so far seen about the role or point of imperfect duties in Kant's theory, that doesn't seem to be their trajectory.

We should in any case be reminded that though these duties can be demanding, they are not all demanding in the same way. Gratitude can be demanding, but not because there's a threat that we will be overwhelmed by the number of occasions that call for it. One might sincerely say: "I owe you everything!" or even "I owe you my life!" What follows isn't easy to say, but as we saw in Chapter 2, the limits to what we can owe in response to a benefit come from something internal to the duty—from what it's about—not from its costs to our balance-sheet of goods.

This prepares us to question whether beneficence in particular is properly understood as demanding in the way the demandingness objection suggests.

---

[12] The painfulness of pain, the brute experience, can make it seem otherwise. Because the point of the pain system is to alert us, to make us stop or avoid, thought experiments isolating the experience of pain from its function are not convincing bases for an argument that we always have a moral reason to minimize pain where we can, other things equal.

This is not to deny the reality of need, which is large. But it is also a necessary element of practical rationality that duties contribute to a coherent deliberative field, and that they are, internally and as a function of their own value, self-limiting. A constant or built-in threat of demandingness could signal a fault in a system of duties. We might then look for a different kind of solution—not all duties are duties of individuals—and a different role for the exercise of discretion in beneficence than just saying "no" to it as a demand.

The Kantian duty of beneficence is especially interesting because its target is drawn from the obligatory end of others' *happiness*: that is, it is not essentially about their survival or their urgent needs. Now, as we've learned, where there is a duty, there is something to be limited or managed. In the case of juridical and perfect duties, it is some act-kind or a deliberative schema. But where there are imperfect duties, the limits take the form of a regimen or discipline, redirecting some tendency, replacing or supplementing natural reasons with moral ones. So the intriguing question about Kantian beneficence concerns the nature of and rationale for a required *discipline* with respect to the obligatory end of others' happiness.

As we examine the imperfect duty of beneficence in the next section, I aim to investigate three additional things. First, the idea that beneficence as a duty of aid or assistance is primarily a duty of individuals directed to other persons (individuals and groups) who are in need. It is often treated as the only duty that is concerned with help or assistance, but there is no compelling reason to think that. Among the things that emerge in the Kantian account of aid is that there are *three* such duties. Their different practical structures, reflecting differences in originating value, allow us to manage the terrain of human need in a more coherent and situationally responsive way. Second, while need is a mark that something might call for assistance, the Kantian view rejects the idea that assistance relates to need in the way food relates to hunger—making something negative, a privation, go away. The arena of concern of the duty is *ends*, not simply needs. This affects what the provision of assistance looks like, which in turn limits the scope of the duty (compare acting for the presenting need of pain or injury and assisting someone with the end of securing rewarding employment—it's not just the immediacy of response or the complexity of means that are different; there is a target that has a place in a life). And third, as an element of a system of duties, beneficence absorbs and reflects the value of other duties on which it structurally depends. It can matter what the context is in which the presenting need shows: whether, for example, it is significant for other moral relationships *who* is the provider of assistance. And, as we will see, because beneficence is not the only duty of assistance, when there are circumstances that introduce a crisis of need—extreme weather events are one kind of example, human-caused famine quite another—the burden is directed to the other duties of assistance whose collective and institutional agents are (or can be) designed to meet it. The individual duty to assist others may still be demanding, but not because there is a straight line from 1 to *n* needy people all having a claim on each of us.

7.2 Kantian Beneficence: What's It For?

Staying with our methodology, we should begin by asking about beneficence: "What's it for?"—what moral value does it serve? I think the answer is not obvious. Even if on every account of beneficence as a duty we are directed to feed starving children, there is more than one way to understand why we are to do that. We can sensibly ask, what, if anything, beyond the alleviation of suffering, are we aiming to accomplish? Why food and not anesthesia? It is natural to respond that while we care about suffering, in ameliorating the situation with starving children we are aiming to preserve life and promote the human good. But then, which sort of good? Is it what the person in urgent need wants now? Her subjective good? Or some objective good: perhaps a good related to the habitat conditions for the rational well-being of persons? And if so then our reasons for feeding the hungry are also reasons to meet needs for education and sustainable community. And that changes how we think about who the "we" is, as well as our understanding of what to do and for whom we should act.[13] It is often clear what I should do if at the end of the month one of my students doesn't have enough to eat. It is also clear when a child requires medical care, though less clear what to do if they aren't getting it. It is equally clear and urgent that inner city children need better schools. And that Uyghurs require a place in the world that will allow them to survive as a people. So what should I or we do?

It is not the aim of a philosophical account of the duties of assistance to answer all of these questions. It should be its aim to provide deliberative resources for placing both need and responses to need in a moral setting broad enough to articulate the different kinds of issues that different sorts of presenting cases and claims press on us.

Kant offers no uniform discussion of beneficence, and at least two quite different arguments for it. One is focused on need, maybe hardship (or "true needs") as the trigger and the reciprocal availability of help as a response; the other is about happiness as it relates to respect for humanity as an end in itself. Both arguments are sketched in the *Groundwork* examples and developed, with some casuistry, in the *Doctrine of Virtue*. Together they offer the framework for a surprisingly sophisticated account of the helping duties. The arguments also engage with the value of this imperfect duty in a way that frames the kind of

---

[13] For insightful work on this and related topics, see Onora O'Neill, *Towards Justice and Virtue* (1996).

discretion the duty allows. That, in turn, sheds light on where the boundaries and bridges are between beneficence and related duties of justice or RIGHT.

The focus of the first argument seems to be on bare facts about the human condition. We are creatures who have needs; we are not by nature self-sufficient; we can be helped. We live among others like ourselves who also have needs; we could help them. These facts register on us. This general possibility of reciprocal helping is the basis for a duty. The argument is present in the *Doctrine of Virtue* (6:451–453), but is more fully presented in the *Groundwork* (4:423).[14]

In the fourth of the *Groundwork* examples that are to show that the formal idea of universal law-giving tracks known duties, Kant identifies a source of volitional inconsistency in a human happiness-pursuer's deciding on grounds of self-interest to ignore the needs of others. While a creature law for us of not helping would be consistent with the laws of nature, a maxim of never helping could not be a self-consistent principle of *rational* willing for *us* because we necessarily will the end of happiness and are permanently vulnerable to needing help. Those who imagine otherwise mistakenly regard the accidents of good fortune as releasing them from the human condition. Since they do will happiness and cannot rationally will to forego help, the universal form of moral judgment commits them to helping (by blocking a happiness-based refusal to help others). The duty commitment (so far) is minimal: that we must sometimes help some others. The idea of the duty is tied to three things: our pursuit of happiness, the limitations of our agency, and the potential resource of others providing help.

The *Groundwork*'s view of beneficence changes tack and deepens in a second argument under the formula of humanity. There Kant adds to the idea of universal law as the form of morally valid maxims the additional idea of rational nature as an objective end (an end in itself) that provides a reflexive norm for rational willing. He argues: only if there is such an end can the idea of willing according to a (universal in form) rational principle, and so moral obligation or duty, be authoritative for us. What binds us to morality is an apparently inescapable conception of the person (of self and other) that implies each of us is to be regarded as an independent and authoritative reasoner.[15] We can disagree and dispute, but we have no valid grounds to subordinate the reasoning of another person to our own, as I would if I deceived you for the sake of my self-interest.[16]

When Kant returns to beneficence, something odd happens. He again starts with the observation that although happiness is the natural end of human beings, contributing to each other's happiness is not required for species survival. *But*, the

---

[14] Rather than deriving the duty, the examples illustrate the form and end of rational willing the argument claims our duties introduce. In doing this they also offer a kind of map to where the elements of duty derivation are to be found: here, in an independent account of happiness as a morally valuable end.
[15] This piece of the argument is not developed until *Groundwork* III. At this point it is a postulate.
[16] That's one way of explaining why a maxim of deceit cannot be a universal law of rational willing.

argument continues, insofar as we regard each person as an end in itself, we not only cannot be indifferent to their happiness, everyone must also "try, as far as he can, to advance the ends of others." Because, he says, "if that representation [of humanity as an end in itself] is to have its *full* effect in me, the ends of a subject that is an end in itself must, as much as possible, also be *my* ends" (G 4:430).[17] That is a very strong conclusion.

A premise of the argument is that "the natural end that all human beings have is their own happiness." The conclusion is that we fail to treat others' *rational* nature, their humanity, as an end in itself if we don't contribute to their happiness by making their ends our own. But why should this follow? From the first beneficence argument we know that none of us can rationally will to forego all help, so if the choice is between a principle of "no help" and "possible help," we are rationally constrained to endorse the latter. But that doesn't get us to making others' ends our own. The missing step lies in the dual characterization of the subject and target of beneficence as *ends*. That turns out to be a big idea.

To see why, we might start with an ordinary distinction. Sometimes all we want is the *state* that is the target of desire (a cup of coffee in hand); other times we have an *end* that includes the target (a morning run to be capped by a stop for coffee at a favored cafe). The difference in success conditions can be important. We want the job offer, and want it to come through a fair assessment of our merits. We won't realize our end if we get the job through well-meaning cronyism. The corrupt uncle may think he's done well by us in getting us the job we want. We should think not. This is not just being picky. We didn't want two things: the offer and a fair assessment; we wanted an offer that reflected an evaluation of our merits.

More formally: When we set and act for ends we represent possible targets of action as good in some way. So if I am to act for your *end*, if your end is to be mine also, it is not merely about my efficient causality. To act for your end is to act in light of the value the end has for you. But if that's right, there is a strain right away in the idea of making others' ends our own. There are values you may have that I do not understand or do understand and disdain. Projects that mean a lot to you but that I find unworthy. Many of the things we take to be central to our happiness are a bit idiosyncratic (to put it nicely). And then there is the Stoic challenge: none of the *elements* of happiness are necessary for us. Since we can often abandon ends we cannot pursue unaided, why is it *morally* incumbent to help for the sake of ends of happiness? Why should that be a duty?

---

[17] The full *Groundwork* text at 4:430 is this: "as concerns meritorious duty to others, the natural end that all human beings have is their own happiness. Now, humanity could indeed subsist if no one contributed anything to the happiness of others while not intentionally detracting anything from it; but this is still only a negative and not positive agreement with *humanity, as an end in itself*, if everyone does not also try, as far as he can, to advance the ends of others. For if that representation is to have its *full* effect in me, the ends of a subject that is an end in itself must, as much as possible, also be *my* ends."

The formula of humanity suggests where to find an answer. It would have us look at the subject of beneficence, the human being, characterized in two ways: as a natural being that has the desire for happiness as a law of its nature, *and* as a rational being who is an end in itself: one whose *telos* is to reason well. That makes the question about beneficence turn on seeing how the first characterization, about happiness, enters being in "positive agreement" with the second, about our rational nature. How could the natural or subjective ends of the human subject that make up her happiness be essential to her *rational* nature?

This framing turns out to be the first step in answering the question we put on hold in the last section about why the *happiness* of others should be an obligatory end. For Kant, the morally relevant fact about happiness is not that it is a state or condition that we want, or even have to want. Looking closely at short passages in the *Groundwork* (4:417–418) and the *Critique of Practical Reason* (5:23–26), what we see first is an account of happiness as a subjectively necessary composite or umbrella end for our lives whose content is made up of our mundane and our more elevated pursuits that we assemble in a defeasible order of expected satisfaction. A contrast is telling. While animal agency is a matter of biology with instinct its organizing principle, human beings are self-organizing agents, each tasked with massaging input from natural, rational, and social sources to form a revisable idea of how they would live, what they count as happiness. To the extent possible, they make themselves into agents of their own idea of the end. The content of the end of happiness can be rich and ambitious, or stunted, as circumstances and imagination allow. It is not a haphazard collection of interests, but a more or less ordered set of subordinate ends: our loves and projects in an updating life plan. We don't act directly for the end of happiness but it sets the idea of an ordered set of subordinate ends whose promotion we value as filling out our idea of living well. Although we can choose against elements of happiness, for morality or for whatever we regard to be a higher good, we can no more abandon the end of happiness than we can abandon our nature.

What this also tells us is that going for happiness is essential to the emergence of effective moral agency. It is the way we develop our practical capacities, that we come to have a personality, gain self-understanding and regulative skills—all things that begin early and develop sequentially, and without which morality would impose an impossible task. If we can't delay gratification, if we don't know how to channel aggression into safe activities, we likely won't do well in the pursuit of happiness, and it will be hard to see anything we don't already care about as a source of significant reasons. Kant also sees the inevitable developmental conflict between happiness and morality as the way the human being comes awake to morality as reason's authoritative principle for organizing our lives for ourselves and with one another as equals. It all begins in the sandbox with that outrageous requirement to share our toys.

The end of happiness thus has two functions in the life of the human being. Subjectively, it supports a principle of self-organization whose success is marked by a person's satisfaction with her life. Its content (what counts as my or your happiness) is diverse, person to person, and success is contingent on available resources, ingenuity, and the actions of other people. Objectively, and at the same time, it prepares us for morality: it is a condition—necessary but not sufficient—for realizing the potential for moral personality in us. Success here is marked by good or correct willing. This does not mean that personal or merely subjective ends are to be replaced by moral ones, though moral ends become part of the individual's practical repertoire and subjective ends come to be evaluated not just in terms of their contribution to happiness but also as they are worthy of pursuit in terms of their contribution, or absence of detriment, to moral well-being. This changes the way we value our ends. A process is set in motion. When all goes well, the development and enhancing of rational and moral abilities continues so that the pursuit of happiness is compatible with and supportive of the requirements of moral personality.

So a first thing we add to the formula of humanity argument is the idea that in regarding the other as an end in themselves, we are to see a practical reasoner engaged in a subjective project that matters to them (as their happiness), and matters morally because it is essential to creating and supporting their moral agency. That is, the pursuit of happiness is both a subjective *and* an objective end. That makes beneficence make moral sense. But it also raises new questions. *How* do we engage with the happiness of others? As the subjects of our helping regard it? Or instrumentally and paternalistically, as promoting the elements that are objectively good for them? And what about limits? Must I promote their happiness as much as I can? Can I limit the costs to me? And within this framework, do I have a choice about whose happiness I promote? If there are limits on the duty here, they should have a different source than our competing desires or preferences. The room for discretion or limits to the scope of the duty should be explained by something about the duty's value.

In the *Doctrine of Virtue*'s telling of the limits or imperfection of the duty of beneficence, Kant gives us some keys to solving for this. He says: We should not compromise ourselves in helping others (it wouldn't be coherent to fall into need in order to meet need); each person gets to decides what counts as happiness for them (it is not a paternalistic duty); we may refuse to support ends we think are harmful for someone (we can avoid complicity with bad choices); and, most interestingly, we can vary the degree of beneficent concern "in accordance with the different objects of [our] love" (*MM* 6:452). This is not, as he earlier alerted us, a permission to make exceptions for ourselves from the duty's requirements, but a "permission to limit one maxim of duty by another (e.g., love of one's neighbor in general by love of one's parents)" (*MM* 6:390).

The first three limits on helping actions are expected and easy to defend. The unexpected example of permitted discretion is about *who* we help. Parents over neighbors. This is not about the burdens of beneficence but about our loves—that they give rise to reasons of permitted partiality. But why would they? The mere fact of relation doesn't seem explanatory. And if it depends on who I care for, would I have permission to act preferentially for a beloved parent but not one from whom I'm estranged? And if my father and my neighbor both have needs, shouldn't it matter that my neighbor's are more urgent? Why isn't *that* the value of the principle I should act on? The trail to follow has us look more deeply at the difference that comes with taking *ends* instead of needs as the object of beneficence.

Were the focus of beneficence on needs, it would be natural to think of ourselves as purveyors of needs-meeting resources. The needs of persons are arrayed before us. They pile up. Facing that, the immediate questions will be about how much of the resources in our possession we have to provide (must we give all that we can?), the range of need that can trigger support (since there is so much urgent need, can non-urgent concerns even get attention?), whose needs must be met, or met first, and the rest of the familiar agony of beneficence casuistry. How can we justify the cost of our child's birthday party or her piano lessons? Concerns about the burdensomeness of the duty and the strains of impartiality (the costs to those we love) are then the natural worries and candidates for the exercise of discretion.

When the focus of the duty is on ends, not needs, we are not self-conceived distributors of stuff and services, but *agents* of ends that are not our own. The duty requires that we cross a barrier of separateness, potentially creating an intimacy that makes ethical demands of its own. The reasons for refusing to help become more complicated (as do those for delegation). There is an *entanglement* of ends and lives that gives an unexpected spin on beneficence as a duty of love.[18] Exercising principled discretion will be essential to making our way through this. Why this should be so is best seen if we step aside from Kant for a while and give some close attention to cases where the ends–needs distinction makes a difference.

The most familiar examples of beneficence start in prescriptions found in old scouting handbooks: returning found and fallen objects; holding doors; carrying packages; helping the elderly. We extend the model to driving people to the airport or hospital, offering a loan to manage financial distress. And then on to rescue cases—rare for most of us in our lives, though not in philosophical discussion. In cases like these it looks as though beneficence is about need and response; one and done.

---

[18] I owe the general moral idea of entanglement to Henry Richardson's more focused use in *Moral Entanglements* (2012).

Now consider a different kind of case. Suppose I come to know through office chatter that George, who has been saving for medical school, finds his goal is out of reach. I realize that I could pay his medical school costs. And I'm willing. How should I think about this? I could ask: Since I have adequate discretionary funds, is this the best use for them if I want to be helpful (after all, I could provide medicine, or meals for many, but then, if George became a doctor he could help a larger number—and I'm off down a familiar rabbit hole). I could also ask: Is George's medical ambition my business? Is it even appropriate for me to help him this way? What would happen to my relationship with George? Would I have a say in his choice of specialization? Such a line of questions wouldn't arise if George was in immediate danger of losing his arm or life. So what should we make of that?

It's a familiar fact that once I initiate help, I can be on the hook for more than I intended. Many helping actions are in passing—I offer directions, give change for a dollar, pick up the book you dropped. But as the presenting need is more serious or complicated, the first step in helping is often not the last. Through our help, we may have intervened in something ongoing that needs to be completed, perhaps in ways not foreseeable. Without meaning to, we become *entangled* in the life of the other person. That's not necessarily a bad thing.

Entanglement can sometimes be essential to helping. It matters for children that their parents or their intimate circle of caretakers act on their behalf in an entangled way.[19] Providing help is part of building a relationship of trust and support that enables a child's healthy moral development. It's not just that I may help my child and not yours; a stranger's help can (sometimes) be intrusive. My child trips, I reach out, but you, a swifter helper, dash in. If there is no real danger, that your help might get there some seconds earlier is not usually a good reason for a stranger to intervene. There is a lot the parent might be doing in helping—providing support, giving instruction. A parent might choose *not* to help as the best response, seeing the episode as a teaching moment. This is not just about cementing the relationship of parent and child, but about the good of the child faced with need in the space of the authority of the parent. The parent looks beyond the immediate need to be met to effects on the person the child will become. Her actions communicate her values (think of all that is being said when a parent helps their child's friend first). This gives us two related things to think about.

Pairing bare need and help won't fully capture what's of value in the moral scene and so what help should provide. And this can tell us why being oriented in helping towards those one is closer to need not be about partiality. In the textbook stranger-helper cases, all we get to see is need; in the relational context, need presents as *embedded in a life*. As we are closer, we know more about a person,

---

[19] Even though helping in some intimate relations feels natural, part of the relationship, it is within the orbit of beneficence and in need of its guidance.

more about her ends, about how this or that interest matters to her now and likely later on. We may let our own experience bear more on the way we choose to help than we would with a stranger. Knowing that a friend needs time to finish an important project I might step in to take on some shareable burden—picking up his child from school. But I might also judge that the friend is letting the project create damaging distance from his child, and then form a different view of what to do. Voicing a beneficence-based refusal to continue helping in this way, I can sustain connection to my friend's ends, perhaps offering some other kind of time-releasing help. The refusal is not about demands on me, but about how I understand another's ends and what they mean in our ongoing relationship. This is what it's like to be agentially connected to another's ends.

Extrapolating from these sketches, beneficence, anchored in the obligatory end of others' happiness, appears to be a *relational* duty.[20] If that's right, we get it backwards if we start with an idea of beneficence as directing us equally to everyone in need so that we require special reason to help or support those we love. It would be hard to justify that. Rather, the focus on *ends* leads to the idea that much of beneficence lives in relationships.[21] That is its home, and the locus of a very different kind of casuistry than the casuistry of impersonal needs' demands. It explains why a rich form of discretion is central to the duty: we need to decide how and whether to act in light of the mix of values and ends that intersect with a presenting need.

We are also led to think about beneficence in a more dynamic way—less about a passive victim and a savior. It can be explicit in a relationship that certain sorts of helping are out of bounds (no monetary loans, for example, but as much of my time as you need). Partners may agree to limit taking on one another's responsibilities (e.g., about adult children from another marriage). A kind of line drawing about ends and needs fixes one's exposure and is a way of settling what the relationship is to be like. One offers help to one's adult children—we always want to help our children!—but where once we sought to support their development, now we help with an eye to avoiding dependence. One helps a spouse with their career, but not in a way that makes the partner a subordinate.

Sometimes a minimal relationship expands because of a simple act of helping, which then changes what one should do. Suppose an elderly neighbor can't locate his medicine—he's misplaced his glasses—and asks for my help. I help, and then find out (because he tells me) that he doesn't remember the dosage. It's obvious that I should extend myself—read the label, call the pharmacy, maybe more. His presenting *need* was to find the missing pills, but his *end* was to take his medicine.

---

[20] So *not* a duty of partiality; though because relational in the way that it is, we have reasons *internal* to the duty of beneficence to sometimes attend more to the ends and needs of intimates.

[21] Much, but not all. I discuss the less relational duties of stranger-beneficence and beneficence-at-a-distance in the next section (7.3).

We can't hive off the one from the other. This is not a point in the metaphysics of actions and events. There is his end, and the fact that what I offer with my help is a fragment of *my agency*, not an Amazon drone. My helping action is not complete if his end is not met. Beneficence comes with a due care responsibility to attend to the location of a need in a life and to shape helping responses accordingly. I probably have to help find the missing glasses as well. But there is also a horizon of completion to a presenting need. It is up to me whether I check on him tomorrow: a question about the relationship I am willing to have.

As helping activity gets more complicated and extended, other issues arise, including, if things go far enough, the question of whether we are now doing something, or a part of something, together. What say should I have? Am I responsible for outcomes? Issues of privacy and tact may press in the opposite direction. It is *your* life; you have a considerable say in how far I may intrude. On the other hand, having invited me in, having accepted my help, if it is obvious that your need is much greater than I knew, we may have to negotiate the new moral situation together—how much of your need you will permit to become my obligation. And then there is a question for you: How much helping from me is consistent with *my* ends being yours as well. Issues of *reciprocal* concern come to the fore.

Where beneficence is relational in its principle, it is to an important degree self-limiting. One of the things that belongs with its entanglements is increasing knowledge of self and other that bears on how much is to be done and by whom. Just as we have the sometimes painful task of assisting our children into their independence from us, so we need a general wariness about patterns of assistance whose routine and comfort exceeds their value. There are pleasures on both sides of the helping relationship that are not good pleasures. We may too readily enjoy the enlargement of our agency that comes with acting for another. It is a temptation to be resisted and not confused with the genuine pleasures we find in being of help. Likewise, even if dependency is unavoidable, it is a danger if welcomed for itself. Gratitude is not the only duty the recipient of assistance has; there is also a requirement not to exploit a willing helper or to indulge in the ease of dependence.

A decision not to go on helping has its own burdens. If it is up to us to decide not to engage in further helping, it is not in the same way up to us how we stop. We may need to give notice if we've been sending a check each month and have reached our limit. We may need to manage a transition to being without help or to find another helper. There are myriad issues of due care that arise as we extricate ourselves from helping.

In these and related ways it makes a real difference that the focus is on *this person in need* and not merely the need a person has. Someone may prefer, and have good reason to prefer, being helped by you rather than by me. Matters of history or confidence or a view towards the way future relationships may develop belong to the decision. The entanglements of helping might reveal information that makes no difference if it's you, but might have disturbing effects if it's me. It may not be trivial to whom one owes gratitude. My graduate student suddenly loses his housing and as it happens there is no one around but me to help. I should help; let him stay at my house. But it is a situation where entanglements are to be resisted, and I should remove myself from the helping relationship as fast as I can (with acknowledgment about why I must and with help finding different housing).

In the ethics of entanglements that arise in helping encounters we come back around to the foundational question about beneficence: what it is about happiness that makes its promotion a condition of treating humanity (our rational nature) as an end in itself. What we have found in the cases is a kind of responsibility taken for another person. Beyond the need that presents there are issues of how the need fits in a life, something that we should make sense of in our helping. And there are also a host of issues on the receiving side, about communication, gratitude, privacy, and reciprocal concern for the ends, the humanity, of the helper. These all speak to there being something more at stake in promoting the subjective end of a person than its being her end. Kant might say: it is the end of an end (one who is an end in itself): an end whose objective value inflects and informs the subjective value of ends to be pursued.

If in regarding the other as an end in themself we are to see a practical reasoner engaged in a project that matters to them subjectively, and matters morally because it is essential to creating and supporting their moral agency, that doesn't mean that when engaged with their subjective ends we are to regard the ends merely instrumentally, supporting them only as far as their successful pursuit contributes to the development or sustenance of moral abilities. If we did that, we would ignore what's of value to the other in their end (and therefore in the means they take): that it belongs to their idea of happiness. My help would, in effect, bypass the others' agency, subordinating their choice to the producing of objective value *in their agency*. Whereas when I provide the help that takes the subjective end seriously, I can connect to objective value *through* what's of value to the other's agency. Only in the latter case do I act for their *humanity*—and for them as a full person. Beneficence thus requires that we support ends and activities holistically, as what they are as chosen (as part of happiness) *and* as they are part of a morally progressing life.[22] As the surrogate agent of another's end, my aim is theirs, *but* I am also responsible for maintaining a connection between their end and moral value (e.g., I might not press forward as hard as they would

---

[22] The duty thus makes an assumption about a person's possible life trajectory. It sets a presumption about how to approach helping a person, one that can have to be adjusted in the face of urgency or limitations of ability or the end of life. The idea of normal functioning that sets the duty does not fully determine its application.

for some end or in the same way or to the exclusion of other ends: entanglement pushes back).

On the relational account of beneficence we have moral reason to support a very wide array of others' activities—*if* they are of value, subjectively and objectively, and *if* we are in (or open to being in) a relational position where it is acceptable to offer our agency to supplement another's, knowing the entanglements that may follow. "Let's go to the movies!" invites a depressed friend out for a nice evening, *and* offers help to sustain necessary social function in a difficult time. It's an offer that depends on a willingness to do a nice thing together knowing it will be muted by the expected effects of mood and perhaps hard conversation.

The point of the duty also informs a standard for judging some ends frivolous or destructive or easily swapped for something else that can be pursued unaided. I can see the frivolous or fungible end's value to you; there's no reason to criticize it or you for having it (there's no call to maximize practical and moral abilities); but I have reason to refrain from supporting your end *as part of* my duty of beneficence—though I am free to join you in collecting skipping stones for the pleasure of it.

Not surprisingly, the relational account affects moral arithmetic. On many needs-centered accounts of beneficence, some number of severe headaches can outweigh one adolescent's struggle with her addiction to recreational drugs. On the ends-focused relational account they might not. If you are in a position either to help her or relieve them, the choices are not in the same moral metric for summing. It is not that her struggle trumps or outweighs their pains. *Your* being in a position to engage agentially with her and her objective end makes a difference. Structurally, it is more like asking whether one should keep a promise or relieve headaches. There is no straight-on summing that can provide an answer. That doesn't mean I should never take helping others as a sufficient reason to break a promise or choose not to help an adolescent given what I can effect for others elsewhere. The relational fact, like the promise, introduces a thread of responsibility that tracks values other than need.[23] We cannot build trust or a community and at the same time be tasked with triage in an emergency room of need.

The lesson we should take from this Kant-inspired investigation of morally required helping is that among persons in need of one another's assistance, relational beneficence is the norm, not the exception. Helping is an activity that typically takes place between ordinary persons leading their lives. People in need talk and reveal relevant things—about the nature and value of their need and the

---

[23] In good ptolemaic fashion, a needs-based account of beneficence can adjust. It can import other metrics—of urgency or life threat, just as under other pressures partiality and burdensomeness are brought in to mitigate the effects of summing. But in being ad hoc—in failing to find a source of the new values in the moral duty itself—such solutions leave the duty with a permanent vulnerability to pressure from extra-moral value of all sorts.

problem it presents. In response *we*, the helpers, also talk—about the resources we have, about our limits and situational contingencies. These are the working conditions of beneficence. In light of this, we would do well to conclude that drowning strangers are not the paradigm case from which to build an account of the helping duty, and writing checks not the paradigm helping action. We do have to rescue drowning persons. We also need to make charitable donations to institutions that serve needy populations. We may have a duty to create and support such institutions. What we should *not* assume is that all these activities are instances of *one* duty of beneficence. Thinking they are is a source of much of the puzzlement that surrounds morally directed helping.

7.3 Beyond Relational Beneficence

When we turn to other cases—stranger helping, or global poverty—we should not just extend the relational account; we will want to know the point of engagement and the value of helping actions in these different settings. Our connection to the happiness of strangers is extremely limited (and not just epistemically: it is potentially intrusive if we presume too much); and where groups of persons are in grave need at a distance, we can't expect to engage each person's ends in order to take sensible steps. The need and the help that fits it may have to be regarded as generic—the target may be whole populations. Alongside but different from relational beneficence, there should be a duty that we might call *humanitarian beneficence*: a duty to help that all of us together have towards all of us. It is an *aggregative* duty: all are implicated as agents of the duty, but, as I'll explain, one by one by one. Its scope includes stranger beneficence, small and large accidents, and some of the immediate need caused by natural disasters. It's a duty that falls under the obligatory end. The aim is to manage a crisis and, if needed, to secure basic conditions for an eventual return to normal life.

The duty is aggregative in the following way. If five of us are crossing a bridge and spy someone drowning, we each have an "activated" humanitarian duty to help. Considerations of efficiency aside, it doesn't matter who helps. If *one* of us succeeds, the duty *we* have is fulfilled; if the one fails, *we* are not done. There may be a division of labor: one goes for a rope; another gets ready to jump in the water. We may figure out a way to act together, making a chain of hands. However, the defining mark of the aggregative duty is that when the one starts to help, they act as part of us; they do not act in place of us: we cannot just go about our business during the rescue attempt.[24] The burden of acting can shift, not the obligation. That is, all of us are obligated, but by accident of ability or location (geographical

---

[24] Just as we don't regard it as okay that I continue casual texting when I reach out to help.

or moral) some are better positioned to act. I think one-on-one stranger beneficence, including rescue cases, should be seen as limiting instances of the humanitarian duty: someone is in need and one of us helping.

There is, as before, room for discretion seated in the value of the duty. Suppose there is a traffic accident, with the five on the street able and prepared to extricate the injured driver, and a sixth nearby who could also help but stays away because she is tending to the needs of her sick child. She does no wrong in remaining with her child even if her deciding otherwise would have made things easier for the others. This is not because she was exempt from the humanitarian duty, or had an overriding special duty to her child, or that she judged the needs of her child to outweigh those of the stranger victim. A person stands in a web of duties some of whose reach is indeterminate. Attending to the traffic injury can be complex and involving for the helpers, whoever they are; a child needs the ongoing attention of their primary caretaker. The space of discretion in the helping duties creates room for judging whether *this* is an occasion when one should, if it is safe, set aside normal relational concerns. If the sixth stays with her child, it matters that she knows there are others who are engaged with the crisis event, able to manage things well enough.[25] There are of course imaginable emergencies when she should join those helping accident victims, even at some cost to her child. The point here is not about fixing outcomes but about the values that are to inform deliberation. Deciding to remain with the child is not providing an extra benefit, not an instance of double-counting. And if the sixth does decide she should help the stranger, she hardly leaves the obligation to her child behind. Indeed, as children get older we both explain why we have to leave them to help a stranger while assuring them that they will be fine until we return.

Stranger beneficence can still generate entanglements, though they are more limited. You stop and help someone at a road accident, call for help, and while waiting, the injured person asks you to call a neighbor so that his dog gets taken care of. You do not need to know the place of the dog in the victim's affections. Having introduced your agency into a situation of indeterminate or open-ended need, the generic end of providing assistance directs you to make the call. It is different if help is targeted at a specific presenting need. You ask if I have jumper cables and I supply them, and then whether I can drive your friend to a meeting. I might do the second thing, but not because I did the first.[26]

---

[25] A further sign that she is in the catchment area of the humanitarian duty is her due care obligation to remain nearby and prepared to do something, if needed, while caring for her child. She might call 911.

[26] There's a difference worth marking between practical and relational entanglement. Sometimes we have to continue on with a task because we've begun it and it takes more steps to complete than we anticipated. Though not always. If I've stopped to help a stranger make a repair and they discover that they are missing a part, I'm not committed to staying while they go to the hardware store (it might be different with a friend). But other times to practically disentangle would cause damage or harm, and

Where very many people are in urgent need as a result of earthquakes, tsunamis, or other natural disasters, all of us are addressed by the humanitarian duty. Some of us may help directly. The aggregate of persons can be involved supporting aid institutions that act on behalf of all of us. Here there is little if any entanglement. It is absent not only because of the mediation of aid institutions;[27] the urgency and immediacy of generic need in extreme conditions precludes it. One of the aims of humanitarian beneficence is to bring a population back to the condition where civic life and relational beneficence can carry more of the burden.

One might question the rationale for such a limit. Surely after a natural disaster there is more to be done: roads and infrastructure that need to be rebuilt, the power grid is down, water and food supply interrupted. Hardly the resumption of normal life. Why hesitate to make this an object of humanitarian assistance? I think the answer is about a different kind of entanglement. One of the criticisms of even the friendliest interpretation of China's 2013 massive multi-decade Belt and Road Initiative was that in offering economic assistance that might well relieve suffering, it posed a threat to local sovereignty as local communities took on a share (even a minority share) of the development costs through loans they might well be unable to repay.[28] Less compromised and more directly humanitarian structural interventions also risk undermining local values and institutions. The issue isn't about leaving things just as they were. There is no moral imperative to do that. It is about the complex task of active appreciation or positive engagement with local values and indigenous trajectories. The worry here is about *negative* entanglement: where helping agents are in no position to engage the ends of others. Beyond the emergency, even generic needs may have local form, creating an impediment to entanglement that preserves autonomy. Some of this is about the scale of the problem and of the helping intervention. At least in theory, micro-loans facilitate choice and independence, empowering women, encouraging education. By contrast, large-scale agricultural interventions that can improve food production may also destabilize and uproot rural communities, alter traditional water sources, and create future debt.[29] The moral logic of beneficence isn't a natural fit with trickle-down benefits: its values direct us to engagement,

---

then maybe I can't do that. Practical entanglement complicates the value space of the subjective balancing of benefits and burdens. (There may be in-between cases where an offer of help verges on a promise to stay the course.)

[27] 1950's campaigns to "adopt" a needy foreign child tried to close this gap through (often) fake personalization: pictures, letters, reports of improved schooling. The episode traded on the emotional power of entanglement. It doesn't just happen to us; making a difference in a particular life is a motivationally potent source of gratification.

[28] A joint China–Laos railway, the Karakoram Highway in Pakistan, a port complex in Sri Lanka, all bring promise of jobs and development. However, defaults on loans will cost some territorial and political control.

[29] The unfortunate consequences of India's "green revolution" and the introduction of genetically modified corn-seed in Mexico are well documented. For some of the complexities and dangers of interfering with water sources, see Sunil Amrith, *Unruly Waters* (2018).

participation, and process, not just outcome measures, even when directing humanitarian aid to needy populations.

In any case, the humanitarian duty, however it is scaled, is *not* the first-order moral response to needs that result from *injustice*: the plight of war refugees or hunger that results from man-made famine. Unlike the needs that belong to beneficence, needs born of injustice support a claim in RIGHT that they be met. The duty to provide aid is then remedial, owed in the first instance and directly by those who cause or support the need-generating crisis. This duty does *not* belong to the obligatory end of promoting others' happiness.

When there are wildfires in California or tornadoes in Kansas, federal disaster relief is called on to repair the damage to that portion of our polity. There is the state's duty to maintain itself (it is the steward or conservator of its resources), and there is the collective's duty to sustain the well-being of its members. By contrast, toxic waste in the rivers from mining or paper milling obligates the polluter to remediate. When that isn't possible, the state (or other public authority) has a back-up duty to protect its citizens from these harmful effects, as it would from any other wrongful assault on the fabric of social existence. The shadow of the original insult remains, and ought to affect the nature of the clean-up as well as the extent and kind of repair to individuals and communities.[30] This is a juridical story, and that reminds us of the expressive component of the moral actions taken under a duty's auspices—what is owed in justice, what is done to remediate the effect of another's fault, when a community aids one of its hurting parts.[31] Things are yet more complicated when aid is at a distance.

Beneficent actions express connection, whether the target is generic or intimately relational. Its deliberative premises involve knowing the other: helping *you* or helping *them* we do not act well if we treat their needs as divorced from their ends. The desire to rebuild, for people to be in a position to continue the trajectory of their lives, has to be weighed heavily. But it must also be compossible with the values of the helping communities. There is no tension in the first humanitarian response to disaster—people need to be fed, clothed, given housing. It is a hard and morally delicate question whether, out of beneficence, a group or community with defining egalitarian values can provide humanitarian support for rebuilding unjust institutions, e.g., ones that include purdah or the exploitation of an ethnic

---

[30] New Orleans post-hurricane Katrina is one of the more grievous failures in this dimension.
[31] If the state owes in justice provision of its citizens' basic needs, when it fails in that duty there can be practical confusion between absorbing the unmet need under relational beneficence (a "we take care of our own" response), and seeing it as prompting the humanitarian duty, managed locally as a matter of efficiency. The difference matters since relational beneficence does not include a standard of equal treatment. We sometimes step in relationally in an emergency—a friend or relative loses their job or incurs a dramatic medical expense—duties overlap, but I think our primary duty here is acting as the state's delegate, and then also as our friend or relative's advocate.

minority.³² And whether, *as an act of humanitarian beneficence*, we can instead place more of our resources where we judge we can be more effective in promoting objective value, even at some cost to a vulnerable population.

If the cause of the demand to meet need elsewhere is injustice, what is to be done should be and be seen to be a response to the moral rupture. Not surprisingly, the related duty is complex. There are different kinds of actor, agency, and authority; national, international, and corporate bodies; histories of war, exploitation, and imperialism. Different histories and different values can affect the landscape of remedial repair. Suppose we have unjustly harmed a community whose values we reject; it is doubtful that we can refuse to compensate or condition remediation on a change in values. On the other hand, we are not without obligation to those who are oppressed, and who may be further oppressed as a result of our remedial action. In the domestic arena, a minority practice that offends may be (locally) lawful. Perhaps the provisional universal right of access to the juridical condition (see section 6.4) can shape humanitarian beneficence (say, by managing the structure of food aid to minimize reinforcing repressive practices). If with the left hand we are required to repair what we've broken, we might double down with the right hand to support emergent reform-minded local institutions. We are not thereby inconsistent. One of the things we expect to encounter in the actual rule of law is that we may be compelled to be neutral despite our moral opposition. That doesn't stop our also trying to effect change.

If the humanitarian duty is not the first-order moral response to needs that result from injustice, as events evolve, the duty of beneficence may still have a role. After the 2015 closing of the Hungarian border in the face of asylum-seeking refugees, decent citizens were left to manage the needs of those unjustly abandoned at the frontier. Their aggregate humanitarian beneficence was a back-up response to the effects of, not a remedy for, injustice. What is to be done follows from the duty that applies. In justice, enacting a policy of resettlement might be called for. But if, as a back-up humanitarian act, a family brings refugees into their home, they respond to a different mix of needs—for shoes, medicine, and food, and also for music and books and a bath. From a distance, we send resources to NGOs to serve as our surrogates, stockpiling clothes and blankets and intermediaries who can interpret and provide representation.

Where global poverty or food scarcity is not an accident or a natural disaster, but the result of a morally malfunctioning global order, the need, though great, again does not directly belong to the duty of beneficence—not to me singly or to us as an aggregate of individuals. It belongs to the agents of the global order (and to us, derivatively, though not merely to us as individuals; corporations and other

---

³² I put the point as a matter of intergroup value relations. I would make the stronger argument, that beneficence itself precludes helping that promotes values inconsistent with the values of the obligatory end.

social entities are implicated as causally responsible agents). We do, however, in justice, as citizens, have a collective duty to support an international political order that will reform patterns of distribution and investment that affect food supply.

The picture that emerges from all this is of a tiered system of duties related to need: the individual's duty of beneficence, a humanitarian duty of the aggregate of persons, and collective duties of justice. Because it is a *system* of duties, there is the possibility of burden shifting. Public elder-care institutions might relieve the increasing burdens of relational beneficence in the face of demographic dispersal, increased longevity, and the costs of medical treatment and palliative care. Justice itself might require a re-alignment of the caretaking relation: I think of the Finnish model that regards public provision of childcare as morally necessary to give child-bearing women access to work and public life.

It is worth emphasizing that there is no common moral currency of need across the system of duties; need is rather a flag or mark that a moral issue is presenting. Homelessness, to take an example, indicates considerable need, but not for only one kind of thing, morally speaking. There is need for shelter, for private space, for domicile—conditions of status recognition; it is also a public health problem. The causes are various: in some places it is neglect or real-estate priorities; in others it is the result of public or publicly supported discrimination. We engage with the need differently depending on the duty that applies. We might subsidize the rent of a relative fallen on hard times, recognizing her need to age in place. Or, like my neighbors during stormy weather, bring blankets and tarps to a nearby homeless encampment. And if the housing system breaks down, we should support the initiation of lawsuits and legislation to secure adequate low-cost housing and address the effects of discrimination.[33] It is always part of our duty as citizens to ensure, as we can, that there is a social world in which persons can realize the value of their humanity, despite illness, bad luck, poor choices, or the effects of structural injustice.

It is not a moral accident or contingency to be overcome that the need we encounter in living our daily lives has an insistent personal quality. Helping each other is part of being connected to one another, of living a social life. The humanitarian duty lacks these features—it can be *you or me* who is its agent today; we may for a time withdraw from its work if other duties press. We swap days at the food bank. We have more time to give in the years after our children leave home. Still, the humanitarian duty could be demanding, and what is required of us in justice even more so. But if that were so, it would not be in the iterated way of making each of us individually responsible for the most need they can meet.

---

[33] A discussion of the related "right to housing" can be found in Chapter 10.

Near the beginning of the discussion of beneficence I asked about the birthday party.[34] Can I spend money to celebrate my child when large numbers of people somewhere are starving? There is something strange about this question. Suppose I know there's a den of thieves or black hat hackers in the neighborhood that the police are aware of but haven't closed down. I could spend the afternoon collecting evidence or working on a petition to my councilman. But safety issues aside, surely I can have the party. Not everything bad is mine to fix. Why think it is otherwise with helping?

Of course, a less all-things-considered momentous crisis with an ailing older parent might call for canceling the party. Relational beneficence can also be very demanding. It is also not a free-standing duty. I should talk to my child if I have to break the party promise. And I need to think about what I can tell my child: concern for a grandparent and concern for world hunger play very differently in the mind of a four-year-old. Should that make a difference in what I decide to do? Relational beneficence suggests that it might. But there are often other options, and we should not forget them. I might call on my reluctant brother to be there for our ailing parent that afternoon so that the party can proceed.

One thing that does *not* follow is that relational beneficence necessarily or inevitably dominates the morality of assistance. Or that, once I get finished with the birthday parties, needy friends, and aging parents, I've pretty much exhausted the helping it is reasonable to ask me to provide, leaving humanitarian assistance a secondary concern, or a large one for those not relationally encumbered. We can resist that narrative. Many of the current concerns we charge to humanitarian beneficence properly belong to the domain of managing the effects of past and present injustice. Victims can demand, as can we on their behalf, assistance that goes well beyond immediate or emergency relief from those responsible for their situation. We are implicated if, as citizens, we are beneficiaries of injustice. However, the response in justice does not tax us as separate individuals—it taxes us, literally, as members of a polity, so in a different register. Where humanitarian beneficence enlarges beyond immediate emergencies is in having to back up failures in remedial justice. But again, humanitarian beneficence is aggregative; the burden is *ours*. And because it is *we* who need to act, we can organize larger scale organizational tools to act as our instrument, and any one of us can contribute more or less as our situation permits. There is something awry if the question I always have to answer is "What more can *you* do *right now*?" We misdescribe the moral situation if we take ourselves to be standing in isolation in a giant field of need.[35]

---

[34] I use a birthday party example rather than, say, paying for a top-tier private college for my child—both things I may well want to do—because the college desire is embedded in a miasma of social inequality that burdens individual decision-making in ways that do not touch the birthday party.

[35] Left unaddressed are persistent issues of global inequality and the detail of ways obligations may be inherited when those to whom they belong wrongfully default. The former issues do not belong to

There are other complexities. Suppose George, my neighbor, falls and needs assistance. I could help him, and so could you, a stranger walking by. We would do the same thing for George—get him back on his feet—but I would act on a relational duty, you a humanitarian one. We should not find this morally odd. In another case I might explain to someone not already involved that I'd rather they, not me, be the one to help, that George has begun to expect more from me than fits our relationship. That can make good sense to both of us.

Now imagine representatives of different interests addressing some large-scale crisis. Some are there because they have responsibility for the crisis; others because injustice is everyone's concern; and still others out of humanitarian duty. It is not obvious that this order is a moral order dictating who should bear the burden of assistance. It might matter to those being assisted that they not enter ongoing relations with parties who have shown no regard for them in the past. That might be inefficient and in some ways morally repugnant because a burdening of the innocent over the guilty. If, as it seems, it also makes some moral sense, there could be reason to develop a system of intermediaries who can make the provision of aid safe—a middle term for managing resources from different players. However the casuistry should go, its point is clear: for those to whom one of the duties applies, discretion is in order in meeting it. The fact of injustice can play a role here, not in setting a perfect remedial duty, but in adding to the exercise of discretion involved in fulfilling an imperfect one.

I began this account of beneficence in order to better understand the discretion that comes with the duty and with imperfect duties generally. I've argued through example and text that the rationale for the permission resides in the value that undergirds the duty. In the duty of beneficence, it is drawn from the dual role of the end of happiness—as an organizing principle of subjective satisfaction and as the vehicle for the emergence of human moral personality. It is the pairing of these values that we engage with in lending our agency to others' ends. The exercise of discretion in how and when we act is then not a permission that benefits us, the potential helpers; it is essential to realizing the value that directs acting on the duty. This doesn't mean that we should keep score—a new rational ability here, a managed weakness there. We act instead with a defeasible grasp of the complexity of the pursuit of happiness, both in the way ends develop and intertwine and in the temporal duration of their effects on agency. That is why we do best for beneficence where we can engage with another's life and be responsive to the value of their ends. The imperfection of the core duty of beneficence might decrease its scope, but it increases the range of concerns that fall under due care in acting for it.

---

the ethics of aid and assistance, although their persistence creates need that does. The latter speaks in favor of limiting the humanitarian duty and against a regime of global sovereignties that resist the logic of imputation.

Where we act for the humanitarian duty, the considerations that inform our exercise of discretion differ. The way we are situated towards the person or persons in need—at a distance, as a stranger, with persons unable to communicate with us—often means we will have to treat ends generically. However, the basic structure of the duty remains. We stand as one among many who can help. The duty gives us a target, its content set by its value. If we come to know more, we may have to do more. If we do not, once we are past the pressure of the presenting need or the emergency, we go exactly wrong when we would do for others what we would have them do for us. That is not ours to say or do, and not what's involved in promoting the ends of others who are ends in themselves.[36]

7.4 Imperfect Duties in the System of Duties

With this much of an account of beneficence in front of us, we encounter a variety of questions that arise from the system nature of the habitat project. Some involve further practical implications of the helping duties, some are about the effect of core ethical duties on other duties in the system. Together they affect the nature and shape of the emerging moral project. There are some loose ends to gather in as well: about the communicative aspect of the duties, the role of due care, the imperfectness of the duty and the supererogatory, and a bit about imputation and responsibility.

It makes sense to start with an "upstream" question about the value carried by the institution of property on which beneficence and the duties of assistance depend. We know that the initial answer to the Kantian "What's it for?" question about property is that it is a morally necessary institution of RIGHT that creates conditions for persons being able to act on and with the material world consistent with innate right. That's the first step, not the complete assignment of value to the institution of property and its regime of rights. Further elements come from the seating of the property right in a juridical system: so a commitment to the rule of law generally and to the conditions for creating citizens who make a regime of RIGHT possible. And since ethical duties also fill out the value of a right, relational

---

[36] Before moving on, there is a textual question that needs attention. Some might wonder whether the three-part account of duties of assistance outruns anything that could be attributed to Kant. I think it does not. In even the most morally spare reading of the *Doctrine of Right*, there is ample material for a rectificatory account of assistance in domestic standards drawn from innate right's anti-subordination values, and, internationally, in entitlements to self-government. *Not* as claims for welfare but claims for justice in rectification. The arguments I've offered for duties of assistance that have international scope are also not distributive in aim, but either humanitarian or, again, rectificatory. The *Doctrine of Virtue*'s "maxim of common interest," a universal duty toward fellow persons in need "united by nature in one dwelling place so that they can help one another" (*MM* 6:453), supports the humanitarian duty, and Kant's account of cosmopolitan right (*MM* 6:351–353) gives reparative justice sufficient international scope. While much more would need to be built out to defend all of the arguments as Kant's, these connections should be enough to keep skepticism at bay.

and humanitarian beneficence introduce an additional system condition that, through the obligatory end that is their source, connects RIGHTFUL possession to the value of humanity in persons generally. This connection affects what it means to regard something as our possession: less about free use in the arbitrary sense—accumulation, monument-building, consumption—and more about our shaping a personal and social life under the guidance of both subjective and objective ends. Whether the moral idea of property will include entitlement to any kind of enduring exclusive possession is no given. Such questions wait on other parts of the system of duties that frame and further articulate property as a moral-juridical power.

This way of fixing content is in sharp contrast with a familiar Locke-inspired picture in which we see ourselves and our property being taxed by morality to provide help to one another. With that starting point it is natural to ask: Will the tax leave us enough for ourselves and for those we care about? We might worry whether we can live a life that makes sense if we are indentured to human need in the large. Or, as many do, we might see beneficence as a private analogue of a public good, where general conformity to the duty, though a burden, creates a reservoir of help to be drawn on when one is in need. Even if we don't use the benefit, it provides security, and those we care about into the future are protected. The duty of beneficence then comes off as a morally mandated (no fault?) interpersonal and trans-generational insurance scheme. Perhaps made better if the scheme were voluntary, or the imperfectness of the duty allowed us to regulate our cost (and our future benefit).

On the moral habitat view, aid and support that draw on what we have are natural extensions of seeing ourselves engaged in a common cooperative endeavor. I gain an understanding of myself as acting for our common cause whether acting for myself or when I stand in for you. I retrieve a dropped tool—whether it's mine or yours. I take an extra shift if something needs to be finished today or if you are ill. I make sure the children are picked up from school—my children and yours. I buy groceries for an ailing neighbor, or drive them to a doctor's appointment. In these we come to see ourselves along with others tasked with creating conditions that are friendly to the exercise of rational and moral agency.

The moral habitat is juridically local and morally part of a larger common project. There are distinct lines of obligation that point to co-citizens and intimates, and others that point to persons elsewhere who lack material and social conditions that support moral standing. A child's or partner's illness can feel like more than we bargained for, but there we are. If we are seriously engaged in a larger common project our exposure is greater. In neither case is there loss of connection to the idea of living our own lives when we have to stop what we are doing or modify our plans to help in an urgency or stand up for decency and justice when they are threatened.

We may pride ourselves as being free and productive persons. But our view of ourselves as free agents co-varies with the full set of duties necessary to support free agency. So if we have substantial duties of assistance *and* recognize that the duties are a piece of the possibility conditions for free agency, that will shape our conception of ourselves as holders of resources as well as our understanding of the moral value of the resources we have. None of this makes each individual a servant of the most impartial good they can effect. It does tell us that we may need to mobilize common resources to secure for ourselves and others the fundamentals for a decent human life. Or to repair injustice. Not an unreasonable demand.

Knowing this, we design institutions to ameliorate and spread the effort of necessary response. The arrangements will not be perfect; there will be defectors. Those who have to do more than their share might take steps to effect a fairer distribution of the burden: defectors can sometimes be brought to care; where responsibility is fairly owed, it is not wrong to impose conditions to meet it. In the face of chronic and increasing need, it would be baldly negligent to assume that it's a matter of unavoidable misfortune ("the poor that we will always have with us"), and that the prevailing system of property and possession, or its interpretation, is an innocent piece of the problem.[37]

This sort of system effect is not a special feature or consequence of beneficence. Many ethical duties in the habitat project can put backwards or upstream pressure on the juridical (infra)structure on which they depend. Consider the innate right to speak one's mind. There are downstream ethical reasons to regard speech as part of a common rational enterprise: what we need to know across the board can depend on the reports of others. Further downstream ethically, that will exclude shaming ridicule as part of criticism, but it won't exclude criticism, even upsetting criticism. The ethical values aren't part of innate right, not close in to primary juridical structures, but in shaping our downstream deployment of speech, they yield upstream pressures that both support and limit public sanctions for how we realize the value of our speech. This leaves room for all the reasons one might want not to legally interfere with (some) ethically wrongful and sometimes even harmful speech. And to juridically limit some harmful public speech (libel or slander) and some private (bullying). It leaves us free, and sometimes obligated, to offer criticism. The work of speech need not be cool and dispassionate: we care, we are incensed, we find things risible. Expressing difficult attitudes isn't incidental to communication.

We get a still richer view of the system effect when we consider the family. Domestic arrangements stand with property as one of the fundamental institutions of RIGHT. Whatever social form they take, because they involve persons in intimate relations (and so vulnerable, physically and morally), and because they

---

[37] For a compelling historical argument to this point see Thomas Piketty, *Capital and Ideology*, (2020).

are likely to be the primary location for the care of children, their (RIGHTFUL) existence depends on juridical relations of obligation.[38] The placement of the family as an element of the juridical state is therefore not an argument for one or another form of domestic relations, but an argument that with respect to whatever modes of intimate dependence we do have, especially those involving children, the state cannot cede final authority to it and can insist on terms and conditions, including resources and protections, for its members. Social forms are moral accidents and have to earn their keep. We should expect that much of the care that is required is continuous with what would be provided out of either love or sense of duty. However, some elements of parental obligation are set by and can be enforced by the state, given its compelling interest in preparing children for their eventual independence and active citizenship. Curricular standards for home schooling fit here. As might some privacy interests of adolescents.

Flowing from a child's innate right (as a person brought into the world destined to be a citizen someplace), are obligations to provide sustenance (of body and psyche) and education (including access to a culture). Descendant duties give parents and primary caretakers constrained authority to manage the child's care and education (*MM* 6:281). What might then follow? Here's an example. The moral education of children requires sustained engagement with the ends of others, some whose ends are like theirs, some not. If moral training were delegated by parents to institutions whose values are inconsistent with that moral goal, the delegation would be wrongful (inconsistent with children's innate right), and constraint on the choice not a violation of any parental right to voluntary association, freedom of speech or religion. Rather than a constraint on domestic speech, we get an argument for public education.

The state may do more. Suppose that the best child science finds that involved caretaking of an infant by both parents during the first year of life is a strong predictor of future emotional stability.[39] And let's assume that as a matter of RIGHT the state could not compel parents to stay home with their children, assuming they have a satisfactory way to meet basic sustenance and education obligations. But the state could permissibly adopt something like Norway's "use it or lose it" package of parental leave benefits that includes a "daddy quota"—a way

---

[38] Children, Kant says, have an innate right to the care of their parents until they are able to care for themselves (*MM* 6:280). Nothing in what brings parents or the family into the purview of RIGHT dictates who the parents are, single or coupled, same sex or variously sexed, natural or adoptive or communally affiliated. Natural or birth parents have no special authority to raise children. On the other hand, no public authority is entitled to distribute children among its preferred caretakers as if pregnancy were just another mode of production.

[39] https://www.nikk.no/en/facts/in-depth/parental-leave. There's reason to doubt the science data here: e.g., we don't know what holds when it's three adults not two, or how gender variation matters. We can assume that it applies to the limited case of the two-parent heterosexual family, treating that case as an instance, not a prototype, and maybe as evidence that there is something detrimental to a young child if one of its primary caretakers (not necessarily male) is mostly absent early on. It can be hard to extrapolate when the instance belongs to a morally compromised arrangement.

of expressing its recognition of the public health benefit of having both parents involved in childcare?[40] If, as has been reported, positive experiences of entangled caretaking do ensue, as well as greater participation by men in family work, the prevailing idea of what a family is and needs will expand as well. This in effect would alter the part of relational beneficence that is in a line of descent from juridical duties concerning the family. So by increasing the opportunity for intimate engagement, the state might enlarge a dimension of a juridically supported ethical duty.

If, as has happened, social patterns of adult intimacy and reproduction change, juridical institutions can and should adjust to the changes in the forms of ethical life. Even if it made sense historically (in some time or place) to treat the natural biological heterosexual reproductive unit as *the* juridical family, the point of juridical relations is not to reinforce the "matter" of choices, in this case the "right" kind of family, but to make the stable intimate relations adults are drawn to having juridically safe for all parties, especially dependent children. Holding that juridical norms about the family should change as social forms change is not to endorse the idea that the permissible follows the actual. The juridical is often a moral check on the variety of social choices people in fact make. There are good reasons to resist juridical recognition of polygamy (given its track record) and it is necessary to prohibit child marriage. The test for the juridical recognition of different domestic arrangements is whether all parties can be made safe from abuse and relations of subordination. Consent and exit have to be real possibilities.

It is an attraction of the habitat system that it aims for visible common value between ethical and juridical practices. This creates a real alternative to ad hoc balancing adjustments between them or permanent subservience of the ethical to dominant external values.[41] The changing interpretation of a juridical institution should both reflect and inform descendent ethical practices. Ideally, robust ethical values fit in the framework of public or juridical recognition.

Common value is particularly important when we act on imperfect duties, given how much we express through the way we act on them. It is not an extraneous fact

---

[40] The idea was to extend already generous parental benefits taken mostly by mothers only if fathers chose to stay home as well. Men who used the benefit as intended (and not just to hire a nanny) reportedly were glad to have had it and valued the changed experience of being a father that came with it. "Nordic research shows that men who take longer parental leave also take more responsibility at home. They are more involved in the care of their children, have better relationships with them and do more unpaid housework. Importantly the men spend time caring for the child or children alone, after their partner has returned to work)." The economics of paid parental leave are said to be wealth promoting for all concerned (equivalent, on one report, to Norway's oil-based wealth fund). Adjustments to a leave policy that were accommodating to adults in non-traditional families would both extend the benefit in a fair way and encourage a more inclusive idea of family.

[41] There remains a risk that numerically or socially dominant practices can exploit juridical institutions to squeeze out morally viable alternative arrangements. Morally transparent institutional design offers some protection from this, though it cannot guarantee against aberrations in what counts as public reason.

about beneficence that we communicate and create through our helping. It is one of the ways we say how we value each other, how we confirm and build relationships, how we regard what we possess. Even in easy rescue cases we express something: that we recognize the need and that just because we are present, we are the one to help. (We sometimes confirm this when we deflect gratitude with "I only did what anyone would have done.") Among the existence conditions of friendship is that friends be willing to help each other. Sometimes, against one's preference, one may need to help a friend *or* let oneself be helped. It can be a moral failure if help to an intimate is given as if to anyone. Someone who rebuffs an attempt at engaged helping is saying a lot.

That we communicate the value we see in our acting affects how we deliberate, how we act or delegate, whether we judge that we have done enough and can move on. As part of the construction of character and community there may be system requirements on dutiful action that it be made clear how discretion was exercised in making choices and in the manner of performance. Failing to do this, or skirting the value we should be tracking as we act, can make an otherwise successful outcome a moral failure.[42]

In the earlier accounts of gratitude and the moral constraints on gifts we saw that both arenas of duty call on us to avoid using what we have in ways that subvert moral relations between persons. In benefiting we are to meet need with an eye to avoiding humiliation and the creation of dependency. Our helping fails if it leaves the recipient feeling diminished. In gratitude we at once accept the benefactor's presence in our life and assert our independence. If we give inappropriately, overstrain the reciprocity of response, or impose unwanted intimacy, our actions communicate a threat to our relationship as equals.

Not all imperfect duties that have to do with material objects are about helping or giving, but they all have an expressive dimension. Having borrowed something from a friend, say a book, I have a perfect duty to return it, and an imperfect duty to care for it while it's in my possession. The different kinds of duty mark different deliberative requirements—one signals that I cannot keep the borrowed thing just because I'd like to (my preferences don't create a transfer of possession); the other signals a responsibility for how the borrowed thing fares. I shouldn't leave it out in the rain if that will ruin it, or dog-ear the pages, though I needn't devote myself to its care. In the typical case, I exercise judgment: about what's normal wear and tear, how much trouble to go to, what the lender's reasonable expectations are (with respect to the object *and* with respect to me). But part of the exercise of discretion is to be open to special features of our circumstances. Knowing my

---

[42] There is in this sense something communicatively off in the "foreign aid" side of humanitarian beneficence that sends necessities packaged with national symbols and flags to say "*from* the US," or "*from* France." We are all bound by the same duty. For one reason or another, not all equally good, only some of us are in a position to help. The resulting division of labor doesn't divide the obligation. The signage obscures the nature of the duty.

friend to be fastidious about their library, I might take special care always to carry the book in a plastic sleeve. I wouldn't violate a right if I didn't take extra care (there were no terms like this in the lending), but if we are friends, I should (unless, perhaps, my friend's fastidiousness has become an obstacle). The richer moral context affects the practical and expressive demands of due care. I can replace a ruined library book with no remainder. Not so for my friend. Here the fact of ownership signals something beyond possession, triggering duties that require more from us in the movement of owned objects between persons.

It's a fair question at this point whether all this complexity is necessary: whether we wouldn't be on safer ground if we relied on a hierarchy of duties. Take care of juridical and perfect duties first, and, as one can, the complicating, expressive, imperfect duties (which, after all, come with permission to exercise discretion about whether and how to act). But that order may not reflect a fixed order of moral value or stringency. In the case of the borrowed book, with the complexities of an anxious bibliophile friend and heavy rains on the promised day of return, shouldn't I violate the perfect duty of return in order to take better care of the object? And why? It may or may not be what my friend wants. It is what I may fairly judge my friend is entitled to—not as a balance of formal duties and permissions but in the order of values that are at stake. I may know better than my friend how things would work out along the different moral paths open to me. I may see both the value of book and the friendship in play. So I decide to delay. And if I turn out to be wrong, it won't be because of a misestimate of the stringency of a perfect duty, but something about my friend that I didn't grasp.

One of the tasks of the duty of due care is to anticipate and manage moral complexity. Seeing stormy weather ahead, I should temper my promises. And where beneficence is at issue, being at the cynosure of others' accumulating needs, we might conclude that we are faced with a challenge that will alter what our lives are about, *or* we might seek help from friends and relatives, explore social resources, seek advice from others who manage similar problems. We might be facing a system failure (think healthcare) and a burden that is properly a task for public morality. So a failure of due care in a different place in the moral system. That doesn't make things easier day to day, but that's not a problem beneficence imposes, though it's a problem beneficence is sometimes left with, however ineffectually. When the social world fails to do its share of the moral work, the effect on individuals can be akin to a natural disaster.

Even where public institutions can manage some of the burdens of need, they don't stand in the same benefiting relation to need that we do on either the relational or humanitarian variants of beneficence. Public institutions are beholden to standards of equality and fairness; they can and should create decent avenues of departure from dependency on social welfare. That can affect the kind or degree of support they provide, making the choice to engage public institutions a hard one. Even so, we might turn to institutions because of the moral condition of private helpers: what happens when elder care falls mainly on women, many of whom are already burdened with childcare. Perhaps some men might step up and assume a greater share of the burden. No doubt they should. But the moral habitat questions are different.

It is not an issue for public institutions if my partner and I divvy-up caretaking burdens in a way that works for us. One of us may come to have a complaint against the other that the division isn't fair and we need to work something out. But if the complaint reflects a social phenomenon, perhaps supported by lots of divvying-up, that can have the effect of excluding a social group from meaningful participation in public life. That's when a policy of "preventive support" is called for. It could be through care-providing public services that take over the burden. It could also be through provision of pay and benefits to those who now privately and "voluntarily" do the caretaking: recognizing as a matter of law that their caretaking is work. What was an ethical duty involving a sphere of discretion can become something juridical, rule-constructed: an entitlement.

It is a moral habitat demand on public institutions to create an environment in which the fundamental values of the moral system can be expressed in people's lives. It is where private or interpersonal morality takes shape, drawing institutionally articulated value into individual lives and relationships. It should not give persons competing sets of moral values. However, the institutions that set the framework and conditions for moral life may play their role well at a time, but then less well as social and economic circumstances change. And if they change, even for the better, that can have disruptive effect on the parts of ethics dependent on them. The challenges this creates for understanding our moral duties will be taken up in Part Three, especially Chapter 11.

Although the account of beneficence outlined in these sections defuses much of the demandingness objection, accumulating burdens do matter. At a certain point, how we respond to the next call for assistance involves a shift from the exercise of discretion to something that looks supererogatory. Choice is exercised in both contexts, but in the one choice belongs to the duty, while in the other we've gone beyond it. Making sense of this sheds further light on choice in moral action and will bring us back to some interesting questions about imputation.

Beneficence contains a deliberative mandate or directive, sensitive to relationships as the arena in which the value of the obligatory end the duty serves is best realized. Choice that belongs to the duty is shaped by this value, though not in any one way: other values may be in play. A decision to help one's uncle can express and develop a relational connection. One is in a position to take on his ends, not just his needs. Vulnerability now enters the relationship. Gratitude may be part of the decision. Your uncle has been there for you in the past; helping him now allows you both to acknowledge and appreciate your independence and competence. It could be an opportunity to spend serious time together. There could also be related indirect reasons: you want your child to understand the importance of sustaining family even when people live at a distance. How much you do or give, for how long, with what kind of openness you have to your uncle's life, are up to you as part of acting on the duty.

Yet you could do more. Since your uncle needs full-time care, you could quit your job and move to Montana to take care of him. Helping him to stay in his home would give him a much better life. Suppose that is what you decide to do. Does this fall within the scope of the imperfect duty as just another exercise of your agent discretion? The decision is a surprise, not what anyone (including you) would have predicted. It would not be unreasonable to say *no* to the move since it involves abandoning your own career, intimates, and friends: changing your life for the sake of another. However, we are free to change or abandon our ends, so long as we take care of our obligations to others and what we owe to ourselves. And caretaking needn't be thought of as brute self-sacrifice. There are the goods of time with the uncle, new skills to acquire, and so on. That suggests the decision could be deliberatively accessible within the duty of beneficence. Then the move is not, even though a surprising and life-changing choice, a supererogatory action. The pull of service to another is at the limit of the relational duty.

It is less clear how to read the classical supererogatory acts of self-sacrifice. Kidney donations, though they change one's body and increase risk of health failure, can reasonably be expected not to upend one's course of life to the degree that the move to Montana would.[43] It is hard to see why the mere fact of taking a risk in order to provide help would move this decision outside the range of beneficence. The move to Montana involves risks as well. Sacrificing one's life for another, by contrast, is about more than taking extreme or risky means. It is not just about doing a lot more. And it would sound perverse to describe "taking a bullet" for someone else as bringing one's agency to bear on another's ends.

In the typology of duties, the discretion that comes with beneficence does much of the work assigned to the supererogatory. But it doesn't extend to the extreme cases. From the perspective of the imperfect duty, giving one's life for another is not just beyond moral requirement, it may be beyond morality's reasons. The moral system that includes imperfect duties doesn't regard our lives as something we can offer to or for others, like a gift. Can we put ourselves in the line of fire to save someone else? Maybe so, but not as an act of assistance. In the film script variant where if A doesn't give herself up, all, including A, will lose their lives—not a case of life-for-life, but an act of making something from an inevitable death— we find acts of courage, but not, I think, beneficence.

If we may set aside our own interests in order to focus on the ends and needs of another, we may not subordinate our agency to their needs. Whatever sacrifices

---

[43] Of course, giving a part of one's body to someone else is momentous for other reasons. For a loved one, the transfer of a part of oneself may seem a natural extension of relationship. It is worth thinking about why altruistic (stranger) donation has become more common and more accepted.

have to be made, the through line of separate agency is to be maintained. The discretion that comes with an imperfect duty does not give us complete authority over the terms of choice. It is a situational descendant of the value marked out by the duty, to be exercised in its terms, bounded by our duties to self. When I focus my beneficent helping on a friend, my discretion does not have the authority of preference: the value that sets the duty is to orient my helping. Within that framework I am to judge whether the friend's need calls for my attention. I can be wrong epistemically; and I can be wrong in the exercise of my discretion: about the need, about the costs to me to in meeting it, about the collateral effects of what I would do. And, as we have seen before, among the ways I can go wrong is in doing too much.

If you exceed the boundaries of the imperfect duty, are the bad effects of that excess imputable to you as their author? Unexpected bad effects may occur whenever you provide reasonable assistance. If you have missed no warning signs and acted with due care, the bad effects don't (imputably) belong to your action. That doesn't mean you will have no further obligation of helping. But if you do, it is likely a result of entanglement and very different from responsibility for an untoward outcome. The latter, not the former, gives rise to a duty of repair. Acting within the framework of the duty you remain protected by its value and so able to withdraw from ongoing assistance in the usual (careful) way if it becomes too burdensome as a result of what happened. That release is not available once you have acted beyond the duty's remit; you are then implicated in the unfolding events. It might seem paradoxical that because of doing more than the duty calls for one can become liable for more than one would have had to bear had one done less. The sense of paradox comes from not recognizing that more is not always morally better, and that other reparative duties may apply once one has acted on one's own authority, beyond the original duty's direction and protection.

One sign of helping too much is making a beneficiary dependent, less able to act on their own. Another is oneself becoming dependent on helping, or creating a relation of co-dependence where what is valued is the generation of need and the opportunity for meeting it. If there is a facilitator of the co-dependence, they are responsible for safely extricating both of the parties. The secondary co-dependent will have obligations as well, but not of repair for going beyond the cone of authorization of the duty.

There are other effects of extending ourselves that alter our available discretion. Suppose I see that if I take the first step in helping, I will have to take a second, and the two together are quite burdensome, though either on its own would not be. I might then be justified in not taking the first step. But if even knowing all this I take the first step, I should take the second. The accumulated burden is not now a reason I can appeal to in deciding whether to take the second step. And that is because in taking the first step, I took its consequences out of consideration.

This points to a further caution in the ethics of benefiting. In the space of need we could meet, we are not doing what we should if we take on the needs of so many that we cannot accept the entanglements created by our first benefiting actions. We misunderstand what beneficence requires if we regard ourselves as cast by the duty as first-responders in the space of need.[44] Imagine a sequence of needy persons presenting—each with a need that calls for second help from the first helper if the first help is to provide its full benefit. Beneficence is not governed by strict principles of triage that require us to move on to someone else once we've stabilized the bleeding part of presenting need. That's a way of thinking that loses the connection between agency and ends central to the morality of benefiting.

Bernard Williams famously called out Kantian theory for the coldness of the helping act motivated by duty.[45] He saw such morally motivated helping as impersonal, small, humanly lacking. Much better for both parties if we are directly responsive to the person and the relationship in our helping. Relational beneficence answers Williams' worry. But what should now be evident is that helping that is unmediatedly directed towards relationships introduces another dimension where things can go wrong—though it is one of excess rather than insufficiency. The problem comes from targeting need, whether it's bare need or your dear uncle's need. To get it right we should act with respect to the need *and* the relationship in light of the moral value marked out by the duties of assistance. None of the duties, and especially not relational beneficence, is cold for being understood and acted on in a moral way.

---

[44] The monetizing of beneficence, especially help at a distance, can create the impression that we are always to be, and always can be, on the front lines of helping. The contrary point is captured well by Maimonides who identifies "the greatest level of charity, above which there is no greater, as supporting a [person] by endowing him with a gift or loan, or entering into a partnership with him, or finding employment for him, in order to strengthen his hand so that he will not need to be dependent upon others." *Gifts to the Poor*, 10.7.

[45] Bernard Williams, "Morality and the Emotions" (1973), 225ff.

8
Tracking Value and Extending Duties

8.1 Casuistry, Due Care, Tracking Value

Among the things we are responsible for in the domain of imperfect duties is tracking a duty's value across differently obligating contexts. If we may, from beneficence, act for intimates over others, it is because we can thereby more fully realize the value of acting for another's ends. However, in circumstances where that difference makes no difference—aid is urgently needed by various distressed populations—restricting aid to groups we favor can exhibit unjustified bias. In a crisis, taking care of those close to us is a first concern, but not the only one; ongoing attention to what warrants or demands our acting isn't optional. So, in the now all too familiar example, if you may save your spouse in a rescue situation, you can't continue *for the same reason* to attend to their less urgent needs when others still need rescue. Even entangling helping may have to be passed on to someone else (with care and explanation) to free up time and resources for doing one's share of the aggregative duty. There is no conflict of duties here. Because the impersonal, the aggregative, and the relational helping duties have the same source value, what we are to attend to is not fixed by what we do first.

There are public variants of the tracking responsibility. If the moral justification of juridical institutions lies in the conditions necessary for the freedom and equality of persons, policies and procedures whose rule is transparent and accessible may have priority over more efficient means that are resistant to public input and oversight. Seeking efficiency by privatization of rule of law vehicles (prisons, courts, tax collection) risks introducing organizational structures and incentives incapable of tracking the values that support the duty they purportedly serve. The challenge is in securing the continuing expression of the value of duties across an extended path of action they govern, especially when the agents involved are differently obligated.[1] That this might be a difficult or costly task is not an inefficiency that directly counts against it.

One might think that this sort of action-affecting value tracking would be limited to imperfect duties because of their built-in space for judgment and discretion. But once we recognize that there is more to a perfect duty than compliance

---

[1] Some are public servants; some beholden to private stockholders. It is not clear how private parties can take on public duties and remain essentially private: that is, private with respect to the reasons that direct what they are to do and the responsibilities they incur in doing it.

with an action-specifying rule—especially where compliance involves more than a single action (or omission) or intersects with other duties, especially other perfect duties—a deliberative door opens. This is not a novel observation and is the root of perfect duty casuistry in hard or unusual or marginal cases.[2] We have a perfect duty not to X (tell lies, push people aside, break promises); casuistical questions ask whether the prohibitions still hold in special circumstances (the harmless social lie; forcing one's way through a crowd in an emergency; when keeping a promise undermines trust). In the periphery of the duty's sphere of application there are situations that do not fit its establishing framework, where conforming to its prohibition can defeat the value the duty represents. Staying with its value, we should in the instance set aside the duty's default rule. Quite often this casuistry of a duty is part of shared or public moral knowledge, and we can be negligently at fault—clumsy, obtuse—for not knowing how to identify and manage those cases.

If the casuistry of perfect duties permits exceptions in some circumstances, the exception is not a license to balance reasons and simply act for the better outcome. Under the duty's authority, we remain connected to its value as we act and take on additional responsibility. We are responsible for what our action communicates—e.g., that our false speaking is not just a lie for some good end (that's not its point or justification). It matters just how we act and what we say as we depart from the duty's default rule. We may owe explanation to other interested parties and must recognize that the convention creates new vulnerabilities (suppose we are caught in a white lie—not only have we failed to protect feelings, we may have brought ridicule to and cheapened our word in a relationship).[3] We may have to take reparative steps (having had to push you aside in the emergency, I have some responsibility for securing care if you are injured, though I did you no wrong; I regret the injury I caused without regretting the deed). And it matters what we communicate to *ourselves* as we act. We might want to interrogate our judgment if the presumptive deviation from the rule of duty gives the wrong kind of pleasure.

We should resist the idea that Kantian casuistry manages a kind of non-ideality in moral life or theory. Its prompt is about the inevitable complexities of human affairs, not about agents' non-compliance with moral requirement. That it can be almost impossibly hard to act in a way that both protects pride and respects truthfulness is a feature of human sociality. We should not lie cavalierly, but rigid truthtelling is its own kind of vice (misrepresenting the value of speech). We might follow Kant in thinking that what we confront in hard cases is not so much a need for a modification of a moral rule but a casuistical *question*: How can we act well here? get it right here? and show respect for moral value. Answers need not

---

[2] This feature of the deliberative import of perfect duties was argued for earlier, in Chapter 6, section 6.3.

[3] On some versions we imagine a social implicature that dictates the "nice hat" answer as a prescribed response to a pseudo-question. The moral vulnerabilities here are tucked away in a differently troubling social framework.

be simple. Perhaps we should adopt a longer view of a relationship to get the priorities right when certain kinds of issues present. We are aiming for more than the single right action in what we do. Thinking of duties atomistically, as directing sequences of complete performances, will often get it wrong about the way a duty introduces its value into our acting.

The duty of due care is often an effective guide. If we may tell some white lies, we must guard against untoward practical consequences that the falsehood makes salient. Sometimes, it will call for taking extra steps—issue a warning, monitoring the flow of information—cautionary actions and attitudes that further constrain acting. It may instead direct us to be gentle or supportive in our truthtelling, or to alert someone that they are not going to hear what they expect. Where the conditions of action turn out to be complex or changing, we may have to adjust our pace, gather new information, engage other people in the project (not a simple thing when we have already departed from the default). Acting with a casuistical permission can frustrate others' expectations, initiating new obligations. We need not have been wrong in our proximate judgment to incur these obligations. We cannot always predict how events will unroll and have no insurance that our intended action will remain adequate to our end or the governing duty's value. Sometimes the thing to do is to back out of a course of action, however reasonable it seemed at the outset. One of the roles of the duty of due care is to keep us attached in judgment and motive to the moral arc, the value, of our duty-responsive actions across unhappy accident and serendipity.

Even where some of the circumstances that call for casuistry are predictable, the deliberative result well known, perhaps recognized in social norms, it is a mistake to regard an entrenched casuistical judgment as modifying the default rule of a duty. Casuistry is not part of a method for articulating a duty, say of truthfulness, that is to be spelled out open-endedly as "tell the truth except when a or b or c or... obtain." If we think of the content of a duty as managing a region of human vulnerability partly by its rule—for performance or deliberation—that provides a kind of protection against tendencies to rationalize and exaggerate, it makes sense for the rule of a duty to continue to put pressure on the deliberating agent even as they sensitively engage the particulars of difficult cases. We might say that in justifying action based on an answer to a casuistical question the agent owns responsibility for the correct reading of the circumstances *and* that the chosen path of action sustains connection with the relevant value. Testimony does not insulate. Others can give advice and their advice can come with good reasons. But the upshot has to be regarded as the agent's own judgment if departure from default rules is to have casuistical justification.[4] This is equally true when the

---

[4] I leave aside the kinds of cases where role position gives one person authority over the actions of another. I am skeptical that any such authority justifies acting contra-morally. There are emergency cases where temporal constraints make giving an explanation difficult or impossible and responsibility is suspended. The bar should be high, and the explanation forthcoming after the doing. Following orders doesn't make it less one's own action, so one needs a moral accounting for what one has done.

exception belongs to common moral understanding. When Socrates points out that returning what is owed is not something to be done when doing so would be dangerous, the example is a reminder, not news.[5] But what is not part of the reminder, but *is* part of the value of borrow-and-return, is the further fact that the object that should not now be returned does not thereby become a possession of the erstwhile borrower. This is part of the reason the actual casuistical authorization is assigned to the agent acting, whether or not the judgment behind it is the result of their own deliberation. Social consensus is no safe harbor. Even if one winds up acting in non-negligent error, it is not unfair to be assigned sanction or blame or remedy. It matters that one's confidence in received opinion is reasonable, or that the source of error arises from a hard to identify mistake of moral fact, but those are mitigating not exculpatory considerations.[6]

Convergence around a kind of case judged to be routinely mishandled by the interpreted rule of a duty will give reason to examine the prevailing understanding of the duty, not add an exception to its rule. There's a reason for thinking of an exception as an *exception*: the form of the case makes it look to belong to the rule (say, about truthfulness in speech in contexts of games like poker or reports about the attractiveness of hats), but its substance is about something else (the pleasure in having a safe space to subvert rules, or, in the second case, staving off unnecessary embarrassment). In exception cases the value the duty protects is under no threat.

In other cases that seem not to be handled well by prevailing moral norms—when to take self-reports of epistemic injury seriously, or when to be truthful to small children or to the very old—what is revealed is an issue with our understanding of the content or value of a duty in application that needs to be excavated and confronted. When that happens, what may be needed is not a modification of the default rule but a rethinking of the duty and the way it sets its terms of requirement. We may experience moral norms changing under our feet, as it were. They can also be changed by a concerted effort of directing public attention to hitherto ignored facts and discounted minority values. There are standing secondary duties to interrogate the reasons for the former and to be vigilant about the causes of the latter.[7]

---

[5] A counter-example in one context is a casuistical exception in another.

[6] Interesting developments in the discussion around testimonial injustice trace this sort of trajectory. There are out and out discriminatory injustices—not listening to women or minorities—and then there is reasonable reliance on statistical regularities in practical decision-making that can screen off effects of a history of discrimination. Cf. Miranda Fricker *Epistemic Injustice* (2007), a touchstone of the first kind of wrong, and Sherrilyn Roush "Epistemic Injustice and the Principle of Total Evidence" (forthcoming) for an exploration of some implications of the second.

[7] None of this makes the duty less real, less objective, a matter of social construction. It is more like medicine and our evolving understanding of illnesses of the body. Something we only now find out makes us realize that the remedy prescribed in our past practice was the very thing masking the underlying cause.

Things work differently with juridical duties. Judgment that the rule fails *in the instance* to protect a relevant kind of claim is not grounds for the parties' making an exception, though it could be an occasion for seeking judicial remedy. The exercise of authorized judgment can in some cases create precedent and thereby alter a rule. Indeterminacy of a juridical rule may require judgment about legislative intent or social purpose. It may need to be revised or replaced. But it is not a part of the value of juridical duties that their rule can be adjusted in the individual's hands to the fine grain of the actual.[8]

Suppose the only way to the fire alarm involves forcefully shoving someone aside. We might think: *ethically* there is a duty here that we not forcibly lay hands on others for the sake of our purposes, and *juridically* the action involves battery: interfering with another's body as a means. Yet we should act. The way the action is allowed by the different duties is not the same. Since the action is not one of acting for "my purpose" in the relevant sense, the ethical restriction is not triggered—*its* stringency is deliberative. The juridical duty is limned by the necessities (and defined limits) of providing juridical protection generally (self-defense lives here). Raising the alarm is itself a juridical duty and has a role in setting the scope of the juridical protection of the body. However, we should not conclude that the ethical duty is idle. *That* there is a right or a juridical duty tells us that the person acting has a particular moral power; however, the correct exercise of that power also has an ethical dimension, from the same root, explaining, in cases of this sort, why due care use of force and post factum explanation and remedy are constituent elements of the rightful action.

The location of the tracking responsibility is different when there is system adjustment or change. Some change will be profound, about who counts as a moral subject or what that entails in the system; some will be remedial, prompted by new knowledge about the effects of material and social arrangements; some will come from changes in our ability to act effectively, both close at hand and at a distance. When change is called for in the higher reaches of the system's structure, given the way duties, public and private, perfect and imperfect, descend from first principles, it is to be expected that it will lead to moral change elsewhere in the system (though not always: the sensitivity of ground-level morality can be unpredictable). This is an obvious fact of social policy-making, less familiar in the way we think about morality as a practice. It can affect how we think about means, which burdens can be placed on individuals, and when it is that moral change requires something like social engineering. Just recognizing that there is a problem won't dictate the locus or kind of change that's called for.

Suppose it remains true that 40 percent of new mothers in the US are unmarried, and that there is a statistically clear connection between that demographic

---

[8] Though an ethical agent can do more: a landlord doesn't have to evict at the moment the law allows it.

fact and childhood poverty.⁹ There is then likely a moral problem, more plausibly a set of moral problems, about a large group of children and their mothers in plain sight, and a moral requirement to change something so that this outcome doesn't repeat as a matter of course. Public attention could be directed at individuals, urging more marriage, or providing free contraception, depending on where it's thought the problem is. Or change could be entertained higher up in terms of making education and job training more accessible. There may need to be other system responses. If it's to be contraception, there may be a threat to religious liberties. If it's pressure to marry, the safety of single mothers in the targeted group may be put at risk as opprobrium attaches to their situation or decision. If women with young children need education or have to work, it is morally negligent not to have publicly funded childcare. But wherever the focal point for change is determined to be, individual and public morality, relational duties and legal requirements, have to function together, tracking value, inside one system of duties.

Given the difficulty of maintaining connection with moral value across social institutions and personal concerns, there is structural need for public criticism and transparency at all levels of the system. Some moral deficiencies can be schooled and individuals learn to do better. Some are entrenched in unjust institutional arrangements that not only control outcomes independent of improvements of individual moral character, they can make morally deficient decisions rational. A status threat to members of a disadvantaged group has to be met by means of uniform public treatment and the elimination of structural disadvantage.¹⁰ Part of the noxious effect of redlining in northern US cities during and after the Great Migration was to translate institutionally imposed segregation in housing (and so also access by black Americans to work, education, and wealth) into a default set of discriminatory attitudes and practices across the board.¹¹ This made interpersonal failure difficult to avoid. The good will of neighbors would not defeat a redlined mortgage loan, or improve schools whose funding was determined by the local tax base. Necessary structural change could create new interpersonal duties as well—duties of attention, anti-discrimination, and status affirming actions at all levels. Where new public duties are implemented and publicly endorsed, they can positively affect sensitivities that over time alter motives. This is not paternalism but an essential element of continuing moral education.

While much of this is common sense, it might be thought surprising in a Kantian theory that any features of the history of an actual system of duties enter an account of what our duties are. If so, it is worth the reminder that even if first

---

⁹ The figure is from the 2018 UN State of World Population Report. Not all unmarried mothers are poor, but a substantial enough number are to make the statistic salient.
¹⁰ Even if a gifted and devoted teacher can make a segregated classroom of comparable value to her students, separate but equal is not a way of realizing what equal standing requires in education.
¹¹ Ta-Nehisi Coates, "The Case for Reparations," *The Atlantic* (June 2014).

principles are a priori and not a function of the situation or capacities of the entities they apply to, since moral principles only make a difference in action if they can be applied by those to whom they apply, the duties we encounter, and the system of duties we may be called on to adjust, have to be shaped to fit the world we live in. We would not do better trying to lay out an ideal system of duties first. The Kantian idea of morality as a system of duties is, after all, a project of giving rational shape to the world we find ourselves in.

Inevitably, no matter how well designed things are, some bad things happen. In the natural order, they happen as they do. In the moral order, they are often a kind of residue from the fitting of one order on the other (because moral actions have their effects in the natural order, even the wisest of agents may be caught in a causal eddy). The effects need be no one's fault; no one must own them as their moral author. If they are serious, they call for a moral response, as would a harm that came about by accident or innocent mistake. It is reasonable, other things equal, for the agent (it may be more than one) who is the efficient cause of a bad outcome to be a first responder. Maybe they could have posted a warning, made the circumstances of their interaction less opaque, taken an extra step. We might think of this as a pragmatics of responsibility independent of imputation. Even if we act reasonably and with due care, when our action falls short, though we don't owe repair, other duties may keep us connected to the untoward events because we are a part of the story of their happening. This kind of tracking, or another kind of entanglement, can arise even with perfect duties. We don't simply get to ignore what we have set in motion because we acted out of duty.

8.2 A Note about Juridical Imperfect Duties

At different moments in the preceding chapters I have alluded to one or another imperfect juridical duty, from the duties of citizens to promote and preserve their own political institutions to the quasi juridical duties we have with respect to systematic denials of innate right elsewhere. Duties in this category are not part of Kant's catalogue, but that's not a reason to deny that they are possible if there are good reasons to think they are needed to fill out the system of duties and make sense of some of our obligations. However, if there are such duties, we need to identify their anchor, their source value. Is there an additional obligatory end that is juridical in aim? If so, it won't be as an extension of the argument for obligatory ends in the *Doctrine of Virtue*. Those are the ends reason in us has to have if it is to be a faculty of ends, able to determine the will (since otherwise reason in us could not be practical (*MM* 6:395)). Innate right is in the background of any juridical duty, but it is not an obligatory end: its value sets terms or limits for descendant juridical rights and duties (e.g., that no domain of RIGHT can support relations of subordination). The answer to the anchor question comes with attending to why in the derivation of duties story juridical duties come first: we can't live together as free and equal persons, or live a fully human life guided by the end of self-perfection, or engage in any serious way with the happiness of others, unless we live in conditions of RIGHT. And that indicates the first fact about the anchor argument: the "we" in the last sentence is not rhetorical.

That is: an essential condition for the development of rational agency in persons is a morally necessary but empirically contingent accomplishment of some "we": securing the conditions of RIGHT, its institutions and distinctive duties.[12] This makes the moral end—realizing the conditions of RIGHT—formally unusual. It is at once obligatory, and so, objectively, an end that each person has to have (in virtue of claims on others they cannot avoid making), but it is also an end that cannot be adopted—cannot give rise to duties—unless it is a common end (for all in a domain roughly identified by unavoidable interaction).[13] In order to be a common end, however, it need not secure the cooperation of those in its domain by their *subjectively* adopting the common end *for* a moral reason so long as they have some subjectively sufficient reason to take the end as theirs (and, of course, the duties that follow don't require acting on a motive responding to the objective end).[14] So there is a moral end that might support imperfect juridical duties. But if the deployment of nonmoral incentives fixes one problem, it sets up another. Since not all agents under the end's authority will have deliberative access to its value, how is an imperfect juridical duty's discretion to be exercised? The solution comes with a demand on juridical institutions: that the value of the objective common end be visible in the institutional structures and strictures of RIGHT: in norms of due process, equal treatment, anti-discrimination, and constitutionally protected freedoms. We should expect an interpretation of the common end's institutional form to show up in the content of imperfect juridical duties.

The idea of such a common end is familiar to us from ordinary activities: an end acted for by all, though not necessarily adopted as an end by all for the same reason. Even so, all can be guided in their acting by an anchoring value. The members of an orchestra can come together through a love of music, or the desire to do something with some specific others, or just the need to make a living through a skill they happen to have. They can cooperate, follow the rules set by the orchestra leader, and so make music together, and even make it well if the conductor is good. There will be differences. Those responsive to the value of

---

[12] This kind of argument is made explicitly in Kant's 1784 essay, "The Idea for a Universal History from a Cosmopolitan Point of View."

[13] At the risk of belaboring the point: *my* subjectively adopting an ETHICAL obligatory end and acting for its duties does not depend on others adopting that end. It is an objective end for all; it need not be a common end.

[14] Kant describes civil society as the cooperative union made by "a will united *a priori*" through an "omnilateral" willing, "presupposing no rightful act for its union" (quoting serially from *MM* 6:263 and 6: 267). The principle uniting the wills is rationally necessary for all of us, so not a matter of voluntary election.

making music together may be more generous to their fellow musicians, more interested, perhaps, in improving musical skills beyond what is necessary for the performance, and, relatedly, critical of those whose connection to the common project is instrumental. They might even have reason to hope that the experience of doing this fine thing together will change the incentive structure of those whose connection to the common enterprise is via extra-musical practical necessity.

So likewise with the members of a polity. Those who grasp the point of their juridical duties needn't regard others' various instrumental reasons for conforming to them as awful or as indicative of faulty moral character (here, instrumental defection is not wrongful because of its motive).[15] If moral stage theory has any merit, one might regard nonmoral reasons for obeying rules of RIGHT as a possible gateway for persons over time recognizing the different values available to them in and through the common project.[16] This is, after all, the way we look at the moral development of children—that is, of all of us. Further, if there is objective necessity to the membership of all in a juridical commons, it is a desideratum on actual juridical duties and institutions that they can make sense to attentive members as conditions for living with others as free and equal persons. This puts an additional premium on avenues of publicity and explicitness.

With this back story in mind, we are in a position to canvass some candidates for imperfect juridical duties. We are looking for moments when qua citizen or agent or official of the state, acting under the auspices of a juridical right or duty requires an exercise of the kind of agent discretion that fits with an imperfect duty. We should first distinguish cases that require judgment, not discretion: where the question to be answered is theoretical, not practical in the imperfect duty sense. For example, one might need to know what the purpose of a piece or element of legislation was in order to figure out where it applies, or the extent and manner of a regulation's enforcement in evaluating a potential venture. Even if there is no fact of the matter discoverable, citizens or officials might have to judge as best they can, working out what makes sense or fits with announced intent or is consistent with past practice. The conclusions reached supplement common understanding about what a rule or regulation calls for.

By contrast, the exercise of discretion that comes with an imperfect duty involves a situational and deliberative moral response, guided but not fixed by the duty's anchoring value. Under the imperfect duty of beneficence I might conclude in one situation of need that I can and should help, but in another, where the need is the same but my circumstances or my relationship to the beneficiary are different, that I should not, or should not if there is someone else

---

[15] One might think they also have reason to worry about such persons staying the moral course. But it is not a foregone conclusion that clarity about a moral end is a stronger bulwark against temptation than wanting to avoid external sanctions.

[16] This is one of the enduring themes of the classical American film form of the western.

who can. What I ought to do can depend on my appreciation of the specifics of my situation. If the accretion of situational readings affects the way "we" come to act, contributing to common understanding of the duty, it is by convergence of circumstances, not by an articulation of the duty's rule. The individual agent acting under convergent common understanding remains responsible for the discretionary shaping of the duty's requirement.

What might we include as juridical imperfect duties? Perhaps this sort of case. Suppose, having a contractual obligation to deliver goods, and knowing that organizing the delivery schedule to facilitate the recipient's needs is not just a good business practice but also shows respect for them and for their enterprise, a business manager integrates the ethical norm into his fulfillment practices. We might think, by analogy, of a public program serving a population that has a serious need and past reason to distrust public services. One could lighten the burden of access, or be a little forgiving about missed deadlines—not as dictated by agency regulation, but as appropriate exercises of discretionary judgment that an agency head or employee might make, given some authority over outcome decisions.

These do not seem to be defining instances of juridical imperfect duties so much as attractive intersections of the ethical and the juridical. That is, an ethical imperfect duty addresses acting under juridical regulation, giving RIGHTFUL actions a fuller moral shape by permissibly inflecting the performance of juridical tasks. The kindness of the clerk managing unemployment insurance applications could be the familiar themed "giving a human face" to the bureaucratic, or it could represent the deeper fact that the juridical is a venue for the exercise of moral agency. This is not just adding value in a contingent way, as it would be were one to play baseball "nicely." While it is not trivial to be polite to an opponent in a competitive game, it also isn't integral to the norms that make the game what it is. Whereas the purpose of the ethical intersection with the juridical is to make the juridical point of application more effective from the moral point of view. The agent/citizen/official acting in this way knows that ethical discretion isn't juridical license, that it doesn't give them permission to boost the access to benefits of a particular group (while it does permit attentive acknowledgment to specific relevant difficulties that may be common occurrences for a specific group), nor permission to benefit some out of personal resources *sub specie* kindly employment counselor. The juridical regime wants morally good agents, not just kind ones. Correlatively, seeing the juridical as a moral locale, a space in which moral agency values and duties have a role, extends individuals' sense of the kind of moral project they are engaged in as citizens. It is not only the amoral and the self-interested who need to see the juridical space as attractive and worth their support.

The intersection introduces limits as well. Moral agents may be inefficient executors of rigid and gratuitously harmful rules. They can be in a good position to see and argue that certain sort of state-sanctioned acts are morally impossible. And aware, if they have adequate moral education, that the spheres are not so separate that what is for good reason strictly impermissible in one sphere can be adopted by the other as a means without express and explicit justification.

We have previously noted some clear cases where discretion is essential to the juridical—viz., intra-juridical duties *of citizens* that have to do with the support and reform of juridical institutions. They are, after all, made institutions, inevitably imperfect and perfectible, inevitably needing to respond to changes in ways the world goes and refinements in understanding while retaining connection to supporting value. There may be no unique direction reform needs to take, though it may be clear that there are some things that must be changed or avoided whatever else happens. There will often be other moral considerations, juridical and ethical, that call for attention and consideration as reform is imagined and implemented. An example might be found in the way common law evolves through adversarial advocacy filtered by adjudicative evaluation about the effect of evolving rules in the system of laws.

We should also look for cases where distinctively juridical values govern regions of decision-making in the use of public resources. Duties that arise from constitutionally-sourced requirements about education, healthcare, or housing would seem to be imperfect in the relevant way. The argument for the duties is drawn from basic structure values, not the contribution to individual welfare. One might think about special education, or occupational retraining—things necessary to create or maintain access to conditions of active citizenship for specific disadvantaged groups (so not for the sake of a well-being value, though well-being is affected). Somewhere in a regime there will be an agent that determines what range of benefits or services is to be provided and to whom and what burdens or costs are to be imposed and on whom.[17] The appropriate outcome is not a given once the problem is identified. Other values will be in the mix: fairness, equality, precedent, the claims of future generations on scarce resources, and so on. What makes this a part of *juridical* duty is the set of values in play in virtue of the common end. What makes the duty *imperfect* is that the answer the situation calls for is not fixed by a rule but is still answerable to the values the duty serves.[18]

Another source of imperfect juridical duties would come from some of the necessary internal repair occasioned by structural injustice.[19] That is, injustice whose source may be all or partly institutional (federal use or sanction of red-lining),

---

[17] I don't mean "agent" only in the individual person sense, but agent in the bearer of responsibility for the duty sense. So it can be a court or an agency or the legislature: something that counts as an accountable public agent.

[18] A question about the direction of action is different from and prior to a question about means.

[19] This and the next paragraph draw on Lawrence G. Sager, "Imperfect Constitutional Duties" (forthcoming) and Lawrence G. Sager and Nelson Tebbe, "Discriminatory Permissions and Structural Injustice" (2022).

or injustices that arise from systematic actions in the private sphere (refusals of commercial or public services based on religious conviction), or cases where the state's explicit permission to privately discriminate encourages just that kind of conduct. How to act for equal treatment of groups subject to subordination and discrimination may require a division of labor with respect to the promulgation and enforcement of statutes, the pragmatics of expressive legislation (not just doing what is right but saying why it is), regions of affirmative governmental support (of venues of speech, for example, to insure fair representation). What brings these actions under imperfect duties is the deliberative task of shaping a response. What is known is that evolved or newly made vivid circumstances implicate basic structure values; what needs to be settled on is a way to (re)shape the powers of the involved agents (public and private) in stable and justice promoting ways. This might involve actions of citizens or courts or legislatures exercising deliberative discretion about when and how to act for some impacted juridical or justice value.

An example of this might be the adoption of Title IX legislation in the US that partially corrected previous civil rights law concerning discrimination based on race, color, and national origin—but not sex. It arose in a political context resistant to passage of the more powerful and far-reaching Equal Rights Amendment (ERA), not merely as a stop-gap or a means, but as a way forward, introducing structural changes in employment and athletics that would be expected to accomplish in substance some part of the ambitions for equality that the ERA would bring if passed.[20] All the marks of an imperfect duty are present. An equal rights value inadequately realized; a challenge to find a path of action that could negotiate competing interests without losing connection to the goal of substantive equality; a suite of value-responsive limited objectives. Whether or not it was the best path, once in place it became a source of rules and directives that would (and did) contribute to the morally necessary change in social understanding of the public significance of gender and sexuality.

In acting for any imperfect duty, success does not come by balancing competing interests, but from a situational appreciation committed to a moral framing of the practical. In the juridical case, it can include judgment about the moral tolerance for limits in the ongoing project of realizing the condition of RIGHT given situational constraints. But the tolerance itself has to have limits. It should be hard to justify restrictions imposed on news venues, even if that would promote social calm, since limiting public access to information violates fundamental conditions of public right. And it shouldn't be hard, not *morally* hard, to see

---

[20] In the words of Senator Birch Bayh, the bill's sponsor: "While the impact of this amendment would be far-reaching, it is not a panacea. It is, however, an important first step in the effort to provide for the women of America something that is rightfully theirs—an equal chance to attend the schools of their choice, to develop the skills they want, and to apply those skills with the knowledge that they will have a fair chance to secure the jobs of their choice with equal pay for equal work." 118 Cong. Record 5808 (1972).

that respect for individuals' faith-based values is consistent with reproductive freedom for women, a condition of their equal public status.[21]

Not last and certainly not least are the duties that are about the recognition of innate right outside one's own juridical home. As argued in section 6.4, this includes state actions directed at other states as well as the actions of individuals and groups taken on behalf of persons at moral risk elsewhere. In all of these cases we find the value-tracking discretion that is the hallmark of imperfect duties.[22]

If this quick canvass is reasonable, we should conclude that there are (at least) straight up juridical imperfect duties, ethically inflected juridical duties, and extra-juridical imperfect duties that track the underlying value of innate right. They are identified by the deliberative structure they introduce. In each case the duty requires discretion in determining the actions called for by the duty, discretion that involves appeal to the duty's supporting value.

And what about motive? With ethical imperfect duties, there is an essential role for the moral motive to maintain the connection in deliberation and choice with the duty's anchoring end or value. The problem here is that while it is defining of the concept of RIGHT that it does not call for our acting from a moral motive—there need not be any action-shaping concern for moral value in our RIGHTFUL actions—it is often important to the work on behalf of juridical imperfect duties that the actions they call for be expressive and communicative about common value, even, on occasion, be symbolic. The point of accommodation for some religious practices is to express respect for these important human commitments. One should expect motive to be essential to this aspect of the juridical project.

The difficulty here is in keeping the different levels of argument separate. We should recall that "moral motive" is a functional notion: it can and often ought to be realized in our psychology, but it can have non-psychological instantiations as well. The function of the motive is to be a deliberative and practical orientation internally connected to the content of a duty, reflecting the duty's moral value or point. In that sense, the moral motive can be realized institutionally, in constitutional mandates, terms or rules of incorporation, or an action-generating entity's regulation by a complex decision procedure. There is no violation of the idea of RIGHT in this. Indeed, it is an important part of the moral critique of a public institution or practice that it has allowed the wrong sort of reason to dictate its decisions, or that it is the captive of special interests, or engages in ad hoc balancing when something like strict scrutiny is called for. Directed at the form of a public

---

[21] It *shouldn't* be hard. Still, for many the conclusion is out of reach. I don't think the explanation lies in hard to follow implications of the system of RIGHT so much as it does in resisting them. Knowing where public reason belongs doesn't tell us how to make the public reason.

[22] It is a little tempting to conjecture that the imperfect juridical duties connected to the end of the condition of RIGHT divide as do the imperfect ethical duties between duties to self and duties to others: that is, duties to sustain and improve the juridical condition at home and duties to act on behalf of the juridical condition elsewhere.

institution, or to the agents who act in its name, what is being criticized is a failure in their decisions and choices to track the value that gives them privilege or legitimacy.[23] It is a failure of motive in the formal or functional sense. A court decision that allows a corporation's asserted religious interests to be the basis for self-exemption from funding employee insurance that includes contraception (as part of federally mandated healthcare) arguably fails in just this way.[24]

---

[23] That is, government actors should act from motives (in this sense) that reflect values underlying juridical norms. (They may also have the moral meta-motive that they should be so motivated.)

[24] See *Burwell v. Hobby Lobby* (2014) (that allows privately held corporations to self-exempt on religious grounds from the contraceptive mandate of the Affordable Care Act). The contrary value was voiced by Justice Scalia, a noted defender of the free exercise of religion, in his 1990 *Employment Division v Smith* opinion where he argued that if protected free exercise extends to any action one might disagree with on religious grounds, law would lose authority.

PART THREE
LIVING IN THE MORAL HABITAT

9
A Dynamic System

The descending matrix of duties, juridical and ethical, perfect and imperfect, extended by entanglement, adjusted by casuistry, and supplemented by the duty of due care, is a complex and dynamic system of moral requirement. It has to be asked: What does all this mean for the very idea of a duty and for the agent acting under morality's authority? Should we now think of these "Kantian duties" as unstable, subject to change over time, their content relativized to context? Are agents expected to track the nuance of relation and entanglement, to know and respond flexibly in terms of the values supporting the presenting duties and entitlements? One of the supposed attractions of a moral theory that involves duties comes from their provision of firm guidance across a wide range of actions and interactions. Is the Kantian agent on the moral habitat account, by contrast, both at sea and on her own? If the dynamic system I've described burdens judgment with one hand and muddies the locus of moral responsibility with the other, that would be a decidedly ironic result even for a revisionary interpretation of Kant's ethics.

The investigations of Part Three address these questions in several different ways. This chapter looks at the claim that morality, as a system of duties, not only can be, but has to be, dynamic. It shows that this is what we should expect if, as Kant thought, morality is a practical science, and like the other sciences has some things that are fixed, if subject to ongoing interpretation, and some things that we take ourselves to know that are not true, or only partially so, or hostage to hidden assumptions which, when uncovered, rightly destabilize our confidence. To give some real form to this idea, Chapter 10 considers what it would mean for a system of duties to absorb the non-obvious idea that persons have a *right* to housing: what the effect would be at the ground level for agents acting, as well as what it would modify in the higher reaches of the theory, including its idea of property. The account I give of the proposed right is only a preliminary sketch, but it is enough to make the dynamic system point, and enough to show that the implications for acknowledging such a right extend our duties beyond borders (section 10.3 discusses the duties owed to the stateless and other refugees that follow from the moral content of the right). Chapter 11 returns to the question of objectivity in a dynamic system, and a related question about the responsibility of agents, both for what they do, given the real possibility that parts of prevailing moral understanding are in error, *and* for the content of the system of duties itself.

* * *

A first thing to say is that to describe a system of duties as dynamic does not mean that everything is in motion. The underlying values and first principles of the system, as well as the broad categories of duty, are constant. General duties (or principles of duty) about the use of property (as distinct from the juridical conditions of ownership) or the stringency of promises or the demands of beneficence are not immediate directives for choice and action but deliberative requirements. Still, they firmly rule out a variety of maxims and actions (typically self-serving exceptions to core or default duties), thereby creating stable moral practice. But in morally complex circumstances (where, say, standard moral protections, or standard interpretations of moral protections, threaten the interests they exist to protect), deliberative requirements are open to input in their premises that reflect morally salient changes in knowledge and circumstances. That degree of dynamism in the system should be a welcome feature.

Again it matters that in this, as with other regions of knowledge and practice, we rarely act alone. We discuss things with reliable others, we try to imagine alternatives that can make common sense, we accept as a constraint that we need to make our actions intelligible—especially to those they will affect—even if that limits the range of choices available to us. Some things we can fix just between us: it's obvious that your need requires more than an equal share and there is enough for us both, even so. But where our interactions are mediated by external social forms, our moral possibilities may be limited by a public understanding of what is morally possible or necessary. Suppose we find moral fault in the way society manages the intersection of gender and work. Passively or actively, it may be the cause of long-term social and economic inequality (no retirement benefits for full-time child or elder care). It creates a biased default setting for authority (both in the style of authority that matters and in the distribution of positions of authority). Suppose that were all of it. It is possible for some to adjust their personal interactions so that they more thoroughly express a commitment to equality. It is possible to have a *good* business in the way one might have a *green* business, instituting procedures and training and goals that tend towards equality in a gender-sensitive way. It is possible, though, perhaps not surprisingly, difficult to change what authority looks like. It is possible, though surprisingly difficult, to adjust default gendered assumptions about who has responsibility for remembering and dividing the work to manage the daily needs of children and the household. The socially determined "voluntary" tends to undermine well-intentioned private adjustments. Beyond the impediments to equality, there are burdens in accounting for what one does, to oneself as well as others, when living in a morally opaque environment.

Such now-familiar observations tell us that we can't just assume being careful and attentive in what we do is enough. For the engaged moral agent it has become part of normal moral concern to worry about how what they do is affected by persistent ground-level inequality and threats to equal standing that have their source in and are supported by background elements of juridical institutions. Just as we diagnose personal wrongdoing by investigating an individual's motives, so we should be prepared to find fault in institutional motives (the embedded values in their rules or procedures) when they favor choice situations that prime persons to fail to act well towards one another. The idea that we can manage or even understand all the strains of interpersonal morality without looking at what is happening elsewhere in the system of duties implies not just a quietism about morality in the large, but also assent to a measure of false consciousness about our own situation.

While obedience to law is a system requirement of juridical duties, the system itself is open to adjustment, from within and constitutionally, and also from within and extra-legally (in targeted disobedience) in cases of its persistent and overt resistance to morally compelling need for change. A desirable state of the system is that it shares the humility of moral agency. Given the complexity of the undertaking, error is to be expected; given the increase in understanding of ways moral distortion gets built in to our institutions, we know that many voluntary choices are in fact indentured, many restrictions on freedom for its own sake will in fact be its enemy (think of voting restrictions "to ensure free elections" and who they disenfranchise). It is a sign of a system of duties' health when individuals are free to collectively assert their authority as citizens and resist—juridically or ethically—inadequate law.[1] It is a normal moral fact that new duties that result, or new interpretations of received duties, will alter the way moral requirement presents at different locations in the system.

This sort of talk about change and adjustment makes most sense in a system of duties not grievously unjust at the root. We are also not to imagine a churn of serious moral requirements, some simply vanishing as new duties pop up, creating moral surprise and consternation even for the best of us. Nonetheless, as we know, we can become aware that lived or articulated morality has blind spots or regions where the implications of underlying moral value have not been adequately drawn out. We are familiar with calls for the extension of rights and obligations to new populations, debates about who counts, who is an equal, what equality requires of us. By the time of the passage of the 19th Amendment to the US constitution in 1920, the problem of women's suffrage didn't catch anyone by surprise. We have come to recognize that there are new or newly conceptualized moral issues to integrate into prevailing moral understanding around actions of large numbers, future generations, the responsibility for climate change. We do not need to resolve whether what we confront is an epistemic development or a practical,

---

[1] In some cases it is not morally possible to act as the law requires (turning in undocumented workers and their children to a morally bankrupt immigration authority). In others, resistance is a call for reform (marching or picketing to protest efforts to disenfranchise a vulnerable class of citizens). The resistant act should be and be visibly directed at an element of public right that is inconsistent with RIGHT's justifying value.

moral, dynamic one. It can be both.[2] Perhaps we always had duties of global justice and didn't register them until we had the means to act, or destroy, globally. Perhaps having a certain level of technology and wealth changes the nature of human agency—certainly our abilities—and so the requirements that can conceivably be ours. Either way, from the perspective of acting agents, if their social world looks at all like ours, there is work that needs to be done, changes made to the system of duties, substantively or interpretatively.

A moral theory can regard this work as a part of its pragmatics (being open to new instruments for acting); it might have a subdivision for managing the inevitably imperfect nature of moral practice. Or, it could regard the work as integral to the very idea of morality: that it is a dynamic practical system designed to sustain connection to fundamental value as it adjusts and reconfigures its action-directing elements as a result of new knowledge, external change, and its own successes (e.g., as advances in accessible healthcare extend our lifespan they usher in a range of moral questions both about what counts as a well-formed life and about how to meet the specific needs of this enlarged demographic). The moral habitat idea belongs here. What it adds is the possibility of moral change taking place at different levels in a system of duties and the associated sensitivity to effects upstream and down. Once we see our moral requirements, our duties, as elements of a system whose purpose is to give a value-driven shape to the human habitat, and thereby to the natural world (even if only negatively, in deciding where not to go, what to leave alone), it will not seem strange that the content of duties should be affected by changes in knowledge and circumstance, sometimes directly, sometimes in ways that depend on the place of a duty in the system.

With this idea comes new kinds of questions. Over time, as the system of duties responds to empirical and epistemic change, there can be alterations in the moral division of labor—concerning who bears a duty and, as a result, about what the duty requires, especially when the bearer of a duty that was private becomes public. As we've seen, even if the rationale for such a change is a matter of efficiency, the change in bearer can yield change in content. A content that was discretionary or dependent on relationships, becomes an entitlement, and then subject to norms of equal treatment. This is familiar in discussions of duties associated with the education of children, care of the elderly, and caretaking more generally. Evaluation of gains and losses needs to be framed in terms of the different loci of obligation.

Consider, as an illustration, the argument for public education. Here is one way it might go, and go wrong. One might think that the moral starting point of reference for education is the family. Even if the family has a duty to raise

---

[2] Since after the fact it will look within the system that what they now ought to do is what they ought to have been doing, the issue at the cusp of change about whether the problem was epistemic or about morality is moot.

independent and competent adults (on various measures of competency), beyond that, family values, the family's resources and interests, appropriately shape the nature and extent of the education provided. Schooling choices will reflect that, with some taking advantage of a public option, if it is available, some not. Suppose that for reasons of social efficiency or economic need, the education of children becomes a public charge—public schooling a state duty. Things change. Now there is a requirement of educational equality or parity. And while public education permissibly can take on public tasks—training for citizenship, for example— there are content constraints on what public education can teach so as to respect the diversity of values brought from the family into this new space. So we get toleration and multiculturalism and celebrating everyone's winter holiday.

Whatever we think about winter holidays, there is reason to think this argument gets the moral story backwards. Once it is practically possible to have public education, it is a moral requirement, not merely an efficiency. That is: there is a requirement both to have the institution *and* to participate in it. Training in the values of equality and independence that mark the moral-juridical community not only cannot be optional, it cannot take place in just any setting. It calls for a degree of common experience so that persons are enabled to meet and register one another's standing as equals across a wide variety of social contexts. And this needs to be set in place early. That righteous parental "*We* don't do that!" can express the right idea but have the wrong scope and authority. The value of public education is not first or not only about uniform pedagogy. It is a response to a moral need for children to separate (some) from the family, to be in schools with open access and diverse populations, comparable resources, and with curricula that embody the values of the common moral project. One could argue: Just as regular and intimate caretaking is a necessary condition for the development of an infant into an individual whose independence as a self is engaged with trusting and valuing others, so training to find common value in diversity, a sense of being one among equals who share responsibility for the conditions of common life, has to be a collective project. Not every moral task can be performed privately. If the quality of public education is good enough, family-based or sectarian arguments for keeping healthy children separate lack traction. Public education is not in competition with private interests in promoting family values and traditions, languages, or religious identities—all of which can be pursued alongside it.[3]

Not all arenas of public moral concern mandate a shift to public institutions even as empirical or demographic changes cast moral doubt on the adequacy of common private practice. While increases in lifespan and patterns of family

---

[3] In this context, it is not easy to see how private or sectarian schools, especially those that resist the values of the common moral project, would have a claim on a share of public educational resources to support their institutional mission. Historically, some sectarian institutions have been important in the rise of liberal traditions and in providing quality education in social sectors where the public system has failed. The history is praiseworthy. It is not an argument for a principled division of labor.

dispersal put pressure on end-of-life caretaking, interpersonal or familial reasons warrant greater permissiveness about who provides care so long as adequate minima are maintained. Nonetheless, since the physical and social limits that often come with aging and infirmity can lead to a kind of servitude in caretakers and dangerous dependency in those cared for, there is not only need for public support and protection, there is reason to locate ultimate responsibility for elder care in the public realm. It should follow that public provision of end-of-life care has to be a viable and available resource. And further, locating the ultimate responsibility in the public realm implies that sectarian institutions and private options have to function within a juridical regime of oversight and protection. However well this is organized, even good solutions may not be permanent. As we understand more and can do more, as we perhaps change our view of what the later years in life are about, our obligations and arrangements may also change.

Rather than making moral practice implausibly complex, this sort of change and adjustment, involving the different strata of duties, rather makes morality more like the rest of the practical domain, where means and ends are interlocked, and the arc of an enterprise may take us beyond anything we foresaw as we began a course of action. Since that sort of complexity *can* make life complicated, we learn to anticipate and prepare, and take notice of institutional processes and inertias. It only seems to be a special problem for morality if we think of our relation to it as primarily about learning the rules and following them, where our chief difficulty is corralling errant motivations that cause us to resist doing what we ought.[4]

In a decent society, one can for the most part rely on customary moral practices and virtues that have been refined over time to negotiate daily life. But not always. Moral life isn't tidy. A welcome favor done yesterday could come to be regarded as an insult tomorrow. We see that a small invasion of privacy could relieve a large anxiety. What to do? Changes in sensitivities make navigating a social scene—a workplace or classroom—complex and fraught. It can be difficult to keep up. No articulation of morality can avert problems of this sort. The idea is that being engaged with a deliberatively responsive and transparent system of duties includes an invitation to rethink and redescribe stubborn problems, to find creative ways consistent with the system's value to respond to unexpected sources of distress and complaint, and to accept responsibility for what happens if we take it upon ourselves to figure out what should be done. As we will see in Chapter 11, this is

---

[4] There is no blurring here of the line between moral philosophy and applied ethics, or between the derivation of duties and the sociology of a group's moral practices. The point is to insist on the need in moral theorizing to include the idea of moral practice (as lived *praxis*)—that we understand its requirements and appreciate that its actual conditions bear on what morality can require. This is the data set that tests the adequacy of moral theorizing. It's also a model that offers a serious response to charges that the limits of a moral theory at its historical moment of emergence just about guarantee its inadequacy in the face of the moving present of moral understanding. It can be part of theory design that it should expect to have to transcend such limits.

far from an invitation to go rogue, or to think that one's unique circumstances afford one special authority to act.

Sometimes, however, the kind of change called for poses a challenge to the system's more fundamental values—to what they are or how they are understood. To see what this might involve, I want to begin an exploration of some parts of the array of moral issues around housing and homelessness that we currently face, both domestically and across national boundaries. In trying to do this within the framework of the moral habitat idea, we will get some measure of the resources I've been claiming it has.

Suppose we live in a wealthy city where there are many individuals and families who are homeless. Many live on the street, some in cars, some in shelters or other forms of transient housing. Domestically, many at the economic and social margins live in threat of eviction, overcrowding, costly but substandard housing, often at punishing distances from available work. There is little dispute that inadequate and impermanent housing has negative effects on mental and physical health, educational success, family life, confidence in the future, a sense of security, and more.[5] It is not a morally possible condition.

Or we might live in a place that is either a proximate or a distal destination for migrants and refugees. Some come because of war, or because the effects of economic and political dislocations, or of climate change, make it impossible for them to work their land or find employment in their home country. Others are fleeing violence directed at themselves or their children. The United National Relief Agency estimates that 70.8 million individuals were forcibly displaced in 2018 (this includes internal displacement as well as migrations across borders). Many wind up in refugee centers, temporary shelters, migrant camps, or in the margins of the temporary housing market. That's also not a morally supportable outcome.

Either scenario presents a toxic stew of moral problems. People are suffering. There are all kinds of need. The causes of the failures are various. There is much fault to be found. Those who are responsible for the situation are often in no position to remedy the need were they to be willing to, which very often they are not. There are issues of beneficence; humanitarian problems; matters of justice; some mix of rights claims. What kinds of needs and claims are recognized and who bears the responsibility for meeting them could have a large effect on a range of duties and as a result, on the moral burdens we have both as individuals and as citizens. As much as any sort of issue can, this one has the potential to reshape both juridical institutions and interpersonal duties.

We could engage the issues by matching the array of problems with known duties that could manage them, and, if necessary, initiate a kind of moral triage:

---

[5] The evidence is not in dispute. For a compelling presentation of the stakes, see Matthew Desmond's *Evicted: Poverty and Profit in the American City* (2016).

assign large-scale suffering to international aid organizations, anything that involves rights to states, provision of material and monetary support to voluntary organizations and individuals as bearers of duties of beneficence. Such a strategy assumes that we can read the nature of the moral problems off the surface suffering and dislocation. We might think we are facing a crisis of unmet welfare needs. And of course that's true. If we are decent, policy planning ensues for increasing the number of beds available to the homeless, providing easier access to food and medical services, and so on. The problem is more complicated if people flood across a border. We face hard questions of priorities and balancing. But what if there is more involved than welfare issues?

Suppose it emerged that the appropriate conceptualization of the problem involved an appeal to a *right to housing*, even what might be called a human right to housing. That would change how we assessed the significance of the need and evaluated responses. We would have to determine what is owed, and by whom, given the relocation of the moral claim. Solutions here would involve much more than further articulation and extension of our welfare duties as we understand them.

Because the right to housing or domicile seems as credible as any right putting pressure on the way we conceive of the system of duties, and since what could be involved in recognizing a right to housing might call for some rethinking all the way back to the basic institutions of RIGHT, it is a good trial case for assessing the dynamic potential of the habitat system.

In considering a possible right to housing, we need to know whether there's room for such a right in the system, and if so, what value or values support it. If it is not essentially about welfare, where is it located in the moral story? As part of the very idea of what property is for, and so tied to the conditions of free action? Might it instead emerge later, alongside access to work, as a component condition of citizenship? The answer will identify the *object* of the right and its related duties by identifying the moral value it serves. The *content*, the juridical and deliberative directives that would make recognition of the right real, will in part be specified by the place of the right in the system of duties (public, private, perfect, imperfect), and the conditions on choice and action that come from the intersection of its value with other elements in the system. And that will in turn tell us about *agent* of the right: who is responsible for it and its correlative duties. A significant part of the answer will point to duties that are public and institutional. But because the system's duties are interconnected, we should also anticipate that the existence of such a right will affect the duties individuals have towards each other.

Although the discussion that follows is hardly adequate to the problem it examines, I am hopeful it digs in deeply enough to give a provisional measure of the kind of moral work that is needed to address it.

10
A Right to Housing

10.1 Property, Hybrid Value, and Second Stage Questions

If there is a right to housing, it will affect property rights, broadly understood. On the Kantian view that I have been exploring, property is anchored in that part of public right that is tasked with securing agents' independence of choice and action (that is, independence from the arbitrary choices of other persons). That is its object. Public right begins its work here by ensuring that everyone has a defensible juridical claim on some place to be and on some material stuff for life and action. If there is to be an institution of *private* property that removes places and material stuff from general availability for exclusive use, then it must be justified by the value that supports public right, and the scope of private property would be limited by the conditions public right introduces. So not every place can be privately owned with rights of exclusion; there needs to be publicly accessible space for free movement; no one can have the juridical status of being propertyless.

In articulating the value of independence as it shapes the institutions of property, the natural emphasis is on freedom from physical interference (with one's body or one's material property). Equally consequential for property, however, is protecting the equal status in citizenship for all (no castes or classes with differential fundamental rights tied to property). It is not a conceptual claim that status values can be affected by the use of material things (think of Hume's golden age). But where there is the possibility of extended possession and exclusion in conditions of limited scarcity, status values can call for constraint on the structures of wealth accumulation and influence.[1] Positively, the conditions of citizenship require real opportunity to secure independence and so anchor entitlements to healthcare and education, among other moral goods. Since such entitlements are not welfare benefits, but provide material support for the actualization of innate right, their costs belong to the the existence conditions for possession.[2]

The result is a public institution shaped by the interpreted value of property that affects the content of terms and conditions for a wide array of social forms

---

[1] One might also find grounds in the freedom to express one's mind that there be access to public space, so limits from that quarter on what can be privately owned and controlled.

[2] Kant himself took the possession of a marketable skill (and not just raw labor)—the mark of independence from others—as the minimum condition for active citizenship. From a more modern perspective, that seems to get things backwards: active citizenship is itself a path to independence.

and practices, from inheritance, to rights of way, mineral and water rights, intellectual property, and so on. Further downstream are conditions on rightful exchange and private action, even gifts, still answerable to the value of freedom as independence. Given the structure and point of basic rights, however, the discretion allowed in their exercise concedes space for actions that conflict with the value of having that discretion. Such actions do not have moral impunity.[3] They are not conflicts with duty (like the giving in a bribe), but a conflict *in* duty: a failure to carry the value of a right into choices the right makes possible—an abuse or misuse of the discretion afforded by a right.[4] If extreme and institutionally reinforced, they can call the right (or its interpretation) into question.

There is another dimension to keep in mind as we think about housing, what it means, what we want from it (socially and personally), where it fits in the system of duties. It's at the convergence of different streams of articulated fundamental value. One might think this is an obviously good thing: more reasons imply more support. But the effect of overdetermination on content is not simply additive: there need be no gain in efficiency; the convergence may or may not create greater urgency; the right might look different in different contexts of application; there may be deliberative inconsistency in what the different sources of a right direct. How this all works out will require some amendment to the moral categories of value combination.

Even in nonmoral cases, a "two birds with one stone" outcome isn't necessarily a straightforward increase in efficiency. By arranging a trip to New York, you get to have a nice vacation and can arrange a visit to your elderly aunt. Both are things you value, though they needn't be on a par. Often one outcome is a bonus that rides on the other: perhaps if the vacation part of the plan falls through, the visit to the aunt is put off. Other times, both values are equal drivers: either will get you to New York. How this plays out affects New York sub-routines. In the bonus case you might say to your children "We are on vacation! And while we are here..." You would plan differently if you had both aims, making sure your vacation priorities left ample time for visiting your aunt. And on some scenarios, the aunt is the lens through which the visit to New York has value for you. Her availability determines what you'll do.

When more than one value or end is at the same time and non-accidentally integral to deliberation and action we can talk of *hybrid content*.

Hybrid content can affect action interpretation. Consider a parental birthday present. There's the desired benefit and the benefit coming from generous parental provision *or* as something owed. The parents can act for one to the exclusion of the other, or they can act for both. Which it is that they do in turn affects matters

---

[3] This limit to discretion was argued for in Chapter 3.
[4] It can be especially difficult to keep track of this when the felt value of an action points in a different direction (one acts for friendship, out of generosity, for the sake of self-expression).

of gratitude, possibly views about how others are to be treated, and it can have a range of effects on how the child regards what is to be done with the good received—what it's for, whether it is a burden, whether it can be passed on to others. It can be important that things be kept overtly separate (so as to avoid "contamination") or, conversely, it can be internal to fully realizing the value of two ends that they be pursued together. It can be an important source of confidence for the parent to have love and duty converge. A child might need the freedom of a purely loving act (something done spontaneously, even taking on some risk). Which content is active is not a matter of the parents adopting a motive or arranging their psychology, but may be about how they see the course of their acting extending over time: what counts as success in giving. It's your birthday and we sing songs and cut cake and act in other ways that will please you. Or, it's your birthday and we promised a song. Also a cake. It's not the same sequence.

We see something similar when means and ends come together in different ways. One can learn music theory while learning to play an instrument, or play by ear and learn theory later, or not at all. The different paths are not equivalent as means to "playing the piano." Not equivalent, but not necessarily one better than another. Which, if either, matters, may depend on a host of evolving contingencies. Needing to abandon performance ambitions for teaching, it may turn out that success came about in the wrong way. Sometimes in choosing a means one alters or settles on an end. Committed to taking public transportation tonight, I've (in effect) decided to have dinner with John and not Jim.

Now, if property lives in the intersection of multiple fundamental values, its deliberative import for action will be shaped by convergent hybrid content that reflects both the independence and equal standing of citizens as well as a variety of the personal and moral needs of agents. Not all elements of the hybrid are equal. A system of property relations may need to limit the freedom of use it values if it would generate an overt or de facto structure of differential civic rights. Likewise, the value to family of inherited wealth is not on a par with the social value of intergenerational equality.

Hybrid content also shapes descendent duties and permissions. Property rights are thought to give their holder permission to refuse to provide means even where there is a duty to help (that I possess some medicine that you need and I don't is thought not to weaken my entitlement to keep it). The conclusion is said to follow from the very idea of the right. We can resist that. It is a conclusion about *content* derived from an account of property rights focused on individual entitlement (on the liberty value of rights). Such a scheme prizes independence above other relevant values. If, by contrast, the institution of property is a vehicle to express and protect *both* independence and equal status, not just of the right holder but of all who are affected by the system, it is hardly clear that the *content* of property rights would have to prize a liberty value for the right-holder over other moral concerns. We shouldn't confuse the logic of the right (its Hohfeldian form) with its *content*. If property rights are a piece of a system whose *object* is a certain kind of moral environment or habitat, these rights, executed in the terms of permissions and entitlements, serve the common habitat purpose. If they do, that explains how the claims of others can imply a limit to right—and not as a limit from outside the well-formed right: derived from the hybrid value, some limits are an element of the content expressed through the right's logical form.[5]

The ideas of property in the different branches of liberal political thought are not free standing. They join a (morality apt) conception of human nature with an initial situation that calls for the institution of property. We have the Lockean idea of separate and equal loci of acquisition from the unowned commons for individual possession and use. There is Rousseau's account of "adroit usurpation" by the strong superseded by rectificatory acts of the general will. And then there is the Kantian idea of equal and independent persons with the end of realizing their separate and common rationality through practical activity, making and doing, that involves possession. It would be unlikely if such different ideas generated the same understanding of the rights associated with the idea of property. Not only are the starting points different, they have competing ideas of what property is for, and so of the content of duties and permissions that need to belong to ownership or use.

It's worth noting in passing that not all accounts of human nature will lend themselves to robust property rights. Suppose we had a starting point where the value of the independence of persons was more radical: through discipline and extremes of internality, one could achieve a kind of indifference to circumstances and so independence from the coercive control by others. A Stoic ideal, where independence as a value does not require that an agent be able to express herself in the world. And suppose further one found the equality of persons in their equal dependence on an alien power (as sinners in the hands of an angry God, perhaps).[6] Such a constricted idea of the value of a person (i.e., of the values that define it as a moral idea) will in turn call for limited duties and permissions, given the powers and possibilities taken to matter (e.g., securing external freedom won't get us more of what matters, nor will assuming innocent until proven guilty). In such a moral environment, there would be no need for robust property rights since there is no special value in the realization of our powers through the making or building that sustained possession makes possible. Wishing to make or improve something would show pride or weakness, of not exercising the power of

---

[5] The deliberative discretion that imperfect duties introduce extends this idea.

[6] There are circumstances in which relying on internality and renunciation might be the best we can do. To build from that fact would be like using the conditions of solitary confinement as a starting point for urban design.

withdrawal from need that is the chief mark of our humanity.[7] Insofar as equality was found in persons' relation to a judging and angry God, mitigating the effects of material inequality might seem to conflict with a divine ordering of things, and envy at others' good fortune a further proof of deficiency, or at least confusion about what counts as real harm. The implausibility of these assumptions highlights the more important implausibility of thinking the familiar ideas of property are independent of any such assumptions.

The Lockean tradition adds to its starting point the challenge of first ownership. We can ask why. It might be thought of as a piece of moral metaphysics, or a normative genesis story. It's also a posture of anxiety. Unless there is a possible (even quasi-) historical story that could make some original sequence of acquisitions and transfers legitimate, property rights are without foundation, mere convention, and if mere convention, then unstable, or vulnerable to radical critique. But why think that?[8] There is something truly extreme in the thought that an argument for an original *possibility* of legitimate ownership is needed, where the worry is not about injustice and exclusion (that's a later problem that might need fixing), but about our very title to live here, to not be guests, or just passing through—to be in the right in the thought that we are entitled to make the world our place. But notice, even if there were a good argument justifying the initial private acquisition of land (for withdrawing it from some prior moral state—the commons), the *content* of the right would not thereby be determined, not for the use of the land, and not for using the form of the land-right as the pattern for property in general. Any property rights story is answerable to the need for organizing relations between persons about things through the moral logic of a right to them. Looked at this way, that the first moral question about property is about the initial division and ownership of the land is an odd convention, suggesting it might be a mask for a different question—about who has a fundamental say about the distribution of the useful things of the world.[9] Since we don't need an origins story to address the content question, we can set this conjecture aside.

There are two distinct stages in Kant's moral account of property.[10] The first tells us the form or shape of property relations: mutual juridical obligations among persons with respect to things. The second stage articulates content: setting the

---

[7] In the moral habitat, by contrast, publicly secured equality mitigates the occurrence of resentment and envy, and for active agents, needing the help of others is not a mark of deficiency or inferiority: we recognize our common humanity as much in needing help as in providing it.

[8] The question of first ownership can be seen as a practical one, about the implementation of the idea: something taken up *after* the justificatory argument is place. This is how Kant regards it. An unintended consequence is to leave any actual system of property more vulnerable to challenge.

[9] In fairness to Locke, what's odd is the *convention*, not his question, raised to support a revolutionary political movement.

[10] Kant uses quasi-historical state of nature language, but he is clear that it is only a mode of presentation or stages of analysis.

terms that determine how having relations of that form will intersect with and affect other moral relations we have. The first stage answer is about the nature of the moral powers property introduces, including a structure of protections from interference. What counts as property accounts for much of what human beings can do. In order for humans to express their rationality in action, for their potential as makers and shapers to be realized, they require stable control over the materials they will work on. Walking in opposite directions on a country path, we can each go where we want by passing to the right (or left)—no rights are needed for use. Where common use isn't possible—suppose your family is walking three abreast in a ceremony while I am out for a morning stroll—I can step aside and cede the space as the balance of reasons directs. This deliberative pattern won't do for the need that property rights meet. If, today, I have begun a productive process—started construction, plowed the field, assembled the pieces—then I need it to be the case that tomorrow things are as I left them (as far as possible), even if in the meantime you could meet some need of yours by using my scaffold for something else, planting your crops in my plowed field, assembling my pieces into your sculpture. In the regions where the structure of right is introduced, deliberation is moved away from the interpersonal balance of reasons. But whether having a right to the scaffold or land or pieces allows me to begin and never finish without foregoing the claim in right to what I left off working on is a further matter. How that goes might depend on the scarcity of the resource involved. Or, concerning an invention, whether my patent blocks your creative use of some technology that I own but don't care to use for anything. Or, if I have finished harvesting, whether I can prohibit a gleaner's access to my fields?[11] These are *second stage* questions about content, the answers to which draw on the full set of hybrid values, including whatever value led, at the first stage, to property as a part of public right.

It is within the framework of a second stage question that I want to look at the moral idea for a right to housing: that is, the right to a secure and stable dwelling, with water and sanitation, access to resources, etc., now widely regarded as one of the basic human rights.[12] It is a right to have and control a material resource, so it is a property right, though not necessarily an ownership right.[13] As currently understood, the right goes well beyond protection of existing housing (where it

---

[11] English common law and many religious codes included gleaning as a kind of primitive welfare right; in some codes, there was even a requirement that farmers leave a corner of their field unharvested. In 1788, a decision in the House of Lords (*Steel v Houghton*) went against the rights of gleaners and declared that a property right offered its owner "absolute enjoyment" of the land. Such events move towards what might be called third stage questions in justice as developing economic and social interests intervene.

[12] Perhaps the original division of land was assumed to carry with it a place to house those who first worked it. There are many hidden assumptions in the just-so origins story.

[13] The right to housing can be satisfied by many legal relations to housing, including renting, so long as housing is affordable, access is non-discriminatory, and there is security of tenure.

might limit the scope of evictions or removals via eminent domain): its satisfaction conditions arguably require the creation of the very objects claimed as a matter of right. International rights documents describe the right to housing as essential for other rights, such as employment and education, as well as for the exercise of the liberties of speech and association.[14] It is at once an anchor of citizenship and a condition for having a personal life. It is a place for rest, the site of family relations (in some places, for friendship as well); it is a location or orientation in the social world, a possible site of work, and a space for personal expression.[15] So more than having a place to live, a roof over one's head. The needs this right meets are not an aspect of natural ethology, not like the hive to a bee or the den to a bear; it is an artifact of a social world in which the absence of modern sanitation and electricity is a form of social disability, not just a disadvantage.

The Kantian approach can tell us quite a bit about the deliberative import of a right to housing, and, by implication, about the way property rights can carry moral value out into the wider space of activities and relationships. Even if the right to housing cannot be realized outside a political scheme, or not in dire economic conditions, like the right to education it transcends any historically particular political organization or economy. It is in that sense what I earlier called a provisional human right (see section 6.4). In the moral habitat scheme, it functions almost like an a priori conceptual claim: where there is a scheme of RIGHT for persons, this must be one of them. So something in the account of fundamental value must lead to it.

The moral content, or deliberative import, of the right to housing is not in the same register as what it is individuals lack when they lack shelter. One question to be answered is in the space of public right, perhaps about whether "we" are obligated to build or supply housing (or just ensure fair access to what is there), about the possible use of rent control to stabilize tenancy, about zoning or other regulations to ensure the construction of affordable housing, and so forth. A second is a question about the kind of control persons should have over this resource. The first leads to practical political questions: how to meet the burden if housing is a basic right; the second is about what is involved in the idea of housing, is it or does it involve a right to a *home*? If it does, which I will assume and explain as we go on, it will add a dimension to the moral shape of a human life. And that

---

[14] The right to housing is among the human rights recognized in the Universal Declaration of Human Rights, elaborated in General Comment 4 to the International Covenant on Economic, Social and Cultural Rights: everyone has a human right not to be homeless. The matter of *domicile* in the world is separate: in a world carved up into nation-states, statelessness is a morally impossible condition.

[15] One of the many dehumanizing features of solitary confinement is denial of this limited expressive control of space. Illegal tent cities are often distinguished by lavish expression of personality, making the loss when they are abruptly bulldozed even more of an assault, involving the intentional destruction of both a place to be and of an identity created in a place.

will, in turn, affect the response we should make to persons in need of the resource we could provide.[16]

In adding to the idea of housing that it should be a home, we move from structures and services to conditions for active living. Guaranteeing some place to be each night only secures shelter. Not everyone wants to have a home. The point of the amplified right is to shift the default condition.

And what is a home? A home need not be a separate dwelling for each person or group of affiliated persons. It is a place where a person or family stably resides and can lead a reasonable, independent life (and so it must have access to work and schools, medical care, etc., as well as sanitation, running water, cooking fuel). Some forms of collective housing tread a fine line here. Refugee camps, for example, can provide elements of housing, but cannot meet the standards the right imposes and only tragically count for some as a home.[17]

If a person has a right not just to housing but housing that is or can be a home, then it is not a service or a mere possession for use, like a piano or car. The value that supports the right to a home is deeper, in a different register. Some have taken this to mean that if one has a home, one can defend it with a level of force that one couldn't use to protect one's piano: an extension of a supposed right of self-defense. A view of the home as like the carapace of the person, without which they are vulnerable, dependent, at the mercy of strangers. It's not a good argument, but it's not wrong to appeal to an idea of deeper value to explain the moral force of maintaining the integrity of a home.

What is wrong here is starting with the right to exclude as defining what the right to housing is. It begs the question, confusing the object with the moral content of the right. The object is to give individuals power or control over some space for living; however, what the content is—the nature and limits of the power—depends on further features of the moral social world. In some places, extending hospitality by taking in any stranger in need is one way the value of having a home is expressed. Elsewhere, the value is taken to lie precisely in being able to exclude others from one's private space without further justification (whether or not it is a nice or a kind or a decent thing to do). Neither convention indicates definitively what the right to housing is about. Both may mark the kinds of value the right can reflect. That is, either or both are candidate articulations of

---

[16] I am indebted throughout this discussion to Christopher Essert's "Property and Homelessness" (2016).

[17] There is arguably an obligation that adults with children have to accept housing offered even at the expense of valued ways of life (so not yet a home). Inducing the Maasai people in Kenya and Tanzania to "winter" in new villages built near to larger towns so that their children, especially their girls, can attend school, engages the shared obligation of Maasai elders to provide for the children, boys and girls, and the larger Kenyan and Tanzanian communities to support these fragile citizens. Here the children's rights have priority over a traditional migrant way of life. There may be other morally possible, even morally better arrangements, but among them is not a refusal to educate to literacy and numeracy or to accept the authority and responsibility of one or another of the states in which they reside.

the right. This may seem paradoxical—that there is a *right* without fixed content, even with possibly incompatible kinds of candidate content. The air of paradox dissipates once one sees that what is fixed is the role of the right in the system of public right. The idea that it's a fundamental right need not rule out contingency at the level of content, and this because content reflects hybrid value and hybrid value can direct different ways of managing a moral need. It is what we might expect as multiple values intersect in a complex social world. Of course not every well-intended argument for form or social configuration that is attempted is going to reach a morally possible outcome. The grasp of hybrid value might be wrong or incomplete, or the articulation of the right's second stage content deliberatively at odds with other central values in the system.

Without begging the question about who or how many live together, or how or whether they are related, it seems important to connect the values that require recognition of a right to housing—the interpreted values of independence and equal status—to our moral understanding of having a home. Is it a space of privacy and authority? Is it a base, a location, from which activity proceeds and to which one returns for rest and repair? What is it to think of a home as a castle (drawbridge and moat?)? In what ways does it matter if the home is the locus of a nuclear family or one is "at home" in an extended affiliative group (think of communes and family compounds). In answering these questions we fix moral content, not once and for all, but in possible configurations of the moral habitat.

While the questions we want to ask should capture the obvious moral tensions around the moral claims that come with having a home, not all questions are on the same moral footing. There are things an individual wants and cares about; there's the moral status of the home; there are the wants, cares, and moral demands of others to use what one has a right to. Maybe I am someone who wants to get on with my business; I resent interruptions and intrusions of all sorts. You like to text whenever you feel like it and are indignant when I don't respond right away. It is morally reasonable that I politely resist. But my resentment about interruption doesn't matter when accidents happen and I am the nearest helper— suppose someone is hurt in the space I call home. If facts about my personal situation continue to have deliberative significance, it's not enough to say that they are my preferences. Compare reasons that point to questions of safety, conflicts with other serious commitments, the easier availability of comparable resources.[18]

Now suppose there are a significant number of people who lack housing. And suppose the lack points to an unmet right to housing. Most think it is obvious that we are not required to make our homes the resource that resolves that deficit.

---

[18] Some of this is geographical. Where people live at great distances from one another, travelers in need landing on the doorstep can't be passed on. The question is very different in a dense urban environment. Living on the 24th floor of a high-rise, what would count as a traveler landing on your doorstep? Issues about neighbors in need will introduce different questions.

But why? The success of Airbnb suggests widespread willingness to live with strangers. If from among those who are well housed a solid fraction took in someone lacking housing, even for a fee, we would go a long way to solving the problem (or one aspect of it). Yet most of us think countervailing reasons of preference and privacy show this to be absurd. But is the moral content that justifies what most of us think about this anything more than an assertion of the bare right to exclude?

10.2 A Housing Story

In what follows, I want to explore a moral narrative that will highlight some elements of the right to housing *as it intersects with* something like the system of property and housing rights familiar in many Western liberal states. Inside the narrative, the right to housing affects how we think about the role of ownership in a moral community and how we understand the value and limits of private action. So, a study in hybrid value. The point of the narrative is methodological. That is, it's not a brief for a particular arrangement of rights and holdings, but rather an occasion to see how the system idea of duties affects both public and private obligations, given certain background assumptions. It remains open to challenge those assumptions as inadequate to moral need. In the meantime, it is of more than passing interest to see what happens when housing is not regarded as a welfare good and instead as a status entitlement.

Here is the moral narrative. I live in southern California where we are always waiting for The Big One. In 1994, the Northridge earthquake shook my neighborhood: some chimneys fell down; there was a fair amount of damage inside homes; the power was out for a couple of days. Where I live, people went outside, checked that no one was injured or in danger, and somewhat nervously we went about our business. Suppose it had been much worse. Suppose a wall of one of the houses to the south of me had collapsed, making it uninhabitable. I know the people who live there, but not well. We occasionally pick up each other's mail. We frequently say hello, but we are not friends; we have not visited in each other's homes. Yet if in the earthquake their wall came down, I'd take them in. I don't see that I'd have a choice (modulo my neighborhood not organizing itself in a different way to manage the crisis).

In a different and equally real California scenario, my neighbors to the south were about to lose their house to foreclosure. Although they were facing eviction, I don't see that I had to take them in (nor did the neighborhood need to act to manage the crisis). I'd say it wasn't my or our responsibility. But how could that be right?[19]

---

[19] The story may be different if the foreclosure is part of the subprime mortgage crisis; maybe not if the problem originates in a single unscrupulous lender. We will take up this thread in a moment.

The resource (my home), the need (my neighbor's loss of hers), and the action I might take to improve the situation (taking my neighbor in), look to be the same in both cases. What is different seems to be the cause of my neighbor's need for housing—earthquake versus financial disorder. That this might make the difference about what to do in response could seem surprising. After all, when I find you in the kitchen, bleeding, it doesn't matter whether you cut yourself or someone cut you, I should do what I can to staunch the flow.

Here are some pieces of an explanation. In the earthquake, something happens to all of us at once; for no apparent reason, some suffer more than others.[20] It's as if we wind up (temporarily) in a state of nature (the institutions of civil society are not working) and so with a common obligation of repair: for a time, and in a limited way, the moral work of civil society devolves on us. The foreclosure, by contrast, is a personal event in the life of my neighbor, a kind of financial disease. Unlike the earthquake, such an event does not change everyone's situation in a way that gives rise to a common obligation.

Now suppose that the foreclosure was the result of the sub-prime mortgage fiasco. It's not just that my neighbor was the victim of a wrongdoing, it is a wrongdoing that I might be said to benefit from—if not directly (in the increased value of my property), then indirectly, from my (likely passive) involvement in the system that protects such wrongful activity. Because as a citizen I share responsibility for a civil society that allows such activity to be lawful, as a citizen I (and my neighbors) have some obligations: in general, to act politically to reverse the injustice, and specifically, for the neighbor, to facilitate the work of civic repair to the extent that's possible. For example: If some of us work for agencies that can provide assistance with housing or refinancing, we might help the neighbors access these resources. Unlike the earthquake case, here the civil framework remains in place and it owns the moral work needed to remedy the injustice it has allowed. Of course in some sense we are civil society. However, *acting as civil society's agent*, it would be inappropriate to take myself to be obliged to lodge my neighbor in my house (as inappropriate as it would be to billet them with someone else).

I can, of course, out of beneficence, bail out my neighbors—lend money, help arrange temporary housing, or, indeed, invite them to stay with me while other arrangements are being made—but I need not, if I have good reason to withhold my hospitality.[21] Perhaps I have small children at home whose care would be upset, or I might be in the midst of completing an important work project that is taking up our spare room. Or, at the limit, I might not feel up to taking on the

---

[20] There's a connection here with the conditions that make insurance sensible.
[21] The reasoning here depends on the existence of public resources—that there is somewhere for them to stay, that the eviction will not land them on the street—so unfortunately, an idealization to make a point.

responsibility of housing strangers. Just as I may say no to taking care of a sick neighbor's child while she goes to work, even though I am home and could do it, so likewise I don't need to take my evicted neighbors in. The discretion I have in beneficence about when and how much I am to help, extends to my home. (The discretion has limits. If cell phone service is down and my neighbor needs to make an urgent call, I cannot appeal to these reasons as grounds for saying no to her using my landline.)

Where my neighbor's loss or threatened loss of her home is the result of personal misfortune, I could, out of compassion, decide to make my neighbor whole—loan or give her the funds to service her mortgage. I act as a surrogate for her impaired agency (at least in this regard). If, however, the loss or threat is the result of an injustice, I cannot repair that part. I can mitigate the consequences, but I don't touch the wrong: something was lost or threatened that should have been protected as a matter of right. This is not a weakness or limitation of beneficence; it's a duty with a different object. If your watch is stolen and I buy you a new watch, even the same watch, there still was a theft. With a new watch on your wrist, you remain fully entitled to file a complaint about the theft and the state has all its reasons to prosecute.

The pieces of explanation that we have been gathering come together around the fact that, considered morally, the value content of housing is realized in having a home of some sort, not in a mere dwelling-place (a hotel room might be that). It is an extension of one's person in civil society—it is our public address and location (a place where we can be reached even when we are not "at home"—something that is not true about a public shelter[22]). It is the public face of both our independence and our common status (as citizen, or at least legal resident[23]). That's why it is something to which persons are entitled as a right, and why the way housing is provided and protected matters so much. Private individuals coming together to build housing units can meet some persons' need for a place to live, but they don't thereby satisfy the entitlement of the right.[24] They can't make tenancy secure, independent of their good will (it's a bit like fostering).

This may seem odd. After all, if I buy housing for you surely I have put you in possession of a home in the morally relevant sense. Parents do this for their children. Habitat for Humanity builds affordable housing as a humanitarian service. How is there a problem here? A house is both a market object and a moral object. Civil society may be set up so that in gaining one you gain the

---

[22] That one can make special arrangements at a hotel to make it one's domicile proves rather than defeats the point. One has to make special arrangements.
[23] Some of the historical anxiety about itinerants and gypsies came from their being regarded as *unheimlich,* and so outside all law.
[24] There are comparable lessons in the early history of labor unions. A benevolent factory owner could decide to raise wages, but in so doing might make his business and his workers more vulnerable to market forces. Unionizing the workforce across an industry gave workers certain rights *and* protected them from the market vulnerability involved in being an outlier.

other—as an efficiency, perhaps, or as an avenue for securing a good without fixing the details of entry. It is an illusion, or a sign that something's gone wrong, if we come to think that what is being bought is the status that, in moral fact, only civil society can provide. The flip side of this is the entitlement: the ability to buy or to rent at arbitrary market rates should not be the *sine qua non* for access to housing sufficient to be a home.

All threats to property are a concern of public morality. Most items of property (watches, pianos) have only market and personal or use value; public morality's aim is to keep such property secure so that its value remains available to the owner. The distinctive role of housing in the civic life of persons gives public morality a different kind of interest—an existential interest. From the point of view of public morality it doesn't matter whether anyone has a piano or a watch. But *unhoused persons* do not have civic existence (lacking a permanent place of abode they typically cannot vote or access a range of civic services; children born in migrant camps may never have their birth registered). Public provision of decent housing is an answer to unwanted homelessness, whatever the source (my bad financial decisions should not deprive me of civic status). It's easy to say that it would be a civic failure to leave the protection of market-value property in private hands. It should be equally easy to say, given the special stake public morality has in the extension and protection of civic status, that it is a public responsibility, a demand of public morality, both to ensure that housing is available to those who lack it, and not to allow otherwise permissible private market activities to substantially burden a condition of public standing.[25]

In the earthquake case, those who remain housed are so by accident, not by entitlement. There is no right of exclusion to stand on, no normal discretion to exercise. The earthquake creates a situation where the assertion of one's independence (by insisting on a right to exclude from what one accidentally has) is at the expense of others' independence. It is something like the assertion of a right of exclusion at the only remaining water hole in the desert: the moral basis for a legitimate assertion, for standing on one's rights, is no longer present. The earthquake puts us (temporarily) outside the civil framework; civil society's moral work (temporarily) devolves on us. We have to take each other in.

On the other hand, because of what a home is, because of its role in creating civic identity, it can't be regarded as a resource that might, if needed, be made available for public purposes (say, by eminent domain or civic billeting). That is why, *so long as* a decent civil society is present, whether one takes others in or excludes them is at one's discretion.[26] In fact, even were a population willing, the

---

[25] That would mean, for example, that those whose housing came under threat from the sub-prime mortgage scandal were owed something as a matter of public morality—most reasonably a fair opportunity to hold onto their homes.

[26] And so, post earthquake, as things normalize and civil society's institutions again take hold, I do no wrong to begin reasserting claims of privacy and possession with respect to my house as my home.

solution to homelessness could not be for each of them to invite people in off the street. Much humanitarian aid can be provided, but homelessness is a problem in the sphere of civic justice.

Which duty one acts on makes a difference. Post earthquake, I may tell a friend whose kitchen was destroyed that he should just come for dinner whenever. In the spirit of relational beneficence, I invite him into my life. If the need around us is great, it activates humanitarian beneficence—*we* need to act; each of us inviting a friend or neighbor won't do—and we should set up a schedule to make sure all who are in need in the neighborhood are fed. But there are limits, temporal and substantive. Once the institutions of public right are back up, the primary responsibility reverts to them.

There are several lessons to draw from all this. Our property rights form a system (and are part of a larger system). Not all points in the system have the same deliberative import. The differences are not primarily matters of weight but of value. We have property rights because authoritative control over some resources is necessary for us to act freely, independently, and productively. Some things over which there are property or property-like rights—our homes, our bodies—have a special place in the system.[27] They are necessary for our having civic standing and for the exercise of our rights generally. This is the first reason why the right to housing is not just another property right: it is the form of our juridical abode. A second reason looks beyond that to housing as a material condition of our agency—a place where we are safe to think and speak, to experiment and be creative with forms of living and relationship, to nurture and be nurtured, and to rest. This is the idea of a home, one that requires (some) privacy, not a place where others can come and go as they have a need for the space and its resources. None of this is about having a large chunk of private property, or a castle. Where our home and our civic status are not fragile, we can safely take on a public role to manage an emergency. But it is also part of due care in taking such measures that they be temporary.[28]

In deliberation about what to do, the right to housing intersects differently with different levels of the moral system. It is a fundamental element of public morality, the basis not only of protections and permissions, but also, of an affirmative requirement, where necessary, of the public provision of housing that meets certain standards (standards set by the values the lie behind the right—independence, civic status—as articulated in current social conditions, so these days including high-speed Internet). The primary duties here fall directly on public institutions and indirectly on citizens through taxation and zoning regulations. Citizens will have

---

[27] There is no doubting that the body is protected by rights, but whether they are akin to property rights is an unresolved question. Hybrid value may play a role in sorting this out.

[28] There are also duties of due care on the other side—e.g., that rules and regulations not be such that beneficent or surrogate public responses to disasters disqualify victims from relief to which they would otherwise be entitled.

more direct duties with respect to this right if they have to take on public roles, as they may have to during emergencies. Further down the system, the public duty both shapes and in turn is completed by elements of private morality. It organizes a region of the content of beneficence: our helping should meet need with an eye to the juridical end of securing housing as a condition of independence. The public duty then also affects the social role of hospitality, constraining generosity. The object of the right (housing that can be a home) can be a source of possible pride and display; it is also a repository of memory. It elicits respect; it is not fungible. Persons may leave one home for another without a back-looking thought; but a public policy that routinely displaces them is a moral failure.

If a significant number of a state's citizens or residents lack access to stable housing—if they are homeless, or vulnerable to cycles of eviction and housing discrimination, or lack housing that is secure and not a threat to health—they are denied what they have a right to, both a human right, but also, descendently, the participatory right of civic membership. Strain on the prevailing system of property rights is not a compelling reason to forego meeting these moral needs. Meeting these needs is a condition of its justification as a system of exclusion.[29]

10.3 Housing Across Borders

Although the primary locus for rights claims about housing is the social order in which persons reside, the arguments behind the claims would seem to range more broadly to the conditions of refugees, unfree migrants, and stateless persons, who often lack not only housing but also shelter, and almost all the basic entitlements of civil status. While the lack of civil location and status is the most pressing moral need, the argument for housing sits alongside arguments for the provision of food, education for children, and healthcare, which don't depend on formal citizenship. If the right to housing straddles the two loci of moral need, it will support what looks like an extension of the humanitarian duty into the outer edges of the domain of RIGHT, and with that, mount a potential challenge from the ethical side to the normative independence of juridical entities, like states. There will be the same normative challenge if it is argued that this is a matter of rights, of provisional human right, that follows from the universal conditions of RIGHT itself. Like the problem of urban homelessness, the issues here go beyond theoretical interest, given the actual and sure to be increasingly large numbers of people at the borders of states making some kind of claim for domicile, for which housing (the first marker of civil status), not just shelter, is essential.

---

[29] Since education and healthcare are not only essential to having an effective human life but necessary for effective citizenship, failure to provide access to them *as a right* is delegitimizing as well.

The question is then this: If the right to housing is connected to innate right, essential to civic status, owed in the first instance to a society's members, who owes what to persons who, because of natural or political disaster, or because of some other pressing need to migrate, can no longer reside where they were and have no claim to be anywhere else? This is a question about the moral claims of *individuals* who present themselves at borders seeking not just entry or temporary asylum, but a new domicile.[30]

To answer this, the basic terms of the habitat theory have to be able to function outside of their initial zone of application. If they can be generative in this way, that's a piece of theory-confirming evidence. What follows is again only a sketch of a position. It is more than a little high-minded. My aim is to provide just enough context and detail to see an argument emerging.

The starting point is the moral idea that all persons have a claim in innate right to rightfully be somewhere, and so in a place where they can secure civic status—that is, a place where their innate right is given juridical and ethical shape.[31] Inside this are the interior claims of equality, independence, and, though indeterminate, rights to work, own property, and as I've been arguing, a right to housing that can function as a home.

If all persons have a claim in RIGHT to be somewhere, there must be some "we" who have a duty to meet the claim. In the circumstance of persons compelled to present themselves at borders, on either of the two most obvious arguments that bear on the question, it is all of us, ultimately, who have the duty, and those proximate to the need who are the first responders. If it's a duty to help, it belongs to humanitarian beneficence, and then ability, efficiency, and proximity pick out the first responders from all of us who are obligated. The other source of the duty to respond would be derived from the moral permission of states to have borders of exclusion.[32] Since, let's suppose, it's a permission necessary to secure the juridical conditions for free action, the moral costs of the permission set a duty that belongs to all who are citizens with respect to all persons. A border, be it a river, fence, or line on a map, is a moral artifice, and whether enforced or not,

---

[30] There are other related threats to civic status that involve injustices and immoralities too complex to address here. These include claims of stateless *peoples*—like the Rohingya, or the descendants of Palestinian refugees—who are prevented by various national actors from having citizenship anywhere. And claims of oppressed minority populations—like the Uyghur Muslims in China—who are deprived of their civil rights because they insist on maintaining a cultural identity.

[31] A further caveat: the discussion that follows does not bear directly on the moral status and claims of indigenous peoples. Prior questions have to be addressed: whether tribes and indigenous nations are states or proto-states, in a moral sense, and even if they are partly dispersed. The standing of members may depend on whether they have duties to provide recognition status, the extent of their right to exclude. All of which is immensely complicated by historical facts of usurped lands, treaty violations, and forced assimilation.

[32] It's not just individual withdrawals of resources from the commons that trigger duties. If some system of property is necessary, and some kind of separate juridical regime is necessary for it, then that limiting, which implicates everyone, carries the moral burden that it not negatively impact innate right.

those who are responsible for its management are our delegates. Their duties are hardly *to* the border, but reflect the values that permit it.

This sets a presumption that where refugees or stateless persons present themselves must count as their *moral* port of entry. They have a claim to a process of recognition: to documents and temporary housing; access to healthcare; legal advice; educational resources and play space for their children. And they have a claim that the nature and duration of their stay at the port of entry not amount to detention.

Not all seeking asylum are stateless. Most are not. Those who are victims of state sanctioned or state tolerated violence, political or social, are the customary seekers of asylum, and should count as stateless from a moral point of view. They arrive where they do as survivors from a moral shipwreck. This class will be vastly expanded if, as it now seems will happen, the effects of climate change render parts of Africa and Central America uninhabitable. That is, if parts of the earth become uninhabitable, that could change the status of existing political arrangements.[33] Those forced to leave have more than claims for hospitality on landing. They cannot be returned to their country of origin without disregard for their human rights (a state or place that fails to make provisional human rights real). Technically they are not stateless, but morally speaking, they have no place to reside.

It may at times be hard to distinguish this condition of unfree migration from that of "free" migrants—those who choose to leave their homes to seek better work, the prospect of economic and social stability for themselves and their families, opportunities for education, and so on. When free migrants move in large numbers, the result can be a humanitarian crisis at borders. Free migrants lack refugee standing in international law. The rationale seems to be that these are the "losers" in economic competition, and so a domestic problem. But there is often a morally significant back story to this form of migration in the various histories of colonialism, resource stripping, exploitative trade policies, and more. The division in the world between rich and poor states is not an accident. If this form of economic migration is an imputable effect of past and present injustices, that shifts the moral location of some of the problem. It supports a claim in international justice to remediate where possible and to regulate development so as not to make it unreasonable for people to reside where they live. People tend to prefer to stay in place if they can support themselves and live decently.[34] At a time of climate change or failure of international justice, however, it seems reasonable

---

[33] The arrangement of nation states is a product of all sorts of historical contingency. The *justification* for there being arrangements is, in a moral sense, timeless—that is, the way things are is dependent for its continuing legitimacy on its solving the problem of civic status for all persons.

[34] It is known that providing nutrition and antibiotics that reduce childhood mortality leads to having smaller families, which reduces risk of maternal mortality, and thereby improves economic prospects for households. Similar results are found with women's literacy, micro-grants, etc. The upshot in both cases is a decrease in both internal and external economic migration.

to act on the presumption that individuals and families who make the trek to borders are not simply choosing to change location.

For the stateless and other refugees who cross borders in search of asylum, because the pathways from state to state are not random—information about how to cross borders is shared social knowledge, and parts of the passage are often controlled by smugglers—in times of crisis large numbers of people will try to move across borders together. That will lead to ports of entry bearing a heavy burden. Where ports of entry are located is often a moral accident (the terminus of traditional migrant work routes or possible water-crossings). Even so, it is not unjust or unfair, not a reason to turn people away. The bar goes up for taking on more than is normally expected, as it does during a natural disaster.

If the burden at a port of entry is chronic because of failures elsewhere, then there is a ground of moral complaint about that, perhaps a claim for compensation. But it supports no entitlement based in the burden to refuse entry. A port of entry has a general claim on other states for resources to maintain the port's services *and* for a commitment to patriate a share of the stateless and asylum-seeking refugees.[35] None of that burden can be shifted to those who arrive: they need expend no extra effort to arrive at a more welcoming or less burdened haven.

In addition to the general (imperfect) duty to patriate, there are further duties not just to compensate but to anticipate—perhaps to build and support what might be called international ports of entry in the spirit of earlier experiments with free cities.[36] Depending on how one understands the moral baseline, this is a complex technical problem, not a moral one.

Rights of states to control their borders and determine the flow of immigrants do not ground a rebuttal to this line of argument. Refugees are not immigrants, or not yet. Whatever the moral argument for there being defensible borders, it isn't an authorization that can secure privilege and preference at the cost of fundamental rights claims. A state is not a family; "homeland" is a meme that often hides its history. If the material world is divided up in such a way that significant numbers have nowhere to be, that calls into question the legitimacy of the division. The ultimate responsibility for how the world is divided is all of ours, a moral fact not dissolved by the further fact that too few have had a say. That's enough for the very existence of stateless persons and refugees to be the

---

[35] A harder moral problem might be whether stateless persons are obligated to accept patriation in willing and safe host countries. Patriation is not in these terms a life sentence. It puts one in line to emigrate, were that desired. Historically, patriation has been directed at individuals and families, but not larger social groups (e.g., towns or sects). This may have to change. An island nation whose land is rendered uninhabitable as result of rising waters has some claim to remain a people. There is anxiety about internal division and resistance to assimilation in the host country. It is not obvious how to balance the different interests in community.

[36] At different times and for different reasons there was the Free City of Danzig, the Free Territory of Trieste, the Shanghai International Settlement, the Tangier International Zone, and a proposal for Jerusalem. Free cities often are part of end-of-war treaties. One of their functions is to manage culturally and ethnically diverse populations without their subordination to any of the previously warring countries.

responsibility of all persons, for their care and for their eventual access to membership in some functioning civil society. Ports of entry or refugee camps are vehicles of transition, not morally possible destinations or "temporary" settlements that last for years, even decades.

This is not an argument for free movement across borders. If a state is a kind of moral unit, a moral habitat, then it may have a limited carrying capacity that's a function of size, wealth, moral, and within reason, civic culture. Although I won't argue for the position here, it seems not out of court for a state to add such considerations to its reasons for regulating non-urgent immigration across its borders. It is, however, a condition of a state's moral legitimacy that it not use xenophobic or racist principles of exclusion; its entitlement to regard itself as a moral unit with morally defensible boundaries already requires that it abjure such considerations from its constituting and regulatory principles. In normal circumstances closing borders to immigrants is often historically incongruous, socially and economically foolish, and an unfortunate encouragement to mistakenly regard an historical entity as a moral form. Even so, there are grounds for some limits to free movement, as well as modest entitlement that those who would freely join adapt to the broad terms of the new country's moral culture, even if that involves some cost to cultural norms they would bring with them.[37]

These limits do not apply to refugees or the stateless. Their condition is one of unfree movement. Their choice to leave where they are is under duress, a response to the many forms of violence, oppression, or natural disaster to which they are subject. They are rendered actually or virtually stateless by their circumstances. They have been thrust into a morally impossible place. This gives them an existential moral claim to reside somewhere—not just to be in a new place, but to be on a path to some form of permanent legal residence with full civic rights, including the right to emigrate.[38] A state's preferences concerning immigration aren't the right kind of reasons to balance against their claims.

As befits a sketch of an argument, I will stop here. The purpose of this brief discussion was to provide evidence that the habitat idea, while inherently local in the way it sets terms for moral living, is not parochial in the scope of its duties, nor insulated by its boundaries from having the content of its domestic duties affected by what happens elsewhere.

---

[37] I offer arguments that support this position in "Morality Unbounded" (2008).

[38] I would argue for citizenship, but that's not necessary for the argument here. Civic rights include the right to stay, the right to travel and return, the right to vote, and access to the same welfare and opportunity resources afforded citizens. In the US, holders of Green Cards have many but not all civic rights—e.g., where locally authorized, they can vote in local but not federal elections (some local jurisdictions don't require US citizenship to vote).

11
Incompleteness and Moral Change

11.1 Moral Change and the Determinacy of Moral Requirement

It is time to return to the questions that launched the discussion of a right to housing. The aim of that discussion was to get a more detailed view of the habitat system of duties at work, and especially to mark the way complex moral features of the context of application can affect the content of rights and duties. Even something as fundamental as the right to property can have its deliberative articulation affected by intersecting moral values (represented by other rights and duties), yielding *hybrid* content for property-based duties and permissions as they are employed. In the other direction, the anchoring values for fundamental moral institutions can require a *second stage* of interpretation as new or differently understood arenas of application throw up questions that are not well accommodated by prevailing understanding of first principles. The moral problem of housing was the laboratory for investigating the dynamic interplay between application, value, and duty content.

The natural next step is to extend the discussion, canvassing in a more thorough way the effects of introducing a dynamic practice into the heart of an account of moral rights and duties. I am particularly interested in two areas of inquiry. One concerns the effect of content variation on the very idea of the determinacy of moral requirement. This includes questions about the objectivity of morals and about the scope of individual or agent responsibility. The second area is about responsibility *for* the content of the system of duties. Some change just happens. Other things ought to be made to happen. But by whom? I will be arguing that there is a neglected imperfect duty here: a duty to be an agent of moral change. Like many imperfect duties, it will not always be the case that there is anything a person is to do; but also like many imperfect duties, it is anchored in a kind of obligatory end, not now of reason itself, but of the moral habitat, that puts its members on notice that the system of duties is of their making and is their responsibility to manage. Attention, invention, and a practice of moral talking are the specific tools that need cultivation.

First, the issues around objectivity, starting with what is fixed, what dynamic. We've seen that some of the fixity we associate with duties is to be found in the higher reaches of the system (its northernmost parts). There we find the first value or values driving the system of duties, values that inform the different descending spheres of right and duty. In the moral habitat account, the values that undergird our free moral agency require real world expression in terms that will secure independence and equal public status. We require authority over our bodies and over some elements of the material world on and through which we can act in a human way. That authority is partly realized in the *form* of property rights. That's a constant. The *content* of property rights depends on what can be property (land and/or made things and/or ideas, but not oceans or persons) and on the kinds of need we have for that kind of authority. That's where we find the right to housing, an authority over something that counts as a home, a right whose satisfaction conditions will depend on contingent features of a moral social world. It is a system increasingly open to adjustment as one goes "south," with some hermeneutical pressure "north" on first principles as the system in application learns more about the order it is bringing about. The specification of the value of free moral agency is not in an abstract concept, but something that takes place over time as we seek to give form to a social world in which we might come to be free and equal moral persons.

We see the same sort of idea in the Rawlsian basic structure where first principles determine the shape and extent of some kind of property rights as part of the necessary institutional structure of a just society. Distributive questions will not be the only ones that need to be resolved. The values of the basic structure show up in downstream judgments about fair wages, exchange, and accumulation. And for that to happen in practice, not just in idea, other structures of the social order need to be in place, that educate and train persons to integrate these values into what they plan and do. There is no expectation of a static outcome. Problems will arise; people have new ideas; downstream laws and regulatory schemes come to be seen as inadequate to their task. It is by participating in this work that the value of the basic structure becomes more granular in the way people conduct their lives. It advances the way they understand what basic institutions like property are for and what it means for them to be equal persons engaged in a moral project of social cooperation.

The idea of the moral habitat is explicitly broader. Its dynamic system structure implies that the possibility of change and even experiment across the different strata of descendent duties should be part of normal moral understanding. That sets up a complicated balancing act. We obviously can't know in advance how far-reaching or how urgent change will have to be for institutions to remain consistent with first principles, *and* we know that persons require a great deal of stability in social practices as a condition of an everyday healthy moral life.

The challenges to institutional design are not a sign of imperfection in the system and need for change is not proof of past failure. Technology solves some problems and then creates others. Questions about integrating new phenomena into our moral space—how could any part of the genome (human or animal) be patentable property?—reach deeply into our understanding of what property is about. Other questions arise because of the moral impact on the world of the way we live. Responding to climate change may require a degree of shared responsibility among civic polities that forces a rethinking of what it means to have independent states.

Even if we can see why the political/juridical side of the moral project might have to be an ongoing site of progressive change, it is hard not to resist the idea of change in ground level interpersonal morality. We assume that answers to most content questions for duties of truthtelling and friendship, beneficence and promise, are known. We don't regard the relationship between promisor and promisee as a place where contingent institutional actions or stresses alter the content of our local obligations. And that's of course largely true.

In making a promise one enters a deliberative space that has a particular moral form. There is a commitment not to alter one's intention according to a running tally of the balance of reasons (and especially not those of bald self-interest). There is a ceding of authority from the promisor to the promisee about who gets to say what happens in the restricted domain of the promise. However, because a promise doesn't stand alone in the moral deliberative field, because the promissory relation interacts with other rights and duties, and with some welfare concerns, because what one can promise and even what can be done is not entirely up to the persons involved, the deliberative import of the *content* of the promise is not completely fixed by its form.[1]

So suppose, right after the earthquake, I promise to take in George and his family if their home turns out to have suffered significant damage. Having made the promise, when George's house is red-tagged, I have an obligation to take him in, even if it is considerably more inconvenient than I imagined when making the promise. Of course I can (and maybe must) decide not to do what I promised if in the meantime my house has suffered serious damage or a family member was severely injured and can't be moved from the extra bedroom. Suppose we think that doesn't amount to *breaking* the promise; perhaps we appeal to the implicit *ceteris paribus* clause for not keeping a promise.[2] Even if I may permissibly not do what I promised to do, that doesn't resolve my responsibility. I can't just walk away. Having promised, I should do what I can to help arrange other accommodation for George and his family. The unkept promise functions as a source of entanglement. I do not need to make George whole, morally or materially (as

---

[1] Some of this enters as conditions of a valid promise. But not all. The promissory duty is not fully accounted for by a rule; it is a deliberative norm with a system-sensitive value premise. See Seana Valentine Shiffrin, *Speech Matters* (2004).

[2] An appeal to a *ceteris paribus* clause is a holding action: it is a way of registering that in some unusual circumstances, perhaps yet to be set out, we might be justified in not keeping the promise. Working out what those circumstances are involves a mix of questions about possibility, permissibility, sacrifice, and conflict with other obligations.

I might have to if I broke my promise), but the fact of the promise creates the kind of agential connection to George that gives his continuing plight special weight in my deliberations going forward.

Things could unfold differently in a different institutional scenario. Suppose that because of actions taken swiftly by our city after the earthquake, there was now high quality temporary housing and easy access to support services for those whose homes were severely damaged. No FEMA trailers for us. Now I think it makes no sense to keep the promise, given the alternative that is markedly better in so many dimensions. Or, if that's too strong, it is at least a question whether the authority my promise cedes to George extends to obligating me to act irrationally, contrary to the very interests that the promise served. I am tempted to say that the change in civic circumstances *evacuates* the content of the promise.[3] It could be that because I stepped forward and made the promise to give George and his family a place to be (not anticipating that there would be a better alternative), or from ongoing reasons of neighborliness or civic friendship, that I should be among those who help George and his family with the move. But if so, it is not as a remedial residue of an unkept promise.

It will be said, correctly, that other considerations can keep the salience of the promise active. Perhaps our families have been close or I have a debt of gratitude; maybe George and his family have already had a rough experience with publicly provided housing in a different city and are skeptical and untrusting of the very institutional structures whose availability seem to evacuate the promise. Is there still a demand on me if George continues to want the help I promised to give? Multiple moral values are in play that don't arithmetically combine. There is the neighborliness and civic friendship that moved me to make the promise. There may be additional relational factors that heighten my beneficent concern. But the reasons that might evacuate the content of the promise are of a different order.

There is in this scene a convergence of duties and moral considerations that shift the valence of the elements entering the deliberative frame. On the interpersonal side there's the promise, as well as matters of friendship and beneficence that point to keeping George's preferences in the forefront of deliberative considerations. But given what George's need is—that it is a need for *housing*—due care widens the range of things we are responsible for as we consider acting on these duties. Specifically, we need to take care that in keeping a promise, or in acting beneficently, that we not neglect intersecting public moral values. This is not just the abiding concern that we not undermine others' independence. The

---

[3] That is—it doesn't make the promise go away, it just no longer has directive content. Here's a simpler case. Suppose after a traffic accident on an isolated road you promise to take care of me—splint my broken arm, stabilize my neck (you took a first-aid course in college). Then a medic shows up. You should now *not* do what you promised; it would make no sense. Here, in withholding your promise, you don't break the promise or even fail to keep it. However you might have an obligation to stay nearby in case further help is needed, the promise to provide care having involved you in the outcome.

choice to act privately in these circumstances might require that we also assume elements of a public role.[4] If it's not just a temporary bed we are offering, but, say, housing in the months until George's house is repaired, we would be taking some responsibility for such things as: where George's children will go to school; what his address will be; making sure that he not be disqualified from receiving public benefits later on by refusing them now. Some of these are things I can't do for George. And that's because in these circumstances private action may not be a morally adequate option given the mix of moral tasks to be managed.[5] This is not a conflict of public and private duties. The hybrid value in meeting the need for housing can take it out of reach of the best intentioned private moral action.[6]

Does this change the *content* of the promissory duty? Or just add more conditions? You can't keep the promise if what you would need to do is immoral, and now, you can't keep it if doing so would jeopardize someone's public status or rights. This misses the point. The deliberative import of the promissory obligation was always open to intersecting moral considerations. The system picture expands the range of what these might be.

If the moral space were constructed out of discrete lines of duty, bottoming out separately in duties of promise, friendship and civic standing, to pick three, it might well be hard to say which direction to take, which duties or values matter more. On the habitat system account, there is a unifying conception of the moral project that explains why, *if* the housing burden is of substantial duration, neither the preferences and relations of the parties, nor the promise, should determine the outcome. What started out as a straightforward promissory relation between persons finds more appropriate moral completion in the delegation of its work to available public institutions. This is not explained by a change in what a promise is as a form of obligating. It is about the range of content-affecting contingencies in which the life of the promissory obligation plays out that include the effects of other intersecting rights and duties and the availability of moral institutions. Habitat duties are open in this way.

A worry might arise here that the understanding of value and duty has segued towards a Kantian analogue of defeasible rule consequentialism. That is, that the

---

[4] There are simple instances of this. The postperson leaves a neighbor's mail in your box by mistake; as a kindness you bring it down the street. It's like other small kindnesses in that being easy to do, easier than alternatives, you just do it. But because its *mail*, part of a public service, you also should deliver it in a timely fashion. Waiting a couple of days if that were easier would still be kind, but it wouldn't be right; and you don't open it or keep track of the senders, even if those boundaries of privacy are not at issue between you and your neighbor.

[5] In seeing this we might wonder whether there is a burden of due care on the other side—e.g., that rules and regulations not be such that beneficent responses to disasters wind up disqualifying victims from relief to which they would otherwise be entitled. This reminds us that due care is not restricted to the province of one level of the system, but is called into play as elements of the moral system are put under pressure.

[6] A different city might make use of private resources, creating guarantees about residency, schooling, services. It's the securing of public status not the provision of public resources that matters.

role of a duty, in this case a promise, is to set a defeasible rule of action that can be (ought to be) set aside when a different course of action would better promote the content-setting value. It is worth being explicit about why that is not an accurate characterization of the argument. First, the underlying value articulated in the content of a duty is not scalar: the shift is not about getting more of the very thing the duty was to provide. Second, although rules of duty are defeasible, we need to keep separate the discretion of the imperfect duty (which is part of a duty's form) and the casuistry that comes with a perfect duty, when circumstances make it that adherence to the rule of the duty *defeats* its point and there is a nearby alternative that preserves it. The cases we looked at earlier were ones where the casuistry directed one *not to* do what the duty required (not tell the truth about that hat and say something blandly nice). But the casuistry could just as easily direct one to a different duty, were that option available. So, third, what one is to do depends on what is at issue where the duty applies. In the current example, the question was whether the final deliberatively salient moral value is presented by the fact of the promise, the preference of the promisee, or the moral demands around housing. The argument was that the challenge to civic status gives priority to meeting the housing need in a public way. It's a situationally adaptive division of moral labor, not a value-increasing departure from the rule of a duty.

The reason the right to housing is complex—not just a set of protections that make the home a moral castle—is because the moral significance of the ways persons dwell in a place is not merely a liberty or security concern. As we come to appreciate the ways family needs and privacy, access to work, education, electricity, water and sanitation have become necessary conditions of viable human living, the scope, distribution, and content of substantive property rights will be under pressure to make room for meeting the right to housing. Ethical duties that draw on the moral content of public right will then also evolve, affecting the requirements of intersecting lateral duties, and at times putting practical and hermeneutical pressure on the principles and values that support their content. Beneficence can overstep; friendship can become an obstacle; personal promises, an indulgence; demographic changes can alter our understanding of independence.

Where the circumstances are such that content from more than one duty is in play, the answer about what we have a duty to do (or a liberty to do) calls for more than inquiry into priority rules and procedures: we need to understand the way the moral structures at each level, vertically and horizontally, interact with each other in realizing the value that sets the system in motion. It makes a difference that the complex right to housing enters the system as a content requirement inside the system of property rights, not as a constraint on it. As a cynosure of input from independence and status values, the right becomes integral to what property is *for*. And that can call for the right to be foregrounded in some social and economic circumstances. The right to housing is not unique in this way. The right to work, and the duties that surround and support it, has come to have similar importance and complexity.[7]

The deliberative import of hybrid value isn't about simultaneously managing the effects of more than one source value; the co-presence of the values *in a context* can present a morally distinctive object. So, analytically, independence and status can be treated separately—one is primarily about authority over choice and action, the other about equality. But human persons are essentially embodied rational and social beings living in a finite material world. Deliberation about us as reasoners has to attend to how our movement in space and place affects where it is that we can speak freely with others. Determining what may be done to and with our bodies has to give special importance to the authority of our consenting speech. So even though independence and equality are separate marks of innate right, in application they come together in a hybrid value that presents the public side of humanity as an end it itself. The value elements are abstract and unchanging. The *form* of descendent duties is to provide protection in the regions of our practical and rational vulnerability. The *content* of the duties reflects both fixed and changing contexts of application in which the hybrid value is realized.

To accept that the content of our duties is in any way empirically responsive entails no form of moral relativism, no awkward vulnerability to hindsight criticism. It is more like site-specific engineering. The anticipated range of weather conditions, geological features, intended uses and available raw materials, all affect the design of bridges. Structural standards and tests have to be adjusted for these differences. Nonetheless, sensible design requires deliberative connection of the right sort to the underlying and invariant principles of mechanics that make the engineering sound and, barring the unforeseen, safe. As time goes on, the structural standards and the materials will improve. As may the conditions in which a span can be attempted. That doesn't mean we act inappropriately when we build according to the standards we have now, even as we know things will evolve. Why should it be otherwise with our duties?[8]

We should expect hard questions about when and how moral change takes place or when it is or should be obvious that prevailing conceptions of moral requirement are not just on the wrong side of something evolving but objectionable and contra-moral in what they require. In some cases we will want to say that

---

[7] As I have noted, this is one of the places where Kant seems to have drawn the wrong inference from actual social conditions. He might have had a point in thinking that there was something about the dependency conditions of day-laborers or the vulnerability of those without a stable home that posed a problem for active citizenship. But he missed the fact that in articulating and realizing a right to work and a right to housing a society can create the conditions for itself in which most all of its adult members can be active citizens.

[8] This fits well with a certain idea of constructivism in morals—that morality is the solution to a practical problem for human beings who regard themselves as free and equal. One could have the view that the elements of the problem are fixed and so therefore is the solution. But one needn't take that view.

the correct ground-level duty simply isn't the duty we thought we had—a ptolemaic problem where we did the right thing in a range of cases, but not from the right principle. And maybe this is what we should say in most cases where we come to reject one way of understanding what we are required to do for another. But not every case is like that. Sometimes a duty as we understand it is incomplete and so leaves us uncertain when we face unfamiliar or conflicted moral terrain. Other times it is our interpretation of the point or value of a duty that misleads, distorting a duty's casuistry. And there are cases where it becomes obvious that what was thought to be a duty was no moral requirement at all, or worse, something that ought not be done.

I think we should accept that there is in principle nothing that counts as a complete or ideal system of duties for human beings. That there is no theoretical point of view from which all that ought to be done is fully determinate or determinable. This is not an epistemic limit, not the result of a parochialism of the moral sensibility at any given time, not something an externalist or realist about moral value should resist. As we better understand the effects of interacting values and institutions, as we gain control of new resources and abilities, we will have new powers, and also new problems, new vulnerabilities. Some things can be managed as extensions of known duties. Some could have been anticipated through careful parsing of counterfactuals. But at the limit, the idea of moral practice should include the possibility that we can have new moral requirements, and that our grasp of familiar duties and responsibilities may need to expand or change to reflect new facts and new understandings.

Should we be concerned that this indeterminateness undermines claims of moral knowledge or the way we make third personal moral judgments across time? Even if certain parts of morality are constant—its forms and basic principles, some brute data about, for example, the wrongness of intentionally harming the innocent—in the less fixed downstream regions of duty wouldn't we worry about the possibility that even being well-intentioned and careful, we may turn out to have gotten something wrong? The possibility of blameless wrongdoing is still wrongdoing and reason not to sleep soundly.

We might try the engineering analogy again. We don't fault the thirteenth-century architects of Notre Dame Cathedral in Paris for using lead in the construction of its roof. They satisfied and surpassed prevailing architectural practices and (let's suppose) couldn't know of the dangers posed by using lead in roofing, and couldn't foresee the effects if there was ever a fire (especially the effects on Paris in the twenty-first century). Still, people were put in harm's way, and for generations were at risk. It is hard to see wrongdoing here, blameless or otherwise. However, in the face of the cathedral roof fire in April 2019 we can fault contemporary fire and building inspectors, contractors, and the French tolerance for smoking on the job. Wrongful negligence was widespread. And then there was a different kind of fault, beyond negligence, in the indefensible failure of Parisian authorities that April day to warn people living nearby of the toxic cloud from the fire and its aftermath. These authorities knew about the dangers of lead. None of this seems hard; accumulating changes in knowledge and circumstance do not interfere with the moral assessments we would make. If we are still worried, we need a harder case.

So let there have been a time when, like the dangerousness of lead roofs, the moral wrongness in discounting the full moral status of some portion of humankind wasn't part of available knowledge. I think we should always be skeptical about such just-so assumptions, but let's just suppose, since that's the way cases are often framed in discussions of relativism in judgment about historical wrongdoing and responsibility. In the well-known cases, we often find inconsistencies that defeat the just-so premise: that a sub-group is at once regarded as "like children" and yet tasked with the moral training of children is strong evidence for the bad faith of the belief.[9] But, is it inconceivable that there have been, or might come to be, cases where entities encountered in exploration or invention strike some as being moral entities while others, without bad faith, judge them as not enough like the normative human to warrant moral standing? Some argue that we are at or approaching such a point now as we enter a new age of artificial intelligence. Can machines be persons? Is being of human gametes, or being flesh and blood, essential to being a person in the moral sense? Or are these characteristics like being white or being male that signal prejudice or small-mindedness, and not a morally relevant distinction? As we broaden what counts as creativity and imagination, the question sharpens. It's not that we are trying to imagine machines being like us; we are trying to broaden the genus of who or what counts morally. Suppose we get it wrong. About race and gender the retroactive defense of not knowing better often doesn't impede negative judgment. What was done was wrong to do. Timelessly so. Ideology, false premises, corrupt reasoning, bad faith behavior. This may be what we will conclude about the treatment of animals. There was nothing we didn't know about their suffering, the complexity of their life forms, etc. Perhaps non-human animals can't be moral *agents*, but that won't speak to whether they are proper subjects of moral concern and duties. It seems harder (for some of us) to imagine the same trajectory in the AI case. But suppose the arguments became compelling, or the AI forms became sci-fi sophisticated, would those of us who lagged be culpably (or blamelessly) at fault? Whatever we think about that, it may not be the only important question to ask. In this perhaps fanciful future, what might be equally important is *when* the question of fault in judgment can arise. Whether there is an "owl of Minerva" problem here. Once common morality changes, ignorance no longer defeats fault. But what about *before*? What kind of responsibility do we have for getting ahead of the curve?

---

[9] In her *A Vindication of the Rights of Woman* (1792), Mary Wollstonecraft exploited the obviousness of this inconsistency to argue, somewhat ironically, for the necessity of women's education.

11.2 The Duty to Be an Agent of Moral Change

I take the assignment of responsibility to be an essential question for the habitat system—not about assignment of blame, but about moral responsibility in the pro-active sense. There is an imperfect duty here, and an important one. A dynamic system of duties is like the agents it is a system for: it does not develop well if it is left to its own devices. Change of the right sort requires agents of change. That is, persons who can see (or be brought to see) what needs to be done (or undone or changed); persons who can act for change intentionally, and from the right motive. It is hard to see how it could not be a duty for all of us to be such agents; though, since this system duty is imperfect, how we engage with it is not likely to be in just one way.

We don't ordinarily think of ourselves as having such a duty. And it is hard at first to say what such a duty could require of us. Obviously it can't be an individual's duty to change the moral system. And we can't have a duty to have only correct moral beliefs about the current state of things. Some may correctly see that *something* needs to change around marriage and family and work, access to education, housing, and power; few of us are in a position to see what might be done, or even where in the system change should begin. Most of us can (eventually) recognize what there was to do *after* things change. It can then seem incredible that it wasn't obvious (and some may realize that it was). That tells us something more about the limits of the moral imagination. Still, even if it's true that some forms of oppression are socially invisible until they begin to be dismantled, one doesn't need to fully reimagine family, child-rearing, work, and other potentially gender-burdened areas of social life to register moral problems. Harm, damage, frustration, depression, intimate violence, are too often in plain view.

There can be fault in not noticing: being blind to things, or too busy, or obtuse, or complacent, or scared. So a first thing that would follow from the imperfect duty to be an agent of moral change is that one work at being attentive and mindful of symptoms of moral distress across the system of duties. A very few are in positions to move common morality or to alter the institutions that frame it. Persons in high social impact roles can initiate inquiries and lawsuits, engage the public in discussion, reform the workings of intermediate institutions. At that level, the rest of us can participate in public fora, vote, and demonstrate. Part of the public recognition of our duty is that there be protected venues for testimony to be heard, not crowded out or threatened, securing freedom to vote and gather. But much of what this duty calls on us to do is within the boundary of everyday moral life.

Suppose someone becomes aware that their normal activity is framed by an institutionally encoded hierarchy that routinely undervalues the contribution of women and minorities. They should give voice to what they see. They can and should evaluate their own practice and the practices of the groups to which they belong and work to change what they can. They can also listen more effectively; share ideas and credit more generously; mentor informally. To be an agent of moral change also requires that we do these things *explicitly*, both as an act of respect and of remedy. It is one way of adding ground level action to the hermeneutic pressure on the governing principles of morally important social institutions.

We act explicitly when it is clear in the way we do what we are doing why we are doing it: what value or values we take our action to embody. We bring our motives to the surface. If a good friend asks for help with a work project, in setting aside what I am doing because I sense his urgency, I should say so, and that it matters that we are available to each other in this way. That allows a friend to make adjustments for my sake. If I can't do what's asked for I will explain and ask if I can do something else to help. Even for intimates who know and trust each other's motives, ongoing explicit conversation keeps the relationship vital. It's a failure of due care not to manage this dimension of our actions.

We don't always act explicitly, in this sense, and sometimes we shouldn't. Suppose I act for someone because no one else will. It's not a bad motive, but expressing it may convey hurtful information. Enabling a student in one's classroom to find their voice needn't carry an explanation of why one thinks they are silent, though there is value in being explicit about the importance of all students feeling safe and free to speak. But what if what tips (not makes) my choice about what to do is some advantage that my participation in a worthy project will bring me. Conveying my impurity of heart might make the group less effective even though my commitment to its work is honest. What one can do, even so, is make it explicit that one has the motivating aim to share ideas or become de facto partners in a common project communicates value and commitment. Being explicit in the relevant way is not the same as being fully transparent.

The claim is not that one needs to be explicit to facilitate change: one can act covertly or indirectly or through misdirection or even by making unnoticed choices that will have a salutary effect. But acting explicitly *is* part of the imperfect duty that situates us as agents of change working in concert with others. Simply: it is what lets others into the conversation. It is a democratic project, in the large and the small.

There is a separate treatise that belongs here, and that I cannot provide, about the special demands of the duty to be an agent of moral change that falls on those in rule-defined social roles—social worker, police officer, judge, legislator—where the principles that give the role special authority are descendent articulations of some region of fundamental moral value. The inhabitants of such roles have responsibility for explicitly maintaining consonance with justifying value as they see their actions affecting the moral environment. The rules defining a social role are tools that can be used well or poorly, left as they are found or sharpened. It is about how a social worker manages a threat of a client's eviction or how narrow the precedent is in a judicial decision. Sometimes providing information about the way a set of rules works can enable those on the receiving end to make the system work better. There is often local authority to make rule application more sensitive to presenting facts. Being explicit here can expand the boundaries of the role for others, making the singular action part of a process.

All individuals have the permanent moral tasks of self-improvement and of improving the circumstances in which they act. If our actions are co-opted, making us cooperators in embedded injustice, the moral demand that we act well, now blocked, can trigger our duties aggregately: to speak out, organize, and support those who are wronged. Among the dark powers of systematic injustice is to make it difficult to see and so to avoid complicity.[10] And when we cannot avoid benefiting from injustice, we may yet incur moral debts to provide or support remedy for its victims.

The duty to be an agent of moral change does not direct us to produce the outcome we think should be the case were the system better. Suppose I am able to provide you with something that both you and I know you deserve but failed to get, as a result of injustice—say, a salary differential between men and women doing the same job. Perhaps I devise a roundabout way to get you the extra money. My action lives in a morally fraught space. I cannot make my action stand for the values that move me. It is neither an act in justice nor one of beneficent concern. The remedial act of justice is not available to me: I don't set salaries. And the beneficent act cannot make it the case that you are treated fairly. And are you to be grateful for a gift in lieu of what you deserve, especially if the rationale for the transaction must remain a secret between us? It is sign of the injustice that I cannot make my good-promoting action explicit—a perverse-feeling reason not to do it.

Sometimes, when the cause of unfair treatment is systemic and some number of us are affected, we can confront indirect efforts to mitigate and together resist being bought off, treating the sub rosa offer as a Trojan gift horse. That is, something we can make explicit and a first step in promoting resistance. It is part of the duty's pragmatics that we are more effective as agents of change when we do not act alone.

Not all actions called for by the duty to be an agent of change are forward-looking. There is also the reciprocal *reactive* part of the moral enterprise—about

---

[10] Though the difficulty here can be exaggerated. The failure named by the "#Me Too" movement has to be seen in light of long-standing and widely reported practices. "Casting couch" exposés appeared in newspapers from the 1930s on, making no dent in the perks and perils of entertainment success. And for the rest of us, it became a trope or meme in film and comedy, which both acknowledged and reinforced the ongoing wrongdoing. For a helpful discussion of this history, see Ben Zimmer, "'Casting Couch': The Origins of a Pernicious Hollywood Cliché," *The Atlantic*. October 16, 2017.

remedy and repair. The two parts are not separate. Responses to wrongdoing and injustice should neither torpedo moral progress nor, in the name of progress, treat past injustice and its effects as something out of reach. Like childhood, the past remains with us, part of who and what we are. The task set by the imperfect duty is for us to both acknowledge and repair in a way that shows respect for how the past shapes the kind of future we can have.

As argued earlier (section 6.2), in the Kantian system of RIGHT, resistance and repair belong to—are a moral effect of—external wrongdoing; they block the completion of or otherwise annul the wrongful action. This is often a task for juridical institutions (thwarting an ongoing wrongdoing, imposing fines or punishment). Just as theft gives no title to stolen property, institutions shaped by discrimination have no inertial claim to stay in place. Insistence that it is unfair and straight up wrongful to frustrate expectations that are the progeny of unjust institutions amounts to the claim that there was no injustice, nothing to remedy (which is not to deny that the expectations can be a due care target of concern). Even if remedy or repair is practically impossible—the wrongful deed really has played out—the failure to have impeded its completion is itself wrongful and requires some remedial response; it can be symbolic. Juridical institutions have a duty, an imperfect duty, to redirect the moral arc of their own wrongful deeds.

When juridical institutions systematically over- or under-reach, they breach a duty to all citizens and members of the polity. Citizens and inhabitants of relevant juridical roles have a duty to respond. Protest and petition, civil disobedience, political works of art,[11] as well as legislative initiatives, judicial leniency, assignment of punitive damages, all belong to the juridical side of remedy and should be carried out under the banner of explicitness.

There can be creative constitutional initiatives introduced without departing from the juridical framework. What they are like often depends on the specifics of culture and accidents of persons in place: who can improvise new social forms that can perform the juridical task of impeding wrongful action, explicitly and openly.[12]

One prominent example of this is found in the ambition of the South African Truth and Reconciliation Commission (TRC). It was built to resonate with the heroic renunciation of personal remedy by Nelson Mandela, given public form through the improvisatory genius of Archbishop Tutu and the members of the TRC. Their accomplishment was to reimagine Mandela's singular act as an

---

[11] Bob Dylan's "Hurricane" is in this sense an influential act of citizen protest that sought redress for the racially compromised murder trial of Rubin Carter.

[12] It is a possibility, at the extreme, that a people finds itself in unjust circumstances beyond the power of extant institutions to remediate or change. Then a particular effort to create a moral habitat will have failed, and individuals are collectively obligated to set out again. Morally speaking, there is no other option. It bears repeating that it is methodologically unwise to start the investigation of duties of reform and repair with such extreme cases. Working out the dimensions of reform and repair that belong to the ordinary life of institutions comes first.

instance of juridical possibility going forward. As I understand the work of the TRC, individual victims of racial injustice were called on to forego the normal path of judicial redress for the crimes against them and to instead engage in a public process involving testimony, confrontation with perpetrators, and acceptance of amnesty for those who would admit what they did as wrongful, with the aim of thereby becoming co-founder-citizens of a new constitutional order rather than victims of an old (dis)order.[13] On a view of justice as a moral virtue and the law as a mere means, it is hard to see this as other than political instrumentalism: convincing those already victimized to suffer unremediated injustice in order to realize a greater good. The habitat system account makes a different sort of room for the TRC in giving individuals ultimate responsibility for the juridical condition (which is not the same as ultimate authority *within* that condition). That fact can support a revisionary casuistry, responsive both to the loss of authority of conventional institutions and to the aspiration to refound the state in a way that would not be possible were "justice" served. The project was a moral revolution from within.[14] For the TRC, it was essential that its terms and processes were made explicit over and over again in the meetings and encounters that were broadcast on the radio in the many regional languages. The public explicitness of the process, the granularity of its application, that it was unhurried (the TRC worked for seven years), together made out its argument to be serving justice in the larger sense though a demonstrably credible practice. That it was not wholly successful as a bridge to an effective juridical reinvention is more cautionary tale than disproof of its argument and aim.

Apart from participation in the discipline of the juridical order, most of us encounter moral repair and redress in the interpersonal world of wrongdoing: we betray trusts and secrets, break promises, fail to live up to the obligations of friendship, act disrespectfully, allow and exploit relations of subordination. (There is also often a moral insult running tandem to a juridical wrong.) In the normal course of things, we use the devices of apology and forgiveness to neutralize the insult of directed wrongdoing. We do work to restore relationships. Where there is material injury or loss, we may repair in kind. Much of this is unaffected by being embedded in a dynamic system of duties.

One region where the dynamic feature of the system makes a difference is in the appeal to external contributory factors to mitigate fault as we make excuses or apologize. Heavy traffic or bad weather made me late; stress at work, lack of sleep made me short-tempered. We still owe apology, but it is lightened by the absence

---

[13] The admission of personal wrongdoing *to the victim* (or survivor) in a formal public setting rescinded the false authority to act that had been a central element of the wrongdoing. It was not a requirement of apology.

[14] For a longer discussion of this idea, see my "Contingency in Obligation" (2007). See also, Lucy Allais, "Restorative Justice, Retributive Justice, and the South African Truth and Reconciliation Commission" (2011). Accounts of the TRC that emphasize forgiveness miss its grand moral ambition.

of insult in the failure—unless we should have anticipated the traffic or weather, not initiated a difficult conversation when we knew we were stressed or tired, etc. Things look different when the external factor belongs to our moral arrangements. Perhaps change is afoot and it has run ahead of us. Caught unawares it might only after the fact be generally obvious that there always were reasonable sensitivities ignored concerning the presentation of race and gender in the classroom; a department chair receives complaints that food ordered for a public reception is not suitable for vegans, though the presence of vegans in the group was well known; it becomes publicly noted that a workplace lacks accommodation for nursing mothers. The examples are all in the moral domain of negotiating power and recognition.

There are standards for acting well in such contexts. Not knowing, not being aware, not thinking enough, not taking extra steps, are marks of a failure to take due care when past practice is being explicitly and reasonably challenged. Especially where exercise of power and authority is encoded in what counts as ordinary, once a credible alert is sounded, there is a duty to make it safe to offer testimony and to treat it as carrying prima facie if defeasible warrant. When failure to attend to or acknowledge an explicit alert is negligent, duties of respect can require that we *not* mitigate apology and remedy by appeal to ignorance of emerging standards of behavior whose significance we missed: once ordinary patterns of behavior are explicitly challenged, we lose the option of arguing from innocence.

There is a change in this to the scope of our responsibility. While revision of common concept and practice is not something that usually happens quickly or that any one of us can bring about on their own, we shouldn't assume that our duties don't change until common concept and practice are reformed. We routinely commit to long-term projects that depend on others: building a house or a city; engaging in research that may take generations to complete. It would be bizarre to think that we couldn't have a duty to act better even when others' needed cooperation was not secured, or that it made no sense to begin a moral project whose realization outlasted our contributory agency. There are things that have to be done in stages.

In light of this, we should see ourselves cast as active participants in an ongoing collective and progressing moral project. There are things that *I* should do because *we* must do something. There are things that the aggregate of persons (the iterated each of us) must work to ensure that *we*, the collective, do. The measure of moral success and failure extend beyond short episodes of individual action. And if we can be in this way be responsible for what others do, we have heightened reason to make common cause with them.

Seeing myself as having a part to play in this common enterprise, I don't see myself as morality's Hercules, but rather as an ordinary person having a set of tasks, some sharply defined, some open in their directive to changing circumstances. In some contexts, acting explicitly moves a duty-directed action into the space of moral conversation. If it is appropriate—e.g., not intrusive, self-congratulatory, preachy—we might want to say why we chose to help *this* person, did more than seems required, or selected a less efficient but more inclusive means, in order to shift the horizon and content of moral action. We put ourselves in less comfortable moral spaces, take advice, offer testimony. We seek out others to act with us. The object isn't to make the moral enterprise grander or our moral lives more strenuous. Some of the problems we will encounter are like discovering that people with peanut allergy are at risk from things the rest of us unthinkingly do, and so we need to change how all of us do familiar things (no peanut anything in the school lunchbox). As with the peanut allergy, not everything that needs to be done can be in the charge of individuals to act well. Alerts and labeling and the ready availability of epi-pens are better served by public regulation and provision: a division of moral labor, not an outsourcing of moral work to an extra-moral agency.

The habitat system is not an arrangement to facilitate—either as modus vivendi or overlapping consensus—diverse conceptions of the good. As a deontological system, it is not in the business of dictating conceptions of the good for individuals or groups, but it is demanding about the coherence of ultimate ends and practices with the first principles and values of the system of duties. Satisfying the demand is a condition of moral conversation, the talking that makes us intelligible to one another.[15] It stands behind the requirement of acting explicitly. Contention about what is permissible, what forbidden, what required, is then about the application and ongoing articulation of the values that are expressed through the habitat's duties. Such disagreement is not a sign of failure or imperfection, but, in the familiar Millian sense, necessary for working out next steps and repairing errors. There's a lot that is not obvious about, e.g., the permissible reach of tax policy, public education, the scope of religious freedom, reproductive rights, and by extension, the shape of interpersonal ethics that fits into the resulting moral topography. But disagreement is not about whether the independence of persons or bodily integrity are first values; they necessarily are. What does not follow is that we see everything or understand everything about independence or about the body from where we stand now.

Suppose we are trying to work through the complexities of reproductive freedom in an intersectional context where for one population of women it means freedom to control when and if one becomes pregnant or has a child, while for another it is about the freedom to have and keep a child without

---

[15] Let me say two things to slow down objections. First, the coherence demand is at a high level of abstraction: rule of law values; respect for persons as equal and independent; etc. Second, lacking that, conversation may be possible, as may be mutual learning and persuasion, but not *moral conversation*, in the sense of cooperatively working out what shared value commitments require.

commitment to or dependence on a genetic father.[16] The complexity won't be resolved through conceptual analysis of reproductive freedom. Each group fixes on a threat to reproductive freedom, though where they see the impediment to their freedom is different because it is shaped by different oppressive social forms. In some parts of the real world this complexity reflects an underlying issue about race. Issues about bodily control tend to be more salient for middle-class white women, those about reproductive independence—getting to decide what a family is—tend to be more vivid to younger black women. Making contraception widely available supports one. Making aid to dependent children more liberal, as well as ceasing to demand child support from an unwilling and unwanted biological partner, supports the other. One group is criticized for being selfish, for wanting control over pregnancy, the other is also criticized for being selfish, but for wanting both a family and independence. The common element is control of women's lives through the imposition of reproductive constraints.

As we see what drives different positions, and what drives resistance to them, not only do we come to see that there is no real conflict between what differently situated women want, we extend our understanding of reproductive freedom as well as the sources and goals of structures of oppressive constraint. Seeing the moral task as determining *which* sets of relations should have the moral-juridical standing of a family not only mistakes the issue, it perpetuates a wrongful norm of reproductive freedom. The source value for this arena of juridical and ethical duties is rather about the preservation of the independence of persons in the context of shared living that may include children. The recognition project for what the juridical family is shouldn't foreclose arrangements that challenge (what should be) suspect norms.

To be clear. It is not part of the idea of the habitat system of duties to offer a complete account of the institutions and relations in a morally ideal world. It is the idea of an ongoing project, not an aspirational state. The old descriptive term "moral science" is useful: a body of practical knowledge that we expect to undergo revision, grow and progress. Some questions do get resolved, but even those answers may be reinterpreted, deepened, as the systematic aspects of the inquiry develop. New issues can come into view carrying a history that needs to be understood and often dismantled. Effectively recognizing the injustice of denying the vote to persons with past felony convictions involves a revision of ideas about what a crime is, so that "criminal" becomes a technical term and not a moral-juridical status assignment.[17] Now we can ask as a rhetorical question: How could "civil death" be an imputable effect of wrongdoing in a moral polity?

---

[16] I am drawing here on interviews reported in Kathryn Edin and Maria Kefalas, *Promises I Can Keep: Why Poor Women Put Motherhood Before Marriage* (2005).
[17] At least sixteen democratic countries allow felons to vote, even while in prison. These countries include Canada, Croatia, Czech Republic, Denmark, Finland, Ireland, Latvia, Lithuania, Macedonia, Serbia, Slovenia, Spain, South Africa, Sweden, Switzerland, and Ukraine. Jason Lemon, "Can Prisoners Vote in Other Countries," *Newsweek* (April 24, 2019).

In the space of moral pragmatics there are costs that need to be factored in that may delay or alter the trajectory of repair and remedy. They enter in the domain of due care where the aim is to secure viable and reasonably enduring solutions to past or emerging moral problems. The politics of change is often combative, introducing a corrosive rhetoric of victory and loss. Entrenched practices can be threatened, destabilizing normal patterns of action in ways that erode agents' confidence in their moral competence. Additions and subtractions to our responsibilities can have far-reaching and difficult consequences. There is a line to monitor between resistance that's appropriate grit in the system and that needs to be acknowledged and accommodated, and resistance as a strategy of forcing compromise, which may be unavoidable in practice, but should be regarded as an imposition, not a normal cost of doing moral business.

The meta-moral posture should be one of humility. We acknowledge epistemic limits and accept that morality has an historical and dynamic dimension. If it informs our reflection on change, it will affect how we assign responsibility and the burdens that come with correcting a moral course. Even the best of us, or especially the best of us, are made uneasy having to negotiate uncertain ground. It can be difficult to accept that a common practice is wrong and at the same time withhold judgments about wrong-*doing* and guilt, about ourselves and about others. The progressive thought is that we would come to have a different sense of what it is to hold ourselves accountable if we understood morality to be a dynamic system of duties rather than a rule-based set of imperatives, and the process of critical reflection and recalibration a part of normal moral life.

That the change that can belong to a moral system is both deliberate and deliberative is consequential. It leads to a practice of discussion and debate, responsive to interests, needs, and grievances, but carried out in terms that are drawn from and reflect first principles. Unlike the parrying of intuitions and cases that comes with stand-alone casuistical reasoning, there's a quasi-democratic feature to this kind of moral colloquy.

Not all moral adjustments are grand in scale. In response to an "epidemic" of school violence, it became policy in the Los Angeles Unified School District to involve the police in student misconduct—from truancy to "willful defiance" to petty theft and minor vandalism. Students were formally cited, often handcuffed and removed from school, and then later required to appear in court where, if found guilty, they entered the juvenile justice system. In 2014, the district adopted a new policy whereby students involved in such missteps would instead "be referred to counseling and administrative discipline rather than being sent to juvenile court."[18] The announced reasons for the new policy exhibit the marks of

---

[18] "Moving Past Zero Tolerance in Schools," *LA Times*, August 20, 2014, editorial.

good judgment (if it was a little late in coming).[19] Looking back, the rationale for "zero tolerance" in schools came to be regarded as the result of panic, underfunded support systems, and covert racism. The effect was to treat behaviors characteristic of adolescence as if they were criminal acts, and the miscreants, criminals. By suspending students and sending them to juvenile court, their access to further education and the possibility of graduation was impeded, and so the very future that is the moral mission of public education was defeated. Under the new policy, students committing minor infractions are to be referred to trained counselors, the district is hiring "restorative justice advisors," etc.—in short, there is a refocusing of the institution's necessary disciplinary role on education rather than on punishment.

This is a case where a collective exercise of moral judgment corrected a faulty decision to treat a class of socially inappropriate behaviors as violations of public right. The correction was not about rebalancing costs or interests. It instead reflected the understanding that, where possible, responsibility for children's development and correction should be with those who can engage with them personally and without threat to their civic status.

It is a natural extension for the duty of due care that it have the role of aligning the revision or adjustment of moral requirements with fundamental moral value *in context*. Whenever a change is made to a familiar regimen, we are, if we are wise, alert to unintended and unexpected effects. Think of a change in diet or exercise, moving to a new city or taking a new job. There are all the explicit changes that are part of our planning—making new arrangements for a child's after-school care, budgeting time and resources for the fact that we will be taking public transportation to work instead of driving, taking on maintenance responsibilities because we are living in a house rather than an apartment. No matter how well we plan and execute, we will not be altogether prepared. If we are wise, we cut ourselves (and others) some slack. We increase attentiveness to physical well-being. We anticipate emotional stress in our children and conflict with a partner. We act in more deliberate and forgiving ways. We would be negligent if we did not. Likewise, as we sincerely engage with a reforming of moral space, due care directs us to attend to the reasons new demands or permissions are hard to integrate into ordinary life and to watch that other values are not compromised in our focus on what is newly exposed and urgent. Again, explicitness in talk and action is a valuable tool.

As a secondary duty, it is a task of due care to ensure that acting as the revised or reformed content of a duty directs still serves the duty's object. Suppose the object of a duty is fair or equal treatment in hiring, and the reasonable revised content for applicant review has the unintended effect of excluding a population

---

[19] Although from the perspective of 2020, it looks prescient. The arc of the moral universe bends slowly.

of concern.[20] Perhaps there needs to be a rethinking of the relevant skill set or the effect on different populations of the shape and demands of a job. In the US, women medical students rarely elect to become surgeons.[21] That might change, surveys indicate, if surgery residencies didn't require twelve-hour shifts, or if the needs of nursing mothers were factored into surgical routine (as other biological needs are), or if there were on-site day care. The argument from the duty of due care is not that these would be good things to do whose costs have to be balanced against other goods, but that if the facts point to gendered impediments, it is morally required to take such steps to remove them.

The imperfect duty of due care marks out a kind of responsibility in moral space that calls for attention and response as things happen. We do not know in advance what due care will require. It can depend on what others do or need or know, on contingent or accidental occurrences, or on the realization that what is routine and thought adequate in some moral sphere is in the instance (or in general) insufficient. And it can depend on what we judge we are able to do, here and now. That's due care in its forward-looking mode. Where there is a morally significant deficit, and means to remedy it are available, choosing not to take that course because of discomfort or cost to some other favored project or just lack of resolve is negligent. That's due care in its assessing mode. There need be no match after the fact with what would have been sufficient beforehand.

Due care keeps one oriented to where one stands in the system of duties. A frustrated counselor in a public welfare office ought not use her own funds to help a needy client, even though the alternative is filling out forms, delay, and the possibility of no help forthcoming.[22] She should not do that any more than she should falsify records for a client's benefit. Efficiency and kindness don't erase the negligence involved in ignoring issues of fairness and public record-keeping. Both are mistakes about the nature of our moral powers. Merely doing good in a bad situation is not to be an agent of moral change.

Here we have an imperfect duty (due care) regulating another imperfect duty (to be an agent of moral change) that tasks us both as agents of the moral public sphere and in our interpersonal lives. For this to be possible, if we are to be responsible for what's done in our institutions' name, it is a condition of due care that the value that supports their authority be visible in the forms of regulation and direction they provide. This is a system truth about the moral content of the relationships we value and of the institutions on which our moral lives depend.

---

[20] As we have learned, considering prior work experience can sound fair unless it already skews against the targeted population. Likewise setting salaries in line with previous salary can seem fair yet compound pay inequity.

[21] Emma Goldberg, "When the Surgeon is a Mom," *NY Times*, December 20, 2019.

[22] It's not always wrong for a public employee to pay for things—teachers sometimes buy supplies that financially strained schools cannot afford. There is a moral failure here, but not of the teachers.

Conclusion
Method and Limits

Having come back around to the ineliminable role of the imperfect duty of due care both in the articulation of the habitat system's duties and for agents who would act well given their location in the system's moral space, we have reached a good place to take stock of what this account has aimed to accomplish and some of what remains to be done.

In the course of motivating, exhibiting, and applying the idea of a system of duties as a moral habitat, I have been treating morality as a subject for a kind of theory (the moral science idea) and as a set of practical concepts and duties that will be used by persons who are members of the habitat. Implicit in this method is the conviction that, a priori first principles notwithstanding, the two parts of the project have to be developed together. This is not a desideratum of theory construction in general. It arises here from the source materials of the account. Once we attend to both the content and object of duties, to the way they introduce value into moral deliberation, it becomes obvious that the theory side has to answer to how these materials are taken up by a community of persons in the various contexts in which they have to act. It is not a further feature of moral action that it is expressive, or that choices in one kind of moral context may be judged by their effects on another. Nor is the aspiration to find coherence between the values of public and interpersonal morality just an added hope. They are integral to the habitat project in its Kantian form.

While the habitat idea does not come from or depend on Kant's moral theory, I have found Kant's theory open to it in the sense that the habitat questions are liberating for rethinking the theory, and for eliciting its system resources that help clarify and extend the habitat idea. Exploiting this synergy has introduced some limits in the account. I have taken over Kantian first principles in their given form: that morality is a reason-based normative system, and that the notion of *innate right* is the appropriate starting point for a system of duties, rights, and obligations suited to the condition of human beings. I've offered no justification for doing this beyond exhibiting their usefulness in laying out a moral theory that is both objective in its fundamental principle and sensitive to the way things work out empirically in its application. For the purposes of this project, that seems sufficient. The test will be in extending the theory's range of application and sustaining the coherence of its defining values under the resulting hermeneutical pressures.

A sought-for advantage in putting this practical pressure on Kant's theory has been to open some new avenues of interpretation of the theory being used. This has led to some refinement of the supposed ambition of the *Groundwork* and a foregrounding of the *Doctrine of Right* in resolving the contents of duty question. The rethinking and reordering of key elements of Kant's moral theory is intended to stand on its own.

One important consequence of using the Kantian approach to lay out the habitat idea is a focus on the human being as a moral agent as the primary subject of moral theorizing. Human beings with certain capacities, separately and in groups, are the bearers of duties and obligations. What they are like, what duties and obligations have to be like for the system to be practical, then has to be central to the investigation. That does not seem to me a controversial assumption. Nor does what follows from it: that the tending of moral agents—their education, their psychological health and stability as persons with duties and obligations, the culture that supports them—should be among our duties. Nothing follows from this about who (or what?) the denizens of the moral habitat are whose interests are of moral concern. It hardly needs saying that "we" are not alone where we reside. And also that the creation of the moral habitat, like the building of houses and roads, the publishing of books, and the making of art, may burden other entities. This makes the answers to the questions that then arise—about the responsibilities that come with habitat construction—no less urgent, but needing to be framed in terms that are in touch with the moral situation of the stewards of any duties that might result. As one says at a point like this: these are issues that will have to wait for another occasion.

In the way the habitat system idea is developed, the primary sphere of duty and obligation is local, not global. It is important that there be sufficient commonality in practice and avenues of communication among persons that they can understand themselves to be making something together. We should expect morality to infuse custom, and so at the ground level to be different in different places. Etiquette, or what's left of it, used to be the most local part of morality. It is now probably the most context specific (from the protocols of international organizations to the rules of online web gaming). I have carried out the discussion using states or nations as the natural habitat form. It is still where we are and so a conceptual convenience. What matters to the account is locality, common law-making, and the possibility of constructive moral conversation among persons living together *and* across boundaries, not the Westphalian nation-state. Still, because it is where we are, it seemed important to take some trial steps in looking at the moral relations and duties that arise in managing borders while maintaining the values of the moral habitat system. I take it to be an advantage of the moral habitat idea that its empirical openness to issues and claims that perturb the givens of its system of duties well suits the increasing interdependence of the once separate regions of the world.[1]

Two notions that are alien to the history of deontological accounts of moral action—moral value and motive—have been central to the account given here. Labels don't matter, but the reasons for the sidelining of these two notions do. Many of the features associated with deontology have their source in a rejection of consequentialism as a form of moral reasoning coupled with an embrace of assumptions about value and motive that belong to the moral empiricism associated with David Hume. When what's good or of value is an object of desire, and motive is something like an active (action-producing) desire for some object, then it will follow that if the standard of rightness for action is not good-promoting, but some other kind of principle, then the motive from which one acts when one acts morally cannot be relevant to its rightness. But this conclusion is far from necessary. There's no reason morality can't be "good for" something without raising the specter of consequential moral arithmetic. And if it can, if there's a notion of value in play in morally correct action, then there's an important role for motive—a "that-which tracks value" in our deliberation, volition, and action—a structural element of our psychology that keeps us practically oriented to what morality requires of us. It's not the way we tend to think of motive; I've argued that we should (and noted, in passing, that Kant did). We might think of motive as the internal analogue of procedural value—arriving at the right result the right way.[2] It is also a notion of motive that is a better fit with psychological theories of human development that see the dynamic changes in the value-objects of affects as essential to the emergence of a healthy human self.[3]

This study began by focusing on a small set of imperfect duties that I thought put instructive pressure on some received views about the structure of moral theory—about wrongness, motive, and system. The path from those initial discussions to the Kantian habitat view and beyond hasn't been exactly straight, and it is far from complete. One thing that I hope has emerged is that imperfect duties are central, substantial parts of the moral terrain, sometimes demanding and often open-ended (rarely does meeting their demands have the finality of the promise kept or the debt paid). They often provide space for us to bring our critical and imaginative faculties to bear on a developing and dynamic moral system that can have both a creative and a regulatory role in our lives.

---

[1] On the general issue of the progressive capacity of some forms of national solidarity, I recommend Kymlicka (2015) and (2020).
[2] And, as I've noted several times along the way, in entities that don't have a psychology, the work of motive is often done through their value-tracking constitutive principles.
[3] Something I argue for in "Other to Self" (2018).

Bibliography

Allais, Lucy (2011), "Restorative Justice, Retributive Justice, and the South African Truth and Reconciliation Commission," *Philosophy and Public Affairs*, 39 (4): 331–363.

Ameriks, Karl (2000), *Kant and the Fate of Autonomy: Problems in the Appropriation of the Critical Philosophy*, Cambridge: Cambridge University Press.

Amrath, Sunial (2018), *Unruly Waters: How Rains, Rivers, Coasts and Seas have Shaped Asia's History*, New York: Basic Books.

Beitz, Charles (2009), *The Idea of Human Rights*, Oxford: Oxford University Press.

Bryson, Norman (1990), *Looking at the Overlooked*, London: Reaktion Books.

Card, Claudia (1988), "Gratitude and Obligation," *American Philosophical Quarterly*, xxv (2): 115–127.

Coates, Ta-Nehisi (2014), "The Case for Reparations," *The Atlantic*, May 2014.

Deligiorgi, Katerina (2012), *The Scope of Autonomy: Kant and the Morality of Freedom*, Oxford: Oxford University Press.

Derrida, Jacques (1999), "On the Gift," in John D. Caputo and Michael J. Scanlon (eds.), *God, the Gift, and Postmodernism*, Bloomington and Indianapolis: Indiana University Press.

Desmond, Matthew (2016), *Evicted: Poverty and Profit in the American City*, New York: Crown Books.

DeWitt, Janelle (2018), "Feeling and Inclination: Rationalizing the Animal Within," in Kelly Sorenson and Diane Williamson (eds.), Cambridge: Cambridge University Press, 67–87.

Edin, Kathryn and Maria Kefalas (2005), *Promises I Can Keep: Why Poor Women Put Motherhood Before Marriage*, Berkeley: University of California Press.

Engstrom, Stephen (2009), *The Form of Practical Knowledge: A Study of the Categorical Imperative*, Cambridge, MA: Harvard University Press.

Essert, Christopher (2016), "Property and Homelessness," *Philosophy and Public Affairs*, 44 (4): 266–295.

Feinberg, Joel (1970), "The Nature and Value of Rights," *Journal of Value Inquiry*, 4: 245–257.

Flikschuh, Katrin (2015), "Human Rights in Kantian Mode: A Sketch," in Rowan Cruft, S. Matthew Liao, and Massimo Renzo (eds.), *Philosophical Foundations of Human Rights*, Oxford: Oxford University Press, 653–670.

Flikschuh, Katrin (2020), "Innate Right in Kant" (unpublished).

Fricker, Miranda (2007), *Epistemic Injustice: Power and the Ethics of Knowing*, Oxford: Clarendon.

Guyer, Paul (2000), *Kant on Freedom, Law, and Happiness*, Cambridge: Cambridge University Press.

Guyer, Paul (2002), "Kant's Deductions of the Principles of Right," in Mark Timmons (ed.) *Kant's Metaphysics of Morals*, Oxford: Oxford University Press.

Henry, O. (1906), "The Gift of the Magi," in *The Four Million*, New York: McClure, Phillips & Co.

Herman, Barbara (2007), "Contingency in Obligation," in Herman, *Moral Literacy*, Cambridge, MA: Harvard University Press, 300–331.

Herman, Barbara (2008), "Morality Unbounded," *Philosophy and Public Affairs*, 36 (4): 323–358; reprinted in Herman (2022a) *Kantian Commitments*.
Herman, Barbara (2011), "The Difference that Ends Make," in Julian Wuerth (ed.) *Perfecting Virtue: Kantian Ethics and Virtue Ethics*, Cambridge: Cambridge University Press. Reprinted in Herman (2022a) *Kantian Commitments*.
Herman, Barbara (2018), "Other to Self: Finding Love on the Path to Moral Agency," Amherst Lectures in Philosophy. http://www.amherstlecture.org/lectures.html. Reprinted in Herman (2022a) *Kantian Commitments*.
Herman, Barbara (2022a), *Kantian Commitments,* Oxford: Oxford University Press.
Herman, Barbara (2022b), "Juridical Personality and the Moral Role of Juridical Obligation," in *Normativity and Agency: Themes from the Philosophy of Christine Korsgaard*, eds. Tamar Schapiro and Kyla Ebels Duggan, Oxford: Oxford University Press.
Honneth, Axel (1995), *The Struggle for Recognition: The Moral Grammar of Social Conflicts.* Trans. Joel Anderson, Cambridge: Polity Press.
Hill, Thomas E. (2002), *Human Welfare and Moral Worth*, Oxford: Clarendon.
Irwin, T. (2004), "Kantian Autonomy," in J. Hyman and H. Steward (eds.), *Agency and Action*, Cambridge: Cambridge University Press, 137–164.
Kleingeld, Pauline (2012), *Kant and Cosmopolitanism: The Philosophical Ideal of World Citizenship*, Cambridge: Cambridge University Press.
Korsgaard, Christine M. (2009), *Self-Constitution*, Oxford: Oxford University Press.
Kymlicka, Will (2015), "Solidarity in Diverse Societies: Beyond Neoliberal Multiculturalism and Welfare Chauvinism," *Comparative Migration Studies*, 3 (17): 1–19.
Kymlicka, Will (2020), "Why Human Rights are Not Enough," *New Statesman*, March 5, 2020, https://www.newstatesman.com/2020/03/why-human-rights-are-not-enough
Laurence, Ben (2014), "Juridical Laws as Moral Laws in Kant's *Doctrine of Right*," in George Pavlakos and Veronica Rodriguez Blanco (eds.), *Practical Normativity: Essays on Reasons and Intentions in Law and Practical Reason*, Cambridge: Cambridge University Press, 205–227.
Laurence, Ben (2018), "Kant on Strict Right," *Philosopher's Imprint*, 18: 1–22.
Maimonides, Moses (circa 1170) "Laws Concerning Gifts to the Poor," *Mishneh Torah*, 10 (7), https://www.sefaria.org/Mishneh_Torah,_Gifts_to_the_Poor
Mauss, Marcel (1925), *The Gift: The Form and Reason for Exchange in Archaic Societies*, W. D. Halls trans., New York City: W. W. Norton Co. (2000).
McAuliffe, K., P. Blake, N. Steinbeis, et al. (2017), "The Developmental Foundations of Human Fairness," *Nature Human Behavior*, 1 (0042): 1–9.
McConnell, Terrance (1993), *Gratitude*, Philadelphia: Temple University Press.
Murphy, Liam and Thomas Nagel (2002), *The Myth of Ownership*, Oxford: Oxford University Press.
O'Neil, Onora (1996), *Towards Justice and Virtue: A Constructivist Account of Practical Reasoning*, Cambridge: Cambridge University Press.
Parfit, Derek (2011), *On What Matters Volume I*, Oxford: Oxford University Press.
Pallikkathayil, Japa (2010), "Deriving Morality from Politics: Rethinking the Formula of Humanity," *Ethics*, 121: 116–147.
Piketty, Thomas (2020), *Capital and Ideology*, Cambridge, MA: Harvard University Press.
Pippin, Robert (2006), "Mine and Thine? The Kantian State," in Paul Guyer (ed.), *The Cambridge Companion to Kant and Modern Philosophy*, Cambridge: Cambridge University Press: 416–446.
Rawls, John (1971), *A Theory of Justice*, Cambridge, MA: Harvard University Press.

Rawls, John (2000), *Lectures on the History of Moral Philosophy,* Cambridge, MA: Harvard University Press.
Reath, Andrews (2006), *Agency and Autonomy in Kant's Moral Theory,* Oxford: Clarendon.
Richardson, Henry (2012), *Moral Entanglements: The Ancillary Care Obligations of Medical Researchers,* Oxford: Oxford University Press.
Ripstein, Arthur (2005), "In Extremis," *Ohio State Journal of Criminal Law,* 2 (2): 415–434.
Ripstein, Arthur (2009), *Force and Freedom: Kant's Legal and Political Philosophy,* Cambridge, MA: Harvard University Press.
Roush, Sherrilyn (2021), "Epistemic Injustice and the Principle of Total Evidence," (forthcoming).
Sager, Lawrence G. (2020), "Imperfect Constitutional Duties" (unpublished).
Sager, Lawrence G, and Nelson Tebbe (2022), "Discriminatory Permissions and Structural Injustice', *Minnesota Law Review.*
Scanlon, T. M. (1998), *What We Owe to Each Other,* Cambridge, MA: Harvard University Press.
Scanlon, T. M. (2008), *Moral Dimensions: Permissibility, Meaning, Blame,* Cambridge, MA: Harvard University Press.
Schapiro, Tamar (2001), "Three Conceptions of Action in Moral Theory," *Nous,* 35 (1): 93–117.
Shiffrin, Seana Valentine (2011), "Immoral, Conflicting and Redundant Promises," in R. Jay Wallace, Rahul Kumar, and Samuel Freeman (eds.), *Reasons and Recognition: Essays on the Philosophy of T. M. Scanlon,* Oxford: Oxford University Press, 155–178.
Shiffrin, Seana Valentine (2014), *Speech Matters: On Lying, Morality and the Law,* Princeton: Princeton University Press.
Shiffrin, Seana Valentine (2017), "The Moral Neglect of Negligence," in David Sobel, Peter Vallentyne, and Steve Wall (eds.), *Oxford Studies in Political Philosophy,* Oxford: Oxford University Press, 197–221.
Smit, Houston and Mark Timmons (2011), "The Moral Significance of Gratitude in Kant's Ethics", *The Southern Journal of Philosophy,* 49 (4): 295–320.
Stone, Martin and Rafeeq Hasan (2022), "What is Provisional Right?" *The Philosophical Review,* 131 (1).
Timmerman, Jens (2012), "Autonomy and Moral Regard for Ends," in Oliver Sensen (ed.), *Kant on Moral Autonomy,* Cambridge: Cambridge University Press, 212–224.
Uleman, Jennifer (2016), "No King and No Torture: Kant and Suicide and Law," *Kantian Review,* 21 (1): 77–100.
Varden, Helga (2020), *Sex, Love and Gender,* Oxford: Oxford University Press.
Walker, A. D. M. (1988), "Political Obligation and the Argument from Gratitude," *Philosophy and Public Affairs,* xvii (3): 191–211.
Weithman, Paul (2006), *Religion and the Obligations of Citizenship,* Cambridge: Cambridge University Press.
Westphal, Kenneth (2016), *How Hume & Kant Reconstruct Natural Law: Justifying Strict Objectivity without Debating Moral Realism,* Oxford: Clarendon Press.
Willaschek, Marcus (2002), "Which Imperatives for Right? On the Non-Prescriptive Character of Juridical Laws in Kant's *Metaphysics of Morals,*" in Mark Timmons (ed.) *Kant's Metaphysics of Morals,* Oxford: Oxford University Press.
Williams, Bernard (1973), "Morality and the Emotions," in Williams, *Problems of the Self,* Cambridge: Cambridge University Press, 207–229.
Williams, Bernard (2005), *In the Beginning Was the Deed,* Princeton: Princeton University Press.

Wollstonecraft, Mary (1792), *A Vindication of the Rights of Woman*. London (manuscript). Reprinted (2009) *Oxford World Classics*.

Wood, Allen W. (2011), "Kant and the Right to Lie Reviewed Essay: On a Supposed Right to Lie From Philanthropy, by Immanuel Kant," *Eidos Revista De Filosofia De La Universidad Del Norte*, 15: 96–117.

Wood, Allen W. (2014), *The Free Development of Each*, Oxford: Oxford University Press.

Zylberman, Ariel (2016), "The Public Form of Law: Kant on the Second-Personal Constitution of Freedom," *Kantian Review*, 21 (1): 101–126.

Index

For the benefit of digital users, indexed terms that span two pages (e.g., 52–53) may, on occasion, appear on only one of those pages.

abilities
    imperfect duties and 123–4, 128, 130
    status in right and 111–12
actions
    action under law, theory of 74
    agency and 69
    attitudes and 58
    authority and 69
    beneficence and 66, 148–9, 163
    imperfect duties and 132, 176
    law of obligation and 101
    moral status of 45, 103
    motives and 59–60, 64, 67–8
    naturalist accounts of 89–91
    obligations and 90–2
    perfect duties and 10, 107
    public institutions and 210
    reason and 65, 182
    right and 90
    supererogatory actions 40–1, 160–2
    values and 64–5
    wrongness and 48–9, 91–2, 123
agency
    actions and 69
    attitudes and 58–9
    beneficence and 139, 141–4
    deliberation and 69
    due care and 65–6
    duties and 58, 128–9
    essential conditions for 171, 202
    ethics and 110–11
    gratitude and 18–19, 18n.13
    happiness and 137, 143–4
    housing rights and 202
    innate right and 110–11
    juridical duties and 73, 173
    motives and 58, 62n.19, 65–6
    obligatory ends and 171–2
    property and 22–3
    rational agency 125–6, 128–30, 143–4, 171
    reason and 48–9, 69, 125–6, 128–30, 143–4, 171

    right and 22–3, 110–11, 171
    self and, duties to 130
    surrogate agency 18–19, 18n.13, 143–4
    values and 143–4, 208–9
agents of change. *See also* moral change
    backward-looking aspects of 219–20
    beneficence and 219
    collective moral project and 222–3
    constitutional initiatives and 220
    due care and 218, 222, 227
    duty to be 217–19
    explicitness required for 217–19
    imperfect duties and 208
    moral change and 217
    moral habitat and 208, 217, 220n.12, 222–3
    motives and 218
    obligatory ends and 208
    pragmatics and 219
    public institutions and 217–18, 220
    reciprocity and 219–20
    repair and 219–21
    responsibility and 217–19, 222
    rules and 218–19
    social roles and 218–19
    systemic injustice and 219
    values and 218–19
aid and assistance, duties of 109–10, 117, 122, 133–4, 148, 151n.35, 153–4, 153n.36, 155, 163, 164
appetites 60, 128–30, 132
Aristotle 29, 42n.32, 86n.7
artificial intelligence 216
asylum seekers 149, 204–6
attitudes 58–9
authority
    abuses of 38–9
    bias in 182
    coercive and 95
    deliberation and 214
    discretion and 46
    gift giving and 38–9
    housing rights and 208–9

authority (*cont.*)
  impermissibility and 46–7
  inequality and 182–3
  justice and 46–7
  limits of individual 42–3, 196–7
  moral habitat and 208–9, 220–1
  promising and 210
  property and 46–7, 208–9
  right and 45–7
  social practices and 182
  wrongness and 39, 45–7
autonomy 80–1, 84–5, 101, 147–8

beneficence, duty of
  actions and 66, 148–9, 163
  agency and 139, 141–4
  agents of change and 219
  aggregative duties and 145–6
  aid duties distinguished from 122
  aims of 134, 144
  casuistry and 141, 152
  complexity of 159
  consequentialism and 10–11
  deliberation and 134, 148–9, 160–1
  demandingness and 10–11, 122, 132–4, 140–1, 151, 160
  dependency on 142, 159–60, 162
  discretion and 141, 146, 152, 160–3
  due care and 141–2
  elder-care and 150
  ends vs. needs and 139
  entanglements and 139–40, 142–3, 146–8, 162
  Formula of humanity and 135–7
  Formula of universal law and 135
  gift giving and 31, 34–5
  good will and 16, 19
  gratitude and 15n.5, 23–4, 25–6, 142–3
  happiness and 133, 134–8, 141, 143–5, 152
  homelessness and 150
  housing rights and 199–200, 202–3
  humanitarian beneficence 145–54, 159–60, 202–3, 204–5
  imperfect duty and 138–9
  juridical duties and 148
  justice and 148–50, 152
  Kant's various arguments for 134–5
  moral habitat and 134, 155
  natural disasters and 147–50
  needs and 133–5, 139–43
  obligatory ends and 133–4, 136, 138–44, 152–3
  permitted partiality in 138–41
  property and 21–3, 79, 114, 155
  public institutions and 148–9, 159–60
  rational nature as end in itself, and 135–6, 143–4
  reciprocity and 135
  refugees and 149, 204–5
  as relational duty 141–2, 144–5, 147–52, 159–60, 163, 202
  remedial beneficence 148–9
  right and 23, 134–5, 148, 153–4
  scope of 133–5, 138–42, 145–8, 151, 163
  self-sacrifice distinguished from 161–2
  states and 148
  stranger helping and 145–6
  success conditions of 136, 158
  supererogatory actions and 160–1
  values and 26, 133, 134–6, 139–41, 144, 146–8, 152–3
blame 45n.40, 130, 166–7, 215–17
bodies 98, 105–7, 113–14, 130, 168, 202, 223
Brown v. Board of Education of Topeka (1952–1954) 62n.19

care, duty of. *See* due care, duty of
casuistry
  beneficence and 141, 152
  gratitude and 20–1, 26–7, 26n.27
  imperfect duties and 11
  knowledge and 164–5
  limits of 166–7
  moral change and 214–15
  non-ideality and 165–6
  obligations and 166
  perfect duties and 108, 164–6
  promising and 212–13
  property and 114
  responsibility and 166–7
  rules and 166–7
  social norms and 166–7
  special cases and 164–6
  suicide and 108
  values and 166–7
catastrophes 147–50, 198–9, 210–11
categorical imperative
  action-description problem of 80–1
  beneficence and 135, 137–8
  categorical imperative procedure, limits of 3–4, 73, 80–4
  derivation of duties and 80–1, 83–5
  empty formalism of 3–4, 80–1
  end in itself and 125–6
  good will and 82–3, 85, 90
  humanity formula of 81, 84–5, 125–6, 135, 137–8
  juridical duties and 101

kingdom of ends formula of 80–1, 83–4, 85
obligations and 101
obligatory ends and 124–6
overemphasis on 73
reasoning and 84
right and 101
universal law formula of 80–5
change. *See* moral change
children. *See also* family
citizens and 155–6
development of 18, 172
gratitude and 16
housing rights and 196n.17
illegitimate children 111n.62
innate right and 111n.62, 155–6, 156n.38
marriage of 115–16, 157
moral education of 156, 216
right and 115–16, 122–3
citizens
children and 155–6
citizenship 114n.72, 122–3, 184–5, 188, 189, 194–5, 203
civil death and 224
civil disobedience and 119
conditions of 189
creation of 153–4
imperfect juridical duties and 119, 122–3, 174–5
housing rights and 202–3
imperfect duties and 119
independence and 155–6, 189n.1
innate right and 119
juridical duties and 170–1, 174
non-citizens and 114–17
obligations and 101–2
property and 189, 191
reform seeking by 119
refugees and 149–50, 183
right to become 207n.38
state aid for 148
work rights and 214n.7
civil death 224
civil disobedience 119, 220
civil society 116–17, 171n.14, 199–202, 206–7
climate change 183–4, 187, 205–6, 209–10
coercion 86n.9, 95–6
communication, duties of. *See also* truthtelling, 52–3, 85–6, 101–2, 108–9, 127–8
conflict of duties 53, 78–9, 164
consequentialism 2–3, 10–11, 75–6, 212–13, 230
constitutional considerations 101–2, 112, 174, 176–7, 183–4, 220
constructivism 214n.8
content (moral content)

beneficence and 153
casuistry and 166–7
categorical imperative and 84–5
deliberation and 87
discretion and 84
due care and 53
gratitude and 26
guidance provided through 56
hybrid content (*see also* hybrid values) 190–2, 196–8, 208, 211–12, 214
imperfect duties and 11–12
juridical duties and 4, 113
moral habitat and 188, 214
motives and 62, 64, 176–7
obligations and 92
obligatory ends and 126
perfect duties and 107
promising and 210–12
property and 154, 189–90, 208–9
right and 86, 96, 104–5
contingency in duties 21–2, 57, 144–5, 150, 196–7
contractualism 114, 120–1
cosmopolitan right 116–17, 153n.36
Critique of Practical Reason (Kant) 82, 137

deliberation
beneficence and 134, 148–9, 160–1
content and 87
derivation of duties and 81
due care and 158–9, 226
duties and 57, 166–7
hybrid value and 214
housing rights and 190, 195–6
imperfect duties and 123–4, 128–31, 158–9
juridical duties and 174
moral habitat and 182
obligatory ends and 128–9, 131
perfect duties and 107
private morality and 28
promising and 210–12
property and 191, 193–4, 202–3, 208
public institutions and 174
rational agency and 30
right and 87–8, 193–4
rules and 33–4, 107–8
self and, duties to 129–30
system and 4, 182
values and 57, 214, 230
demandingness
beneficence and 10–11, 122, 132–4, 140–1, 151, 160
gratitude and 16, 132
imperfect duties and 9–11, 132

demandingness (*cont.*)
  limits on 9–10
  moral habitat and 132–3
  objections based on 132–3, 160
  relationships and 27
deontology 2–3, 76, 104–5, 223, 230
derivation of duties
  assumptions and 81
  categorical imperative and 80–1, 83–5
  deliberation and 81
  freedom and 93
  good will and 81
  happiness and 135n.14
  innate right and 97–8, 110, 114, 116, 127–8, 214
  juridical duties and 108–9, 112–13, 170–1
  moral habitat and 80, 86
  moral basic structure and 86
  problem of 80–1, 96
  public law and 81
  right and 85–9, 96–8
  willing and 83–5
Derrida, Jacques 36n.14
desires 59–60, 106, 124–5, 138
dignity 20n.17, 27, 74n.1, 120
disadvantaged groups 169, 174
discretion
  authority and 46
  beneficence and 141, 146, 152, 160–3
  content and 84
  due care and 47–8
  freedom and 38–9
  gift giving and 39–41, 47
  gratitude and 160–1
  housing rights and 199–200
  imperfect duties and 10–11, 132, 158, 176
  impermissibility and 38–9
  juridical duties and 172–4
  property and 189–90
  public institutions and 160
  right and 45–6
  as space of risk 38–9
  wrongness and 38–9, 45–6, 48–9
division of moral labor 73, 120–1, 158n.42, 212–13, 222–3
Doctrine of Right (Kant)
  assistance duties in 153n.36
  content in 229
  derivation of duties in 87, 93
  innate right in 96–7
  juridical duties in 81, 97–100
  persons moral condition in 89, 93
  right defined in 94
  state coercion in 86n.9, 94–5
  Universal Principle of Right in 85–6, 96
  vulnerability in 89
Doctrine of Virtue (Kant)
  assistance duties in 153n.36
  beneficence in 134–5, 138
  deliberation in 122, 131–2
  derivation of duties in 93, 123n.1
  duties to self in 108–9, 128–30
  humanity in 81, 85–6
  imperfect duties in 122–4, 128, 130–1, 158–9
  limits of imperfect duty in 138
  obligatory ends in 93, 123–6, 128–9, 131, 170–1
due care, duty of
  as accessory duty 53
  agency and 65–6
  agents of change and 218, 222, 227
  beneficence and 141–2
  caution in acting and 50n.1
  conflict of duties and 53
  content and 53
  contextual nature of 50–1, 54, 57, 65–6
  deliberation and 158–9, 226
  discretion and 47–8
  equality and 226–7
  failing conditions of 52–4
  forward-looking mode of 227
  guidance provided by 166
  housing rights and 202, 212n.5
  imperfect duties and 54, 131
  importance of 11, 50, 54
  knowledge and 227
  moral change and 226–7
  moral habitat and 227, 228
  motives and 47–8, 50–1, 54–9, 64–5, 166
  necessary means, distinction from 52–3
  negligence and 51–2
  other duties, relation to 50, 53–4, 53n.5, 227
  overview of 51–4
  perfect duties and 54
  pragmatics and 225
  promising and 56
  property and 113
  reasoning and 55–6, 65–6
  responsibility and 50–1, 227
  right and 54, 119–20
  role of 153, 166
  as secondary duty 50, 53
  standards, absence of 53–4
  success conditions of 158–9
  understudied nature of 11
  values and 50, 54–5, 57, 65, 166, 226–7

duties. *See also* derivation of duties; imperfect duties; perfect duties; *specific duties*
  acting according to 70
  acting from 69–70
  agency and 58, 128–9
  aggregative duties 145–6
  aims of 73–5, 77–8, 128–30
  atomistic conception of 165–6
  authority and 165
  citizens and 119, 122–3
  communicative aspect of 153, 158
  conflicts of 78–9, 164, 189–90
  deliberation and 57, 166–7
  exceptional cases and 165–7
  first principles for 4
  good will and 81
  independence and 80
  motives and 50–1, 54–9, 69–70, 176–7
  obligatory ends and 123–4, 127–8
  ordering of 159
  refugees and 117
  relations between 4, 9–10, 73
  rules and 56, 166–7
  values and 56–8, 65–6, 68–70, 74–5, 77–8, 165–7, 192–3
  vulnerability and 128–30, 166–7

education 156, 184–5, 195, 223, 225–6
elder care 139, 150, 185–6
end in itself
  beneficence and 135–6
  categorical imperative and 125–6
  happiness and 134–5, 143–4
  humanity and 81, 84–6
  obligatory ends and 124–6
  reasoning, rational nature and 84–5, 135–7, 143
ends. *See* obligatory ends
Engels, Friedrich 100n.35
entanglements 139–40, 142–3, 146–8, 162–3, 170, 181
equality. *See also* inequality
  due care and 226–7
  gratitude and 18–19, 26–8
  humanity and 96
  independence and 185, 214
  innate right and 214
  moral habitat and 5, 193n.8
  property and 189, 191–3
  public institutions and 159–60, 164
  status-equality 28
  values and 175, 185
ethical duties. *See* duties

etiquette 13–14, 50, 229–30
exceptions 10, 24n.24, 45n.38, 73, 108, 139, 165–8

family. *See also* children
  changes in social patterns of 157
  innate right and 99–100
  juridical family 157, 224
  moral habitat and 223–4
  obligations and 155–6
  as other than a purely private entity 99–100
  parental leave and 156–7
  parents and 155–6, 156n.38
  public education and 184–5
  reproductive freedom and 223–4
  right and 155–7
  states and 155–7
  vulnerability and 155–6
Feinberg, Joel 89n.13
formula of humanity 81, 84–5, 125–6, 135–8
freedom
  derivation of duties and 93
  discretion and 38–9
  gift giving and 39–40
  independence and 189–90
  innate right and 96–7, 111–12
  juridical duties and 102
  moral causality and 93
  moral habitat and 120–1, 183
  natural causality and 93
  property and 189–90
  reproductive freedom 175–6, 223–4
  right and 93–6, 130–1
  of speech 38–9, 97, 108–9, 112, 155–6
  states and 95, 100, 103
  of thought 189n.1
  values and 38–9
Fricker, Miranda 167n.6
friendship 27, 40–1, 65, 131–2, 157–9, 211–12, 221

general will 95n.24, 192
gift giving
  anonymous gifts 34n.9, 43
  anthropological accounts of 29, 36
  authority and 38–9
  beneficence and 31, 34–5
  burdens created by 41–2
  charitable gifts 43
  competition in 37n.20
  complexity of 35
  consent and 38
  discretion and 39–41, 47
  expectations surrounding 36

gift giving (*cont.*)
  expressive dimension of 35–6, 40
  friendship and 40–1
  giving too much 29–43, 46–7
  gratitude and 15, 18–19, 25n.25, 30, 33, 41–2
  impermissibility and 38–9
  importance of 11, 31
  inequality and 39–40, 42, 46–7, 49n.45
  moral dimensions of 34, 36–8, 43
  privacy and 37–8
  property and 32, 36–7, 39–40, 114
  public institutions and 36
  reciprocity and 31, 40
  refusal of the gift and 42
  relationships and 31–2, 35–41, 43, 46–7
  rules and 31, 33–4, 42–3, 47
  social practices and 32, 36, 42–3
  success conditions of 40, 158
  supererogatory actions and 40–1
  willing and 32–3
  wrongness and 29–34, 38–40, 46–7
"The Gift of the Magi" (O. Henry) 35n.12
good will
  acting from duty and 69–70
  beneficence and 16, 19
  categorical imperative and 82–3, 85, 90
  derivation of duties and 81
  gift giving and 40
  gratitude and 19–20, 33
  motives and 58–9
  right and 102, 111
gratitude, duty of
  acknowledgment and 15–16
  agency and 18–19, 18n.13
  beneficence and 15n.5, 23–7, 142–3
  casuistry and 20–1, 26–7, 26n.27
  children and 16
  debts of gratitude and 13–14, 16–17, 18n.11, 19–22, 19n.16, 22n.20, 24, 26–7
  definition of 13, 14n.2
  demandingness and 16, 132
  dependency and 19–20
  discretion and 160–1
  equality and 18, 26–8
  friendship and 27
  gift giving and 15, 18–19, 25n.25, 30, 33, 41–2
  good will and 19–20, 33
  imperfect duties and 13, 24–6, 131
  importance of 11, 24–5
  independence and 26–7
  inequality and 18–20
  injustice and 19
  justice account of 16–17, 20–1
  limits of 13n.1

  motives and 15n.6, 69
  obligatory ends and 123–4
  other duties, relation to 20–1, 26, 28, 79
  property and 21–4, 26, 28, 79
  public morality and 24, 28
  reciprocity and 13–15, 17
  relationships and 27
  right and 22–3
  scope of 13–15, 14nn.2,3, 17–19, 18n.12
  success conditions of 158
  surrogate agency as status threat and 18–19
  thanking and 16
  traditional view of 24n.23, 27
  values and 17, 26–8
Groundwork of the Metaphysics of Morals (Kant)
  agency in 110
  authority conditions of moral requirement in 85n.6
  beneficence in 134–5
  categorical imperative and formulas in 73, 80–5, 135–8
  content of duties in 229
  criticism of 82
  derivation of duties in 80–5, 90
  examples in 82–4
  good will in 81–4
  happiness in 137
  kingdom of ends in 83–4
  limited aims of 81–3, 85, 90
  maxims in 90
  moral appraisal in 82–3
  moral worth in 69
  obligatory ends in 125–6
  wrongful reasoning in 84
Guyer, Paul 102n.41

habitat. *See* moral habitat
happiness
  agency and 137, 143–4
  beneficence and 133–8, 141, 143–5, 152
  categorical imperative and 138
  derivation of duties and 135n.14
  end in itself and 134–5, 143–4
  obligatory ends and 123–4, 126–7, 138, 140
  of others 123–7, 137–8, 170–1
  rational nature and 136–8, 143–4
  self and, duties to 130
healthcare 109–10, 159, 174, 176–7, 184, 189
helping. *See* beneficence
hermeneutics 3, 76–7, 208–9, 213, 217–18, 228–9
highest good 78n.3
homelessness

INDEX 241

beneficence and 150
discrimination and 150
housing rights and 188
moral problems associated with 187
moral triage and 187–8
needs and 150
negative effects of 187
as not a morally possible condition 187
welfare issues and 187–8
housing rights
 agency and 202
 basis of 188
 beneficence and 199–200, 202–3
 children and 196n.17
 citizens and 202–3
 civil society and 201–2, 204
 complexity of 213–14
 definition of 194–5
 deliberation and 190, 195–6
 discretion and 199–200
 due care and 202, 212n.5
 as entitlements 198, 200–1
 exclusion rights and 196–7, 201
 home in, moral status of 196–7
 homelessness and 188
 imperfect duties and 3
 independence and 194–5, 202–3
 innate right and 204
 international recognition of 194–5
 moral habitat and 181, 188, 195, 212
 natural disasters and 198–9
 needs for 194–5, 197–8
 practical questions of 195–6
 promising and 210–12
 property and 3, 189, 201, 203, 208–9, 213–14
 public institutions and 200–3
 public morality and 200–3
 refugees and 188, 196, 203–4
 responsibility and 198–9
 right and 188, 194–7, 203
 satisfaction of 194n.13
 stateless persons and 204–5
 values and 190, 196–8, 200, 208–9, 211–14
 vulnerability and 203
humanitarian beneficence 145–54, 159–60, 202–5
humanity
 definition of 96
 end in itself and 81, 84–6
 equality and 96
 humanity formula 81, 84–5, 96, 125–6, 135, 137–8
 moral law and 96
 right and 96, 153–4

human rights 114–17, 205
Hume, David 59n.14, 60n.15, 118, 189, 230
humility 183, 225
hybrid values 190–2, 196–8, 208, 211–12, 214

imperfect duties. See also *specific imperfect duties*
 agents of change and 208
 choice afforded by 9, 25–6
 citizens and 119
 communicative function of 158–9
 definition of 1, 24–6
 deliberation and 123–4, 158–9
 demandingness and 9–11, 132
 discretion and 10–11, 132, 158, 176
 distinguishing features of 25–6
 gratitude and 13, 24–6, 131
 guidance provided by 1, 68–9
 importance of 1, 9–11, 122–3, 130–2, 157–8, 230
 innate right and 2, 109–10
 juridical imperfect duties 122–3, 173, 176
 objections to 9–10
 obligatory ends and 122–4, 127–8, 130–2
 perfect duties, relation to 1, 5, 10, 109, 159
 public institutions and 112n.65, 122–3, 164
 responsibility and 9–10, 164–5, 176
 right and 88, 119–20, 122–3
 scope of 9–10, 50, 68–9
 success conditions for 131, 175–6
 typical theories on 10–11
 values and 1, 132, 157–8, 164–5
 vulnerability and 130
 wrongness and 45
impermissibility
 authority and 46–7
 context insensitivity of 44–5
 definition of 44–5
 discretion and 38–9
 doing too much and 29–30
 exceptions and 45n.38
 gift giving and 38
 innate right and 2
 moral policing and 45
 not impermissible but wrong 29, 39, 43–5
 permissibility and 45
 wrongness and 1, 29, 39n.25, 40n.26, 43–5, 48–9
independence
 agency and 103
 citizens and 155–6, 189n.1
 duties and 80
 equality and 185, 214
 freedom and 189–90
 gratitude and 26–7

independence (cont.)
  housing rights and 197, 202–3
  innate right and 113, 116
  moral habitat account and 208–9
  property and 24, 26, 189, 191–3, 201
  right and 87, 93–4, 96, 112
  self-defense and 103
  values and 26–7, 185, 189, 197, 213–14
inequality. *See also* equality
  authority and 182–3
  economic inequality 182, 192–3
  gift giving and 39–40, 42, 46–7, 49n.45
  global inequality 151n.35
  gratitude and 18–20
  moral habitat and 116–17
  property and 21–2
  public morality and 23–4
  stateless persons and 205–6
  wrongness and 40
ingratitude 13–14, 20, 37–8
injustice 19, 150, 164, 174–5, 183–4, 219
innate right. *See also* right
  abilities and 111–12
  agency and 110–11
  application of 110
  authorizations of 96–8, 111
  bodies and 98, 105–6, 110
  child marriage and 115–16
  children and 111n.61, 155–6, 156n.38
  citizens and 119
  civic status and 204
  communication and 111–12
  derivation of duties and 97–8, 110, 114, 116, 127–8, 214
  domestic unions and 99–100
  equality and 214
  family and 99–100
  freedom and 96–7, 111–12
  housing rights and 204
  imperfect duties and 2
  independence and 113, 116
  juridical duties and 97, 99–100, 104–5, 108–9, 170–1, 176
  moral habitat and 100–1, 110, 116–18, 120–1, 228–9
  non-citizens and 114–17
  obligations and 112, 118–19
  perfect duties and 104–5, 107–9
  property and 2, 98–9, 105, 109–10, 113, 153–4, 204n.32
  provisional universal rights and 114–18, 120–1
  refugees and 117, 204
  states and 100–1, 114n.71, 117–18
  values and 113, 155, 214

intellectual property 108–9, 189–90
intentions. *See* motives

juridical duties
  actions and 101
  agency and 73, 100, 171
  articulated juridical duties 113
  beneficence and 148
  categorical imperative and 101
  citizens and 170–1, 174
  cultural variation and 110n.58
  derivation of duties and 108–9, 112–13, 170–1
  discretion and 172–4
  ethical duties and 73, 104–5, 107–8, 168
  exceptions to 168
  freedom and 102
  imperfect duties and 122–3, 172
  innate right and 97, 99–100, 104–5, 108–9, 170–1, 176
  juridical conditions and 98–9, 112–16, 118–20, 204–5, 220–1
  juridical imperfect duties 122–3, 173, 176–7
  juridical institutions 85–7, 157, 164, 174, 220
  motives and 101, 171
  obedience to law and 183
  obligations and 78n.4, 101–2, 118–19
  obligatory ends and 170–2
  perfect duties and 107–9
  powers and 93–6, 100, 153–4
  property and 109–10, 153–4
  public institutions and 171, 174
  responsibility and 168–9
  self-defense and 4, 103–4
  structural injustice and 174–5
  system of 97
  values and 100–2, 168, 171–4, 176
justice
  authority and 46–7
  beneficence and 148–50, 152
  distributive justice 46–7
  gratitude and 16–17, 20–1
  historical context and 149
  moral habitat and 150
  moral personality and 2–3
  needs and 149
  provisional universal rights and 149
  refugees and 149
  reparative justice 153n.36
  structural injustice 150, 174–5, 219

Kantian ethics
  agent-centered nature of 78
  aims of 77–8
  animals and 76

collectivity problems and 76
conflicts of duty and 78-9
deliberation and 79
derivation of duties problem in 80
difficulty of interpreting 5n.4
hermeneutics and 76-7
highest good and 78n.3
housing rights and 3
moral theory and 76-8
motives and acting from duty in 69
need for new approach to 3-5
reasoning agents and 48-9, 135
revision of 1-3, 2n.1, 73
second nature and 78
standard objections to 73, 76, 110, 163
system of duties and 78-9
values and 73, 77-9
kingdom of ends formula 80-1, 83-5

Laurence, Ben 102n.42
Lectures on Ethics (Kant) 4
Lockean approach to property 21-3, 36-7, 154, 192-3
lying 18, 76, 82, 108-9, 127-9, 166

Maimonides 163n.44
Mandela, Nelson 220-1
marriage, child 115-16, 157
Metaphysics of Morals (Kant)
  action under obligation in 90-1
  agency in 110-11
  deliberation in 110-11
  derivation of duties in 81, 85-6, 110-11
  design of 85, 110-11
  duties of ethics in 85-6
  duties of right in 85-6
  moral causality in 90-3, 92n.19
  moral habitat and 81, 89-90
#Me Too movement 219n.10
migrants 116, 187, 201, 203, 205-6
moral agency. *See* agency
moral authority. *See* authority
moral change. *See also* agents of change
  animals and 216
  casuistry and 214-15
  causes of 214-15
  due care and 226-7
  incompleteness of 214-15
  knowledge and 216
  mistakes and 214-16
  moral habitat and 168, 183-4, 186
  politics of 225
  technology and 214-15
moral competence 66, 130, 225

moral complexity 28, 159, 183, 186
moral concerns 76, 79, 88-9, 182-3, 185-6, 191-2, 216
moral content. *See* content
moral conversation 222-3
moral discretion. *See* discretion
moral doubt 185-6
moral habitat
  agents of change and 208, 217, 220n.12, 222-3
  aims of 123, 186, 228-9
  assumptions of 229
  authority and 208-9, 220-1
  beneficence and 134, 155
  citizens and 183
  complexity and 186
  constraints of 116-18, 228-9
  content and 188, 214
  contractualism and 120-1
  cooperation and 154-5
  criticism of 181, 223n.15
  definition of 1-2
  deliberation and 182
  demandingness and 132-3
  deontological theory and 230
  derivation of duties and 80, 86
  due care and 227, 228
  dynamism of 3, 181-2, 186-7, 209-10, 221-2
  equality and 5, 193n.8
  explanatory power of 77n.2, 81, 120-1, 157, 184, 204, 229
  family and 223-4
  freedom and 120-1, 183
  free movement and 207
  as hermeneutic 3
  housing rights and 181, 188, 195, 212
  humility and 225
  incompleteness of 184, 215
  independence and 208-9
  inequality and 116-17
  injustice and 183-4
  innate right and 100-1, 110, 116-18, 120-1, 228-9
  justice and 150
  locality of 229-30
  moral change and 168, 183-4, 186, 225-6
  motives and 64, 66, 69, 230
  objectivity and 181
  obligations and 212
  obligatory ends and 223
  pragmatics and 184, 225
  promising and 212
  property and 191-2, 202, 208-9
  provisional universal rights and 118, 195

moral habitat (*cont.*)
  public institutions and 155, 157, 159–60, 220–1, 223–4
  repair and 220–2
  responsibility and 181, 217, 220–1, 229
  right and 86–7, 100–3, 130–1, 195
  system of duties and 3, 118, 150, 153, 184, 225
  technology and 111n.63, 118n.76, 183–4, 209–10
  unifying conception within 212
  values and 4–5, 120–1, 157, 187, 208–9, 228, 230
moral labor 73, 120–1, 158n.42, 212–13, 222–3
moral life 9, 11, 111, 160, 165–6, 186–7, 209, 217, 225
moral luck 52n.2
moral personality 69, 73, 86–7, 100, 138, 152
moral powers 74, 89–90, 97, 100, 111, 127–9, 168, 193–4, 227
moral practices 182, 186–7, 215
moral relativism 214, 216
moral repair 155, 162, 174–5, 199, 219–21, 225
moral science 224, 228
moral stage theory 172
moral standing 96, 154, 216
moral status 2, 45–6, 88–9, 94, 103, 197, 216
moral worth 69–70
moral wrongness. *See* wrongness
motives
  actions and 59–60, 64, 67–8
  agency and 57n.10, 58, 65–6
  akrasia and 64
  motive-involved wrongdoing and 67–8
  competitiveness and 60–1
  definition of 59
  desire model of 59–60
  development of capacity for 63, 67
  due care and 47–8, 50–1, 54–9, 64–5, 166
  duties and 50–1, 54–9, 69–70, 176–7
  failure and 66, 176–7
  implicit bias and 63–4
  instinct, analogy with 60
  juridical duties and 171
  moral habitat and 186, 230
  moral motives 60–8, 176–7
  motive-involving duties 55–6, 64–5
  motive-involved wrongdoing 67–8
  naturalist account of 60–2
  negligence and 55, 56n.8, 62n.19
  psychology and 104, 176–7
  public institutions and 169, 176–7
  rational agency and 61, 64, 64n.22, 67
  responsibility and 63–4, 66

  right and 176–7
  self-defense and 104
  self-interest and 61
  system motives, kinds of 62–4
  as system state 59–62
  values and 60–2, 64–8
  variation across agents 67
  wrongness and 48–9

natural disasters 145, 147–50, 206–7
needs
  beneficence and 133–5, 139–43, 150
  gift giving and 34–5
  homelessness and 150
  housing rights and 194–5
  injustice and 19, 149
  motives and 60–2
  partiality and 140–1
  personal quality of 150
  physical needs 60–2
  public morality and 23–4
  wants distinguished from 34–5
negligence (duty of non-negligence)
  accident distinguished from 53
  attention and 52
  caution in action and 52n.2
  definition of 51
  harm and 51
  knowledge and 215–16
  legal dimensions of 51
  moral dimensions of 51–2
  motives and 55, 56n.9, 62n.19
  reasoning and 55–6
  responsibility and 51
  values and 55, 65
19th Amendment 183–4
non-citizens 114–17

objectivity, moral 181, 208–9
obligations
  actions and 90–2
  casuistry and 166
  citizens and 101–2
  family and 155–6
  housing rights and 199
  innate right and 112, 118–19
  juridical duties and 78n.4, 101–2
  laws of 91, 101
  as moral events 90–1
  moral habitat and 212
  moral incentive and 92, 101–2
  persons and 91
  property and 118–19
  right and 118–19, 127–8

obligatory ends
   agency and 171–2
   appetites and 128–30
   beneficence and 133–4, 136, 138–44, 152–3
   categorical imperative and 124–6
   definition of 123–4, 170–1
   duties and 123–4, 127–8
   end in itself and 124–6
   ethical duties and 127–30
   free action and 124–6
   gratitude and 123–4
   happiness and 123–4, 126–7, 137–8, 140
   imperfect duties and 122–4, 127–8, 130–2
   innate right and 170–1
   juridical duties and 170–2
   moral habitat and 125n.4
   necessity of 124–5
   reason's interest in, and 124–7
   reciprocity and 131–2
   right and 125n.4, 170–1
   rules and 128
   self and, duties to 128–30
   self-perfection and 124, 126–7
   source of 124–5
   subordinate ends and 124
   suicide and 129
   types of 124–7
   values and 65, 123–5, 128, 130–1, 136, 190–1
   vulnerability and 130
On Liberty (Mill) 125n.4

pain 61, 131–4
Parfit, Derek 67–8
particularism 79n.5
patriation, right of 206, 206n.35
perfect duties. See also *specific perfect duties*
   actions and 10
   bodies and 105
   casuistry and 108, 164–6
   content and 107
   definition of 104–5
   deliberation and 107
   due care and 54
   exceptions to 107–8, 164–5
   gratitude and 13
   ground of obligation and 108
   imperfect duties, relation to 1, 5, 10, 159
   innate right and 105
   juridical duties and 104–5, 108–9
   motives and 104–5
   obligatory ends and 129–30
   property and 109–10
   reasoning and 104–5, 107, 165
   responsibility and 164–5, 170
   right and 104–5, 107
   rules and 164–5
   special cases and 164–5
   values and 104–5, 107, 164–5
personality, moral 69, 73, 86–7, 100, 138, 152
Plato 108–9
polygamy 157
possessions. *See* property
practical reason. *See* reason
pragmatics 184, 219, 221, 225
primary duties 47–8, 50, 52–3, 68–9, 109, 202–3
privacy 37–8, 56, 66, 142, 155–6, 187, 202, 213
private morality 20, 28, 202–3
promising
   aims of 56
   authority and 210
   casuistry and 212–13
   ceteris paribus clause for 210–11
   content and 56, 210, 212
   contract and 109n.57
   deliberation and 210–12
   due care and 56
   dynamism of 210–11
   evacuation of promises and 211
   gift giving and 32
   gratitude and 211
   housing rights and 210–12
   moral habitat and 212
   motive of duty and 69
   natural disasters and 210–11
   promise-keeping and 4–5, 56, 69, 91–2
   promissory duties and 56, 79, 81, 212
   relationships and 56
   responsibility and 210–11
   rules and 210n.1, 212–13
   structure of 56
   unkept promises and 210–12
   values and 4–5, 56, 211–13
property
   abandoned property 113
   agency and 22–3
   aims of 94–5, 98–9, 153–4
   authority and 46–7, 208–9
   beneficence and 21–3, 79, 114, 155
   bodies and 105
   casuistry and 114
   citizens and 189, 191
   content and 154, 189–90, 208–9
   deliberation and 191, 193–4, 202–3, 208
   distribution questions and 209
   division of 193–4
   due care and 113
   equality and 189, 191–3
   exclusion rights and 189, 203

property (*cont.*)
  freedom and 189–90
  gift giving and 32, 36–7, 39–40, 114
  gratitude and 21–4, 26, 28, 79
  housing rights and 3, 189, 201, 203, 213–14
  human nature and 98–9, 192–3
  independence and 24, 26, 189, 191–3, 201
  inequality and 21–2
  innate right and 2, 98–9, 105, 109–10, 113, 153–4, 204n.32
  intellectual property and 193–4
  juridical duties and 109–10, 153–4
  Lockean view of 21–3, 36–7, 154, 192–3
  moral habitat and 191–2, 202, 208–9
  necessity of 153–4, 209
  perfect duties and 109–10
  private property 189, 202
  promising and 109–10
  public institutions and 155, 189–90
  right and 23, 95n.25, 153–4, 189, 193–4
  scarcity and 189, 193–4
  states and 109–10
  taxes and 109–10, 154
  values and 26, 39–40, 109–10, 113, 153–4, 189–92, 208–9
Ptolemaic theories 60n.15, 75–6, 144n.23, 214–15
public education 156, 184–5, 195, 223, 225–6
public institutions
  actions and 210
  agents of change and 217–18, 220
  beneficence and 148–9, 159–60
  constitutionally sourced requirements and 174
  criticism of 169
  deliberation and 174
  dependency on 159–60
  disadvantaged groups and 169, 174
  discrimination and 169
  division of moral labor and 160
  equality and 159–60, 164
  gift giving and 36
  housing rights and 200–3
  imperfect duties and 112n.65, 122–3, 164
  innate right and 112
  institutional design and 54, 81, 209–10
  juridical duties and 171, 174
  moral habitat and 155, 157, 159–60, 220–1, 223–4
  motives and 62n.19, 169, 176–7, 182–3
  property and 155, 189–90
  public servants in 164n.1
  responsibility and 164–5, 170, 174n.17
  self and, duties to 130n.10
  structural change to 148–9, 169
  values and 164, 174
public morality 22–4, 28, 89–90, 97, 159, 200–3
public reason 108–9, 176n.21

Rawls, John 2–3, 22n.20, 62n.19, 83–6, 209
Reason (reasons, reasoning)
  actions and 65, 182
  agency and 48–9, 69, 125–6, 128–30, 143–4, 171
  balancing of 44–5, 165
  beneficence and 135, 137
  categorical imperative procedure and 84
  co-reasoning and 48–9
  deliberation and 132–3, 193–4
  demandingness and 132–3
  due care and 55–6, 65
  end in itself and 84–5, 135–7, 143
  gift giving and 32–3
  happiness and 136, 143
  impermissibility and 44–5
  innate right and 118–19
  juridical powers and 100
  morality as authoritative principle of 137
  motives and 61, 64, 67
  negligence and 55–6
  obligatory ends and 124–7, 129–30, 170–1
  perfect duties and 104–5, 165
  practical reason 47–8, 69, 90, 98–9, 118–19, 132–3, 138, 143–4, 170–1
  public reason 103n.43, 108–9, 176n.21
  rational nature and 78, 84–5, 88–9, 125–6, 132, 135–7, 143
  reasonable person standard and 57–8, 67
  self and, duties to 129–30
  values and 62, 64–5, 64n.22
  willing and 95n.23
  wrongness and 44–5, 48–9
reciprocity 13–15, 17, 31, 40, 102, 131–2, 135, 219–20
redlining 174–5
refugees. *See also* stateless persons
  beneficence and 149, 204–5
  camps for 206–7
  citizens and 149–50
  civic status and 204
  duties and 117
  estimation of number of 187
  exclusionary borders and 204–7
  free cities and 206
  free movement and 207
  housing rights and 188, 196, 203–4
  innate right and 117, 204
  justice and 149

moral port of entry and 205–7
moral problems associated with 187–8
refusal of 206
resettlement of 149
responsibility and 206–7
welfare issues and 187–8
relationships
  demandingness and 27, 151, 160–1
  gift giving and 31–2, 35–41, 43, 46–7
  gratitude and 27
  norms of connection within 27
  promising and 56, 210–12
relativism *See* Moral relativism
religious accommodations 176
reproductive freedom 175–6, 223–4
responsibility
  agents of change and 217–19, 222
  assigning of 217
  casuistry and 166–7
  due care and 50–1, 227
  housing rights and 198–9
  humility and 225
  imperfect duties and 9–10, 164–5, 176
  imputation and 91–2
  juridical duties and 168–9
  moral change and 221–2
  moral habitat and 181, 217, 220–1, 229
  motives and 63–4, 66
  negligence and 51
  objectivity and 181
  perfect duties and 164–5, 170
  promising and 210–11
  public institutions and 164–5, 170, 174n.18
  rules and 168–9
  shared responsibility for stateless persons and refugees 206–7
  tracking responsibility 164–5, 168–70, 176
Richardson, Henry 139n.18
right. *See also* housing rights; innate right; *specific rights*; states
  acquired right 97–8, 98n.32, 99n.33
  action under obligation and 90
  agency and 22–3, 110–11
  aim of 85, 89, 94–5
  authority and 45–7
  beneficence and 23, 134–5, 148, 153–4
  categorical imperative and 101
  children and 111–12, 115–16, 122–3
  coercion and 95–6
  common end and 95, 171
  contract and 99
  cosmopolitan right 153n.36
  cultural variation and 115–16
  definition of 86n.8, 94

deliberation and 87–8, 193–4
derivation of duties and 86–9, 96–8, 104–5, 114
discretion and 45–6
domestic union and 99–100
due care and 54, 119–20
ethical duties and 2, 85–6, 89–90, 153–4
family and 155–7
freedom and 93–6, 130–1
good will and 89, 102, 111
housing rights and 188, 196–7, 203
humanity and 96, 153–4
imperfect duties and 88, 119–20, 122–3
independence and 87, 93–4, 96, 112
innate right 93–4, 96–7
moral habitat and 86–7, 89–90, 100–3, 130–1, 195
motives and 176–7
obligations and 118–19, 127–8
obligatory ends and 125n.4, 170–1
omnilateral will and 95, 97–8, 118–19, 171n.14
perfect duties and 104–5, 107
powers, moral and juridical, and 95, 100, 127–8
priority of 89–90, 107
property and 23, 88, 95n.25, 98–9, 153–4, 189, 193–4
public morality and 22–3
reciprocal conditions of 94, 100
rightful interference and 95
self-defense and 103–4, 104n.44
state of nature and 94
universal law and 94, 96
universal principle of 94–6, 101–2
values and 87, 93–4, 96, 127–8, 153–4, 176, 183n.1
vulnerability and 95, 115
willing and 87n.11, 90
right of entry 205–7
right of patriation 206, 206n.35
Ripstein, Arthur 97n.29
Rousseau, Jean-Jacques 78, 86n.9, 95n.24, 192
rule consequentialism 212–13
rule of law 97, 101–2, 112, 149, 153–4, 164
rules
  agents of change and 218–19
  alterations to 168–9
  casuistry and 166–7
  deliberation and 33–4
  duties and 56, 166–7
  exceptions to 164–8
  obligatory ends 128
  perfect duties and 164–5

rules (*cont.*)
  promising and 210n.1, 212–13
  responsibility and 168–9
  values and 75–6, 168
rule utilitarianism 75–6

Scanlon, T. M. 39n.25, 120n.79
self-defense
  definition of 103
  independence and 103
  interest and 4
  juridical duties and 4
  motives and 104
  private individuals and 4, 103–4
  private right to 104
  public reason and 103n.43
  right and 103–4, 104n.44
  self and, duties to 130
  state of nature and 103–4
  states and 103–4
self, duties to
  agency and 130
  appetites and 129–30
  deliberation and 129–30
  happiness and 130
  importance of 129–30
  obligatory ends and 128–30
  public institutions and 130n.10
  reasoning and 129–30
  self-defense and 130
  self-harm and 130
self-governance 24
self-interest 82–3, 82n.1, 84, 104–5, 135
self-perfection 85, 123–8, 130, 170–1
Seneca 13–14, 25n.25
sex and marriage 99n.34
Socrates 166–7
South African Truth and Reconciliation Commission (TRC) 220–1
speech, freedom of 38–9, 97, 108–9, 112, 155–6
stateless persons. *See also* refugees
  asylum seekers as 205
  causes of 205–6
  climate change and 205
  exclusionary borders and 206–7
  free cities and 206
  free migrants and 205–6
  free movement and 207
  housing rights and 204–5
  inequality and 205–6
  moral port of entry and 205–7
  patriation of 206, 206n.35
  refusal of 206
  responsibility and 206–7

state of nature 23n.21, 94, 103–4, 112–13, 199
states
  authority and 95
  beneficence and 148
  citizens and 148
  coercive power of 103
  duty to be part of 95–6
  ethical duties and 156–7
  failed states 113, 115
  family and 155–7
  freedom and 95, 100, 103
  housing rights and 203
  innate right and 100–1, 114n.70, 117–18
  juridical duties and 97
  moral powers and 100
  omnilateral will and 95, 97–8, 118–19, 171n.14
  property and 109–10
  public health and 156–7
  self-defense and 103–4
  suicide for reasons of state 108
  vulnerability and 95
status, moral 2, 45–6, 88–9, 94, 103, 111–12, 169, 197, 216
Stoicism 136, 192–3
Strawson, Peter 58–9
structural injustice 150, 174–5, 219
subordination 40, 89, 93, 98–9, 125–6, 129, 157, 171, 174–5, 221
suicide 108, 129
supererogatory actions 40–1, 160–2
surrogate agency 18–19, 18n.13, 143–4
systemic injustice 150, 174–5, 219

technology 117n.75, 209–10, 214–15
Thomas Aquinas 15n.6
trust 27, 31, 35, 82, 140, 185, 218
truth-telling 69, 97n.28, 101–2, 108–9, 165–7
Tutu, Desmond 220–1

universal law formula 80–5
universal principle of right 94–6, 101–2
universal rights, provisional 114–18, 120–1, 149, 195

values
  actions and 64–5
  agency and 143–4, 208–9
  agents of change and 218–19
  anchoring values 171–3, 208
  articulated fundamental values 190
  beneficence and 26, 133–6, 139–41, 144, 146–8, 152–3
  casuistry and 166–7

deliberation and 57, 214
due care and 50, 54–5, 57, 65, 166, 226–7
duties and 56–8, 65–6, 68–70, 74–5, 77–8, 165–7, 192–3
equality and 175, 185
freedom and 38–9
gift giving and 46–7
gratitude and 17, 26–8
happiness and 138, 143–4
housing rights and 190, 196–8, 200, 211–14
hybrid content of 190–2, 196–8, 208, 211–12, 214
imperfect duties and 1, 132, 157–8, 164–5
independence and 26–7, 185–6, 189, 213–14
innate right and 113, 155, 214
juridical duties and 100–2, 168, 171–4, 176
moral habitat and 4–5, 120–1, 157, 187, 208–9, 228
motives and 60–2, 64–6, 64n.22, 67–8
negligence and 55, 65
obligations and 101–2
obligatory ends and 65, 123–5, 128, 130–1, 136, 190–1
perfect duties and 104–5, 107, 164–5
promising and 4–5, 56, 211–13
property and 26, 39–40, 109–10, 113, 153–4, 189–92, 208–9
public institutions and 164, 174
reason and 62, 64–5, 64n.22
responsiveness to 64–5
right and 87, 93–4, 96, 127–8, 153–4, 176, 183n.1
rules and 75–6, 168
tracking of 164–5, 168–70, 176
vulnerability and 120–1
virtues 29, 43–4, 186–7, 220–1
vulnerability
 content and 166–7, 214
 duties and 166–7
 ethical duties and 89–90
 family and 155–6
 housing rights and 203
 imperfect duties and 130
 innate right and 111
 motives and 64
 obligatory ends and 130

right and 95, 115
states and 95
values and 120–1

wealth 10, 46–7, 112, 183
well-being 78–9, 127, 134, 138, 148, 174, 226
"What is Enlightenment?" (Kant) 108n.52
white lies 165–6
Willaschek, Marcus 102n.41
Williams, Bernard 110, 163
willing. *See also* good will
 definition of 95n.23
 derivation of duties and 83–5
 general will 95n.24
 gift giving and 32–3
 good will and 70
 happiness and 138
 moral law and 95n.23
 motives and 58
 omnilateral will 95, 97–8, 118–19, 171n.14
 reason and 95n.23
 right and 87n.11, 90
 states and 95
 unilateral will 94
 usurpatory will 32–3
Wollstonecraft, Mary 216n.9
wrongness
 actions and 29, 91–2, 123
 agency and 48–9
 authority and 39, 45–7
 blame and 45n.40, 215
 conditional wrongness 39
 context sensitivity of 44–5
 discretion and 38–9, 45–6, 48–9
 doing too much and 29–34
 gift giving and 29–34, 38–40, 46–7
 impermissibility and 1, 29, 39n.25, 40n.26, 43–5, 48–9
 inequality and 40
 knowledge and 215–16
 moral policing and 45
 motives and 48–9, 67–8
 not impermissible but morally wrong actions 29, 39, 43–5
 public institutions and 182–3
 reasoning and 48–9